AF839939

'This book deals with the constitutional adjudication of ten European peak courts and their compliance with European norms from the perspective of the financial crisis, terrorism and migration. The shelf-life of the findings will be long, because these challenges, and the non-compliance with European values seem to stay with us.'

Gábor Halmai, Professor and Chair of Comparative Constitutional Law at the European University Institute, Florence

'This book presents a remarkable overview in new developments in constitutional adjudication, a field in permanent evolution and constant pressure from diverging issues, including fundamental rights at a time of growing security concern, legislative reforms under conditions of financial crisis and the extension of supranational law. Covering many relevant controversies, this book invites further research and debate.'

Otto Pfersmann, EHESS (Institute for Advanced Studies in Social Sciences), France

New Challenges to Constitutional Adjudication in Europe

In the past few years, constitutional courts have been presented with new challenges. The world financial crisis, the new wave of terrorism, mass migration and other country-specific problems have had wide-ranging effects on the old and embedded constitutional standards and judicial constructions. This book examines how, if at all, these unprecedented social, economic and political problems have affected constitutional review in Europe. As the courts' response must conform with EU law and in some cases international law, analysis extends to the related jurisprudence of the European Court of Justice and the European Court of Human Rights. The collection adopts a common analytical structure to examine how the relevant challenges have been addressed in ten country specific case studies. Alongside these, constitutional experts frame the research within the theoretical understanding of the constitutional difficulties of the day in Europe. Finally, a comparative chapter examines the effects of multilevel constitutionalism and identifies general European trends.

This book will be essential reading for academics and researchers working in the areas of constitutional law, comparative law and jurisprudence.

Zoltán Szente Professor, Research Chair, Institute for Legal Studies, Hungarian Academy of Sciences; Professor of Constitutional Law, National University of Public Service, Budapest, Hungary.

Fruzsina Gárdos-Orosz Senior Research Fellow, Director of the Institute for Legal Studies, Hungarian Academy of Sciences; Associate Professor, National University of Public Service, Budapest, Hungary.

Comparative Constitutional Change

Series editors:

Xenophon Contiades is Professor of Public Law, Panteion University, Athens, Greece and Managing Director, Centre for European Constitutional Law, Athens, Greece.

Thomas Fleiner is Emeritus Professor of Law at the University of Fribourg, Switzerland. He teaches and researches in the areas of Federalism, Rule of Law, Multicultural State; Comparative Administrative and Constitutional Law; Political Theory and Philosophy; Swiss Constitutional and Administrative Law; and Legislative Drafting. He has published widely in these and related areas.

Alkmene Fotiadou is Research Associate at the Centre for European Constitutional Law, Athens.

Richard Albert is Professor of Law at the University of Texas at Austin.

Comparative Constitutional Change has developed into a distinct field of constitutional law. It encompasses the study of constitutions through the way they change and covers a wide scope of topics and methodologies. Books in this series include work on developments in the functions of the constitution, the organization of powers and the protection of rights, as well as research that focuses on formal amendment rules and the relation between constituent and constituted power. The series includes comparative approaches along with books that focus on single jurisdictions, and brings together research monographs and edited collections which allow the expression of different schools of thought. While the focus is primarily on law, where relevant the series may also include political science, historical, philosophical and empirical approaches that explore constitutional change.

Also in the series:

Democratic Decline in Hungary
András L. Pap
ISBN: 978-1-138-05212-3 (hbk)

Participatory Constitutional Change: The People as Amenders of the Constitution
Edited by Xenophon Contiades and Alkmene Fotiadou
ISBN: 978-1-472-47869-6 (hdk)

New Challenges to Constitutional Adjudication in Europe

A Comparative Perspective

Edited by
Zoltán Szente and Fruzsina Gárdos-Orosz

Routledge
Taylor & Francis Group
LONDON AND NEW YORK

First published 2018 by Routledge

2 Park Square, Milton Park, Abingdon, Oxfordshire OX14 4RN
52 Vanderbilt Avenue, New York, NY 10017

Routledge is an imprint of the Taylor & Francis Group, an informa business

First issued in paperback 2019

Copyright © 2018 selection and editorial matter, Zoltán Szente and Fruzsina Gárdos-Orosz; individual chapters, the contributors

The right of Zoltán Szente and Fruzsina Gárdos-Orosz to be identified as the authors of the editorial material, and of the authors for their individual chapters, has been asserted in accordance with sections 77 and 78 of the Copyright, Designs and Patents Act 1988.

All rights reserved. No part of this book may be reprinted or reproduced or utilised in any form or by any electronic, mechanical, or other means, now known or hereafter invented, including photocopying and recording, or in any information storage or retrieval system, without permission in writing from the publishers.

Notice:
Product or corporate names may be trademarks or registered trademarks, and are used only for identification and explanation without intent to infringe.

British Library Cataloguing-in-Publication Data
A catalogue record for this book is available from the British Library

Library of Congress Cataloging-in-Publication Data
Names: Szente, Soltâan, editor author. | Gâardos-Orosz, Fruzsina, editor author.
Title: New challenges to constitutional adjudication in Europe : a comparative perspective / edited by Zoltân Szente, Fruzsina Gârdos-Orosz.
Description: New York, NY : Routledge, 2018. | Series: Comparative constitutional change | Includes bibliographical references and index.
Identifiers: LCCN 2017041772 | ISBN 9781138057890 (hardback)
Subjects: LCSH: Constitutional law--European Union countries. | Judicial review--European Union countries. | Constitutional courts--European Union countries.
Classification: LCC KJE5053 .N49 2018 | DDC 342.4--dc23
LC record available at https://lccn.loc.gov/2017041772

ISBN: 978-1-138-05789-0 (hbk)
ISBN: 978-0-367-89360-6 (pbk)

Typeset in Galliard
by Taylor & Francis Books

Contents

Contributors

Balaguer Callejón, Francisco is Professor of Constitutional Law at the University of Granada and Jean Monnet Professor ad personam of European Constitutional Law and Globalization.

Birkinshaw, Patrick is a Professor of Public Law and the Director of the Institute of European Public Law at the University of Hull.

Canotilho, Mariana is Professor of Public Law at the Universities of Coimbra and Minho and Legal Adviser of the President at the Portuguese Constitutional Court.

Ciolli, Ines is Associate Professor of Constitutional Law at Sapienza University, Department of Legal Sciences, Rome.

Delzangles, Beatrice is *Maitre de Conferences* in Public Law at the University Paris-Dauphine, PSL Research University and Member of the *Centre de recherches Droit Dauphine*, CR2D.

Gardasevic, Djordje is an Associate Professor of Constitutional Law at Zagreb Law Faculty, University of Zagreb.

Gárdos-Orosz, Fruzsina is Senior Research Fellow and Director of the Institute for Legal Studies, Center for Social Sciences of the Hungarian Academy of Sciences and Associate Professor at the National University of Public Service, Institute of Constitutional Law, Budapest.

Granat, Miroslaw is Professor of Constitutional Law at Warsaw II University and Former Judge at the Polish Constitutional Court from 2007 until 2016.

Groppi, Tania is Professor of Public Law at the University of Siena.

Hourquebie, Fabrice is Professor of Public Law at the University of Bordeaux. He is Head of the Doctoral School of Legal Studies and Secretary General of the French Association of Constitutional Law, AFDC.

McEldowney, John is a Professor of Law at the School of Law, University of Warwick.

Mehde, Veith is a Professor of Public Law and Administrative Science at the Law Faculty of Leibniz University Hannover.

Szente, Zoltán is a Professor of Constitutional Law at the National University of Public Service, Institute of Constitutional Law, and Research Chair at the Institute for Legal Studies, Center for Social Sciences of the Hungarian Academy of Sciences, Budapest.

Verpeaux, Michel is a Professor of Public Law at the University Paris 1. Panthéon-Sorbonne.

Varju, Márton is Senior Research Fellow at the Center for Social Sciences of the Hungarian Academy of Sciences, Budapest, and Senior Lecturer at the University of Debrecen, Faculty of Law.

Vlachogiannis, Apostolos is a Ph.D from the University of Paris 1. Pantheon Sorbonne and Teaching Assistant at the Hellenic Open University.

Cited judicial cases

Croatia

U-I-179/1991.
U-I-673/1996.
U-I-884/1997.
U-I-131/1998.
U-I-1156/1999.
U-III-661/1999.
U-I-2566/2003.
U-I-2892/2003.
U-I-3789/2003.
U-I-296/2006.
U-I-2012/2007.
U-I-4516/2007.
U-III-4182/2008.
U-I-448/2009.
U-I-602/2009.
U-I-1710/2009.
U-IP-3820/2009.
U-I-18153/2009.
U-IIIB-1373/2009.
U-III-64744/2009.
U-I-3597/2010.
U-I-5813/2010.
U-I-2871/2011.

France

Décision n° 2003–467 DC du 13 mars 2003.
Décision n° 2009–588 DC du 6 août 2009.
Décision n° 2010–613 DC du 7 octobre 2010.
Décision n° 2011–625 DC du 10 mars 2011.
Décision n° 2014–373 QPC du 4 avril 2014.

Décision n° 2014–374 QPC du 4 avril 2014.
Décision n° 2014–439 QPC du 23 janvier 2015.
Décision n° 2015–713 DC du 23 juillet 2015.
Décision n° 2015–478 QPC du 24 juillet 2015.
Décision n° 2015–715 DC du 5 août 2015.

Germany

1 BvL 1/09 (2010)
1 BvL 3/09 (2010)
1 BvL 4/09 (2010)
1 BvR 357/05 (2006)
BVerfGE 1, 14 (1951)
BVerfGE 6, 389 (1957)
BVerfGE 24, 367 (1968)
BVerfGE 33, 303 (1972)
BVerfGE 34, 269 (1973)
BVerfGE 43, 291 (1977)
BVerfGE 46, 160 (1977)
BVerfGE 54, 148 (1980)
BVerfGE 65, 1 (1983)
BVerfGE 73, 339 (1986)
BVerfGE 86, 390 (1992)
BVerfGE 88, 203 (1993)
BVerfGE 89, 155 (1993)BVerfGE 95, 1 (1996)
BVerfGE 95, 96 (1996)
BVerfGE 105, 313 (2002)
BVerfGE 108, 282 (2003)
BVerfGE 112, 50 (2004)
BVerfGE 115, 118 (2006)
BVerfGE 120, 274 (2008)
BVerfGE 124, 199 (2009)
BVerfGE 126, 400 (2010)
BVerfGE 129, 124 (2011)
BVerfGE 131, 239 (2012)
BVerfGE 132, 179 (2012)
BVerfGE 133, 59 (2013)
BVerfGE 133, 277 (2013)
BVerfGE 134, 366 (2014)
BVerfGE 135, 317 (2014)
BVerfGE 138, 296 (2015)
BVerfG 2 BvR 2/08
BVerfG 2 BvR 987/10
BVerfG 2 BvR 1390/12
BGHSt 39, 1 (1992)

BGHSt 40, 218 (1994)
BGHSt 40, 241(1994)

Greece

AP 23/1897.
CoS Plen 668/2012.
CoS 866/2002.
CoS 1511/2002.
CoS 2165/2002.
CoS Plen 1663/2009.
CoS 3838/2010.
CoS 693/2011.
CoS 1620/2011.
CoS 668/2012.
CoS Plen 1283/2012.
CoS Plen 1285/2012.
CoS Plen 1972/2012.
CoS Plen 187/2013.
CoS Plen 460/2013.
CoS Plen 3354/2013.
CoS Plen 413/2014.
CoS Plen 1906/2014.
CoS Plen 1116–1117/2014.
CoS Plen 2115/2014 .
CoS Plen 2192/2014.
CoS Plen 2307/2014.
CoS Plen 3177/2014.
CoS Plen 3410/2014.
CoS Plen 4274/2014.
CoS Plen 4741/2014.
CoS Plen 2287–2290/2015.
CoS Plen 2288/2015.

Hungary

903/B/1990. AB határozat
17/1992. (III. 30.) AB határozat
26/1992. (IV. 30.) AB határozat
64/1993. (VI. 3.) AB határozat
11/1995 (III. 5.) AB határozat
1138/B/1995. AB határozat
867/B/1997. AB határozat
51/2001. (IX. 15.) AB határozat
1053/E/2004. AB határozat

36/2005. (X. 5.) AB határozat
61/B/2005 AB határozat
66/2006. (XI. 29.) AB határozat
72/2006. (XII. 15.) AB határozat
2/2007. (I. 24.) AB határozat
9/2007. (III. 7.) AB határozat
109/2008. (IX. 26.) AB határozat
32/2008 (III. 12.) AB határozat
87/2008. (VI. 18.) AB határozat
143/2010. (VII. 14.) AB határozat
184/2010. (X. 28.) AB határozat
37/2011. (V. 10.) AB határozat
13/2013. (VI. 17.) AB határozat
23/2013. (IX. 25.) AB határozat
32/2013. (XI. 22.) AB határozat
8/2014. (III. 20.) AB határozat
9/2014. (III. 21.) AB határozat
20/2014. (VII. 3.) AB határozat
34/2014. (XI. 14.) AB határozat
3194/2014. (VII. 14.) AB határozat
2/2015. (II. 2.) AB határozat
12/2016. (VI. 22.) AB határozat
13/2016. (VII. 18.) AB határozat
22/2016. (XII. 5.) AB határozat
3098/2016. (V. 24.) AB határozat
3103/2016. (V. 24.) AB határozat
3130/2016. (VI. 29.) AB határozat
3150/2016. (VII. 22.) AB határozat
3151/2016. (VII. 22.) AB határozat
3167/2016. (VII. 1.) AB határozat
3222/2016. (XI. 14.) AB határozat
3272/2016. (XII. 20.) AB határozat

Italy

no. 15/1982.
no. 404/1988.
no. 10/1993.
no. 198/2000.
no. 105/2001.
no. 252/2001.
no. 222/2004.
no. 223/2004.
no. 372/2004.
no. 379/ 2004.

no. 201/2005.
no. 224/2005.
no. 300/2005.
no. 432/2005.
no. 156/2006.
no. 50/2008.
no. 148/2008.
no. 306/2008.
no. 11/2009.
no. 29/2009.
no. 209/2009.
no. 10/2010.
no. 76/2010.
no. 121/2010.
no. 134/2010.
no. 187/2010.
no. 269/2010.
no. 299/2010.
no. 316/2010.
no. 40/2011.
no. 61/2011.
no. 61/2011.
no. 329/2011.
no. 70/2012.
no. 115/2012.
no. 192/2012.
no. 2/2013.
no. 40/2013.
no. 62/2013.
no. 10/2015.
no. 22/2015.
no. 230/2015.
no. 275/2016.
no. 95/2017.

Italian Supreme Court

no. 316/2010.

Poland

2008 K44/07.
K 9/12, OTK ZU no. 11/A/2012.
no. K 21/14, OTK ZU, no. 9/A/2015.
no. K 34/15, OTK ZU no. 11A/2015.

Portugal

no. 287/1990.
no. 683/1999.
no. 509/2002.
no. 306/2003.
no. 188/2009.
no. 154/2010.
no. 338/2010.
no. 399/2010.
no. 396/2011.
no. 353/2012.
no. 594/2012.
no. 187/2013.
no. 474/2013.
no. 602/2013.
no. 794/2013.
no. 862/2013.
no. 413/2014.
no. 572/2014.
no. 574/2014.
no. 575/2014.
no. 141/2015.
no. 296/2015.
no. 3/2016.

Romania

1533/2011

South Africa

First national bank of SA Ltd t/a West bank v. Commissioner, 2002 (4) SA 768 (CC).

Spain

Constitutional Court (Tribunal Constitucional de España)

STC 47/1984.
STC 107/1984.
STC 99/1985.
STC 115/1987.
STC 199/1987.

STC 147/1988.
STC 71/1994.
STC 242/1994.
STC 237/1998.
STC 31/1999.
STC 95/2000.
STC 48/2003.
STC 95/2003.
STC 5/2004.
STC 6/2004.
STC 236/2007.
STC 259/2007.
STC 260/2007.
STC 261/2007.
STC 262/2007.
STC 263/2007.
STC 264/2007.
STC 265/2007.
STC 103/2008.
STC 126/2009.
STC 31/2010.
STC 62/2011.
STC 113/2012.
STC 138/2012.
STC 10/2014.
STC 42/2014.
STC 215/2014.
STC 24/2015.
STC 31/2015.
STC 49/2015.
STC 93/2015.
STC 138/2015.
STC 211/2015.
STC 259/2015.
STC 26/2016.
STC 62/2016.
STC 90/2017.
SCJ 85/2003.
SCJ 176/2003.
SCJ 99/2004.
SCJ 110/2007.
SCJ 112/2007.
SCJ 43/2009.
SCJ 44/2009.
SCJ 126/2009.

Spanish Supreme Court (Tribunal Supremo de España)

TS 197/2006.

United Kingdom

R v Hampden (1637) 3 St Tr 825.
Scott v Scott [1913] AC. 417.
Local Government Board v Arlidge [1915]. 120.
Zamora [1916] UKPC. 24.
Liversidge v Anderson [1942] AC. 206.
Conway v Rimmer [1968] UKHL. 2.
Norwich Pharmacal Co v The Customs and Excise Comrs [1974] AC. 133.
Maunsell v Olins [1975] AC. 373.
Laker Airways [1977] 1 QB 643 (CA).
R v Secretary of State for the Home Dept. Ex p Hosenball [1977] 3 All ER 452 (CA).
Council of Civil Service Unions v Minister for the Civil Service [1983] UKHL. 6.
Secretary of State for Defence v Guardian Newspapers [1984] 3 All ER. 100.
AG v Guardian Newspapers Ltd (No 2) [1988] 3 All ER. 545.
R. v Secretary of State for Transport ex parte Factortame Ltd., (No.2). [1991] 1 AC. 603.
R v Secretary of State for the Home Department ex parte Fire Brigades Union [1995] 2 AC. 513.
R v Secretary of State for the Home Dept. ex parte McQuillan [1995] 4 All ER. 400.
Home Secretary v Rehman [2000] 3 All ER. 45.
Whaley v. Lord Watson of Invergowrie [2000] SC.
Home Dept v Rehman [2001] UKHL. 47.
R *(Abbasi) v Secretary of State for Foreign Affairs* [2002] EWCA Civ 1598.
R v Shayler [2002] UKHL. 11.
Thoburn v Sunderland City Council [2003] QB. 151.
A v Secretary of State HD [2004] UKHL. 56.
R v H [2004] UKHL. 3.
A et al v Secretary of State HD [2005] UKHL. 71.
A v Secretary of State HD [2005] 3 All ER 169 (HL). 56.
Jackson v Attorney General [2005] UKHL 56 [2006] 1 AC. 262.
Roberts v Parole Board [2005] UKHL. 45.
Al Skeini v UK Secretary of State etc [2007] UKHL. 26.
Charkaoui v Canada (2007) 1 SCR. 350.
R *(Al-Jedda) v SoS D* [2007] UKHL. 58.
YL v Birmingham City Council [2007] UKHL. 27.
Bancoult No 2 v Secretary of State for Foreign Affairs [2008] UKHL. 61.
R *(Bancoult No 2) v SoS FA* [2008] UKHL. 61.
R *(Corner House Research & Ors) v The Serious Fraud Office* [2008] UKHL. 60.
R (Gentle) v Prime Minister et al [2008] UKHL. 20.
B (Algeria) etc v Secretary of State for the Home Department [2009] UKHL. 10.

HM Advocate v McLean [2009] HCJAC. 97.
Secretary of State v AF [2009] UKHL. 28.
Bin Yam Mohamed [2010] EWCA Civ 65.
Cadder (Peter) v HM Advocate [2010] UKSC. 43.
Guardian News Media [2010] UKSC. 1.
HM Treasury v Ahmed No 2 [2010] UKSC. 2.
McInnes v HM Advocate [2010] UKSC. 7.
Ali v SoSHD [2011] EWCA Civ. 787.
Al Rawi et al v Security Service et al [2011] UKSC. 34.
Axa General Insurance and others v The Lord Advocate [2011] UKSC. 46.
Axa General Insurance and others v The Lord Advocate [2011] CSIH. 31.
Fraser (Nat Gordon) v HM Advocate [2011] UKSC. 24.
Home Office v Tariq [2011] UKSC. 35.
SoS HD v CD [2011] EWHC. 2087.
W (Algeria) v SoSHD [2012] UKSC. 8.
Bank Mellat v HM Treasury No 1 [2013] UKSC. 38.
Bank Mellat v HM Treasury No 2 [2013] UKSC. 1052.
Osborn v The Parole Board [2013] UKSC. 20.
Secretary of State for Foreign and Commonwealth Affairs v Assistant Deputy Coroner for Inner North London [2013] EWHC 3724 (Admin).
Smith v Ministry of Defence [2013] UKSC. 41.
Guardian News and Media Ltd v AB, CD [2014] EWCA Crim. 1861.
Kennedy v Charity Commission [2014] UKSC. 20.
R (HS2 Action Alliance Ltd.) and others v Secretary of State for Transport [2014] UKSC. 3.
R (Litvinenko) v Home Secretary et al [2014] EWHC 194 (Admin).
R (Lord Carlile QC) v SoS HD [2014] UKSC.
R (Sandiford) v Secretary of State [2014] UKSC. 44.
Bank Mellat v HM Treasury [2015] EWCA Civ. 39.
Keyu and others v Secretary of State of Foreign and Commonwealth Affairs and others [2015] UKSC. 69.
Kiani v Secretary of State of the Home Department [2015] EWCA Civ. 776.
Pham v Secretary of State for the Home Department [2015] UKSC. 19.
R (Sarkandi) v Secretary of State for Foreign etc Affairs [2015] EWCA Civ. 687.
Guardian News & Media Ltd v R & E. Incedal [2016] EWCA Crim. 1861.
Human Rights Watch v Secretary of State for F&CA [2016] UKIPTrib 15_165 C-H.
Ministry of Defence v Iraqi Citizens [2016] UKSC. 25.
Privacy International v Secretary of State for F&CA [2016] UKIPTrib 14_85 C-H.
R (Miranda) v Secretary of State for the Home Department et al [2016] EWCA Civ 6.
Secretary of State for Home Affairs v HM Coroner etc [2016] EWHC 3001 (Admin).
Youssef v Secretary of State for Foreign etc Affairs [2016] UKSC. 3.
Abd Ali Hameed-Waheed v Ministry of Defence and Serdar Mohammed v Ministry of Defence [2017] UKSC. 2.

Belhaj et al v Straw et al [2017] UKSC. 3.
Belhaj & An'r v Straw et al [2017] UKSC. 3.
Rahmatullah v MoD [2017] EWHC 547 (QB).
Rahmatullah (No 2) v Ministry of Defence [2017] UKSC. 1.
R (Miller) v Secretary of State for Exiting the EU etc [2017] UKSC. 5.
R (Privacy International) v IPT [2017] EWHC 114 (Admin).

United States

US Supreme Court

The Prize cases, 2 Black (67 U.S.) 635 (1863).
Home Building and Loan Association v Blaisdell, 290 U.S. 398 (1934)
West Coast Hotel Co. v Parrish, 300 U.S. 379 (1937)
Adkins v Children's Hospital, 261 US 525 (1923)

US Appeal Court of Appeals for the Ninth Circuit

State of Washington et al v Donald J. Trump President et al No 17–35105 CA Ninth Circ 9/02/2017.

European Court of Human Rights

Lawless v. Ireland App no 332/57 (ECHR, 1 July 1961)
Klass and others v. Germany App no 5029/71 (ECHR, 6 September 1978)
Airey v. Ireland App no 6289/73 (ECHR, 9 October 1979)
Sporrong and Lönnroth v. Sweden App no 7151/75 and 7152/75 (ECHR, 23 September 1982)
Malone v UK App no 8691/79 (ECHR, 2 August 1984).
X. and Y. v. Holland App no 8978/80 (ECHR, 26 March 1985)
Leander v Sweden App no 9248/81 (ECHR, 26 March 1987)
Soering v United Kingdom App no 14038/88 (ECHR, 7 July 1989)
Observer and Guardian App no 13585/88 (ECHR, 26 November 1991)
Vilvarajah and others v United Kingdom App nos 13163/87,13164/87, 13165/87, 13447/87 and 13448/87 (ECHR, 30 October 1991)
Margareta and Roger Andersson v. Sweden App no 12963/87 (ECHR, 25 February 1992)
Chahal v United Kingdom App no 22414/93 (ECHR, 15 November 1996).
Johansen v. Norway App no 17383/90 (ECHR, 7 August 1996)
Hornsby v Greece App no 18357/91 (ECHR, 19 March 1997)
Zana v. Turkey App no 18954/91 (ECHR, 25 November 1997)
Caloc v. France App no 33951/96 (ECHR, 20 July 2000)
Larioshina v Russia App no 56869/00 (ECHR, 23 April 2002)
Khocklich v Moldova App no 41707/98 (ECHR, 29 April 2003)
Broniowski v. Poland App no 31443/96 (ECHR, 22 June 2004)

Hirst v UK App no 74025/01 (ECHR, 6 October 2005)
Öcalan v. Turkey App no 46221/99 (ECHR, 12 May 2005)
Siliadin v. France App no 73316/01 (ECHR, 26 October 2005)
Stec and Others v United Kingdom App nos 65731/01 and 65900/01 (ECHR, 6 July 2005) *Hutten-Czapska v. Poland* App no 35014/97 (ECHR, 19 June 2006)
Ramirez Sanchez v. France App no 59450/00 (ECHR, 4 July 2006)
Scordino v Italy (No. 1) App no 36813/97 (ECHR, 29 March 2006)
Salah Sheekh v the Netherlands App no 1948/04 (ECHR, 11 January 2007)
Saadi v. Italy App no 37201/06 (EHCR, 28 February 2008)
Salduz v Turkey App no 36391/2 (ECHR, 27 November 2008)
A. and Others v. United Kingdom App no 3455/05 (ECHR, 19 February 2009)
A v UK App. no. 100/1997/884/1096 (ECHR, 23 September 1998)
Ciovica v Romania App no 3076/92 (ECHR, 31 March 2009)
Daoudi c. France App. no 19576/08 (ECHR, 3 December 2009)
Meidanis v Greece App no. 33977/06 (ECHR 22 August 2008)
Zouboulidis v Greece App no. 36963/6 (ECHR 25 June 2009)
Daoudi c. France App no 19576/08 (EHCR, 3 décember 2010)
Galotskin v. Greece App no 2945/07 (ECHR, 14 January 2010)
Kennedy v UK App. no 26839/05 (ECHR, 18 May 2010)
Vassiliou Athanasiou v Greece App no 50973/08 (ECHR, 21 December 2010)
Agrati and Others v Italy App no 43549/08 (ECHR, 7 June 2011)
Al Skeini v UK App no 55721/07 (ECHR, 7 July 2011)
Al-Jedda v UK App no 27021/08 (ECHR, 7 July 2011)
Maggio and Others v Italy App nos 46286/09, 52851/08, 54486/08 and 56001/08 (ECHR, 31 May 2011)
Mihăieş and Senteş v Romania App nos 44232/11 and 44605/11 (ECHR, 6 December 2011) *M.S.S. v. Belgium and Greece* App no 30696/09 (EHCR, 21 January 2011)
Babar Ahmad and others v United Kingdom App nos 24027/07, 11949/08 and 36742/08 (ECHR, 10 April 2012)
Del Río Prada v Spain App no 42750/09 (ECHR, 10 July 2012)
El-Masri v The Former Yugoslav Republic of Macedonia App no 39630/09 (ECHR, 13 December 2012)
Glykantzi v Greece App no 40150/09 (ECHR, 30 October 2012)
Hirsi Jamaa and Others v. Italy App no 27765/09 (EHCR, 23 February 2012)
Michelioudakis v. Greece App no 54447/10 (ECHR, 3 April 2012)
Glykantzi v Greece App no 40150/09 (ECHR, 30 October 2012)
Kuric and Others v. Slovenia App no 26828/06 (ECHR, 26 June 2012)
M.S. v Belgium App no 50012/08 (ECHR, 31 January 2012)
Nada v Switzerland App no 10593/05 (ECHR, 12 September 2012)
Othman (Abu Qatada) v. United Kingdom App no 8139/09 (ECHR, 17 January 2012)
Scoppola v Italy App no 1226/05 (ECHR, 20 June 2012)

Aswat v United Kingdom App no 17299/12 (ECHR, 16 April 2013)
Conceição Mateus and Santos Januário v Portugal App nos 62235/12 and 57725/12(ECHR, 8 October 2013)
Da Conceicao Mateus and Santos Januario v. Portugal App no 62235/12 and 62235/12 (EHCR, 8 October 2013)
Koufaki and Adedi v. Greece App no 57665/12 and 57657/12(EHCR, 7 May 2013)
Nencheva v Bulgaria App no 48609/06 (ECHR, 18 June 2013)
N.K.M. v Hungary App no 66529/11 (ECHR, 14 May 2013)
R. Sz. v Hungary App no 41838/11 (ECHR, 2 July 2013)
Zarzycki v Poland App no 15351/03 (ECHR, 12 March 2013)
Zolotas v Greece App no 66610/09 (ECHR, 29 January 2013)
Al Nashiri v Poland App no 28761/11 (ECHR, 24 July 2014)
Frith and Others v UK, App no 47784/09 (ECHR, 16 August 2014)
Hassan v UK App no 29750/09 (ECHR, 16 September 2014)
Husayn (Abu Zubaydah) v Poland App no 7511/13 (ECHR, 24 July 2014)
Kuric and Others v. Slovenia App no 26828/06 (ECHR, 12 March 2014)
Mennesson v. France App no 65192/11 (EHCR, 26 June 2014)
Mohamed v. France App no 21392/09 (EHCR, 25 March 2014)
Nagla v Latvia App no 73469/10 (ECHR, 16 July 2014)
Preda and Others v. Romania App nos. 9584/02, 33514/02, 38052/02, 25821/03, 29652/03, 3736/03, 17750/03 and 28688/04 (ECHR, 29 April 2014)
Sharifi and Others v. Italy and Greece App no. 16643/9 (ECHR, 3 November 2014)
Trabelsi v. Belgium App no 140/10 (ECHR, 4 September 2014)
Da Silva Carvalho Rico v. Portugal App no 13341/14 (EHCR, 1 September 2015)
Mahamad v. France App no 48352/12 (ECHR, 15 April 2015)
McHugh and others App no 51987/08 (ECHR, 10 February 2015)
Ouabour v. Belgium App no 26417/10 (ECHR, 2 June 2015)
Sharifi and Others v. Italy and Greece App no 60104/08 (EHCR, 21 January 2015)
Khlaifia and Others v Italy App no 16483/12 (ECHR, 1 September 2015)
Vékony v. Hungary App no 65681/13(ECHR, 13 January 2015)
Armani da Silva v UK App no 5878/08 (ECHR, 30 March 2016)
Khlaifia and Others v Italy App no 16483/12 (ECHR,15 December 2016)
Nasr and Gali v Italy App no 44883/09 (ECHR, 23 February 2016)
Szabó and Vissy v. Hungary App no 37138/14 (ECHR, 12 January 2016)
R Zakharov v Russia App no 47143/06 (ECHR, 6 October 2005)

Court of Justice of the European Union

Case C-6/90 and C-9/90 *Francovich v Italian Republic* [1991] ECLI:EU:C:1991:428
Case C-213/89 *The Queen v Secretary of State for Transport, ex parte Factortame* [1990] ECLI:EU:C:1990:257

Cases C–65 and 111/95 *R v Home Secretary ex p Shigara and Radiom* [1997] ECR I-3343

Cases C-402/05 P and C-415/05 P *Yassin Abdullah Kadi and Al Barakaat International Foundation v Council of the European Union and Commission of the European Communities* [2008] ECLI:EU:C:2008:461

Case C-76/10 *Pohotovosť* s.r.o. v Iveta Korčkovská [2010] ECLI:EU:C:2010:685

Case C-618/10 *Banco Español de Crédito SA v Joaquín Calderón Camino* [2012] ECLI:EU:C:2012:349

Case C-411/10 and Case C-493/10 *N.S. v Secretary of State for the Home Department and M.E. and Others v. Refugee Applications Commissioner & Minister for Justice, Equality and Law Reform* [2011] ECLI:EU:C:2011:865

Case C-508/10 *European Commission v Kingdom of the Netherlands* [2012] EU: C:2012: 243

Cases T-541/10 and T-215/11 *ADEDY Spyridon Papaspyros and Ilias Iliopoulos v Council of the European Union* [2012] ECLI:EU:T:2012:626–627

Case C-61/11 *Hassen El Dridi alias Soufi Karim* [2011] ECLI:EU: C:2011:268

Case C-398/11 *Thomas Hogan and Others v Minister for Social and Family Affairs, Ireland and Attorney General* [2013] ECLI:EU:C:2013:272

Case C-415/11 *Mohamed Aziz v Caixa d'Estalvis de Catalunya, Tarragona i Manresa (Catalunyacaixa)* [2013] ECLI:EU:C:2013:164

Case C-430/11 *Sagor* [2012] ECLI:EU:C:2012:777

Case C-434/11 *Corpul Naţional al Poliţiştilor v. Ministerul Administraţiei şi Internelor (MAI) and others* [2011] ECLI:EU:C : 2011:830

Case C-522/11 *Procura della Repubblica c. Abdoul Khadre Mbaye* [2011] ECLI: EU:C:2013:190

Case C-462/11 *Victor Cozman v Teatrul Municipal Târgovişte.* [2011] ECLI: EU:C:2011:831

Case C-134/12 *Corpul Naţional al Poliţiştilor – Biroul Executiv Central (în numele şi în interesul membrilor săi – funcţionari publici cu statut special – poliţişti din cadrul IPJ Tulcea) v Ministerul Administraţiei şi Internelor and Others* [2012] ECLI:EU:C:2012:288

Case C-128/12 *Sindicato dos Bancários do Norte and Others v BPN – Banco Português de Negócios SA* [2013] EU:C:2013:149

Case C-264/12 *Sindicato Nacional dos Profissionais de Seguros e Afins v Fidelidade Mundial – Companhia de Seguros SA* [2014] ECLI:EU:C:2014:2036

Case C-297/12 *Criminal proceedings against Gjoko Filev and Adnan Osmani* [2013] ECLI:EU:C:2013:569

Case C-293/12 *Digital Rights Ireland Ltd v Minister for Communications, Marine and Natural Resources and Others and Kärntner Landesregierung and Others* [2014] ECLI:EU:C:2014:238

Case C-370/12 *Thomas Pringle v Government of Ireland and Others* [2012] ECLI:EU:C:2012:756

Joined Cases C-537/12 and C-116/13 *Banco Popular Español SA v Maria Teodolinda Rivas Quichimbo and Wilmar Edgar Cun Pérez and Banco de Valencia*

SA v Joaquín Valldeperas Tortosa and María Ángeles Miret Jaume [2013] ECLI:EU:C:2013:759

Case C-26/13 *Árpád Kásler and Hajnalka Káslerné Rábai v OTP Jelzálogbank Zrt* [2014] ECLI:EU:C:2014:282

Case C-34/13 *Monika Kušionová v SMART Capital, a.s.* [2014] ECLI:EU: C:2014:2189

Case C-265/13 *Torralbo Marcos v Korota SA and Fondo de Garantía Salarial* [2014] ECLI:EU:C:2014:187

Case C-280/13 *Barclays Bank SA v Sara Sánchez García and Alejandro Chacón Barrera* [2014] ECLI:EU:C:2014:279

Case C-333/13 *Elisabeta Dano and Florin Dano v Jobcenter Leipzig* [2014]. ECLIU:C:2014:2358

Case C-342/13 *Katalin Sebestyén v Zsolt Csaba Kővári and Others* [2014] ECLI: EU:C:2014:1857

Joined Cases C-482/13, C-484/13, C-485/13 and C-487/13 *Unicaja Banco, SA v José Hidalgo Rueda and Others and Caixabank SA v Manuel María Rueda Ledesma and Others* [2015] ECLI:EU:C:2015:21

Case C-665/13 *Sindicato Nacional dos Profissionais de Seguro e Afins v Via Directa – Companhia de Seguros SA* [2014] ECLI:EU:C:2014:2327

Case C-8/14 *BBVA SA v Pedro Peñalva López and Others* [2015] ECLI:EU: C:2015:731

Case C-49/14 *Finanmadrid EFC SA v Jesús Vicente Albán Zambrano and Others* [2016] ECLI:EU:C:2016:98

Case C-62/14 *Peter Gauweiler and Others v Deutscher Bundestag* [2015] ECLI: EU:C:2015:400

Case C-67/14 *Jobcenter Berlin Neukölln v Nazifa Alimanovic and Others* [2015] ECLI:EU:C:2015:597

Case C-169/14 *Juan Carlos Sánchez Morcillo and María del Carmen Abril García v Banco Bilbao Vizcaya Argentaria SA* [2014] ECLI:EU:C 2014:2099

Case C-309/14 *Confederazione Generale Italiana del Lavoro (CGIL) and Istituto Nazionale Confederale Assistenza (INCA) v Presidenza del Consiglio dei Ministri and Others* [2015] ECLI:EU:C:2015:523

Case C-362/14 *Maximillian Schrems v Data Protection Commissioner* [2015] ECLI:EU:C:2015:650

Joined Cases C-381/14 and C-385/14 *Jorge Sales Sinués and Youssouf Drame Ba v Caixabank SA and Catalunya Caixa SA (Catalunya Banc S.A.)* [2016] ECLI:EU:C:2016:909

Joined Cases C-584/10 P, C-593/10 P and C-595/10 P *European Commission and Others v Yassin Abdullah Kadi* [2013] ECLI:EU:C:2013:518

Case C-300/11 *ZZ v Secretary of State for the Home Department* [2013] ECLI: EU:C:2013:363

Case C-650/13 *Thiery Deligne v Commune de Lesparre-Médoc and Préfet de la Gironde* [2015] ECLI:EU:C:2015:648

Joined Cases C-203/15 and C-698/15 *Tele2 Sverige AB v Post-och telestyrelsen and Secretary of State for the Home Department v Tom Watson and Others*

Part I

Conceptualising pressure and change in constitutional adjudication

1 Introduction

Contemporary challenges of constitutional adjudication in Europe

Zoltán Szente and Fruzsina Gárdos-Orosz

1 Research questions and presumptions

At the very end of the twentieth century, after the defeat of the communist regimes in Central and Eastern Europe, in the course of gradually deepening European integration, and as a result of the technical revolution that has created unlimited access to information, one may hope that a new age of rationality and prosperity would come about worldwide or, at least in the Western world, as all the conditions for well-informed decisions on essential social and political issues appear to be given.

Yet, today there is quite a general belief that we live in a post-rational epoch. From the spread of populism and 'illiberal democracies' even in the modern constitutional states to Brexit, or from the earth-shaking effects of the world economic crisis to Al-Qaeda, several factors cause fear and uncertainty today.

Whatever we might think about the real grounds for these fears, it is true that in recent years modern governments have had to face many serious and new challenges.

Not surprisingly, the challenges discussed in this book have become the subject of mainstream academic literature. A substantial amount of books and journal articles have dealt with such new challenges as the world financial crisis, terrorism, inland security, migration and other country-specific issues as well as their effects on the national and supranational legal systems. As these challenges have arisen fairly recently, the first general or comparative books have just started to be published. Usually, such works concentrate on a specific topic, for example, the world financial crisis,[1] terrorism[2] or migration.[3] These have raised a number of ongoing and open discussions worthy of attention and further consideration in an era explicitly referred to by some scholars as the 'century of challenges', wherein transformative changes in the natural and social world are triggered by technological and industrial developments that are 'increasing cultural and social tensions among peoples within and between states'.[4]

Though the subject matter of this book is not a new or a further inquiry into these societal problems, it focuses on their constitutional effects. We examine how these challenges have affected the constitutional jurisprudence of the courts in some European countries and also the jurisprudence of the European courts. Our focus is not on exploring the challenges themselves, but on investigating the related constitutional adjudication – in relation to these current worldwide challenges.

In the past few years constitutional courts and other national high courts adjudicating constitutional matters have had to cope with these new challenges. The world financial crisis, the new wave of terrorism, mass migration and other particular problems have wide-ranging effects not only on public policy and the day-by-day life of people but also on the old and embedded constitutional standards and judicial constructions as well. Our book examines how, if at all, these developments have affected the constitutional review in Europe. In new situations constitutional courts have to give responses to the constitutional questions of unprecedented social, economic and political problems. Furthermore, all the answers must conform with EU law and with some pieces of international law. Therefore, our analysis extends to the related jurisprudence of the European Court of Justice and the European Court of Human Rights.

Courts inevitably have had to reconsider their own older ideas and legal doctrines and arguments in their case-law that had been elaborated to handle other challenges in the past decades.

And, although the outcome of these judicial processes might differ depending on the subject matter, the international context, national traditions and constitutional conventions and other factors, our underlying assumption is that all constitutional courts and other high courts have some basic options:

- to use the existing and/or traditional judicial constructions, doctrines and interpretive tools based on the well-elaborated and permanent jurisprudence;
- to modify some well-established practice or adjust it to the new circumstances; or
- to seek essentially new approaches, abandoning or reinterpreting some constitutional principles and practices.

In fact, these are not exclusive alternatives that can be clearly separated from each other but, rather, they indicate some of the basic directions or choices that the courts may have made. Thus, the next basic research question of this project is whether these courts have changed their jurisprudence in order to meet these new challenges, or have they have resisted this. If constitutional jurisprudence has changed, the nature and extent of these changes need to be studied.

Finally, the book aims to give general and contextual explanations for the examined constitutional jurisprudence at two different levels. First, the country studies seek to highlight the reasons for the change or continuity of constitutional adjudication. Beyond analysing national solutions, some comparative chapters examine the effects of multilevel constitutionalism – for instance, the role of judicial dialogue, or the influence of the European Court of Justice and the European Court of Human Rights in related constitutional matters. Second, the comparative part of the book aims to identify general European trends and characteristics.

In sum, the core questions of our book are: Have the 'new challenges' in the various European countries changed the constitutional jurisprudence of constitutional, European and other high courts, or not? If yes, how did the interpretation of these courts change? What factors and circumstances determine whether a court has modified its case-law and how can the change or stability of the constitutional jurisprudence in the different countries be explained?

Ultimately, the book is an invaluable contribution to the contemporary scholarly debate on the values of European constitutionalism studying the well-embedded principles and requirements under specific, and sometimes, extraordinary circumstances. Our underlying argument is that we can learn much about modern constitutional values by testing their stability and viability in times of unprecedented pressure. The book provides an insight into the contemporary ideas on constitutional justice and the present role of constitutional adjudication in Europe. Beyond this, the eventual way of how judicial bodies react to the unprecedented pressures and modern challenges can be an excellent test for the suitability and adaptability of both the constitutional review as a process and the constitutional (or other equivalent) court as an institution, and, in this way, our results contribute to the everlasting scholarly debate on their legitimacy. The range and volume of literature on constitutional comparison has been increasing and some researchers even speak about the 'Renaissance' of this method.[5] One of the most frequently discussed topics is constitutional adjudication including its institutional aspects[6] and methodology.[7] However, very recent constitutional jurisprudence on contemporary challenges has yet to be explored from a comparative perspective.

2 Conceptualising 'challenges' to contemporary constitutional justice

This book focusses on 'new challenges' and 'pressures' as social phenomena which can potentially affect constitutional adjudication in the various European countries. In our understanding, the relevant challenges are those that have brought about serious social, political and/or economic/financial difficulties in recent years and that have had constitutional implications. These are, primarily:

- the world economic/financial/debt crisis,
- terrorism and inland security,
- migration;

complex concepts themselves that can be divided into further (partial) problems. In fact, all the 'challenges' discussed here have caused diverse and complex crises with multiple societal, political, economic and cultural effects. For example, the economic and financial depression that began in 2008[8] has several different dimensions like fiscal, financial and debt crisis. In addition, other challenges, which most European countries have had to cope with, have engendered further crises and problems; migration waves, for example, have raised financial, cultural and social difficulties in the transit as well as the host countries.

However, this is not a full list. There are some other pressures that affect European countries selectively, or even particular problems which occur only in one or a few countries, such as political secessionism or the controversial relationship between national and European Union law. Furthermore, there are some other global challenges, from climate change to the endangering of biodiversity, that do not have primary constitutional implications in Europe.

Constitutional systems evidently must face, from time to time, special challenges – products of the constantly developing societies. Constitutional justice evolves along this change as it is the main function of the constitutional courts and other judicial bodies conducting reviews to reconcile the opposing societal interests and ambitions with established standards of constitutionality or in particular cases arbitrate these conflicts. The constitutional review of legal acts, and the adjudication of individual complaints against arbitrary legislative, governmental or judicial actions, are specialised legal instruments to fulfil these tasks. Thus, at a first glance, there is nothing special in the fact that nowadays the courts deal with different matters than before. Yet, the problems listed above represent special challenges, as they embody a whole series of social, political and economic problems which are not limited to one or two countries, but raise general concerns that most European countries must cope with. Moreover, as new challenges frequently entail great risks and dangers, their treatment often calls for extraordinary policy measures and special legal tools. Under such circumstances, courts are under tremendous pressure to give a green light to these unusual, and sometimes extraconstitutional, measures that are necessary to remedy the apparent dangers.

As we have emphasised already, our work concentrates on the constitutional jurisprudence in relation to certain selected challenges where the criterion of selection was the constitutional relevance of the particular problems in the reference states. The same phenomenon can trigger different constitutional responses in the various jurisdictions. If we want to understand the reasons for the different judicial responses to the same challenges, we should take the differences of legal structures, etc, into consideration. The constitutional relevance of these major contemporary problems cannot be denied, even if it can emerge in different ways. One of the most general features of the relevant constitutional issues is that they frequently involve extraordinary measures or emergency powers. The most exigent social challenges can easily be transformed into a constitutional crisis when unusual legal tools are made permissible for the government. Most constitutions acknowledge the inevitability, or, at least, the possibility of crisis management tools and the need for expansive state powers to cope with them. The public interest to overcome these problems therefore can trump individual rights. Through the classical words of Thomas Jefferson,

> The laws of necessity, of self-preservation, of saving our country when in danger, are of higher obligation. To lose our country by a scrupulous adherence to written law, would be to lose the law itself, with life, liberty, property and all those who are enjoying them with us; thus absurdly sacrificing the end to the means.[9]

However, as John Finn shows, Jefferson's thesis is an answer to a wrong question, because

> [w]hether we should suspend a constitution in the interest of self-preservation is a different question than whether standards derived from the basic principles of constitutionalism restrain the exercise of powers of emergency.[10]

Studying the relevant constitutional jurisprudence, it can hardly be denied that the primary job of constitutional courts is to restrain the emergency powers of the government which might be extraordinary limiting basic rights and liberties in an unusual way, but cannot be extra-constitutional. As the German Federal Constitutional Court declared in a landmark decision, '[T]here are constitutional principles that are so fundamental … that they also bind the framers of the Constitution'.[11]

Although the use of extraordinary power can and has to be constitutional, as its exercise must be subject to legal control and restraint, it is certain that there is an inherent tension between the need for the rights limitation in order to handle special situations and problems, and the constitutional order aiming at safeguarding and widening the individual rights and liberties. Thus, the contemporary challenges claiming legal responses are also special challenges to the constitutional systems of the various countries in which constitutional and other high courts have a preeminent role.

Sometimes the constitutional implications of these special situations and challenges can easily be recognised, whereas in other cases the constitutional relevance is more indirect.

As to the world economic and financial crisis, since its beginning in 2008, constitutional courts have often been asked to resolve challenges on the constitutionality of various measures adopted by the political branches in the areas of budgetary constraints, financial stabilisation and other economic policy measures. The courts have been inescapably involved in the public debates about the relevant legislation, as the financial austerity programmes embraced, among others, liberalisation measures in the labour market, restrictions of welfare expenditures and the reduction or withdrawal of certain social rights and vested interests. These measures frequently inflicted or limited property rights, social and welfare rights and produced challenges to the principle of equality. Though in some countries property rights were severely restricted (e.g. by imposing special taxes or nationalisation of private pension funds), the public sector was often a primary target of austerity programmes by means of reducing the wages of public servants or curtailing social benefits in an effort to reduce public expenditure. Social policy considerations and social rights have proved to be the loser in the whole process of economic recovery in a number of countries.

Constitutional courts have been asked on multiple occasions to adjudicate not only the national legislation and domestic policies implementing measures of economic adjustment, but also on international agreements such as the Fiscal Compact, or the European Financial Stabilisation Mechanism, even if some legislation adopted in the EU legal framework has entirely escaped judicial review,[12] as the EU law may not be overruled by national courts. In some countries, like Greece or Germany, discussed in this book, the EU-level financial recovery programmes, such as rescue packages and stability mechanisms, have given rise to heavy constitutional controversies, even though they had a different nature and depth in the various constitutional systems. For instance, in order to offer financial rescue to Greece, and, in this way, to preserve the stability of the Eurozone, some EU Member States established the European Financial Stabilisation Mechanism,[13] and the European Financial Stability Facility. According to these mechanisms, the financial assistance given to the participant countries was subject to specific conditions which affected the sovereignty of the respective Member States. These conditions require the respective countries to implement budgetary restrictions, to submit financial adjustment programs and empowered some EU institutions to control their economic and fiscal policy.[14] Since the EU is working on the perpetuation of the common economic policy, these mechanisms and many other tools of EU-level financial policy and control may encroach on all member countries' economic sovereignty, because these policy instruments entail not only policy transfer from the Member States to the EU but also the transfer of some financial competences from the nation states to the EU institutions falling traditionally within the scope of responsibility of national authorities, like the tightening of control over government deficit and state debt of all member states.[15] Fiscal policy and taxation have been traditionally integral parts of national sovereignty, so any change in the distribution of these powers affects unavoidably the legislative powers of national parliaments, the economic and financial policy-making competences of governments as well as the responsibilities of some other public bodies from constitutional courts to national banks. Moreover, all these national authorities may exercise their sovereign powers only within the existing legal frameworks, which guarantee not only the legality but also the legitimacy of these competences. The same issue raised different constitutional concerns in Germany, where the guarantees of the democratic decision-making process and the integrity of the budgetary powers of the Parliament (*Bundestag*) were at stake. The German Federal Constitutional Court expressed in its ruling on the Lisbon Treaty of the EU in June 2009[16] that the eternal clauses of the German Basic Law (*Grundgesetz*) contain the fundamental constitutional principles of Germany defining its constitutional identity which may not be violated by the transfer of sovereign rights to the EU institutions. One of these principles is democracy in which the Parliament has a special significance, among others in budgetary issues. This was the focal point of the later jurisprudence of the *Bundesverfassungsgericht* when it decided on the constitutionality of the Monetary Union Financial Stabilisation Act in 2011 (authorising the loans granted to Greece),[17] and in its judgement on European Stability Mechanism,[18] stressing that public revenue and spending belongs to the constitutional state by which it can shape public policy democratically. In Poland, as reported by the relevant chapter of this book, some other constitutional principles like equality and the social justice were challenged, whereas in Hungary the harsh restrictions of certain vested rights and property rights brought about constitutional controversies.

As a matter of fact, though certain legal tools were constitutionalised in order to avoid judicial review, some other new constitutional provisions that came about as reactions to the financial crises have widened the scope of constitutional review. The former can be exemplified by the explicit limitations of the competence of constitutional court in public finance (such as in Hungary), the latter relates to the emergence of the principle of 'balanced budget' and debt-brake rules (designed to avert structural imbalances in state budget) in the constitutions.

All in all, the world financial crisis has been one of the major challenges raising the number of diverse constitutional issues with which the constitutional courts have been faced.

Terrorism as a threat to the inland security has been another great constitutional challenge. The social and political danger of terrorist attacks is beyond any doubt: These crimes are political actions which attempt to generate a state of affairs that can ultimately lead to the overthrow of government, and by producing massive intimidation, they have a social dimension generating fear in many people. All these features of terrorism explain why terrorist crimes are seen to inflict more harm than common crimes and why they should be punished more severely.[19] The new forms of terrorism, for example, suicide bombings, blind massacres that kill as many innocent people as possible understandably horrify citizens, as too does the new phenomenon of 'neighbour terrorism' where the terrorist attack is committed by a country's second- or third-generation own citizens rather than by foreigners who do not have any connection or emotional bond with the given country. Under such circumstances, the people are easily willing to accept that this sort of extraordinary threat justifies extraordinary measures in order to defend life and order. The remedy of the high risk of terrorism requires special precautionary measures which may legitimately limit fundamental rights. Therefore, the average person can easily be ready to give a broad mandate to the government to combat terrorism. In Hungary, for example, which has not been affected by terrorist acts so far, the Parliament adopted a constitutional amendment in June 2016 introducing the 'terrorism state of emergency' as a new form of special legal orders providing the government with the right to suspend existing laws and to take other 'extraordinary measures' that depart from existing laws in the event of a terrorist attack or a 'significant and direct danger of a terrorist attack'.

In addition, the danger of terrorist attacks, and especially those committed terrorist acts, incite immediate and hard counteraction by governments and politicians who try to meet real or deemed social expectations to provide a firm and determinate answer to terrorism. In France, only three days after the terrible terrorist attack in Paris on 13 November 2015, the French president made a proposal before both Houses of Parliament assembled in Congress at Versailles to amend the Constitution in a way that was inconceivable beforehand (such as the possibility to strip nationality from a French citizen, while all laws since the Third Republic prohibited the deprivation of nationality from those who had born in France).[20] However, this might lead to a vicious circle, with each successful attack creating a demand for more repressive laws, and so on.[21]

It is easy to see that the main constitutional risk is that in times of the danger of terrorism the balance can be shifted between freedom and security at the expense of individual rights. Although different countries follow different policies, the most usual ways of combatting terrorism are as follows. The first strategy is based on the conventional wisdom that criminal law is an effective instrument in the fight against terrorism because harsher punishments will deter the terrorists from committing their actions. According to this deterrence-based argument, terror attacks should be separately criminalised, with punishments more severe than for common crimes.[22] Another strategy focusses on preventative tools and instruments that try to control the level and state of inland security; the idea is that the threat of terrorism can be successfully handled by early police intervention at the preparatory stage of a terrorist act, and thus focussing on detection and disruption of the ongoing actions. A third strategy – typically followed in the USA – rests on the attitude of treating all terrorists as enemy combatants, which justifies the war on terror using the military to strike at terrorist threats.[23] This strategy presumes that domestic laws and the normal operation of law enforcement authorities are insufficient to adequately combat and protect against the threat of terrorism.

As a matter of fact, all the usual antiterrorism strategies raise constitutional concerns. It is a common danger that fighting terrorism can lead to excessive and disproportionate limitation of individual rights or to unjustified restriction of freedoms of certain communities. Furthermore, the criminalisation of terrorism usually encourages the authorisation of the Government with extra policing powers to gather evidence, special processes to assist trials or imposition of enhanced penalties, and can result in the harsh and unfair treatment of defendants. The preventive strategies frequently applied are detention without trial, data-mining, the seizure of assets, arrest and interrogation[24] even in the case of simple suspicion. Perhaps the instruments of a US-style war on terror would be the greatest challenge to constitutional normality; however, the use of military forces is not typical in Europe, even if it is not unprecedented for certain tasks (e.g. for security services or border guards).

The core problem is what rights and to what extent should these be sacrificed to overcome a danger. The exaggeration of security risks can lead not only to the disproportionate use of state force but also to the exercise of the increased power for other purposes as well. Thus, privacy, due process rights, property rights and other liberties can be unreasonably restricted. Indeed, not only are the citizens' rights and freedoms at stake but also the rights of those who are suspected to be terrorists – however difficult it is to protect the rights of those who, let say, have committed attacks against random people. Likewise, special laws and extraordinary measures can undermine the legitimacy of the constitutional system and the protection of individual rights particularly when they are not only temporary responses but have long-term effects.

In sum, the basic constitutional question is how to keep a balance between the competing interests of safeguarding individual (and group) rights and increasing the effectiveness of law enforcement in fighting terrorism; constitutional courts frequently cannot escape from the responsibility to adjudicate the justification and proportionality of the applied methods and legal tools in the European constitutional democracies. Needless to say, allowing repressive laws for greater security is a primary political issue – nevertheless, courts must have the final say as to whether the particular legal tools are compatible with the constitutional order, or not.

The threat of terrorism and the claim for the protection of inland security are often linked to the problem of migration. The mass migration that has affected a number of recipient European countries in recent years has generated a lot of concerns. One of these fears is that the migrants can destabilise the political and economic order of the affected countries. Migration often generates security problems both in the transitory and the target countries; irregular migrants often violate border regulations and reside in the recipient states without registration and legal status and in these ways they challenge the rule of law and legal order. Their emergence and presence frequently bring about fear, anxiety and distrust and is a source of insecurity.[25]

Another common fear is that the strangers of foreign cultures may cause social and cultural conflicts even once they are accepted in a local community. In most cases, migrants have a different identity from that of the receiving society, which can represent a security threat to the societal identity of the recipient community.[26]

Besides these fears, there is an economic dimension to migration, with multiple effects on the recipient country. Hence, many fear that the newcomers will take away their jobs and acquire undeserved social and welfare services at the expense of local taxpayers. In fact, mass migration can put a major burden on a country's social welfare and health care system and cause a lot of administrative tasks and problems.

However, our interest involves the constitutional aspects of all these issues; more precisely in the stability or changeability or the relevant jurisprudence of constitutional courts. Evidently, several aspects of migration may raise constitutional questions and may be brought to courts. First, 'migration', as a general term, encompasses several groups of people whose members have different legal status. Refugees who have escaped from civil war and harsh oppression by authorities, and who seek protection outside their country of origin, have the universal human right for asylum, so they have a legal claim for being accepted at least in the first safe state. But even before somebody may attain refugee status, everybody has the right to apply for such legal standing as well as to a fair trial, and, beyond that, every migrant has obviously the right to be handled in a humane and fair way.

Because migrants can have several different legal statuses and rights, the governments may legitimately treat them differently. This is a sensitive issue in itself where it is particularly important to provide protection for fundamental human rights, because those who have left their home and seek a new life in a foreign country are by nature in a vulnerable position, especially if the recipient community looks at them with distrust and repugnance. The general mistrust and aversion towards migrants can easily be exploited by politicians for political gains, frightening the public with 'illegal immigration hordes' or to see terrorists in every migrant.

So, the legal conditions established for the respective procedures, the circumscription of the rights and freedoms of migrant people, or the delimitation of the European Union and its Member States' competences all are matters which reach constitutional courts. In this field, there must also be a delicate balance between the legitimate interests of the states for security and the reasonable and non-discriminatory treatment of the various groups of migrants.

The world economic crisis, international terrorism and mass migration are only representative examples of worldwide challenges that have constitutional implications and can trigger several constitutional controversies. Countries might have other modern challenges that demand judicial responses such as regionalisation or secessionist movements in Spain, or the controversial co-existence of the EU and the national law in Britain. The analysis of the judicial responses to these special problems can also be considered to be the proper tools for assessing the state of constitutional jurisprudence in the 'age of challenges'.

3 Research methods

This book analyses all these things from a European comparative perspective. In the course of the research design, we selected countries that have been deeply affected by the challenges we conceptualised for this project. For this reason, the following countries are examined:

- Croatia
- France
- Germany
- Greece
- Hungary
- Italy
- Poland
- Portugal
- Spain
- United Kingdom.

These countries represent different (common law and civil law) legal cultures and legal systems. Their judicial structures and systems of constitutional adjudication also differ from each other. Among them, there are old and well-established democracies and post-communist countries with moderate traditions of constitutional democracy. But all of them are members of the European Union (although the UK is currently in the process of leaving the EU) and they all share the fundamental principles and values of the European constitutionalism, where the legitimate power of government is constitutionally limited (even though in different ways and institutional settings). Therefore, they are undoubtedly comparable with each other when the legitimacy and performance of constitutional control is at stake.

Since the same challenges may occur in different ways and may have different constitutional effects in the various countries, which may face specific internal problems as well, the authors of the national studies were free to choose what judicial cases or problems they present and to analyse the change/stability of constitutional justice in their own countries. Some give a wide picture on very recent constitutional jurisprudence, as most challenges have already reached the constitutional court in their country. Others concentrate on a single major issue, either because they consider it to be characteristic of the state and attitude of national system of constitutional adjudication, or because not all the problems listed here have been dealt with by the constitutional (or equivalent) court.

Certainly, there are no objective criteria to measure the changeability/stability of constitutional jurisprudence. In reality, it is often not possible to compare the old and new interpretive practices of the courts because the current challenges have no precedents in constitutional case-law. But even if this is the case, the structure of argumentation and the preferred method of constitutional interpretation can be compared with the previous practice, and the use of the earlier case-law can also establish an assessment of the change versus stability of constitutional adjudication. It is also true that constitutional amendments or the emergence of a new legal environment may be the source of changes in jurisprudence, even though the legal development and the improvement of interpretive practice of judicial tribunals are quite natural things. Consequently, the change or continuity/stability of constitutional jurisprudence cannot be evaluated in itself, but only when studying the whole context. Of course, if a court modifies its case-law just because of political pressure, or if the new wave of judicial deference is based on institutional (self)interest, the change can be objected for good reason. However, the alteration of the judicial practice can be the result of a justified correction or renewal of old and obsolete interpretive practices, or legitimate adaptation of jurisprudence to the new social circumstances. This is true also in the stability/continuity dimension. So, the justification of the maintenance versus reform of the previous judicial case-law has a crucial importance not only for the scholarship but also for the courts themselves that have to preserve their own legitimacy as ultimate guardians of constitutional values.

Acknowledgements

Finally, we owe special thanks to the French Embassy in Hungary, the Center for Social Sciences of the Hungarian Academy of Sciences and the Francophone University Centre of the University of Szeged which generously supported our research project, and the preparation of this publication. This book reports on the results of an international research project that was financed and assisted by the National University of Public Service and the Institute for Legal Studies at the Center for Social Sciences of the Hungarian Academy of Sciences to which we are also grateful.

Notes

1 Contiades (2013); Iglesias-Rodríguez, Triandafyllidou and Gropas (2016); Morrison (2016).
2 Akhgar and Brewster (2016); Kaunert and Léonard (2013); Richards (2015).
3 Bilgic (2013).
4 Noonan and Nadkarni (2016) 2.
5 See the new wave of literature on comparative constitutional law Hirschl (2013), Tushnet (2014).

6 Harding and Leyland (2009); Comella (2009); Brewer-Carías (2011); , Mazmanyan and W. Vandenbruwaene (2013); Hübner (2013); de Visser (2014).
7 Kapiszewski and Silverstein (2013); Groppi and Ponthoreau (2014).
8 Conventionally, the collapse of Lehman Brothers on 15 October 2018 is held as a definitive moment of the world financial crisis.
9 Jefferson (1893) 279–80.
10 Finn (1991) 22.
11 BVerfGE 1, 14 (1951).
12 Fabbrini (2016) 107.
13 The EFSM was activated not only for Greece, but in the early 2010s for Ireland and Portugal as well.
14 Tuori and Tuori (2014) 91.
15 Ibid. 105.
16 BVerfG, 2 BvR 2/08.
17 BVerfG, 2 BvR 987/10.
18 BVerfG, 2 BvR 1390/12.
19 Meliá (2011) 119.
20 Duhamel (2016) 3.
21 Ackerman (2006) 2.
22 Meliá (2011) 116.
23 Beckman (2007) 165.
24 Walker (2007) 1400.
25 Bilgic (2013) 19.
26 Ibid. 163.

Bibliography

Ackerman, Bruce, *Before the Next Attack. Preserving Civil Liberties in an Age of Terrorism* (Yale University Press 2006).

Akhgar, Babak and Brewster, Ben (eds), *Combatting Cybercrime and Cyberterrorism: Challenges, Trends and Priorities* (Springer 2016).

Beckman, James, *Comparative Legal Approaches to Homeland Security and Anti-Terrorism* (Ashgate 2007).

Bilgic, Ali, *Rethinking Security in the Age of Migration: Trust and Emancipation in Europe* (Routledge 2013).

Brewer-Carías, Allan R. (ed.), *Constitutional Courts as Positive Legislators. A Comparative Law Study* (Cambridge University Press 2011).

Comella, Víctor Ferreres, *Constitutional Courts & Democratic Values* (Yale University Press 2009).

Contiades, Xenophon (ed.), *Constitutions in the Global Financial Crisis. A Comparative Analysis* (Routledge 2013).

de Visser, Marthe, *Constitutional Review in Europe. A Comparative Analysis* (Hart 2014).

Duhamel, Olivier, 'Terrorism and Constitutional Amendment in France' (2016). *European Constitutional Law Review*, Vol 12, No 1.

Fabbrini, Federico, *Economic Governance in Europe – Comparative Paradoxes and Constitutional Challenges* (Oxford University Press 2016).

Finn, John E., *Constitutions in Crisis. Political Violence and the Rule of Law* (Oxford University Press 1991).

Groppi, Tania and Ponthoreau, Marie-Claire (eds), *The Use of Foreign Precedents by Constitutional Judges* (Hart 2014).

Harding, Andrew and Leyland, Peter (eds), *Constitutional Courts. A Comparative Study* (Wildy, Simmonds & Hill Publishing 2009).

Hirschl, Ran, *Comparative Matters – The Renaissance of Comparative Constitutional Law* (Oxford University Press 2013).

Hübner Mendes, Conrado, *Constitutional Courts and Deliberative Democracy* (Oxford University Press 2013).

Iglesias-Rodríguez, Pablo, Triandafyllidou, Anna and Gropas, Ruby (eds), *After the Financial Crisis – Shifting Legal, Economic and Political Paradigms* (Palgrave MacMillan 2016).

Jefferson, Thomas, 'Letter to John V. Colvin, September 10, 1810', in Paul Leicester Ford (ed.), *The Writings of Thomas Jefferson*, 10 vols (G. P. Putnam's Sons 1893), vol. 9.

Kapiszewski, Diana and Silverstein, Gordon (eds), *Consequential Courts: Judicial Roles in Global Perspective* (Cambridge University Press 2013).

Kaunert, Christian and Léonard, Sarah (eds), *European Security, Terrorism and Intelligence Tackling New Security Challenges in Europe* (Palgrave MacMillan 2013).

Meliá, Manuel Cancio, 'Terrorism and Criminal Law: The Dream of Prevention, the Nightmare of the Rule of Law' (2011). *New Criminal Law Review*, Vol. 14, No 1.

Morrison, Fred L. (ed.), *Fiscal Rules – Limits on Governmental Deficits and Debt* (Springer 2016).

Noonan, Norma C. and Nadkarni, Vidya, 'Introduction: A Century of Challenges', in Norma C. Noonan and Vidya Nadkarni (eds), *Challenge and Change. Global Threats and the State in Twenty-first Century International Politics* (Palgrave Macmillan 2016).

Popelier, Patricia, Mazmanyan, Armen and Vandenbruwaene, Werner (eds), *The Role of Constitutional Courts in Multilevel Governance* (Intersentia 2013).

Richards, Anthony, *Conceptualizing Terrorism* (Oxford University Press 2015).

Tuori, Kaarlo and Tuori, Klaus, *The Eurozone Crisis. A Constitutional Analysis* (Cambridge University Press 2014).

Tushnet, Mark, *Advanced Introduction to Comparative Constitutional Law* (Edward Elgar 2014).

Walker, Clive, 'Keeping Control of Terrorists Without Losing Control of Constitutionalism' (2007). *Stanford Law Review*, Vol. 59, No. 5.

2 The resistance of constitutional standards to the new economic and social challenges and the legitimacy of constitutional review in a contemporary European context

Michel Verpeaux

Today, one of the most exigent problems of constitutional law is whether the fundamental constitutional standards can resist social, technical and economic changes or, to the contrary, need to adapt to these new circumstances. Constitutional resistance to challenges is likely to trigger the modification or redefinition of the interpretation methods discernible in constitutional case-law with regard to fundamental rights, such as the necessity of proportionality.

These challenges, which are diverse in their nature, pose a threat to the existing balance or status quo. So far, constitutions have been facing crises that have taken the shape of threats to constitutional balance, associated rather with threats to the public order – by uprisings or social unrest from within, or from outside, especially by invasions. The nature of these new threats presented as 'economic and social challenges'[1] has changed significantly and they are likely to be external to the State; however, they might not originate from any other States but from less defined forces.[2]

At this point in time, the disturbances are more insidious and more indirect: threats posed by the economic and financial crisis, stock market crashes and massive migration flows, or from terrorism by different groups originating from a variety of situations. We must not forget the crises related to climate risks or to the pollution of the environment either.

Whatever the origin of these threats, resistance means to preserve and maintain the principles that could serve as a bulwark against new challenges. These principles, the denomination of which states that they are 'constitutional', have to be sufficiently established in order not to be hindered by challenges. Otherwise, essential concepts might undergo mutations that may lead constitutional justice to adapt to the changing conditions and to social challenges. Such an adaptation, if it exceeds a specific threshold, carries the risk of infringing even the best-established constitutional principles.

The word 'standard' may take on various meanings but, in any case, it refers to general, permanent rules likely to apply to all situations encompassed by these standards. On the one hand, standards might be rules developed by the judge to facilitate and supervise their own jurisprudence, and in this case, those rules are at the same level as constitutional rules, or below them. In those cases, we are talking about rules of judicial creation that the judge gives themselves and that correspond to instruments enabling the judge to find a more coherent and constant expression to their jurisprudence. These standards are of the same value as the judge's jurisprudence, at best.

On the other hand, the constitutional standards may surpass the single frame of a constitution or constitutional case-law, and may indicate the norms that should appear in a constitution, whatever the country in question or the prevailing situation. This category could include, for example, the recognition of a basis of unquestionable – or minimum – fundamental rights, the need for the guarantee of a fair trial or any other standard considered to be fundamental. Thus devised, these standards have to be considered as imposing on the judge. Their objective is, in fact, to prevent the States from disregarding or ignoring them, precisely in special circumstances, such as the crises enumerated in the title.

Whatever their definition, the standards are devised to be means of resistance or bulwarks to oppose challenges. Against these challenges, the protection by standards may be external to the constitution; however, it can also be enshrined in the constitution itself.

1. Meta-protection

In order to protect constitutional principles, we need to identify the existence of constitutional standards likely to impose upon State authorities, and that, in turn, raises the question of their enforceability.

1.1. The existence of standards

The definition of these standards means, first of all, to define the level on which they are developed. Universal standards, which are valid in every country, reinforce the idea that some sort of world heritage may exist – a concept that would be more fitting than the conventional natural law doctrine in the sense that it does not emanate from metaphysical or 'natural' forces, but from specific facts taken from texts that exist in reality, and based on which a synthesis can be created. This synthesis fits in the debate between positivism and natural law, only in new terms.

The contemplated standards must be sufficiently close to one another to be comparable against the same system of references. This concept has accompanied the ever-growing consideration for fundamental rights and concerns qualified as universal in as much as they would be the conditions of the rule of law.[3] It was in the context of defending these rights that such a concept could be developed, and the Second World War and its barbarity has played a powerful role in that. The present age seems to feel less strongly about them, precisely in the face of the rise of new threats. It is true that, in the absence of a text specifying with certainty and in an evident manner for all what common heritage is, the interpretation of these seemingly customary rules is subject to discussion, which leads necessarily to the weakening of the rules' value and to doubts over their existence. The reference to standards should not make us forget about the pejorative assessment of the term 'standardisation', which evokes a form of impoverishment or levelling out.

One of the difficulties of recognising global or universal standards is, of course, the determination of the conditions enabling a standard to be considered as such and recognised by all States. In the – likely – case in which they are not recognised by all, the principle of the lowest common denominator could suffice to enshrine a standard.

It is doubtlessly easier to imagine standards developed at a regional level, in the framework of the European Union or the Council of Europe. Article 2 of the Treaty on the European Union signed in Lisbon on 13 December 2007 is very enlightening in this regard:

> The Union is founded on the values of respect for human dignity, freedom, democracy, equality, the rule of law and respect for human rights, including the rights of persons belonging to minorities. These values are common to the Member States in a society in which pluralism, non-discrimination, tolerance, justice, solidarity and equality between women and men prevail.

Article 6 of the same treaty[4] declares under § 3 that

> Fundamental rights, as guaranteed by the European Convention for the Protection of Human Rights and Fundamental Freedoms and as they result from the constitutional traditions common to the Member States, shall constitute general principles of the Union's law.

Thus is declared, outside written law, the recognition of these constitutional traditions the origin of which is left in uncertainty, the substance of which, however, seems to be binding for the States, even though these traditions originate from the States themselves. In certain ways, it is a form of 'constitutional *ius cogens*', called for by its supporters and feared by its opponents. As the *ius cogens* recognised in international law and often translated by the term 'peremptory norm', these standards constitute binding law; that is, principles deemed to be universal and superior and that will underpin the peremptory norms of a general constitutional law.[5]

As regards constitutional standards, might it be more accurate to speak about international or supranational consensus in the European context? Failing to designate directly applicable rules, these standards could constitute the objectives the constitutions should reach. Even though the standards tally with good practices or traditions common to the States, giving them a written form, nevertheless, may prove to be necessary, if only to ensure their propagation and their guarantee. There is also the issue of their respect, necessary so that they can respond to the challenges.

1.2. Legally binding standards

Envisioning a common heritage allows establishment of a benchmark or a comparison against which State constitutions can be juxtaposed. When revolutions happen, for example in the case of the Arab revolutions after 2011, the consequence is that proclaiming to draft a constitution is not enough anymore: it must conform to certain ideals or principles. This means that a form of constitutional engineering might exist.

Tailoring constitutions to meet the current needs may go back to two origins. On the one hand, the constituent power itself may want to call constitutional rules into question in order to align them with new circumstances. On the other hand, the constitutional judge or the interpreter of the constitution – where it exists – might be required, whether they like it or not, that is, under the pressure of crisis situations, to interpret constitutional rules in the light of these challenges, stressing the needs qualified as constitutional, such as the protection of the public order, the continuity of the State or the life of the nation. Even if these concepts might not be expressly laid down in the constitutional text, they are, however, at the core of every political organisation, without any need to be inscribed, and would be deduced from other constitutional rules. Take, for instance, Article 5 of the French Constitution, the second subparagraph of which states that the President of the Republic 'shall be the guarantor of national independence, territorial integrity and due respect for Treaties'.[6] The French Constitutional Council acknowledged this concept and ruled that

> in this situation and in absence of directly applicable constitutional or organic provisions, it would appear to be the clear responsibility of the Parliament and the Government, within the sphere of their respective competences, to lay down all the financial measures necessary to ensure the continuity of the nation's life.[7]

In this case, it was only about compensating the absence of vote on the finance law within the time allowed by the Constitution (Article 47). In the event of a more severe crisis, the concept of the 'continuity of the State' would have even more reasons to be used.

To tackle these temptations, the standards must have a binding nature, and thus the question arises: What body would have the power to impose them on the States tempted to withdraw from them in the face of new threats or challenges.

The first answer we might think of is a supranational judge within the UN framework, like the International Criminal Court. Of course, the States would have to accept its jurisdiction, which is hard to imagine. On a regional level, the European Court of Human Rights seems to be more appropriate and better accepted.[8]

In absence of a real jurisdiction the decisions of which impose on the States, there are observing or 'advisory' bodies such as the Commission for Democracy through Law – known as the Venice Commission – a consultative body of the Council of Europe regarding constitutional questions. Its mission is to help Member States wishing to bring their legal and institutional structures into line with European standards and international experience in the fields of democracy, human rights and the rule of law. Its website specifies that it 'also helps to ensure the dissemination and consolidation of a common constitutional heritage' and that it plays 'a unique role in conflict management, and provides "emergency constitutional aid" to states in transition'.

In an even less binding fashion, the dialogue of jurisdictions with common legal and cultural traditions might play a role. An institution like the Association of the Constitutional Courts Sharing the Use of French Language (ACCPUF) can play a crucial role through the dissemination of the rules shared by their constitutional courts. The language barrier or, on the contrary, a shared language – as well as the culture accompanying it – can work as a brake or an accelerator of this dissemination. We must not forget the role of constitutional pilgrims, more or less voluntarily spreading the good word of constitutionalism.

Secondly, at the level of the national judge with sufficient authority, these standards can be compared against the behaviour of the States tempted to disrespect them. This second possibility raises the question of the constitutional judge's freedom and of the limitations that might apply to them. The limitations are the consequence of rules existing outside of state rules, including constitutional rules, and this poses the issue of the relationship between supranational and constitutional standards. A number of constitutions proclaim the equality of these two rule categories, such as the Constitution of the Slovak Republic, in which subparagraph 2 of Article 1 states 'The Slovak Republic acknowledges and adheres to general rules of international law, international treaties by which it is bound, and its other international obligations'. This article is set forth in greater detail by Article 154c of the same Constitution:

> International treaties on human rights and fundamental freedoms which the Slovak Republic has ratified and were promulgated in the manner laid down by a law before taking effect of this constitutional act, shall be a part of its legal order and shall have precedence over laws if they provide a greater scope of constitutional rights and freedoms.

Such is not the case in France where the highest courts or tribunals unanimously declare that in the absence of any text relating to this, the 'supremacy … conferred upon international commitments is not applicable domestically to constitutional provisions' (Council of State, Assembly, 30 October 1998, Sarran, Levacher and others). As for the French Constitutional Council, it ruled that 'it follows in particular from its Article I-5, relating to the relationship between the Union and the Member States, that this denomination has no effect on the existence of the French Constitution and its place at the top of the domestic hierarchy of norms' (decision n° 2004–505 DC of 19 November 2004, Treaty establishing a Constitution for Europe).

Thus, the obligation derived from the respect of constitutional standards, assumingly external to the national constitution, depends, to a large extent, on the place of the constitution in comparison with other, namely supranational norms, and on the way the constitutional judge interprets these relationships.

2. Constitutional self-protection

The constitution itself can prescribe and organise mechanisms we might qualify as internal, in order to protect the rules considered more important within the text, so that they can resist the challenges eventually threatening the constitution better than others. The other way being constitutions might consider making temporary adjustments to the constitutional rules in order to meet specific needs.

2.1. Supra-constitutional provisions

To have constitutional standards within a constitution, there needs to be a constitution first. Should it be written? The answer is a priori negative and a written constitution offers no guarantee of stability – consider the United States for refuting the French example, characterised by chronic instability despite the written nature of French constitutions. However, the written form does offer the advantage of enabling a more direct approach to the constitution the contours of which are, hence, more accessible.

The respect of these standards depends also on the content of the constitution. It can be a purely technical text or it may have more developed material contents, including a number of core principles akin to real standards. Enshrining substantive rules permits better resistance to challenges, by countering crisis situations through solemn principles. Nevertheless, this observation is not as straightforward as it seems, for the rules of procedure help prevent too hasty or easy modifications of constitutional rules. Thus, the question of constitutional rigidity or flexibility arises, the former guaranteeing stability and resistance.

Resistance can come from rules within the constitution, which would include not supranational rules, but those with constitutional value and that impose on constitutional rules of lesser importance, hence the suggested term 'supra-constitutional'. This is the case in several countries: subparagraph 5 of Article 89 of the French Constitution stipulates a prohibition: 'The republican form of government shall not be the object of any amendment'. Other constitutions prohibit the revision of certain provisions considered more essential than others. Such is the case of the German Basic Law where Article 79 § 3 declares 'Amendments to this Basic Law affecting the division of the Federation into *Länder*, their participation on principle in the legislative process, or the principles laid down in Articles 1 and 20 shall be inadmissible'. Paragraphs 2 and 3 of Article 9 of the modified Constitution of the Czech Republic of 16 December 1992 provide that '(2) The substantive requisites of the democratic rule of law is inadmissible. (3) Interpretation of legal rules may not authorize the removal or endanger the foundations of a democratic state'.

Article 60 § 4 of the Constitution of the Federative Republic of Brazil of 5 October 1988 contains provisions the amendment of which is inadmissible and what Brazilians call 'stone-clauses' (*clausula petrea*), also referred to as 'eternity clauses'. They include the federative form of State, the characteristics of direct, secret, and universal vote, the separation of powers and individual rights and guarantees.

The existence of these norms the permanency of which is entrenched raises several questions: the first issue pertains to the power of review disposed to modify these provisions in order to circumvent the prohibition, which supposes that the derived or secondary constituent power is not distinguished from the original constituent power. The second raises the question of the constitutional judge's role with regard to constitutional revision laws. The French case of the Constitutional Council's categorical refusal to control constitutional laws by reason that there is no text that would confer such powers upon it might be isolated and is not without controversy.

2.2. The constitution adjusting constitutional norms

In reverse, constitutions might provide for previously established assumptions, cases in which extraordinary or derogatory constitutional mechanisms exist in order to protect the constitution itself. These measures are, thus, designed as temporary and are intended to bring back constitutional order. In their nature they are similar to dictatorship, which, in the time of the Roman Republic, conferred full powers upon an extraordinary magistrate in order to address major disturbances as efficiently as possible, after a military disaster or during a domestic political crisis, for instance.[9]

More recent constitutions structure crisis and emergency situations. Such is the case of Article 16 of the French Constitution of 1958, heavily inspired by the situation that the invasion by German troops brought about in France in 1940. Its first subparagraph provides that

> Where the institutions of the Republic, the independence of the Nation, the integrity of its territory or the fulfilment of its international commitments are under serious and immediate threat, and where the proper functioning of the constitutional public authorities is interrupted, the President of the Republic shall take measures required by these circumstances, after formally consulting the Prime Minister, the Presidents of the Houses of Parliament and the Constitutional Council.

The Hungarian Constitution regulates a certain number of extraordinary situations, called 'Special Legal Orders', from which the common rules of State of Siege and State of Emergency are derived (Arts. 48 to 50). The same Constitution also provides for the situation of State of Preventive Defense (Art. 51) or for that of Unexpected Attack (Art. 52). Nevertheless, these provisions are all aimed at situations that we could qualify as 'classic' threats to the constitutional order or as aggressions. The scenario referred to as 'State of Danger' under Art. 53 provides that

> In the event of a natural disaster or industrial accident endangering life and property, or in order to mitigate the consequences thereof, the Government shall declare a state of danger, and may introduce extraordinary measures laid down in a cardinal Act.

Subject to further analysis, it seems debatable that these legal orders could respond to the challenges set out in the proposed subject.

The Basic Law of Germany also mentions a state of defence, regulated under Article 115. This provides that

> Any determination that the federal territory is under attack by armed force or imminently threatened with such an attack (state of defence) shall be made by the Bundestag with the consent of the Bundesrat. Such determination shall be made on application of the Federal Government and shall require a two-thirds majority of the votes cast, which shall include at least a majority of the Members of the Bundestag.

The circumstance of attack by armed force does not provide a solution to all the situations covered by economic and social challenges.

We see that the present contribution raises far more questions than answers. However, it is the nature of an introductory chapter to open space for reflection. Furthermore, many of these answers depend on the constitutional judge's role, on their place within the institutions and on their relationship with other public authorities and other jurisdictions, both State and supranational, namely within the frame of Europe. For constitutions, these fragile documents, only make sense if they have an efficient and independent guardian.

Notes

1 For the conceptualization see Szente and Gárdos-Orosz, Introduction (2018) in this book.

2 In this regard, the Islamic State (IS) is emblematic, for in order to justify under international law the strikes targeted at the territory of a real State in which IS had taken hold, the question arises: What is it legally? The question of responding to the threats posed by terrorism originating from a foreign State, for example Syria, arises within the terms of Article 51 of the Charter of the United Nations, which states the following: 'Nothing in the present Charter shall impair the inherent right of individual or collective self-defence if an armed attack occurs against a Member of the United Nations, until the Security Council has taken measures necessary to maintain international peace and security. Measures taken by Members in the exercise of this right of self-defence shall be immediately reported to the Security Council and shall not in any way affect the authority and responsibility of the Security Council under the present Charter to take at any time such action as it deems necessary in order to maintain or restore international peace and security'.

3 On this subject, see Disant and Lewkocicz (2017).

4 Furthermore, Article 6 refers to the Charter of Fundamental Rights of 7 December 2000 recognising it as having the same legal value as the treaties.

5 This concept is defined by the Vienna Convention of 23 May 1969 under Article 53: 'For the purposes of the present Convention, a peremptory norm of general international law is a norm accepted and recognized by the international community of States as a whole as a norm from which no derogation is permitted and which can be modified only by a subsequent norm of general international law having the same character'.

6 The full text of Article 5 reads: 'The President of the Republic shall ensure due respect for the Constitution. He shall ensure, by his arbitration, the proper functioning of the

public authorities and the continuity of the State. He shall be the guarantor of national independence, territorial integrity and due respect for Treaties'.

7 Decision n° 79–111 DC of 30 December 1979, Law authorising the Government to continue collecting the existing taxes and duties in 1980, recital 2.

8 On this topic, see the chapters of Groppi (2018) and Delzangles (2018) in this book.

9 The dictator was nominated by one of the two incumbent consuls after the Senate had approved in principle the dictatorship. Without doubt, the most famous was Lucius Quinctius Cincinnatus, consul in 460 BC, dictator twice in 458 and in 439 BC, because he represented the Roman ideal of traditional virtues, leading a simple life and capable of devoting himself to the patriotic cause.

Bibliography

Delzangles, Beatrice, 'The negotiating function of the European Court of Human Rights: Reconciling diverging interests born from new European challenges', in Zoltán Szente and Fruzsina Gárdos-Orosz (eds), *New Challenges to Constitutional Adjudication in Europe* (Routledge 2018).

Disant, Mattheau and Gregory Lewkocicz, *Vers des standards constitutionnels mondiaux* (Bruylant 2017).

Groppi, Tania, 'New challenges for constitutional adjudication in Europe: What role could the 'dialogue of courts' play?', in Zoltán Szente and Fruzsina Gárdos-Orosz (eds), *New Challenges to Constitutional Adjudication in Europe* (Routledge 2018).

Szente, Zoltán and Gárdos-Orosz, Fruzsina, 'Introduction – Contemporary challenges to constitutional adjudication in Europe', in Zoltán Szente and Fruzsina Gárdos-Orosz (eds), *New Challenges to Constitutional Adjudication in Europe* (Routledge 2018).

Part II

Coping with challenges by national courts

3 Croatian constitutional adjudication in times of stress

Djordje Gardasevic

Introduction

In the following text I shall give an overview of some of the most important cases which hopefully will shed some light on how exactly the Constitutional Court of the Republic of Croatia has acted when faced with situations of crisis and whether, in such contexts, it has been changing its practice that had been developed in 'peaceful' times. In the next section (War, security and terrorism) I will describe some constitutional experiences related to the, so far, only full-blown 'war' crisis which in Croatia occurred in the first part of the 1990s and will then proceed to explain further developments in the context of new security challenges that have appeared in recent years. As it will be shown, these two periods are quite revealing for examining the position of the Court in dealing with legislative attacks on rights and rule of law in security issues. Though in the context of real 'war' the Court showed extreme deference to emergency measures, in recent years it seems to have taken quite a different approach. In the latter sense, the case of the Law on Criminal Procedure from 2012 shows that the Court, when reviewing legislation regulating the balance between security and liberty, is able and willing to apply some rather strict scrutiny standards. The overall situation in this field, however, is far from clear and any general conclusion on how the Court will act in future cases of imminent and serious threat to the constitutional order might be quite premature. The main issue stems from the fact that basic modern legislative acts that deal with security matters in Croatia have not so far been examined by the Court and hence there is a lack of 'evidence'.

In section 2 (Financial crisis and economic policy of the state) I review some of the major decisions of the Court concerning legislation enacted, or intended to be enacted, in the context of the last global economic crisis. Here, I am give three examples that describe the Court's position on tax policies and in the context of organisation of work in the public sector (the 'outsourcing' case). Taking into account that constitutional adjudication in such matters, as opposed to personal and political rights, usually allows for wider regulatory discretion of political branches of Government, the deference with which the Court showed in those cases might have been expected and still could be expected in future. What is of particular interest here, however, is that the Court addressed some hard questions and at least tried to interpret some of the basic constitutional formulations (concepts of 'social state', 'social justice', 'social rights' and 'exclusive powers' of regulation of the Parliament and the Government).

This brings me to some special remarks I wish to give in this introductory section. From strictly an institutional point of view, the modern Croatian Constitutional Court was established with the Constitution of 1990.[1] Two later amendments of the document, in 2000 and 2010, further expanded the Court's powers, raised the number of its justices to thirteen and prescribed that the justices are elected by the Parliament with a two-thirds majority. More precise details regulating the Court's composition, powers and procedures are also contained in the Constitutional Law on the Constitutional Court of the Republic of Croatia which has a constitutional status.[2] It may be said that these normative developments affecting the Court were not a result of any particular crisis as such, but were more a part of wider attempts to, respectively, reconstruct the whole constitutional system after a coalition of parties won parliamentary elections in 2000 and when the country was generally preparing to enter the European Union. From an institutional point of view, therefore, major developments regarding the Court in the last 15 years have taken place through its constantly evolving case-law. In this area, several observations can be made.

Firstly, the modern Court has throughout time gradually abandoned its practice to review mainly the legality of by-laws only and has extensively started to scrutinise laws as such.[3] In this way, undoubtedly, it started to impose some restrictions to the legislator itself and, consequently, firmly posited itself among other branches of government.[4] Secondly, the Court has also started to frequently apply relevant standards of the international protection of rights and freedoms, most importantly the European Convention on Human Rights. In addition, a significant influence on its reasoning may be seen in the quite usual references to comparative law as well as to opinions given by the Venice Commission.[5] Thirdly, the principle of proportionality, as the central feature of judicial review by the Court, was included in the Constitution with amendments to its text in 2000. However, it was actually the Court itself which had already one year earlier interpreted the proportionality principle to be an 'inherent' element of the constitutional system in general.[6] And finally, especially in recent years, the Court has developed some special concepts of constitutional interpretation, such as the 'objective order of values', 'structural unity' of the Constitution or the theory of 'unconstitutional constitutional amendments', which allow it to interpret the law beyond strict textual limitations or show its activism.[7]

1. War, security and terrorism

Similar to many examples, the Croatian 1990 Constitution was to a significant extent influenced by the context of emergency, anticipated as a possible outcome of political turmoil in which the former Yugoslavia found itself at the time.[8] Consequently, the Constitution-makers, mainly inspired by the French 1958 model, decided to adopt a semi-presidential system with relatively strong presidential powers; although in the overall scheme, at least formally, both parliamentary and judicial mechanisms of review over presidential emergency decrees were nonetheless preserved. The first test of those powers came quite shortly after the enactment of the Constitution when the President of the Republic issued a number of emergency decrees having force of law and regulating a wide variety of issues, including the restrictions of constitutionally protected rights and freedoms.

Following the constitutional challenge of those decrees, in 1992 the Constitutional Court delivered one decision in which it was dealing with three principal issues: the presidential power to unilaterally proclaim an emergency; its power to enact measures having retroactive application; and its power to restrict rights and freedoms independently from the fact that the Parliament was all the time in session.[9] The Court rejected all arguments submitted by the applicants and summarised its conclusions in just a few paragraphs. As to the first issue, it established that the President had an independent constitutional power to declare the state of emergency should he or she estimate it necessary. As to the second, the Court concluded that the President, in issuing emergency decrees, was not restrained by constitutional prohibitions regulating retroactivity because such prohibitions were in the constitutional text foreseen only for cases in which the Government had a power to enact decrees on the basis of delegation of authority in normal circumstances. And as to the third issue, the Court simply stated that the President had an independent power to act. The Court's reasoning regarding the first and the second problems might be accepted, at least because it was based on textual interpretation of the Constitution. It should be stressed, however, that in reference to the third issue the Court completely ignored the strict constitutional command that any emergency restriction of rights and freedoms was to be carried out by the Parliament and by the President only if the Parliament was not able to convene. In fact, the Court gave no further explanation for such a "switch" whatsoever, except for having taken into account that emergency decrees were in the meantime approved by the legislative body. An emergency model based upon the elements of clear unilateral executive exception, its subsequent parliamentary ratification and resulting hugely deferential ('process-based')[10] judicial validation that the Croatian Constitutional Court adopted in this case is by no means unknown in comparative practice.[11] Actually, such a 'liberal model' of 'emergency powers'[12] might be typical for constitutional systems in their rudimentary form in which, despite some formal constitutional proclamations, there exists neither a true concept of 'fundamental rights' nor an effective system of judicial review.[13]

Up to this date, this had been the only Croatian experience with 'emergencies' in the narrow sense of the word. Since then, however, the constitutional arrangements concerning both the separation of powers principle and protection of fundamental rights have developed significantly. For the separation of powers, the major change occurred with the constitutional amendments of 2000 which imposed that for most emergency actions a counter-signature of the Prime Minister to decisions of the President of the Republic is required. As for the protection of fundamental rights, as briefly described in the introduction, this has also undergone significant developments inspired by the influence of foreign and international law and other legal materials, by the application of new standards of judicial review and interpretation and by a general decision of the Court to become an institution that imposes limits on parliamentary law-making.

What general conclusions, then, can one make when evaluating these lines of constitutional developments in the field of possible security measures involving 'war' or other similar threats to the public order? Again, since there has been no real experience of wartime measures since the 1990s, it must first be said that all such conclusions are by definition premature. However, it could be said that in future cases of such a serious nature emergency decision-makers would be faced with somewhat important obstacles. In other words, constitutional protection of fundamental rights and freedoms in Croatia in the past 15 years has constantly been evolving in a way as to give those rights a position of judicially enforceable constitutional rules. Seen in the context of 'fundamental rights', it means that 'rights' and 'freedoms are no longer just political standards but, rather, are legal prescriptions that (legally) bind the will of the legislature. At the same time, this also means that they must bind the executive when the executive, during states of emergency, acts in its legislative capacity. In short, judicial review mechanisms would certainly have to make a difference. And as to the issue of separation of powers, mutual agreements between the Government and the President of the Republic, secured through the requirement of counter-signature in cases of emergency decrees, would surely foster additional protection. Nevertheless, it must be stressed here that the Croatian Constitution still empowers the President of the Republic to 'take care of regular and harmonized functioning and stability of the state government'.[14] Even though this provision has never been used on any occasion, one may easily foresee its application in emergency contexts. In absence of any interpretation of the mentioned norm by the Constitutional Court, this may give rise to serious concerns.[15]

Leaving aside general constitutional issues, there remains a need to evaluate some contemporary developments in the legislative field as they are related to the problem of security. Focussing on major laws thereof, several conclusions can be made.

Firstly, important acts in their present form were mainly enacted prior to most recent international events involving terrorism, military threats or migrations and cannot therefore be qualified as a direct response to them. This, for instance, is the case with the Law on Security-Intelligence System of the Republic of Croatia of 2006, the Law on Police of 2011, the Law on Prevention of Money Laundering and Financing of Terrorism of 2012 and the Law on Defence of 2013. One significant exception to this is the Law on International and Temporary Protection of 2015, which replaced the prior Law on Asylum of 2007 and that was primarily adopted in order to implement various EU legislative acts in the field.

Secondly, this, however, does not mean that some of these laws could not provoke constitutional concerns both in reference to protection of rights and freedoms and in the separation of powers. For instance, the Law on Defence anticipates the need to regulate airplane hijack scenarios but it only prescribes that the use of the Armed Forces in situations which require armed action against civil airplanes that endanger sovereignty and national security of the Republic of Croatia would be regulated by a special law.[16] Such a law has not yet been enacted and, should that happen, it would remain to be seen whether it would bring to the surface constitutional disputes similar to other internationally known cases.[17]

On the other hand, the Law on Defence and the Law on the Control of State Borders were amended in March 2016 as a direct response to the migration crisis and this case also reveals some problems. In fact, the latter Law prescribes that in exceptional cases, when the Ministry of Interior or the Prime Minister determine that it is necessary for security or humanitarian reasons, Croatian Armed Forces may provide assistance in protection of state borders, in accordance with the Law on Defence. In such cases the military must act under the instructions of the state police. At the same time the Law on Defence prescribes that the decision on the use of Armed Forces in such cases is made by the Government on the motion of the Minister of Defence and with prior approval of the President of the Republic. The Croatian Constitution indeed allows for this type of cooperation between army and police but it expressly limits it to situations of emergency as they are enumerated in the Constitution.[18] Since the enumeration includes states of war, an immediate threat to the independence and unity of the State, severe natural disasters and situations in which the governmental bodies are prevented from performing their constitutional duties regularly, it is obvious that other broadly defined security and humanitarian reasons are clearly excluded from the list and this is the first major problem here. The second problem is that the amendment to the Law on Defence, by limiting the role of the President to prior approval, significantly restricts presidential powers of control over the use of the Armed Forces. And this actually may be contrary to the constitutional provision that defines the President as the military commander-in-chief; thus, supposedly, the one who must be able to maintain supreme control thereof at all times. Therefore, such types of legislative changes in the domain of security issues, inspired by the actual crisis, should sooner or later come under the review of the Constitutional Court, which brings me to the third observation I would like to make here.

Thirdly, therefore, it must be noted that none of these previously mentioned laws has yet been subject to judicial review by the Court. Hence, there can be no firm conclusion on the attitude of the Court to possible constitutional attacks on these laws. However, there have been two quite notable exceptions to this, which shed significant light on the Court's stance: the Law on Public Assemblies and the Law on Criminal Procedure.

1.1 The 2011 Decision on the Law on Public Assemblies

The Constitutional Court made one significant reference to the problem of terrorist threat in its decision on the constitutionality of the Law on Public Assemblies, delivered in 2011.[19] This Law contained one specific provision that prohibited public gatherings in close proximity to the seats of or the places where certain state institutions (Parliament, Government, Constitutional Court and President of the Republic) resided. The prohibited range was set at 100 metres from those places.

This actually meant that the prohibition included a complete area of one of the central squares in the Croatian capital and the measure itself for years provoked public outrage. In striking down the Law in this part, the Court argued that 'state measures for prevention and suppression of terrorism are legitimate ones, but that they always must be proportional to the nature of necessity for a restriction in each particular case', that they 'must not be directed against various means of civil disobedience or demonstration and must never be used for achieving particular political, religious or ideological aims'. In addition, the Court insisted that the 'fight against terrorism must never be an excuse for justifying arbitral conduct of authorities which restricts human rights and fundamental freedoms guaranteed by the Constitution'. Taking into account that the institutions around whose seats the Law imposed prohibition on assemblies may often be the objects of terrorist attacks, the Court thus accepted that such prohibitions could be accepted on the basis of a legitimate aim for restrictions but only when subject to strict proportionality requirements. Nonetheless, the Court declared the Law invalid because it ruled that the measure imposed was rather extensive and that alternative, less restrictive means (i.e. a narrower perimeter of exclusion) were therefore possible. Additionally, the Court decided that the legal distinction between various forms of public assemblies, according to which some manifestations in the restricted area were still allowed, lacked any reasonable and objective justification. This case deserves attention because it confirms that the Court, in the field of political rights and freedoms, is ready to apply stricter forms of judicial scrutiny; those approaches that in the Croatian constitutional adjudication are usually reserved for personal and civil rights and that are by no means typical for review of economic or social legislation.

1.2 The 2012 Decision on the Law on Criminal Procedure

The Law on Criminal Procedure as it applies today was enacted in 2008. After that the Law was extensively amended several times but it must be stressed that the major change occurred in 2012 when 43 of its articles, completely or in part, were declared invalid by the Constitutional Court.[20] Because in Croatia in the past two decades there have been no military conflicts or major terrorist attacks of the sort that have occurred in other European countries, it may be contested that the Law was principally inspired by such type of crisis. I am taking this case under examination nevertheless because it does reveal certain important messages in the field of security issues that the Constitutional Court addressed to the legislator. By far the most far reaching instruction appeared in relation to the constitutional concept of human dignity and the inevitable accompanying problems of torture and maltreatment. Of course, all types of torture, maltreatment and cruel or degrading treatment or punishment are prohibited by the Constitution and those prohibitions are, moreover, qualified as non-derogative.[21] However, in the case of constitutional provisions on dignity itself the picture was, at least until the 2012 Decision, somewhat blurred by the fact that the Constitution does not expressly protect dignity as an absolute and general right in a way as, for instance, in the

German Basic Law. This fact, however, does not mean that the Constitutional Court has never given any guidance to interpretations on various constitutional provisions regulating dignity and the mentioned cases of prohibited conduct. For instance, in reference to article 23 of the Croatian Constitution, which, among other things, generally prohibits 'maltreatment', the Court has explained that the article: implies an absolute prohibition; that prisoners still retain all the rights and freedoms conferred to them by the European Convention on Human Rights; that measures imposed by imprisonment may not exceed an 'inevitable element of sufferance or humiliation' which is implied in a legitimate state treatment of prisoners; and that there are certain positive obligations of the state to provide conditions that respect essential guarantees of human dignity.[22] The main problem here, however, is that the Court has so far been delivering its decisions in this area only in cases where applicants were lodging constitutional complaints against individual legal acts in particular judicial cases, and not against laws formally enacted by the Parliament.[23] Consequently, these cases cannot be seen as directly binding on the legislature and bear no general meaning for what the Court has to say on legislative attacks on dignity.

From the particular point of human dignity, the major issue for the Court in the 2012 case involving the Law on Criminal Procedure was to examine the special provision regulating inadmissibility of illegal evidence. The category of illegal evidence, apart from that obtained by infringement of various national and international provisions guaranteeing prohibition of torture or cruel and inhuman treatment, extended also to cases where it could be collected in infringement of constitutional, legal and international legal guarantees on the rights of defence, right to dignity, reputation and honour and the right of inviolability of personal and family life. However, for these latter cases, the Law provided one crucial exception: Such evidence was permissible in cases involving serious crimes and where the infringement of a particular right, by taking into account its severity and nature, was substantially less than the gravity of a crime. Such a balancing procedure was declared unconstitutional by the Court, which first invoked the argument that illegal evidence principally aims at infringement of fundamental rights and then reasoned that even though other rights contained in the contested provision (the rights of defence, reputation and honour and inviolability of personal and family life) could allow for their weighing against public interests, the same could not be accepted for the right of dignity. Concluding that, contrary to other cases in this context, the right of dignity represents an absolute and non-derogative right, the Court interpreted that such a conclusion derives implicitly from several constitutional provisions,[24] including the one prohibiting torture and cruel and inhuman treatment exactly in context of states of emergency.[25] As for other provisions of the Law on Criminal Procedure that the Court in this case struck down, some additional points may be stressed. The Court thus invalidated a provision which prohibited an accused person to choose to be represented by a lawyer for whom there was only a 'basic suspicion' that he or she participated in commission of a money laundering criminal act. The Court insisted that in such cases both a stronger legal standard of suspicion, a 'founded suspicion', must exist and that acts qualifying as related to money laundering should be precisely enumerated in the Law so as to include only the acts of a most severe nature, implicitly those that are connected to terrorist activities. Similarly, the Court held unconstitutional provisions that, without further specifications, generally empowered the State Attorney or investigation judge to order surveillance of communication between an arrested person or a defendant and their lawyers, interpreting that such a serious measure requires both a precise definition of criminal acts for which one has been arrested or accused in the first place and its application only in most serious situations, including ones related to terrorism. Unconstitutionality was also found in a provision that empowered the Minister of Justice, acting together with Ministers of Interior, Health and Defence, to prescribe detailed conditions on keeping, erasing, processing and controlling information gathered by molecular-genetic analysis. This part of the Law was seen by the Court as breaching the requirement that such processes must be prescribed by a law, in the strict meaning of an act enacted by the Parliament in a legislative procedure. The Court also held invalid a provision that made an exception to the rule that defendants should be informed on evidence gathered in initial phases of the criminal procedure but only discovered in its later phases. The exception made it possible not to reveal such evidence in cases where this could harm an investigation in other process against the same defendant and the Court again said that such a measure should be limited only to situations involving terrorism or similar extremely serious criminal acts.

In sum, this short overview of the case involving the review of the Law on Criminal Procedure shows the Court's determination to cope with hard cases of legislative attacks on constitutionally protected rights and freedoms in delicate security contexts. As to the precise question of whether the Court's position in this particular case revealed a new direction in its practice, few observations should be made. On one hand, it is quite clear that the Court in its approach used rather strict tests of scrutiny, involving examination under various steps of the proportionality scheme (prescription by law, legitimate aims, proportionality in the strict sense as balancing), as well as references to relevant Strasbourg case-law. From the general point of view, it should be stressed that the Court here only applied the tools of review that have already been construed by the Court itself in its earlier case-law. Thus, for instance, the modern proportionality scheme was judicially developed already in 2000 when the Court posited that the test should be performed in three steps, each one respectively verifying whether the restrictive measures are appropriate for achieving the desired legitimate aim, whether they have the least restrictive effect and whether they are proportional to the objective sought in the strict sense of the word.[26] In addition, as already shown in reference to the cases involving the interpretations of article 23 of the Constitution, by the time this particular Decision was delivered stricter forms of judicial scrutiny had already been established as possible tools in the Court's arsenal.

On the other hand, however, it seems that the principal underlying point of the whole case can be seen from the fact that the Court openly revealed its willingness to engage in judicial activism so as to interpret some rights in a way as to extend them to their outer limits. This surely is the case of human dignity, which obviously may be relevant for future potential cases in the context of security, such as the airplane hijack scenario mentioned above.

2. Financial crisis and economic policy of the state

Contrary the problem of civil and political rights, it has for a long time been the stance of the Croatian Constitutional Court to allow wider legislative discretion in regulating rights and liberties that come to be qualified as economic, social or cultural. Thus, for instance, despite the strict constitutional command that all laws regulating rights and freedoms in general should be enacted as 'organic' laws, requiring a qualified parliamentary majority for their adoption,[27] the Court, arguing that in absence of stricter instructions almost any law could be said to address some rights, interpreted that this command extends only to such laws whose basic function is to define and regulate civil and political rights.[28] This differentiation, being made despite the strict letter of the Constitution, was thus offered as a clear judge-made construction although it must be stressed that in itself it was not made under any particular influence of concrete financial crisis circumstances. Expectedly, however, the Court had already in 2000 started to consider that the constitutional guarantee of ownership must be interpreted quite widely so as to include various property or economic interests, including legitimate future interests of parties that their property would be protected.[29] The final turn to a detailed type of judicial scrutiny in this field occurred in 2009 when the Court adopted the approach according to which any interference in property rights must secure a just and careful balance between them and opposing public interests and must have a 'rational proportionality relationship' between the means to be achieved and measures that are applied as restrictions.[30]

2.1 The 2009 Decision on the Law on Profit Tax and the Law on Income Tax

The issue of legislative competences in the realm of economic policy related to financial crisis may here first be observed in relation to the Constitutional Court's rulings dealing with tax measures. The general position of the Court in this specific context was revealed in 2009 when the Court was asked to rule on the constitutionality of the Law on Profit Tax and the Law on Income Tax. In this case the problem arose because the two laws prescribed that certain subjects, either *ex lege* or on their own will, had the option to choose whether to pay relevant taxes according to the first or the second model. This, in the applicants' view, led both to discriminatory effects and the breach of the principle of equity in the distribution of tax burdens.[31]

In a rather deferent ruling, the Court first invoked the general constitutional provision that empowers the Parliament to independently, in accordance with the Constitution and law, decide on the regulation of economic, legal and political relations in the Republic of Croatia.[32] It then said that its principal position was that the legislative body was independent in regulating the tax system of the Republic of Croatia and that at the same time it had to make sure that tax obligations were determined and distributed to all tax payers equally as to their economic strength, which meant in accordance with the request of an equal distribution of tax burden. The Court further stressed that the notion of 'tax' represented public revenue whose types, levels, ways of calculation and paying as well as other issues relevant to its proper application were questions to be determined by law. As a result, the Court pointed out that it had no power to review the suitability of a certain tax model, especially not its justification and appropriateness, and that the constitutional issue may not be related to the examination of different types of taxes, tax rates or tax benefits. Moreover, the Court insisted that it had no power to challenge the Parliament's decision to alter the taxation system or to answer the question as to why the Parliament prescribed the possibility or obligation for taxpayers to choose to be bound by either of the two different regimes.[33]

2.2 The 2009 Decision on the Law on Special Tax on Incomes, Pensions and Other Revenues

However, the first real test for the Croatian tax system and legislative powers exercised in the context of economic crisis in the proper sense of the word came some time later that year when the Parliament enacted the Law on Special Tax on Incomes, Pensions and Other Revenues. In short, this Law prescribed that certain categories of taxpayers had to pay additional tax designed to provide means for the Government to combat the economic crisis which by 2009 had already had a significant effect in Croatia. The Law was designed to last 17 months at most and was, as a special measure, therefore of limited duration. However, this provoked significant revolt and more than 35,000 applicants challenged its constitutionality. In the Decision of 17 November 2009[34] the Constitutional Court examined the impact that the Law had on the constitutional concept of the 'social state' and referred to constitutional guarantees of prohibition of discrimination, equality before law and equality and equity in tax matters, as well as the general principle of proportionality and its special expression in the field of public expenses.

In reference to the principle of equality, the Court first emphasised that the Law was actually not the only regulation that imposed obligations on taxpayers to contribute to the state budget through special tax and pointed out that yet another law was also in the meantime enacted, thus covering additional group of taxpayers who were not initially covered by the contested Law.

In dealing with claims that the Law impinged upon the constitutional definition of Croatia as a 'social state', which is worked out through specific social rights and in which social justice makes up part of the highest values of the constitutional order serving for interpretation of the Constitution as a whole,[35] the Court first gave some general viewpoints. Its conclusions on this matter principally established that, taken together, these concepts implied general duties of the State both to protect the acquired levels of social security as such as well as to guarantee that social security guarantees are provided equally. However, the Court then stressed that all three concepts have a rather abstract nature that may be seen through the fact that the Constitution itself, most often expressly, leaves all social rights for further regulation to the Parliament which itself in this field has a wide margin of appreciation to decide how to legislate.

From a technical point of view, this part of the applicants' constitutional attack was based on the claim that the Law 'endangered existence of the poorest parts of population', but the Court found that the regulation provided for specific exceptions by which certain categories of citizens with lowest incomes were not required to pay the imposed tax. Moreover, the Court accepted the proposition submitted during the case by the Government that the objective of the Law was to allow the State to fulfil its general obligations, including those stemming from its duty to 'maintain the achieved level of social benefits in context of the economic crisis'. In addition, the Court further reviewed the legal definition of the lowest level of citizens' incomes serving as the threshold by which their duty to pay the special tax was activated. To this specific end, the Court referred to the principle of proportionality and examined the problem in four steps.[36]

The Court first established that any 'regulation in tax matters *prima facie* interferes with basic constitutional rights' and, as such, requires that there is some 'particularly important (qualified) interest' for such interference. This legitimate interest was then found to be proven in the Parliament's concern to 'maintain the stability of the State financial system in conditions of economic crisis' through securing in a short period of time an actual income without which there would be no chance for the State to perform its constitutional duties. Secondly, the Court concluded that the contested Law was directly related to the achievement of public financial stability and, moreover, that it was only a part of broader legal measures (i.e. various means for restricting public expenditures, amendments to other laws) adopted with the same goal. Thirdly, the Court found that the Law was not unacceptably restrictive because only around two-thirds of employed persons and around one-fourth of pensioners were actually required to pay the special tax. In addition, the Law was found to be proportional to the aim because of its limited duration. In this context the Court also instructed the Government to carefully observe further developments related to economic crises and, should it become possible and necessary, proposed that Parliament should either readjust tax rates so as to decrease them or to abolish the Law completely even before the intended period of its duration. And, fourthly, the Court found that the new Law did not impose financial burdens that could be seen as too excessive for citizens because it was applicable only to those categories who were earning more than the amount of minimal pay guaranteed in Croatia during the period for which the Law was intended to be applied.

2.3 The 2015 referendum initiatives

Probably the most striking example of the Court's approach to legislation in the context of economic and social crisis came with its rulings on the constitutionality of two referendum initiatives in 2015. The cases are rather similar and I am therefore here focussing on one of them (the so-called referendum on the ban of outsourcing). It shows a kind of hidden judicial deference in the field because, although it did give rather extensive interpretations of various issues, the Court left some problems untouched and allowed for wide regulatory discretion of both the Parliament and the Government.[37]

In December 2013 the Croatian Government officially started to pursue its plan through which the provision of 'complementary and non-basic services' (further: technical services) in state and public institutions and bodies would no longer be carried out by the persons employed in such institutions and bodies, but would rather be given to private subjects, or, in other words, outsourced. As a reaction to this, trade unions organised an initiative for a referendum on which a new Law on Carrying Out Complementary and Non-Basic Services in the Public Sector would be enacted. The Law itself would prescribe both that these technical services are carried out only by those employed in the public sector and that the measure of outsourcing thereof is prohibited. As a result of this initiative, the Government publicly announced the withdrawal of its plan. Nevertheless, the trade unions in July 2014 requested the Parliament to call the referendum and in February 2015 the Parliament decided to put the issue before the Constitutional Court.

The most intriguing part of the Court's reasoning in this case came with its interpretation of delimitation between the exclusive constitutional powers of state bodies (the Parliament and the Government) and the (remaining) powers of the people which may be carried through a referendum.

Although the Court admitted that in the Croatian constitutional scheme 'the constitution-maker did not expressly enumerate issues which are within the exclusive competence of the bodies of representative democracy', it reasoned that they nevertheless 'derive from the entirety of the Constitution' and then stated that the Government had 'the exclusive constitutional power and obligation to propose the state budget and the annual accounts' and that the Croatian Parliament 'had the exclusive constitutional power and obligation to adopt the state budget'.[38] In addition, the Court also stressed that the Government was constitutionally empowered 'to direct and control the operation of the state administration, to direct performance and development of the public services, and to take care of the economic development of the country'.[39] On the other hand, the Court argued that 'direct democracy is, by the Constitution, permissible and legitimate, but not primary and ordinary way of deciding on the regulation of economic, legal and political relations in the Republic of Croatia' and then construed two general rules: that the adoption of laws on a referendum is not allowed when these laws are (a) either not in accordance with the legal system as a whole or (b) when the laws are directed to regulating issues that, either explicitly or from the entirety of the Constitution, fall within the exclusive competence of the bodies of representative democracy.

The Court then went on to examine the proposed Law and found that it actually contained two general bans: a ban of outsourcing of technical services and a ban of them being carried out in any way other than by those who are employed in the public sector. Qualifying these two bans as 'blanket' prohibitions,[40] the Court came to the conclusion that the Law was contrary to the legal system as a whole on account of several grounds. First, because its principal outcome would be to prevent the Parliament and the Government from pursuing any further modifications of the legal (labour) model regulating the status of those performing technical services in the public sector (bans as preventive or *a priori* measures). Second, because the bans contained in the Law would be of a 'more permanent nature, because they would be prescribed by a law enacted on a referendum' (bans as 'permanent' measures). Third, because these bans would be applied automatically (*ex lege*) and would prevent any possible changes in the field 'as long as such legal bans are in force' (bans as 'automatic' measures). And, fourth, because the bans would be applied 'unselectively', as they would 'cover all the bodies and institutions that make [up the] public sector' and 'their application would not depend on the nature of an activity or work undertaken by these bodies and institutions' (bans as 'unselective' measures). Furthermore, the Court concluded that qualified as such the bans (i.e. as *a priori*, automatic, unselective and permanent measures) also 'prevent changes in the organization of optimal labor law models for complementary and non-basic services in the public sector, in terms of economic capabilities of the State' and that they directly influence

> the functionality of the State and the budget framework in processes of economic, social, political and administrative reforms for which – according to the Constitution – bodies of representative democracy, and not the Organizational Committee [committee organising popular initiative] or a group of employees whose partial interests that Committee intends to protect, bear full responsibility.

To this the Court also added the view that labour law models generally are inherently changeable and that any permanent prohibitions thereof through blanket legal bans not only do not have a legitimate aim but are also 'contrary to both the purpose and the constitutional concept of state and public services in a democratic society'.

All this, as I already stressed, led the Court to conclude that the proposed Law was contrary to the Croatian legal system as a whole. And as to the issue of the exclusive powers of the state bodies, the Court shortly concluded that the mentioned blanket prohibitions were contrary to the Constitution because they would 'restrict the Government and the Parliament in framing the state budget'. The Court's only argument was that, since salaries and other material remunerations for those employed in the public sector are reserved in the state budget, the Government and the Parliament would be that way bound by the Law.

Apart from all that, in the concluding remarks the Court yet gave an additional two announcements, revealing further elements pertaining to its view of the whole case. On one hand, it pointed that

> the use of referendum in order to achieve an a priori and preventive prohibition of future changes of the existing legal regulation, which itself is neither in the course of a process of change nor there exists a formalized or institutional

> intent of the Government to change it, is not – from the rule of law aspect – in accordance with the Croatian legal order as a whole.

Regarding this, the Court actually rejected to review any of the rather serious arguments submitted by the organisers of the initiative that the proposed measure of outsourcing would, in breach of constitutional principles and particular rights, jeopardise social security standards, discriminate employees affected by the measure, as well as their rights to work and proper remuneration for work done. And on the other hand, the Court stressed the following:

> By not entering into the issues of expediency and appropriateness of various possible measures of outsourcing of complementary and non-basic services in the public sector, the Constitutional Court determines that the competent state bodies (the Croatian Parliament and the Government) are constitutionally empowered to carry out such measures at any time and without any special conditions which would derive from the Constitution, except for the respect of democratic procedures and general conditions which are imposed upon the institutional regulators of social relations by the rule of law.

3. Conclusion

This short review of the Croatian Constitutional Court's attitudes to legislative regulation in times of crisis may be summarised in just a few remarks. In the situation of full-blown war, experience points to the extremely deferential position of the Court, marked primarily by its concern to deal only with procedural matters. This process-based approach, based on the concept that in extreme types of cases courts should refrain from substantive review of decisions made by political branches of Government and should therefore merely verify if certain formal conditions for applying emergency measures existed, is typical of the interpretive practice of the Court. This is the main message one may read from the Court's 1992 Decision.

Truly, since the early 1990s the Croatian constitutional system has changed in several aspects. Though the 2000 amendments to the Constitution improved some important checks-and-balances safeguards against wide presidential emergency powers, including those of law-making, the concept of constitutionally proclaimed rights and freedoms has gradually become a system of fundamental rights by which the Court reviews not only by-laws or individual judicial and administrative decisions but also the legislative acts of the Parliament. In addition, in the last 15 years the Court has also developed as an institution that is capable of applying various principles and methods of constitutional interpretation, most notably the principle of proportionality and the systemic reading of the Constitution. Those particular developments might give some fuel to hopes that in future the Court will have a stronger position in cases of extreme crisis. At the same time, modern global security issues in Croatia are present and are addressed by relevant legislation. This may clearly be seen in the example of the 2016 amendments to the Law on Defence and the Law on the Control of State Borders, made in direct reference to the migration crisis. But since neither these two acts nor other major laws in this field have been put under abstract constitutional review, the main problem for a proper evaluation of the Court's position is hence the lack of evidence. The case of the Law on Criminal Procedure from 2012 may indicate that the Court, in its review of core liberty rights, is willing to apply strict scrutiny method but the main problem is that such a 'criminal law model' is usually the first victim of contemporary conditions in which terrorism is often qualified as a threat of a sui generis quality to which regular rules do not apply.

On the other hand, the Court's general approach in reviewing economic and social legislation has continuously been largely deferential, although this claim is subject to some rather important specifications. Typically, as it was indicated by its June 2009 Decision which can here be taken as the paradigm of the Court's stance to these issues in periods not directly affected by a full economic crisis, the Court mostly qualifies those matters as falling within the general constitutional regulatory powers of the Parliament. In other words, such matters are deemed to be of political nature and the Court is willing to examine only whether particular measures have a discriminatory character.

That the Court, however, could engage itself into a more thorough type of scrutiny in this area was confirmed by its Decision of November 2009. Notwithstanding the fact that the Law on Special Tax on Incomes, Pensions and Other Revenues survived the constitutional attack, the Court then gave its reasoning based on several important grounds, most notably on its careful application of the proportionality principle in quite a strict form. As shown before, proportionality of such type was in previous times mainly used by the Court in order to review encroachments upon civil or political, rather that economic, social and cultural rights and freedoms and this can be a sign that the Court is gradually extending its review powers in other constitutional fields. Moreover, such an approach of the constitutional justices may indeed have been provoked by the seriousness of the moment, burdened by the overall economic and social pressures which themselves were undoubtedly requiring more detailed analyses from the bench. When further compared with its June Decision, it may be observed that on this particular occasion the Court did undertake some additional checks as well. Although the Court declined to view the constitutional concepts of 'social state', 'social justice' or even 'social rights' as something more than general policy guidance to lawmakers, it nevertheless posited that, taken together, they alone do have some independent constitutional meaning. This can be observed through the fact that the Court required not only that economic burdens be distributed equally, but also in a way not to endanger some already established levels of social security. This, in other words, means that apart from the general constitutional principle of equality the Court started to view such problems from the point of liberty as well.

When, however, the Court dealt with an outright economic measure proposed in the midst of the full crisis, exemplified by its 2015 Decision on the constitutionality of the referendum on outsourcing, the Court took quite a different direction and, through focusing on the interpretation of some specific constitutional powers given to political branches, gave the Parliament and the Government an extremely secured position. Such a significant relaxation of the Court's review standards, by which serious allegations that the proposed measure would result in derogations of various social and economic security standards were simply omitted from the analysis, surely deserves appropriate warnings.

Notes

1 Here I refer to the Constitutional Court of the Republic of Croatia as it was, as a separate institution, included into the 1990 Croatian Constitution. However, the Constitutional Court has existed in the Croatian constitutional system since 1963.
2 For the English translation of these two documents, see http://www.sabor.hr/important-legislation0001, accessed 15 August 2016.
3 According to J. Omejec, the former Chief Justice of the Croatian Constitutional Court, the modern Court's history may be divided in two major formative periods: Whereas in the first one (1991–2000) the Court was principally focused on resolving constitutional complaints (review of constitutionality of individual legal acts), in the second (2000–) it started to extensively scrutinise laws in abstract review procedures. Omejec (2013) 74–89.
4 This conforms with other comparative developments which affirm the fact that the 'constitutional', as opposed to regular 'judicial' review, is characteristic to modern constitutional courts. Thus, for instance, Kommers argues that in the Federal Republic of Germany this came only with the contemporary notion of Rechtsstaat as envisaged by the 1949 Basic Law. See: Kommers (1997) 36–37. For some additional observations made by the former Chief Justice of the Croatian Constitutional Court, who argues that until 2000 the Court mainly reviewed the legality of particular judicial decisions and that its analyses were, similarly to ordinary courts, strictly formal and based on 'rude textual or grammatical positivism', devoid of any contextual and teleological approach, see: Omejec (2013) 79.
5 Omejec (2013) 74–91.
6 See, for instance, the decisions of the Constitutional Court of the Republic of Croatia: U-I-673/1996, 21 April 1999; U-I-1156/1999, 26 January 2000. Some case-law of the Court (in English) is available at http://www.usud.hr/en/case-law, accessed 14 September 2016. The proportionality principle was already included in the original 1990 Croatian Constitution, but was only applicable to restrictions of rights and freedoms in the case of states of emergency. See: Constitution of the Republic of Croatia 1990, article 17. On this, see also: Bačić (2009) 359–360.
7 On the German concepts of the 'objective order of values' and 'structural unity', for instance, see Kommers (1997) 45–48. See also the decisions of the Croatian Constitutional Court: U-I-3789/2003, 8 December 2010; U-I-3597/2010, 29 July 2011.
8 For the following description of the context in which the Constitutional Court, reviewing presidential emergency decrees, delivered its decision in 1992, see also Gardašević (2014) or a shorter version of the same paper Gardašević (2016).
9 Decision of the Croatian Constitutional Court U-I-179/1991, 24 June 1992.
10 For this approach, see Issacharoff and Pildes (2005) 161–197.
11 In this respect not surprisingly, the possibility of directly comparing the Croatian example with the American experience goes back as early as to the Civil War period. See the *Prize cases, 2 Black* (67 U.S.) 635 (1863).
12 For this, see Lobel (1988–1989).
13 In addition to what has already been said, it should be emphasised that in its Decision from 1992 the Croatian Constitutional Court did not examine a separate problem of whether the issued emergency decrees conformed to the principle of proportionality, although, according to the then valid Constitutional Law on the Constitutional Court, it already had a power to resolve issues that themselves were not raised by applicants. As

shown, thus, the Court's approach in this case remained concerned primarily with procedural matters.

14 Constitution of the Republic of Croatia 2013, article 94/2.

15 For a theoretical interpretation of Article 94/2 of the Croatian Constitution, requiring application of an extremely strict form of proportionality principle thereof, see Smerdel (2015a, 2015b).

16 The Law on Defence, Article 57.

17 In this context, for instance, see decisions of the German and Polish constitutional courts: Federal Constitutional Court, 1 BvR 357/05, 15 February 2006; The Constitutional Tribunal of the Republic of Poland, Judgment of 30 September 2008 K44/07.

18 Constitution of the Republic of Croatia, articles 17 and 101.

19 Decision of the Constitutional Court of the Republic of Croatia U-I-296/2006, U-I-4516/2007, 6 July 2011.

20 Decision of the Constitutional Court of the Republic of Croatia U-I-448/2009, U-I-602/2009, U-I-1710/2009, U-I-18153/2009, U-I-5813/2010, U-I-2871/2011, 19 July 2012.

21 The Constitution of the Republic of Croatia, article 17/3.

22 See Decision of the Croatian Constitutional Court: U-III-64744/2009, 3 November 2010. See also the Decision U-III-4182/2008, 17 March 2009.

23 This has been the case not only with article 23, but also with other relevant constitutional provisions, such as article 25/1 (which states that 'Any arrested and convicted person shall be accorded humane treatment" and that "the dignity of such individual shall be respected'), articles 29/3 and 29/4 (which state that 'An admission of guilt may not be coerced from a suspected, accused or indicted individual' and that 'Evidence obtained illegally may not be admitted in court proceedings') and article 35 (according to which 'Respect for and legal protection of each person's private and family life, dignity, reputation shall be guaranteed').

24 The Constitution of the Republic of Croatia, articles 23/, 25/1 and 35.

25 The Constitution of the Republic of Croatia, article 17/3. In addition, this case is quite comparable with similar comparative cases in which protection of life and dignity as related to maltreatment and other prohibited acts in security related contexts has an utmost importance. For a characteristic 'executive unilateralist' approach in this sense, which relies upon the 'rule-exception' scheme of confrontation between allowing 'grave evils' and achieving 'greater goods', and which consequentially argues that emergencies may necessitate coercive interrogation, that it should be regulated similarly to other 'harmful governmental tactics' and that it should not be prohibited by judges invoking constitutional constraints, see: Posner and Vermeule (2007) 183–215. For an opposing view, for instance, see: Cole (2009).

26 Decision of the Constitutional Court of the Republic of Croatia U-I-131/1998, 3 February 2000; Decision of the Constitutional Court of the Republic of Croatia U-I-884/1997, 3 February 2000. In the first Decision the Court analysed the problem of appropriate judicial protection in the case of infringement of individual autonomy (compensation of damages in terms of publication of information in public media and related to guarantees of protection of private and family life) whereas in the second it was dealing with the freedom of association. One may also notice here that this approach of the Croatian Constitutional Court to the proportionality principle actually follows the German model. On this see: Kommers and Miller (2012) 67.

27 The Constitution of the Republic of Croatia, article 83.

28 Decision of the Constitutional Court of the Republic of Croatia U-I-2566/2003, U-I-2892/2003, 28November 2003.

29 Decision of the Constitutional Court of the Republic of Croatia U-III-661/1999, 13 March 2000.

30 Decision of the Constitutional Court of the Republic of Croatia U-IIIB-1373/2009, 7 July 2009.

31 The Constitution of the Republic of Croatia, articles 14/2 and 51.
32 The Constitution of the Republic of Croatia, article 2/4.
33 Decision of the Constitutional Court of the Republic of Croatia U-I-2012/2007, 17 June 2009.
34 Decision of the Constitutional Court of the Republic of Croatia U-IP-3820/2009, 17 November 2009.
35 The Constitution of the Republic of Croatia, articles 1 and 3.
36 The Constitution of the Republic of Croatia, articles 16 and 51/1.
37 I am here giving a shorter version of my wider presentation of the case which may be found in: Gardašević (2015).
38 The Constitution of the Republic of Croatia, articles 113/2, 81/3 and 91.
39 The Constitution of the Republic of Croatia, article 113/6–8.
40 When referring to the concept of 'blanket prohibitions', the Court furthermore stressed that, in cases dealing with 'the functioning of the state and its apparatus …' such prohibitions 'may lead to automatic and non-selective limitation or repeal of a possibility of changes without which there can be no progress in the implementation of necessary economic, social, political and administrative reforms …'.

Bibliography

Bačić, Petar, 'Konstitucionalizam i sudski aktivizam – ustavna demokracija između zahtjeva za vladavinom većine i protuvećinskog argumenta' ['Consitutionalism and Judicial Activism – Constitutional Democracy Between Requests for the Majority Rule and the Countermajoritarian Argument'] (2009). Dissertation, Law Faculty, University of Split.

Cole, David D. (ed.), *The Torture Memos: Rationalizing the Unthinkable* (New Press 2009).

Gardasevic, Djordje, 'American Lessons Learned – European Future Rethought?' (2014); www.jus.uio.no/english/research/news-and-events/events/conferences/2014/wccl-cmdc/wccl/papers/ws1/w1-gardasevic.pdf, accessed July 15 2016.

Gardasevic, Djordje, 'American Lessons Learned – European Future Rethought?' (2016). 66 *Collected Papers of Zagreb Law Faculty* 1, 61–86.

Gardasevic, Djordje, 'Constitutional Interpretations of Direct Democracy in Croatia' (2015). 12 *Iustinianus Primus Law Review*, 7, 1–50.

Issacharoff, Samuel and Pildes, Richard H., 'Between Civil Libertarianism and Executive Unilateralism: An Institutional Process Approach to Rights During Wartime', in Mark Tushnet (ed.), *The Constitution in Wartime – Beyond Alarmism and Complacency* (Duke University Press 2005) 161–197.

Kommers, Donald P., *The Constitutional Jurisprudence of the Federal Republic of Germany* (2nd edn, Duke University Press 1997).

Kommers, Donald P. and Miller, Russel A., *The Constitutional Jurisprudence of the Federal Republic of Germany* (3rd edn, Duke University Press 2012).

Lobel, Jules, 'Emergency Power and the Decline of Liberalism' (1988–1989). 98 *Yale Law Journal*, 1385–1433.

Omejec, Jasna, 'Odgovornost ustavnog sudstva za ustavne norme', in Arsen Bačić (ed.), *Ustavna demokracija i odgovornost* (Hrvatska akademija znanosti i umjetnosti 2013).

Posner, Eric A. and Vermeule, Adrian, *Terror in the Balance – Security, Liberty and the Courts* (Oxford University Press 2007).

Smerdel, Branko, 'Promemorija za Predsjednicu Republike' (2015a). *Jutarnji list* (Zagreb, 15 December 2015).

Smerdel, Branko, 'Može li nas državni poglavar izvesti iz blokade?' (2015b). *Informator*, 6397, December 21.

4 Remarks on the case-law of the French Constitutional Council in relation to new challenges

Fabrice Hourquebie

The context of the jurisprudence of the French Constitutional Council is composed of many challenges imposing on the constitutional judge. However, is the judge 'sensitive' to these challenges linked to the multifaceted crisis? Do these modify – in the sense of widening or narrowing – the French constitutional judge's interpretation?[1]

Currently, it is the function of the French Constitutional Council in the grip of the crisis that we need to look into, touching quickly on the challenges it is faced with (1) and then considering the ways these challenges were able to retroact on the reasoning and the sense of the judge's decisions (2).

1 The challenges facing the French constitutional judge

I identify the challenges before going on to examine what they imply for the Constitutional Council.

1.1 The challenges

These challenges are of several kinds; I will refer to some of them without aiming to be exhaustive. However, I should like to give some reference points. They seem relevant to our study for they are either related to current, exceptionally heavy – domestic or international – political, economic, social or societal issues, and/or have a special resonance in the Constitutional Council's case-law. In the field of public order and domestic security, recent events have been clearly dominated by the fight against terrorism, with a debate on the adoption of a French Patriot Act following the attacks against Charlie Hebdo. Laws relating to domestic security have been following one another for a decade (cf. notably the 2003 Internal Security Law; the 2011 Law on Orientation and Programming for the Performance of Homeland Security; and most recently the 2015 Law on Security Intelligence). The question of balancing interests arose every time, thus the constitutional judge had to adjudicate the issue of acceptable degree of derogations between individual freedoms on the one hand – such as the right to privacy – and the requirement of homeland security and safety of persons on the other hand.

On the more societal level, the constant challenge that is facing the French Republic, and that has been renewed by the fight against terrorism, is a challenge of integration and, consequently, of reconciling religious freedom with the constitutional principle of secularism; a principle reaffirmed by the legislator in the 2004 law regulating the wearing of symbols or clothing conspicuously indicating religious belief in public schools and colleges, and also a principle which later served as political justification or pretext, depending on point of view, for the adoption of the 2010 Law Prohibiting the Concealment of the Face in Public Spaces. The Constitutional Council, uncommonly initiated jointly by the president of the National Assembly and the president of the Senate, had to give its interpretation of the law against the very particular background of combatting terrorism and the identification of French nationals involved in the jihad.

In economic and fiscal matters, national issues in the field of competitiveness, economic recovery and decline of the public debt associated with the economic crisis in the countries of the European Union, have prompted the legislator to adopt several texts encouraging to conclude public–private partnership contracts, promoting an ever more liberal approach to the economy that the Council, as we will see, had to manifest in its case-law. It is also, however, the concept of 'exceptional contribution' on high income or of temporary surcharge on corporate income tax that was at the heart of political debate, since the legislator had adopted those schemes in several successive budget laws (for 2013, 2014 and 2015). Given that, the aforementioned laws have called upon the Constitutional Council both regarding a prior review and preliminary rulings on constitutionality.

Finally, the question of economic recovery has had social repercussions, since the legislator sought to adjust the rhythm of working hours, allowing for shops to be open on Sundays, which has to this day been significantly derogatory and regulated by French labour legislation. Thus, as early as 2009, the legislator adopted a law reaffirming the principle of Sunday rest with the purpose of adjusting the derogations to that principle – which the law of the Minister for Economic Affairs Emmanuel Macron (the 2015 bill for growth, activity and equal economic opportunity) came to loosen by increasing the number of and assumptions for derogations.

1.2. Implications

For an easier understanding of the issues the Constitutional Council had to face, here I would like to recall that France has a system of concentrated constitutional review, ensured by the Constitutional Council, established in 1958. Until 2008, the French Constitution[2] only allowed for *a priori* control of laws' constitutionality – notably since 1974 – if referred by at least 60 members of Parliament and Senators (thus, the parliamentary opposition). The constitutional amendment of 23 July 2008 introduced the mechanism of preliminary rulings on constitutionality,[3] which indirectly allows every individual, in the event of dispute, to challenge the violation of a constitutional right or freedom by a legislative provision.

Reflecting upon whether or not the aforementioned challenges have an influence on the case-law of the Constitutional Council naturally comes down to asking whether and to what extent they impact the constitutional judge's work methods, but also, and in particular, their reasoning, the statement of reasons for their decision and, finally, the style the constitutional decision is written in. However, reflecting upon whether the constitutional judge eventually takes these challenges into account also means in a unique way to ponder the place of extra-legal considerations in the decision making of the Constitutional Council. In other words, it is to measure on what scale the economic, social or societal parameters (that Hart qualifies as 'secondary rules'[4] and McCormick calls 'second-order justifications')[5] may have repercussions on the solution reached by the constitutional judge. Turning towards these extrajudicial factors in the legitimising procedure points to a consequentialist reasoning of the constitutional judge.[6] This reasoning might sound familiar to the common law judge, notably because of their well-established social role, however, it will seem more alien to the French Constitutional Council, and more generally to the judges of the continental legal tradition who rely more on the hypothetical-deductive reasoning method.

2. The impact on the development of constitutional case-law

Here I should like to mention a few decisions of the Constitutional Council, in particular concerning the challenge of public order and of security (Section 2.1), as well as the more social issue of Sunday work (Section 2.2), to see what lessons can be learned on the function of the constitutional judge (Section 2.3).

2.1. Homeland security decisions

The challenges regarding maintaining public order and security through the fight against terrorism demonstrate best the way the judge uses the proportionality test and the technique of interpretative reservations constructively at the same time to salvage the provisions with regard to the overriding goal pursued by the legislator, without loosening the vise of its control.

In the Decision of 7 October 2010 (Law Prohibiting the Concealment of the Face in Public Spaces)[7] the legislator held that the practice of concealing the face in public spaces may pose a danger to public safety and disregards the minimum requirements of life in a society.[8] In passing the Law, the legislator completed and generalised rules that had been, until then, reserved for specific situations, in order to protect the public order.

The Constitutional Council carried out the proportionality assessment it exercises constantly to determine whether the law ensures a conciliation that is not patently disproportionate between protecting the public order and guaranteeing the protected constitutional rights. On the one hand, the Constitutional Council ruled that, in this particular case, the conciliation was not patently disproportionate, having regard to the objectives set out by the legislator, and taking into account the weak sanction imposed in the case of breach of the rule determined by the legislator. On the other hand, however, the Constitutional Council ruled that the ban on the concealment of one's face in public spaces shall not constrain the exercise of religious freedom in places of worship that are open to the public (interpretative reservation).

In the Decision of 13 March 2003 (International Security Law)[9] thirteen directive or neutralising interpretative reservations were issued and a proportionality test was carried out showing a tighter control and displaying the will not to constitute a substitute for the legislator's discretionary power. In the Decision of 10 March 2011 (Law on Orientation and Programming for the Performance of Homeland Security)[10] fourteen non-conformities with the Constitution were found in articles, paragraphs or subparagraphs, out of which five were reviewed *ex officio* and thus censored: a sign from the Council that the fight against terrorism shall not allow derogations from the fundamental freedoms beyond a certain threshold, the ceiling of which has, nevertheless, been undoubtedly raised with regard to the exceptional nature of the period.

In the process of the priority preliminary ruling on constitutionality (*question prioritaire de constitutionnalité*, hereinafter: QPC) of 23 January 2015 (deprivation of nationality)[11] the Council rules that the provisions in dispute conform to the Constitution by referring explicitly to the need to fight terrorism – which enables the legislator to play the card of the constitutional guarantees of equality for its own advantage, and to validate the proportionality between the commission of a terrorist act and the loss of nationality. First, individuals who have acquired French nationality and those to whom French nationality was granted at their birth are in the same situation, however, the difference in treatment established with the goal of fighting terrorism does not breach the principle of equal treatment.[12] Second, considering the particularly serious nature of terrorist acts, the Council considered that the contested provisions imposed a sanction with the character of punishment that was not patently out of proportion with the gravity of these acts and which did not infringe the requirements of Article 8 of the 1789 Declaration.

In the Decision of 23 July 2015 (Law on Security Intelligence),[13] the Council identified seven unconstitutionalities. However, it also validated the provisions of the Code on homeland security that deal with 'extreme emergency', turning this need into a reference parameter of control. The need for public security and for combating terrorism and the supervision envisaged by the legislator will thus enable the validation of the Homeland Security Code's provisions on the real-time transmission of technical data on the use of technical devices enabling real-time localisation and on collecting such data.

In QPC of 24 July 2015 (administrative access to internet connection data),[14] the provisions of the Homeland Security Code relating to the administrative authority's access to connection data were declared to be constitutional, as the legislator has provided sufficient legal guarantees of supervision in the framework of the national security and counter-terrorism goals.

2.2. Social matters

The challenge in social matters surrounding Sunday rest demonstrate clearly the judicial policy of conciliation between freedoms and economic and social needs, where the judge ensures the protection of employee rights while avoiding to place excessive restrictions on entrepreneurial freedom, and does so whether or not at a time of crisis.

In the Decision of 6 August 2009 (Law on Sunday Rest),[15] the Council considers that the two new derogatory regimes from Sunday rest are consistent with the Constitution – it invalidated, however, another derogation in the light of the principle of equal treatment. In QPC of 4 April 2014 (conditions for night work),[16] a decision of constitutional conformity, the Council declared the following:

> Given that allowing night work is exceptional and has to be justified by the need to preserve the continuity of economic activity or socially necessary services, the legislator carried out a conciliation which is not flagrantly disproportionate between entrepreneurial freedom, which follows from Article 4 of the 1789 Declaration, and the requirements of both the tenth and the eleventh subparagraphs of the Preamble of 1946 [which specifically guarantee rest and free time].

In QPC of 4 April 2014 (suspending the derogations from Sunday rest granted by the prefecture),[17] the objective was to examine the assumptions of suspensory appeal against the derogations granted by the prefecture from the Sunday rest provided for in an article of the Labour Code; this article was declared unconstitutional, as the contested provision disregarded the constitutional requirements on the guarantee of rights that follow from Article 16 of the 1789 Declaration. In addition, the judge used their power to abrogate immediately. Later, in the Decision of 5 August 2015 (Law on Economic Growth and Activity)[18] five unconstitutionalities were raised, but none regarding the provisions on derogations from Sunday rest.

2.3. Lessons learned about the function of the judge

In these two series of examples, the Constitutional Council is faced with taking into account a reality that obliges it to adopt a pragmatic or even realistic approach.

Furthermore, the realistic approach does not justify the violation of the applicable constitutional law or the excessive derogation from the constitutional requirements. Rather than accepting derogations that would be specific and related to the circumstances of the crisis, it seems that the Constitutional Council, as usual, remained in the field of the conciliation between freedoms, even if it means shifting the balance, when doubts about constitutionality arise, in favour of the legislator to enable them to meet the objectives of maintaining the order or fighting against terrorism, for example.

Faced with the circumstances of the crisis, now more than at other times, the Council performs a balancing exercise between interests; a kind of 'multifactor balancing test'[19] that the South African constitutional judges use, for example, but not just that. Such a weighting of freedoms enables the Council to give a dynamically evolving interpretation of the constitutional text – 'living constitutionalism'[20] – which supports the idea that the Constitution has to be interpreted in a dynamic sense, depending on the trends apparent in society (cf. the Italian doctrine of the living law), without, however, relinquishing the field of hypothetical-deductive reasoning firmly anchored in the constitutional foundations.

In any case, even though the Council's voluntary self-limitation regularly leads to reminding everyone that it does not have general discretionary powers identical to those of the Parliament, the Council, faced with security, economic or social challenges, seems to extend its review to the provisions that are submitted to it.

For this purpose, the Council uses almost the same techniques in a priori and a posteriori disputes (which leads in fact to the relativisation of the opposition between these two types of constitutional review in France) and the same grounds stated that we find in the above-mentioned case-law:

- The use of objectives enshrined in the Constitution (a category of constitutional standards not prescribed by law), sometimes referred to as 'dismantling the general interest'. The Council holds that these objectives, including the protection of the public order or the respect for the individual person's freedom and the freedom of others, are all objectives assigned by the Constitution to the legislator in order to make the rights and principles of constitutional value more effective; in reality, it increases the reference standards of the Council's control;
- Directive interpretative reservations ordering law enforcement authorities (legislator, regulatory powers, judicial authorities) to enforce the law in line with the constitutional requirements set out; great many interpretative reservations have been identified in the framework of fight against terrorism;
- The challenge posed by terrorism and, we will see, the financial challenge demonstrates well the development of the Council's case-law on the ratchet effect. In fact, in the field of freedoms, 'the Council has renounced to impose a "no-return" rule on the legislator'[21] (abandoned in this field since 1986). Thus, the legislator can 'modify or even abrogate earlier texts regarding freedoms by substituting them with other provisions where necessary'.[22] The consequence of the strict application of the ratchet effect would have been a legislation that is always protective towards fundamental rights and hence every legislative progress would have been constitutionalised. This 1) could have only been realised at the expense of other, equally fundamental rights and would have hindered the correct use of the conciliation method; and 2) would have led to the entrenchment of the relationship to constitutionality by making it impossible to take into account certain economic, social or societal developments while determining the level of protection of such rights.

The security, economic and social challenges place the Constitutional Council under pressure; however, they also turn the constitutional judge into the last counterweight of the legislator,[23] especially in a time of crisis. The balance of fundamental rights depends on that.

Notes

1 This study does not deal with the decisions of the Constitutional Council that were rendered under the state of emergency (Article 36 of the Constitution) declared following the series of terrorist attacks that had struck France (after the attack against the newspaper Charlie Hebdo); case-law that has endeavoured to maintain a form of balance between security and freedom in a context of continuous threat to the safety of the State.
2 Art. 61.
3 Art. 61–1.
4 Hart (1976).
5 McCormick (1996) 117.
6 Consequentialism would be to justify the solution or the interpretation of a text by the consequences that a contrary solution would entail; see Hourquebie (2014) 2.
7 Décision n 2010–613 DC du 7 octobre 2010.
8 It also held that women who conceal their faces, voluntarily or otherwise, are in a situation of exclusion and inferiority, clearly incompatible with the constitutional principles of freedom and equality.
9 Décision n 2003–467 DC du 13 mars 2003.
10 Décision n 2011–625 DC du 10 mars 2011.
11 Décision n 2014–439 QPC du 23 janvier 2015.
12 It ruled that the taking into account of acts committed prior to the acquisition of French nationality and the extension of time limits adopted in 2006 conform to the Constitution. It was noted in particular that the 15-year timeframe between the acquisition of French nationality and the alleged acts only applied to particularly serious crimes.
13 Décision n 2015–713 DC du 23 juillet 2015.
14 Décision n 2015–478 QPC du 24 juillet 2015.
15 Décision n 2009–588 DC du 6 août 2009.
16 Décision n 2014–373 QPC du 4 avril 2014.
17 Décision n 2014–374 QPC du 4 avril 2014.
18 Décision n 2015–715 DC du 5 août 2015.
19 Cf. *First national bank of SA Ltd t/a West bank v. Commissioner*, 2002(4) SALR 768 (CC).
20 Ackerman (1995).
21 Mazeau (2005).
22 Ibid.
23 Hourquebie (2004).

Bibliography

Ackerman, Bruce, 'The living constitution', in Eivind Smith (ed.), *Constitutional Justice Under Old Constitutions* (Kluwer Law International 1995).

Hart, H. L. A., *Le concept du droit* (Bruxelles 1976).

Hourquebie, Fabrice, *Sur l'émergence du contre-pouvoir juridictionnel sous la Vème République* (Bruylant 2004).

Hourquebie, Fabrice, 'L'argument conséquentialiste dans les décisions de justice' (2014). *Les Cahiers de la justice*, n° 2, 199–216.

MacCormick, Neil, *Raisonnement juridique et théorie du droit*. Les voies du droit (PUF 1996).

Mazeau, P. Erevan, (2005). www.conseil-constitutionnel.fr/conseil-constitutionnel/root/bank_mm/pdf/Conseil/20051001erevan.pdf; last accessed on the 25 October 2016.

5 Beware of disruptions

The *Bundesverfassungsgericht* as supporter of change and anchor of stability

Veith Mehde

Post-war Germany has been built on ruins: actual rubble as well as moral devastation and guilt. The war that Germany caused led to widespread destruction of its cities. After the war, a significant part of the population were refugees or displaced persons and an even larger part of the population had elected, supported or tolerated a system that caused a war and murdered millions of people. Under these circumstances, it can be considered extremely lucky – if only for the Western part of the country – that the Western allies not only were prepared to co-operate with the newly elected political leaders of the Federal Republic but – the United States in particular – actively helped to improve the economic situation. While the eastern part of Germany became part of the sphere of influence of the Soviet Union with a soviet-style political system, the strategy with regard to the Federal Republic was a firm integration of the country in the West on the basis of the democratic decisions of the citizens. European integration led to a situation in which a sovereign state had to cope with the fact that many decisions were taken at another level of government or, in other words, that in certain policy areas the role of the state institutions was reduced to taking part in the decision-making processes of the European Union. Nevertheless, the constitutional challenges in this respect were quickly accepted and the Federal Constitutional Court (*Bundesverfassungsgericht*) paved the way for the full integration into the European legal system.[1]

1 The system of constitutional adjudication in Germany

The system of adjudication of constitutional matters could be called centralised, but at the same time – paradoxically – there are very good reasons why, from another perspective, the only appropriate description is 'highly decentralised'. Though the second interpretation could be a consequence of the undeniable fact that Germany is a federal state comprising 16 states (*Länder*) with their own constitutional systems, the first interpretation would mainly have to focus on the factual impact of the adjudication of the *Bundesverfassungsgericht*.

All 16 *Länder* have their own constitutions. Art. 28 para 1 sec. 1 GG reads as follows: 'The constitutional order in the *Länder* must conform to the principles of a republican, democratic and social state governed by the rule of law, within the meaning of the Basic Law'.[2] It is generally accepted that this leaves the *Länder* with a lot of options regarding the specific design of their systems of decision-making.[3] Consequently, the *Länder* have established Constitutional Courts. The number of cases they have to deal with almost exclusively depends on the question if constitutional complaints on the basis of an alleged breach of basic rights can be filed. If this type of procedure should be introduced it is for the legislature in the respective Land to decide. In states where this is not the case, the protection of human rights ultimately rests with the *Bundesverfassungsgericht.* In the *Länder* in which the law does not comprise constitutional complaints, the *Länder* Constitutional Court deals exclusively with matters relating to the organisation of the state institutions as well as complaints by local governments that allege a violation of the right to local self-government as enshrined in all *Länder* constitutions that have local governments – e.g. all *Länder* apart from the city states (Berlin, Bremen, Hamburg). As local government law is part of the powers of the *Länder* legislatures, the legal reasoning is mainly produced by the Constitutional Courts at that level. The *Bundesverfassungsgericht* decides on matters relating to this right only rarely.

The formal decentralisation of constitutional adjudication is overshadowed by the sheer amount of cases on which the *Bundesverfassungsgericht* has to decide, on the one hand, and the importance the Court rulings have both in the perception of the general public and of the community of professionals in the respective area of the law. Apart from questions that, because of the specific nature of certain constitutional provisions at the *Länder* level, can even theoretically only come up in the Constitutional Court of the respective Land, the judgements of the *Bundesverfassungsgericht* are by far the most important source of legal reasoning in the interpretation of the Constitution. It is one of the remarkable facts of the practical functioning of the German political system that generally the chances to develop different solutions are not used. As a consequence, it is regarded as normal that the Constitutional Courts of the *Länder* quote the *Bundesverfassungsgericht* extensively and that they generally follow its lines of reasoning.[4] For the justification of their own reasoning they also tend to quote, if relevant precedents exist, Constitutional Courts from other *Länder*.

The *Bundesverfassungsgericht* is not the German Supreme Court. According to Art. 95 para 1 GG, '(t)he Federation shall establish the Federal Court of Justice, the Federal Administrative Court, the Federal Finance Court, the Federal Labour Court and the Federal Social Court as supreme courts of ordinary, administrative, financial, labour and social jurisdiction'. In contrast to this, the *Bundesverfassungsgericht* is the highest authority only in the application of the constitution. Art. 93 para 1 GG enumerates the procedures which result in the jurisdiction of the *Bundesverfassungsgericht.* Major cases regarding the constitutionality of laws have often reached the Court on the basis of Art. 93 para 1 No. 2 GG. According to this, the *Bundesverfassungsgericht* shall rule

> in the event of disagreements or doubts concerning the formal or substantive compatibility of federal law or Land law with the Basic Law, or the

compatibility of Land law with other federal law, on application of the Federal Government, of a Land government or of one fourth of the Members of the *Bundestag*.

Apart from periods in which the respective federal government was elected and supported by a grand coalition – a coalition of the two parties most MPs belong to and that therefore have a very large majority in the *Bundestag* – there have been opposition factions in the *Bundestag* with a share of more than a quarter of the seats. In these cases, it has often been an instrument of opposition politics to fight against certain projects not only from a political perspective but also to deny the constitutionality of the government's plan. To ask the *Bundesverfassungsgericht* for a review of the respective law gives further credibility to the claim of unconstitutionality. Moreover, there are always governments in some of the *Länder* that have party affiliations that are different from the one of the federal government and hence these may consider involving the *Bundesverfassungsgericht* on the basis of the above-mentioned Art. 93 para 1 No. 2 GG.

The by far highest number of cases that have to be decided by the *Bundesverfassungsgericht* are constitutional complaints. According to Art. 93 para 1 No. 4a GG the *Bundesverfassungsgericht* shall rule 'on constitutional complaints, which may be filed by any person alleging that one of his basic rights or one of his rights under paragraph (4) of Article 20 or under Article 33, 38, 101, 103 or 104 has been infringed by public authority'.

2 Challenges in the history of the Federal Republic

Generally, the *Bundesverfassungsgericht* stresses the continuity of its reasoning. In his 1982 book on the development of the constitution, Brun-Otto Bryde, a legal scientist who later became a judge of the *Bundesverfassungsgericht*, pointed out that cases in which the *Bundesverfassungsgericht* assesses its own judgements in a critical manner were practically non-existent.[5] Bryde describes the fact that the Court hardly ever having to decide exactly the same question twice to be the reason why it is difficult to assess the role of the *Bundesverfassungsgericht* in the development of the Constitution.[6] It is a routine part of judgements that precedents are quoted and that an essential part of the argument is how the reasoning from these judgements is in line with the one in the case under discussion. Nowadays, it seems almost unthinkable that the Court could explicitly distance itself from previous judgements. It is much more likely that the reasoning, especially the deduction of the rule applicable in the respective case is based on precedents, while in the application of the rule[7] the differences to the previous case are stressed. However, change does take place.[8] In the area of basic rights and with regard to the legal status of political parties, the *Bundesverfassungsgericht* did change directions, and hence some of the earlier judgements can be regarded as obsolete.[9] This is, though, clearly a phenomenon from the early days of modern constitutional reasoning by the *Bundesverfassungsgericht*. The respective doctrine first needed to be developed. Therefore, the following analysis focusses on judgements from the 1970s onwards with a clear focus on those that were given after 1990; that is, after reunification.

2.1 The challenges of terrorism and family law

One of the challenges can be linked to two periods in the history of West Germany: Terrorism first became an important topic in the 1970s. Some of the attacks have become part of the collective memory: for example, the hostage-taking and murder of members of the Israeli delegation at the Olympic Games in 1972 and the killing of the head of the Federal Prosecution Service Siegfried Buback as well as the abduction and subsequent murder of the head of the German Employers' Association, Hans-Martin Schleyer – both in 1977. The last two cases were perpetrated by the Red Army Faction (RAF), a German terrorist group. While this group was over time renewed by new members – it is still spoken of the different 'generations' of the RAF – who committed crimes even decades after the group was founded, the main challenges after 2001 relate to the modern forms of terrorism. The Constitutional Court has been very much involved in the creation of the legal foundations for the fight against all these forms of terrorism – if only by judging some of the powers given to the security services to be in violation of basic rights.[10]

An area of particularly remarkable changes has been family law and some closely related fields. As in most Western countries social attitudes and subsequently also the law on the question of gender equality have changed over the years. The *Bundesverfassungsgericht* played a major role in the implementation of Art. 3 para 2 of the *Grundgesetz* (GG) ('Men and women shall have equal rights') while the majority of the members of Parliament apparently did not seem to recognise a need to change for example a law that gave the husband a privileged role in the relationship of the spouses.[11] This constellation was reversed with regard to the criminal liability for abortion. While Parliament pressed for a reform of the originally very strict provision of the Penal Code, the *Bundesverfassungsgericht* in two landmark cases rejected the changes – in the first case – in total, in the second case it called for changes while generally accepting the regulatory approach.[12]

A particularly massive change has occurred in the attitudes regarding homosexuality. In 1957, the *Bundesverfassungsgericht* regarded the criminal liability for male homosexual activity as constitutional.[13] Since then, homosexuality has become more and more accepted.[14] The changes can also be traced in the law: The part of the Penal Code making homosexual activities a crime was deleted in 1969.[15] In 1994, the last aspects of the discrimination of male homosexuality were erased from the Penal Code.[16] The attempts to end the discrimination of homosexuals were not restricted to criminal law. The main topic at the turn of the millennium was equal access to a legal status for couples.[17] The first step in this respect was the introduction of civil unions[18] that were not regarded as marriages (although in everyday language it is not unusual to talk of the 'wedding' of homosexual couples).

2.2 The reunification of Germany and the government's criminality in the GDR

The historical challenge that stands out in the German constitutional history is the reunification. In October 1990, more than four decades after the creation of two states on German territory, the German Democratic Republic and the shortly before founded 'new' states ('neue *Länder*' became the quasi-official term for them) joined the Federal Republic. The pressures of these discussions about the possibility of a new constitution led to a commission that the *Bundestag* as the federal parliament and the *Bundesrat* as the representation of the *Länder* governments introduced jointly. This commission suggested some – rather moderate – changes to the Constitution.[19] Despite the fact that the reunification took place under the Constitution that had been in place for over 40 years in the West, the integration of a territory in which the consequences of an undemocratic system were still more than noticeable – including violations of human rights especially in dealing with people that were not in favour of the regime – created a massive challenge. A number of these challenges concerned the judicial system and ultimately became questions the *Bundesverfassungsgericht* had to answer.[20]

The Federal Republic had to integrate not only a country of 18 million people and to cope with the extraordinary economic differences leading to massive transfers from the West to the East, but also to deal with the aftermath of life in a dictatorship and violations of human rights perpetrated by people who had worked for or otherwise helped the regime. In a number of cases, the judicial system had to decide on matters that had happened in the GDR. As the frequently used term *Vergangenheitsbewältigung*[21] – the process of coming to terms with the past – shows, this was a particularly difficult topic for the judiciary to face. It was a widely perceivable belief that this second case of dealing with a dictatorship in the history of the Federal Republic would have to take place under much more scrutiny and with much more sense for the responsibility of state officials than had been the case in the first instance in the 1950s. Still, the rule of law brings about restrictions also in dealing with the history of a state that had not accepted the rule of law and human rights in practice. From a political or perhaps psychological point of view an impression of a *Siegerjustiz* ('winners' justice') had to be avoided – the word characterising a situation in which the 'winning' system would punish the members of the 'losing' system.

Cases of particular interest concerned the prosecution of the people in Eastern Germany who were responsible for crimes under the old system. Art. 103 para 2 GG states that '(a)n act may be punished only if it was defined by a law as a criminal offence before the act was committed'. The criminal justice system nevertheless dealt with a number of cases of *Regierungskriminalität* (government's criminality). Considering that the system – despite its name – could by no means be called democratic, the punishments imposed for election fraud might seem to be the most surprising ones.[22]

According to the figures published by the Federal Commissioner for the records of the State Security Service of the former German Democratic Republic[23] at least 136 people were killed when they tried to cross the Berlin Wall. The death toll at the border between the GDR and the Federal Republic in total is estimated to be 872. The *Bundesverfassungsgericht* had to decide on the basis of constitutional complaints from three members of the National Defence Council of the GDR who had been regarded as responsible for a number of deaths at the border and had been convicted for manslaughter or for inciting or abetting manslaughter.[24] One member of the border patrol forces of the GDR who had shot and killed – together with another soldier – a person trying to flee to the West filed a complaint following his conviction for manslaughter.[25]

The highest criminal court of the Federal Republic, the *Bundesgerichtshof*, rejected the notion that a possible justification under the law of the GDR could have any legal relevance for the questions under discussion[26] and the *Bundesverfassungsgericht* followed this line of reasoning.[27] The idea was that the implementation of a rule that prohibited a crossing of the border under all circumstances could not be regarded as a justification for the killing of the people trying to cross the same border. This argument was based on two pillars: First, the so-called *Radbruchsche Formel* (Radbruchs's formula),[28] that the name-giving German philosopher had developed to describe the boundaries of the binding character of law creating blatant injustice – a question he dealt with in the context of crimes committed in the Nazi era that in his opinion had to be regarded as illegal even if the law itself stated the opposite.[29] International human rights, as the second pillar, were used to identify the specific content of the otherwise highly abstract *Radbruchsche Formel*.[30] Although it did not explicitly use the formula as a means to reject the validity of the provision of the GDR law justifying the shootings at the border,[31] the Court stated – in very brief manner[32] – that the application of the formula by the *Bundesgerichtshof* was in compliance with the *Grundgesetz*.[33] The result was summed up by the sentence that 'the factually existing justification for the killing of 'border violators' is irrelevant because it is a materially worst injustice'.[34] Therefore, it seems right to say that the Court did not invent the line of reasoning but it integrated the reasoning of the *Bundesgerichtshof* into its own arguments.

2.3 Improving the infrastructure in the former GDR

Another great challenge faced by the political system and the judiciary in the process of reunification was the disastrous state of the infrastructure in the former GDR that now had become the eastern part of the reunited Germany. In order to speed up the planning process for a central railway connection between Berlin and the western part of Germany, the *Bundestag* passed a law in which the building of the tracks was permitted. In other words, instead of the planning by administrative act on the basis of abstract legal provisions, the legality of the planning was established by the law itself. As this planning was also the basis for the necessary expropriations, the *Bundesverfassungsgericht* in its judgement[35] not only applied Art. 19 para. 4 s. 1 GG ('Should any person's right be violated by public authority, he may have recourse to the courts') but also the right to property (Art. 14 para 1 s. 1 GG). The Court follows a long-established line of reasoning[36] that expropriation by law as opposed to the one by administrative act is constitutional only in narrowly defined cases.[37] Therefore, the constitutionality becomes a question of sufficient justification. This gives the Court the chance to take into account the special situation in which the planning process did take place. The Court argued that 'the reunification created an extraordinary situation. For the set-up of the economy in the new *Länder* the installation of the traffic infrastructure was and is indispensable'.[38] The delay that would have been caused by a planning process overseen by the administration compared with the one by the legislature is explicitly described as a considerable disadvantage for the common welfare.[39]

2.4 Abortion

As in many countries, the debate about the legality of abortions in Germany has been a highly emotional one. Two major changes in the law have ultimately led to decisions of the *Bundesverfassungsgericht*. The first judgement dates back to 1975.[40] The year before, an amendment to the Penal Code had made legal abortions in the first 12 weeks of the pregnancy. In the mentioned judgement, the *Bundesverfassungsgericht* stopped this reform and judged the respective provisions of the Penal Code to be unconstitutional. Art. 2 para 2 s. 1 GG ('Every person shall have the right to life and physical integrity') served as the basis for this judgement. The *Bundesverfassungsgericht* applied this right to the unborn child.[41] From there, the argument is developed in two steps: First, the Court interpreted the right as not only guaranteeing freedom from interference by the state but as demanding active steps to protect human life.[42]

What was more remarkable was the second step: The Court had to ask how far this obligation of the legislature would go.[43] In this case, the *Bundesverfassungsgericht* decided that the scope for decision-making by the legislature was very much reduced. As a consequence, abortions could only be regarded as legal in the cases of a threat to the life and a severe threat to the health of the pregnant woman, pregnancy resulting from rapes, severe disabilities of the child and severe social difficulties on the side of the pregnant woman, while in all other cases abortion had to be made a criminal offence – at least in the absence of an equally effective sanction.[44]

The reunification brought together the liberal abortion laws of the GDR with the system based on criminal law in the West. In the treaty between the Federal Republic and the GDR on the unification, the parties had agreed to pass legislation on the topic (Art. 31 para. 4). The provision also made it obligatory to create an improved system of counselling and improved social security for pregnant women. The *Bundesverfassungsgericht* had to deal with the fact that the legislative solution was in conflict with the first ruling of the same Court. In this case, the

Bundesverfassungsgericht did not deny this but started by saying that 'the law-maker, when developing a new concept for the protection of the unborn life not only can but has to evaluate the experience from legal practice and to align its concept for the protection with these'.[45] The Court that had less than two decades before declared a criminal punishment obligatory in all cases without proper indication now concludes that 'different forms of a far-reaching protection for the unborn life in criminal law have not been able to prevent abortions from becoming and remaining a mass occurrence'.[46] So it is basically the experience following the application of a law that the *Bundesverfassungsgericht* essentially had designed that gave the same Court the justification to open the door for a different approach and to state an obligation of the legislature to evaluate the experiences. While the first argumentative step from the earlier decision is being made – the state's obligation to protect the unborn child – the second one – a duty to use criminal law as a deterrent – is missing in the 1993 decision.[47] On this basis, the Court stated that the legislature's assessment was not to be criticised from a constitutional point of view, that the threat of punishment does not only fail to influence women in a conflict to decide against an abortion but has rather the opposite effect 'because the pregnant woman experiences her conflict as something personal and defends herself against assessments and appraisals by third parties'.[48] It is impossible to evaluate the impact this had on the legal opinions of the different judges. While the topic itself had not lost its controversial character, it seems plausible that – as was indeed explicitly mentioned in the legal argument[49] – the experience in the West played an important role – at the time of the judgement no judge could have the serious impression that the concept of protection as established by the Court in the first judgement was, in fact, effective.

2.5 Same-sex partnerships

The discussions about the legal status of homosexual couples have followed a similar path as in most Western countries. The first steps were taken by the red-green coalition at the beginning of the century by introducing the possibility of civil unions and by giving these unions certain – but by no means all – rights that before were reserved to married couples.[50] The *Bundesverfassungsgericht* had to decide if the status introduced for the benefit of homosexual couples was in contradiction with Art. 6 para 1 of the constitution stating that '(m)arriage and the family shall enjoy the special protection of the state'.[51] Not surprisingly, the Court decided that the necessity of a 'special protection' for one legal status did not require that the other had to have certain disadvantages.[52] While it did not consider to change the definition of marriage, which is still a union between one man and one woman,[53] the status of marriages was regarded as unaffected by the introduction of a similar status for homosexual couples.[54]

Nevertheless, in the following years the *Bundesverfassungsgericht* became the main promoter of equality between – still exclusively heterosexual – marriage and civil unions of homosexual couples.[55] The tool for this was not the above-mentioned Art. 6 GG but Art. 3 para 1 GG which reads: 'All persons shall be equal before the law'. According to a long-established line of judgements, it is – without sufficient justification – unconstitutional not to treat equally what is essentially equal. By giving civil union many of the rights and of the mutual obligations married couples have, the legislature opened the door for stating that with regard to certain aspects these two legal statuses are essentially equal. Therefore, the legal situation of same-sex civil unions had to be further improved although the definition of marriage remained completely unchanged.

The *Bundesverfassungsgericht* declared unconstitutional that the law compensating the victims of crimes did not include the partners of a civil union when one of the partners is killed and the surviving partner does not take up adequate employment in order to be able to look after the children of the couple.[56] It also decided on the rules regarding certain areas of the pension system of the civil service,[57] inheritance tax,[58] real estate transfer tax,[59] certain benefits the state grants to civil servants' families[60], the lacking ability of partners of a civil union to adopt the child the partner had adopted ('successive adoptions')[61] and the privileged position married couples have in income tax law.[62] In all these cases, the *Bundesverfassungsgericht* ruled the law granting certain privileges to married couples to be in violation of Art. 3 para 1 GG because civil unions were not given the same legal position. The legislature therefore had to ensure that in the mentioned areas the remaining differences between married couples and the partners of civil unions were abolished. The gradual convergence of the two legal positions started with a decision by the legislature which was then taken further on the basis of the case-law of the Constitutional Court. Therefore, one might conclude, as Jörg Benedict has in an article on the constitutional protection of marriage, that Art. 6 para 1 GG stands 'like a monument' that reminds one of former times.[63] It should also be mentioned that while the definition of marriage was not changed, the word 'family' as mentioned in Art. 6 para 1 GG was explicitly applied also to the partners of a civil union and a child – even if only one of the partners is a parent in the legal sense – under the condition that the union is permanent and is lived as an all-embracing community.[64] As a consequence of a law passed in July 2017, same-sex couples have equal right to marry.

3 Recent challenges to the jurisprudence of the *Bundesverfassungsgericht*

3.1 Teachers with headscarves

As in many European countries, the population of the Federal Republic is increasingly diverse. One of the topics the *Bundesverfassungsgericht* was faced with in this context concerned the question if female teachers were allowed to wear a headscarf as an element of their Muslim faith while teaching in state schools. In 2003, the *Bundesverfassungsgericht* had determined that the state legislatures were allowed to decide on the extent of religious references in schools as long as the religious freedoms of teachers as well as of pupils, the right of the parents and the neutrality of the state in religious matters were considered adequately.[65] In a 2015 decision, the other senate (chamber) of the *Bundesverfassungsgericht* decided in a very similar case that the law could not generally prohibit outer appearances of teachers that showed symbols of religious beliefs.[66] According to this decision, the basis of such prohibitions can only be concrete hazards to conflicting constitutional provisions (again the rights of pupils and parents, state neutrality in religious matters).[67] The respective rules have to apply to all religions equally.[68] It could be argued that the first attempt to hand back the decision to the legislatures had not led to acceptable results and therefore forced the Court to state more precisely the principles the state legislatures had to apply.[69] It has to be noted, though, that while commentators pointed out the differences between this decision and the previous one,[70] the Court itself did not see any necessity to explain why it felt free to modify the rules compared with the precedent.

3.2 European debt crisis

Germany is one of the few countries in Europe with an economy that recovered very quickly after the crisis of the years 2008/09. The amount of taxes generated soon rose to new record highs. In this context, the *Bundesverfassungsgericht* was faced with the challenge to further develop its stance on European integration and especially on the consequences of European monetary union. The main topics can be defined quite clearly. The establishment of the European Stabilisation Mechanism (ESM) and namely the German participation in it led to a case that can be called historical not least because of the number of constitutional complaints. One group of lawyers filed complaints for no fewer than 11,693 persons.[71]

The key element of the legal reasoning seems to be the challenge to save the budgetary powers of the *Bundestag*. The Court would regard it as a violation of the electoral rights of citizens if a transfer of budgetary powers led to a loss of budgetary responsibilities on the side of the *Bundestag*.[72] This loss was regarded as unacceptable even in the cases in which the transfer of budgetary powers was part of an intergovernmental governance mechanism.[73] This mainly implied that it was unconstitutional to take part in systems leading to financial obligations that cannot be assessed beforehand by parliament exercising its budgetary powers.[74] While these conditions, at first sight, seem to be an obstacle in the process of creating an international institution granting loans to states that have difficulties to find lenders on the capital markets, the *Bundesverfassungsgericht* decided that the constitutional requirements were met,[75] so that the German participation in the 'rescue packages' remained uncompromised. The focus clearly was on the institutional setting. The judgements thereby are part of an interplay involving the *Bundestag* and the *Bundesverfassungsgericht* that both try to establish further participation rights of the *Bundestag*.[76] It also becomes clear that the urgent character of the situation was no justification for an erosion of the powers of the *Bundestag*. In the end, the legal reasoning was based on a clear – although not explicit – rejection of the idea of the necessity for different rules for the crisis mode.[77] The *Bundesverfassungsgericht* does not base its decision on the fact that it is taken in a particularly critical situation and there is not even a hint that the graveness of the crisis might justify changes in the interpretation of the constitution. In other words, the challenge was reduced to a factual one that did not change the legal questions.

Indirectly, the crisis, however, led to a novelty in the legal system of the Federal Republic: Faced with constitutional complaints against the Outright Monetary Transaction programme, the *Bundesverfassungsgericht* decided to ask for a ruling by the ECJ.[78] It was the first time the Court had done so, thereby taking its 'co-operative relationship with the ECJ', which it had famously made a cornerstone of its 1993 judgement regarding the constitutionality of the Maastricht Treaty,[79] to a new level. When the ECJ accepted the actions of the European Central Bank,[80] the *Bundesverfassungsgericht* did not object.[81]

3.3 Terrorism

As already mentioned, Germany experienced two different periods in which the challenge of terrorism was a major issue. In 1977 the *Bundesverfassungsgericht* had to decide if the federal government was obliged to release terrorists from prison who other terrorists had demanded in exchange for the release of the abducted head of the German Employers' Association Hanns-Martin Schleyer. The Court ruled that there was a comprehensive obligation of the authorities to protect human life.[82] Nevertheless, the rights of the abductee did not extend to releasing the terrorists from prison. The Court decided that the obligation existed towards all citizens and that therefore the authorities had to have the power to decide each situation individually as otherwise the state would lose its capacity to protect its citizens.[83] Within days of the ruling, Hanns-Martin Schleyer was murdered.

After September 11 2001, the legislature passed a number of laws that were part of the fight against the new forms of terrorism. Numerous reforms – all aimed at improving the capacities of the police and other security agencies to track terrorist plots and thereby to prevent terrorist activities – have almost invariably been the object of constitutional complaints. One judgement clearly stands out: In 2005 a law was put into force that allowed the German army under certain, narrow conditions to shoot at and to bring down planes that were captured by terrorists who intended to use the plane as a weapon against persons.[84] It does not need further explanation that the scenario behind this rule is the one that happened in New York in September 2001. The *Bundesverfassungsgericht* regarded this as a violation of the basic right to life (Art. 2 para 2 s. 1 GG) in connection with the basic right of human dignity (Art. 1 para 1 s. 1 GG) insofar as this would cause the death of people other than the terrorist.[85]

Most of the legal problems concerned very detailed questions about how surveillance of telecommunication including the online search on computers could take place and how information gathered in various contexts could be saved in databases and used from there.[86] Therefore, the *Bundesverfassungsgericht* has had many possibilities to draw clear lines that the legislature could not cross. Typically, the *Bundesverfassungsgericht* accepts the approach chosen by the legislature but regards certain particular elements as unconstitutional. Secret surveillance of personal computers was regarded as possible in principle but the particular law as insufficiently clear and disproportionate.[87] The central anti-terrorism-data-gathering system could be installed but some elements regarding the gathering and the further use of the respective information were ruled to be in violation of basic rights.[88] In this context, the Court stated a prohibition in principle: The intelligence agencies are generally not allowed to pass on information that they have gathered to the police force.[89] According to this judgement, the exchange between the two for the purpose of operative measures by the police can only be justified by outstanding public interests.[90] In the judgement from April 2016, the *Bundesverfassungsgericht* had to assess the constitutionality of the law empowering the *Bundeskriminalamt*, the agency created by the federal level with a special expertise in information collection and international co-operation.[91] The *Bundesverfassungsgericht* regarded a number of rules authorising surveillance and the later use of the collected information as too far-reaching. The Court accepted, though, that data collected for one purpose can be used for another one if certain, narrow conditions are met.[92]

The lines of reasoning as such were generally not new. The most important norms that were applied and therefore determined the result of the respective cases can be found in the principle of sufficient clarity and precision of the laws permitting the interference with the basic rights on the one hand and the principle of proportionality on the other hand.[93] Both principles – precision and proportionality – are deduced from the *Rechtsstaatsprinzip*, which is probably best translated as 'the rule of law'. The problem with these two benchmarks lies in the fact that they are very vague and therefore very difficult to apply. This is particularly problematic when the legislature has to predict what kind of approach the *Bundesverfassungsgericht* will regard as constitutional.

Worth mentioning in this context is that the *Bundesverfassungsgericht* 'invented'[94] a new basic right in order to define an area of behaviour protected by the constitution, although the text of the constitution does not give any hint that this right might be included. In this, it followed its own example. Quite early in the history of the Federal Republic certain questions concerning privacy had to be decided by the courts. The right to privacy is not included in the constitution. As a functional substitute, the *Bundesverfassungsgericht* used Art. 2 para 1 GG and Art. 1 para 1 GG in order to establish the *allgemeines Persönlichkeitsrecht* ('general right of personality').[95] In 1983, in the context of complaints against a planned census, it decided that part of the general right of personality implied a right to informational self-determination.[96] In 2008, the *Bundesverfassungsgericht* had to decide on the legality of the online surveillance of personal computers. The Court took the opportunity to add another specification deduced from the same general right of personality, the 'basic right to confidentiality and integrity of information technology systems'.[97] The Court described it as a basic right that is only applicable when no other basic right – especially the above-mentioned right to informational self-determination, the right to privacy of correspondence, post and telecommunications (Art. 10 para 1 GG), and the inviolability of the home (Art. 13 para 1 GG)[98] – guarantees, although not without boundaries, protection in the respective cases.[99] The other basic rights mentioned are defined in a way that leads to a diagnosis according to which the other, above-mentioned basic rights do not protect against certain elements of the process of surveillance of personal computers.[100]

4 Arguments and methodology

The previously discussed developments lead to the question if there have been changes in the legal reasoning or in the methods applied by the *Bundesverfassungsgericht*. Essentially, the answer is a clear 'no' on both counts. While the results in the cases were not easy to predict, the lines of reasoning that lead to them have always been rooted in the general methodology. Arguments dealing with 'crisis' or 'changes' have, if used at all, been integrated into those already known.

4.1 Ignoring the 'crisis-argument' (in general)

The changes described in this article follow different kinds of logic. Only one of them could be clearly identified as changing the type of argumentation. In the other cases mentioned, the element of change comes into play because of the extraordinary character of the case as such i.e. of the legal constellation the courts were faced with. In other words, there was no need to explicitly change the legal reasoning because the case was different from previous ones. Bryde stated already in 1982 that the bulk of the judgements of the *Bundesverfassungsgericht* dealt with questions that, until then, had not been answered and that it dealt with them by considering and referring to previous judgements.[101] This kind of situation can be identified in a number of cases, Many of them were a consequence of the challenge of reunification.

The 'crisis-argument' or arguments to this effect – new constitutional rules for new challenges – have rarely been used and even then normally only in the application of long-established norms and not as part of a modification of the existing rules. Namely, in a case, when according to the traditional case-law a justification for certain action is needed, the recourse to the extraordinary character of the challenge of reunification seemed appropriate, if only as the answer to a question – the justification of a certain act – that has to be asked in all cases. Even in a situation as extraordinary as this, it clearly seems to be the case that part of the *Bundesverfassungsgericht*'s self-defined role is the one as an anchor of stability. It stands to reason that such an anchor is needed particularly when the sea is rough.[102] Therefore, continuity in the legal reasoning is not surprising but rather seems to be an essential element of the self-perception of the Court.

In a category of change, that mainly concerns the impact of the judgements in practical terms, the *Bundesverfassungsgericht* reacted to the creation of the particular legal status available to homosexual couples. Though leaving the definition of marriage unchanged, the *Bundesverfassungsgericht* became, in effect, the main actor in the process of gradually closing the gap between the legal privileges of married couples and the legal consequences of these civil unions. Therefore, the legislature itself provided the opportunity for a new approach by creating a status whose legal consequences could be compared with the ones of traditional marriage and that seemed sufficiently similar. The disruptive character of the change did not originate from the legal reasoning of the Court but from an act of parliament. The respective judgements did not change the interpretation of the non-discrimination clause of the constitution and the Court therefore did not, in a strictly legal view, side with any of the diverse political opinions in this respect. It could be regarded as a general tendency that the Court tries to find ways to develop the argument in a specific case with as little impact in other areas as possible.

4.2 Continuity in methodology

The methodology applied in the above-mentioned judgements also shows no signs of disruptive changes. What stands out from the point of view of methodology is the recourse to legal philosophy which is, of course, not something the Court would consider on a regular basis. It has to be said, though, that this approach was not invented by the *Bundesverfassungsgericht* but rather originated from the judgements by the criminal courts that were the subject of the constitutional supervision. The argument stating special necessities of the economy in East Germany is in accordance with the general legal reasoning: It was included in a question that is always asked in cases of expropriation as part of the justification for the interference with the right of property and that therefore is not significant in a methodological perspective. It is an obvious and therefore not surprising approach to look for the justification also in the challenges brought about by extreme differences between the 'old' and the 'new' *Länder*. Because all kinds of justifications have been applied, this certainly does not amount to new legal doctrines or new methods. The same can be said with regard to the other areas of reasoning covered in this analysis, which might seem surprising or extraordinary considering the cases under discussion or the results, but they do not leave the established lines of reasoning by the *Bundesverfassungsgericht*.

The second aspect that is worth mentioning is the 'invention' of new basic rights – not without foundation in the constitution but certainly with an intention to channel discussions in a direction that according to the written basic rights might have led to a different line of reasoning. In this sense, the Court has acted not only as an interpreter of the constitutional law but also as an innovative force. Even in this context, it could well be argued that this happened out of an undeniable necessity; that is, the fact that certain principles – namely, privacy, data protection and the protection of personal computers against surveillance – are not explicitly protected by the Constitution while their importance seemed undeniable and undoubtedly in conformity with the values as set out by the constitution. It therefore seemed to be an obvious solution to merge two basic rights into one with specific legal features. Even in this case, the Court made sure to attach the 'new' basic right to two existing rights that each itself had left marks in the case-law of the Court. Therefore, it would be hard to argue that the respective decisions, apart from the fact of the inventions of the basic rights as such, contained a particularly innovative methodology.

The attempt to avoid anything that resembles disruptive changes in the legal reasoning is also exemplified by the fact that the Court uses numerous quotes from previous judgements. In this way, it seems as if it wanted to prove the continuity in its own legal reasoning. Brun-Otto Bryde concluded that by quoting only those parts of previous judgements that support the present one, the Court makes its own judgements look more consequential than they are, leaving it to dissenting opinions as well as to academic discussions to point out where contradictions to earlier judgements might lie.[103] It has to be said, though, that this is an analysis of the first three decades of constitutional reasoning in which certain aspects of the reasoning that later became established first had to be developed. In the decades after that the Court's reasoning could be based on a far better-established methodological foundation.

5 Conclusion

The discourse about topics of constitutional significance in Germany is dominated by a very strong *Bundesverfassungsgericht.* It has the authority to interpret the constitution. Its legal reasoning has a large impact that is much bigger than the legal requirements demand. One of the consequences of this outstanding role in the discourse about constitutional law seems to be a self-imposed obligation for continuity. The essence of the case-law generally is not dominated by disruptive changes but rather by a cautious development in the underlying interpretation of principles. The search for changes that can be pinned to a particular situation to which the *Bundesverfassungsgericht* would have reacted by referring to the extraordinary character of the situation or the necessities of a particular change in the factual world has been unsuccessful and it had to be unsuccessful. The Court prefers to let changes in its judgements – even where they occur – appear as a consequence of already established lines of reasoning.

Concerning the subject matters it seems possible to diagnose a greater willingness to be – in the different, above-mentioned ways a Constitutional Court has at its disposal – part of changes in attitudes about social matters than to surrender to pressures originating from crises like the European debt crisis and terrorism. The *Bundesverfassungsgericht* has in parts actively caused changes, mainly by preventing discrimination – originally of women, then of same-sex partnerships and of persons with certain religious faiths – or at least uphold legislative decisions like a more liberal law on abortion. In other areas the Court seems to be much more hesitant. Even the reunification only led to certain adaptions and not to a new constitutional law or different standards. The challenges of terrorism and the European debt crisis were no exception to this development. In fact, it seems impossible to claim that the questions underlying the respective decisions would have been answered in any way differently without the impact of the crisis.

Notes

1 See especially BVerfGE 73, 339 ff.; 89, 155 ff.; 123, 267 ff.

2 English translations of Articles of the *Grundgesetz* follow https://www.gesetze-im-internet.de/englisch_gg/englisch_gg.html#p0142; website last visited 9 November 2016. 'Land law' refers to the law of the 16 states, the 'Basic Law' is the constitution of the Federal Republic and it will be referred to as 'the constitution' in this article.
3 See Mehde (2014) para 31.
4 For an analysis of this in regard to the interpretation of the right to local self-government see Mehde (2012), para 25 ff.
5 Bryde (1982) 163.
6 Bryde (1982), 164.
7 For an analysis of these two different parts of judgements see Lepsius (2015) 119 ff.
8 See e.g. Voßkuhle (2004), 456; Würtenberger (2007), 82 ff.
9 Bryde (1982) 164 f.; Voßkuhle (2004), 456.
10 See C.V.
11 See Hohmann-Dennhardt (2015) 414 f.
12 See C.III.
13 BVerfGE 6, 389 ff.
14 See Benedict (2013) 482.
15 Benedict (2013) 484 f.
16 Benedict (2013) 485.
17 See C.II.
18 Gesetz zur Beendigung der Diskriminierung gleichgeschlechtlicher Gemeinschaften: Lebenspartnerschaften v. 16.2.2001, BGBl. I 266.
19 See Deutscher Bundestag (1993).
20 See C.I.
21 See e.g. Dreier (1997) 421.
22 See BVerfG NJW 1993, 2524 f.
23 Bstu.bund.de/DE/Wissen/DDRGeschichte/MfS-und-Mauer/Flucht-Mauertote/_node.html, last visited 9 November 2016.
24 BGHSt 40, 218 ff.
25 BGHSt 40, 241 ff.
26 BGHSt 39, 1 (14 ff.); 39, 168 (184 f.); 40, 218 (232); 40, 241 (244 ff.).
27 BVerfGE 95, 96 (135 ff.).
28 For a summary of the background of the formula see Dreier (1997), 423 ff.
29 BVerfGE 95, 96 (135 ff.).
30 BVerfGE 95, 96 (135).
31 Dreier (1997), 428.
32 Schwill (2002) 93.
33 BVerfGE 95, 96 (135).
34 BVerfGE 95, 96 (136); translation by the author.
35 BVerfGE 95, 1 ff.
36 BVerfGE 24, 367 (398 ff.); 45, 297 (331 ff.).
37 BVerfGE 95, 1 (22).
38 BVerfGE 95, 1 (23), translation by the author.
39 BVerfGE 95, 1 (23 f.).
40 BVerfGE 39, 1 ff.
41 BVerfGE 39, 1 (36 ff.).
42 See BVerfGE 39, 1 (42 ff.).
43 BVerfGE 39, 1 (44 ff.).
44 BVerfGE 39, 1 (49 ff.).
45 BVerfGE 88, 203 (265) – translation by the author.
46 BVerfGE 88, 203 (265) – translation by the author.
47 See Schulz (1994) 41 f.

48 BVerfGE 89, 203 (265) – translation by the author; the implementation of the law that was the reason for the judgement had been stopped by a preliminary ruling by the same Court, BVerfGE 86, 390 ff.
49 Geiger and von Lampe (1994) 25.
50 Gesetz zur Beendigung der Diskriminierung gleichgeschlechtlicher Gemeinschaften: Lebenspartnerschaften v. 16.2.2001, BGBl. I 266.
51 For a comparison of the reasoning of the Bundesverfassungsgericht and the European Court of Human Rights see Maierhöfer (2013).
52 BVerfGE 105, 313 (348).
53 BVerfGE 105, 313 (342); 112, 50 (65).
54 BVerfGE 105, 313 (342 ff.).
55 See Reimer and Jestaedt (2013) 468 f.
56 BVerfGE 112, 50 ff.
57 BVerfGE 124, 199 ff.
58 BVerfGE 126, 400 ff.
59 BVerfGE 132, 179 ff.
60 BVerfGE 131, 239 ff.
61 BVerfGE 133, 59 ff.; according to Brosius-Gersdorf (2013) 169 the judgement is 'another milestone' toward equal treatment of marriages and civil partnerships.
62 BVerfGE 133, 377 ff.
63 Benedict (2013), 481.
64 BVerfGE 133, 59 (82 ff., Para 60 ff.).
65 BVerfGE 108, 282 (309).
66 BVerfGE 138, 296.
67 BVerfGE 138, 296 (335 ff., Rn. 101 ff.).
68 BVerfGE 138, 296 (348 ff., Rn. 128 ff.).
69 Volkmann (2015), 1091 has found the convincing formula that while one senate trusts the democratic legislature, the other one rather trust itself (translation by the author).
70 Sacksofsky (2015) 807 f.; Volkmann (2015), 1090 f.; Wolff (2015), 491 f.
71 BVerfGE 135, 317 (319).
72 See especially BVerfGE 129, 124 (177 ff.); 135, 317 (399 ff., para 161 ff.).
73 See BVerfGE 129, 124 (179); 135, 317 (400, para 162 ff.).
74 BVerfGE 129, 124 (179); 135, 317 (401, para 163).
75 BVerfGE 129, 124 (183 ff.); 135, 317 (405 ff.; para 176 ff.).
76 See Daiber (2014) 820.
77 See the respective critique by Nettesheim (2012) 1413.
78 BVerfGE 134, 366 ff.; critical: Mayer (2014); No. 2 of Vol. 15 (2014) of the *German Law Journal* is a special edition with a number of different analyses on the OMT decision of the *Bundesverfassungsgericht*. The journal can be found online: http://www.germanlawjournal.com (last visited 9 November 2016).
79 BVerfGE 89, 155 (175).
80 ECJ Judgement of 16 June 2015, Case C-62/14 – *Peter Gauweiler and Others v. Deutscher Bundestag*.
81 BVerfG NJW 2016, 2473 ff.
82 BVerfGE 46, 160 (164).
83 BVerfGE 46, 160 (165).
84 § 14 Abs. 3 Luftsicherheitsgesetz vom 11.1.2005, BGBl. I S. 78 ff.
85 BVerfGE 115, 118 ff.
86 For an analysis of the 'milestone' cases see Bull (2015) 627 ff.
87 BVerfGE 120, 274 ff.
88 BVerfGE 133, 277 ff.; the main argument for assuming a violation being, again, the principle of proportionality; see Käß (2013) 711 f.
89 BVerfGE 133, 277 (329, para 123).
90 BVerfGE 133, 277 (329, para 123).

91 BVerfG, NJW 2016, 1781 ff.
92 BVerfG NJW 2016, 1781 (1800; para 275 ff.).
93 BVerfGE 120, 274 (315 ff.); 133, 277 (320, para 105 ff.); BVerfG NJW 2016, 1781 (1783, para 93 ff.).
94 Bull (2015) 652 points out that the Court did not invent a new basic right but rather found a word for a dimension of the general personality right.
95 See especially BVerfGE 54, 148 (152 ff.); the civil courts had developed the notion of an 'allgemeines Persönlichkeitsrecht' some time before the *Bundesverfassungsgericht*, see BVerfGE 34, 269 ff.
96 BVerfGE 65, 1 ff.
97 BVerfGE 120, 274 (302).
98 Sceptical regarding the necessity of a new basic right: Bull (2015), 652 ff.
99 BVerfGE 120, 274 (302).
100 BVerfGE 120, 274 (308 ff.).
101 Bryde (1982) 165.
102 See Badura (2014), para 17.
103 Bryde (1982) 163.

Bibliography

Badura, Peter, 'Verfassungsänderung, Verfassungswandel, Verfassungsgewohnheitsrecht', in Josef Isensee and Paul Kisrchof (eds), *Handbuch des Staatsrechts, Band XII* (3rd edn, C.F. Müller 2014), 591.

Benedict, Jörg, 'Die Ehe unter dem besonderen Schutz der Verfassung – Ein vorläufiges Fazit' (2013). 68 *JuristenZeitung* 477–487.

Brosius-Gersdorf, Frauke, 'Gleichstellung von Ehe und Lebenspartnerschaft' (2013). 5 *FamFR* 169.

Bryde, Brun-Otto, *Verfassungsentwicklung – Stabilität und Dynamik im Verfassungsrecht der Bundesrepublik Deutschland* (Nomos 1982).

Bull, Hans Peter, 'Grundsatzentscheidungen zum Datenschutz im Bereich der inneren Sicherheit', in Robert Chr. van Ooyen and Martin H.W. Möllers (eds), *Handbuch Bundesverfassungsgericht im politischen System* (2nd edn, Springer 2015) 627.

Daiber, Birgit, 'Die Mitwirkung des Deutschen Bundestages an den Maßnahmen zur Eindämmung der Staatsschuldenkrise im Euroraum' (2014). 67 *DÖV* 809.

Deutcher Bundestag, 'Bericht der Gemeinsamen Verfassungskommission' (1993). BT-Drs. 12/6000 of November 5th 1993.

Dreier, Horst, 'Gustav Radbruch und die Mauerschützen' (1997). 52 *JuristenZeitung* 421–434.

Geiger, Julia and von Lampe, Claudia, 'Das zweite Urteil des Bundesverfassungsgerichts zum Schwangerschaftsabbruch – BVerfG, Urteil vom 28. Mai 1993–2 BvF 2/90, 4/92, 5/92 – Ein Schritt vorwärts, zwei Schritte zurück' (1994). 16 *Jura* 20–30.

Hohmann-Dennhardt, Christine, 'Das Bundesverfassungsgericht und die Frauen', in Robert Chr. van Ooyen and Martin H.W. Möllers, Martin (eds), *Handbuch Bundesverfassungsgericht im politischen System* (2nd edn, Springer 2015), 413.

Käß, Robert, 'Das Urteil des Bundesverfassungsgerichts zum Antiterrordateigesetz – Trennung der Grundrechtssphären und informationelles Trennungsprinzip' (2013). 144 *BayVBl.* 709–712.

Lepsius, Oliver, 'Entscheiden durch Maßstabsbildung', in Robert Chr. van Ooyen and Martin H.W. Möllers (eds), *Handbuch Bundesverfassungsgericht im politischen System* (2nd edn, Springer 2015), 119.

Maierhöfer, Christian, 'Homosexualität, Ehe und Gleichheit: Ein Missverständnis im Dialog der Gerichte' (2013). 40 *EuGRZ* 105–113.

Mayer, Franz C., 'Rebels without a cause? A Critical Analysis of the German Constitutional Court's OMT Reference' (2014). 15 *German Law Journal* 111–146.

Mehde, Veith, 'Art. 28 Abs. 2', in Theodor Maunz and Günter Dürig (eds), *Grundgesetz-Kommentar* (Beck 2012).

Mehde, Veith, 'Art. 28 Abs. 1', in Theodor Maunz and Günter Dürig (eds), *Grundgesetz-Kommentar* (Beck 2014).

Nettesheim, Martin, 'Verfassungsrecht und Politik in der Staatsschuldenkrise' (2012). 65 *NJW* 1409–1413.

Reimer, Philipp and Jestaedt, Matthias, 'Anmerkung' (2013). 68 *JZ* 468–472.

Sacksofsky, Ute, 'Kopftuch als Gefahr' (2015). *DVBl* 801.

Schulz, Lorenz, 'Verschlungene Wege des Lebensschutzes. Zum zweiten Abtreibungsurteil des BVerfG' (1994). 14 *Strafverteidiger* 38.

Schwill, Florian, 'Zur Anwendung der Radbruchschen Formel in der Rechtsprechung des Bundesverfassungsgerichts' (2002). 85 *KritV* 79–97.

Volkmann, Uwe, 'Dimensionen des Kopftuchstreits' (2015). 37 *JA* 1083–1094.

Voßkuhle, Andreas, 'Gibt es und wozu nutzt eine Lehre vom Verfassungswandel?' (2004). 43 *Der Staat* 450–459.

Wolff, Heinrich Amadeus, 'Anmerkung' (2015). *BayVBl.* 489.

Würtenberger, Thomas, 'Verfassungsänderung und Verfassungswandel: Von der nationalen zu einer globalen Perspektive', in Ferdinand Kirchhof, Hans-Jürgen Papier and Heinz Schäffer (eds), *Grundrechte und Rechtsstaat, Festschrift für Detlev Merten zum 70. Geburtstag* (C.F. Müller 2007), 77.

6 From submission to reaction

The Greek Courts' stance on the financial crisis

Apostolos Vlachogiannis

Everything must change
so that everything can stay the same.

(*Il gattopardo*, Giuseppe Tomasi)

Introduction

Greece is one of the few European countries that has not yet succumbed to the sirens of the model of constitutional justice described by Kelsen before the Second World War and adopted by most countries in its aftermath. Instead, it has a long-standing tradition of judicial review similar to the American one (i.e. decentralised, *a posteriori*, incidental, concrete and declaratory control).[1] The first judgment of the Supreme Court near the end of the nineteenth century that declared a law unconstitutional was in 1897[2] and subsequently the interpretative declaration with regard to Art. 5 of the Constitution of 1927 solemnly recognised this power.[3] It follows that for more than a century, Greek courts of every type, jurisdiction and hierarchy – i.e. not only the three highest courts (the Council of State [Συμβούλιο της Επικρατείας, hereafter: CoS], the Supreme Court [Άρειος Πάγος, hereafter: AP] and the Court of Audit) – have exercised a check on the legislative power by refusing to apply laws which have been voted by Parliament but are however deemed unconstitutional.

In this context, judicial review of legislation has been a constant feature of Greek constitutional law.[4] Despite the establishment of the Special Supreme Court [Ανώτατο Ειδικό Δικαστήριο, hereafter: SSC] that has the power, under special conditions prescribed by article 100 of the Hellenic Constitution, to invalidate laws,[5] the 'true constitutional Court' of Greece is without doubt the CoS. Since 1929, when it started functioning, it has exercised an extended control of legislative measures; and especially since 1975 it has been considered the 'guardian of the Constitution'.

During the past five years, Greece has been undergoing a serious economic crisis which has put to test its legal, political and social institutions. The global financial crisis which started in 2008 has been qualified as an 'unprecedented disaster' that has influenced constitutional orders to a great extent.[6] However, in Greece the impact of the crisis was tremendous from the beginning and has embraced every field of activity. According to former President of the CoS, P. Pikrammenos, the effects of the Greek financial crisis were universal and catalytic.[7] The crisis brought a violent interruption of the previous situation, which created a predominant feeling of discontinuity and anomaly and led practically to the dismantling and reversal of the *status quo*. As a consequence, rules guaranteeing normality and everyday harmony were suddenly indefinitely suspended and, in this context, arose the risk that this acute situation would demand solutions at all cost and that the economic and financial necessities would be considered as the basic reason for a (*de facto*) violation of existing rules. As a conclusion, static rules of legality were to be measured against the efficiency of extraordinary legislative measures, this confrontation taking place 'under the auspices' of the notion of general interest.[8]

The two crucial moments which need to be retained are 2010, when the first memorandum[9] became an act of law[10] and 2012 when the second memorandum[11] was voted – the third memorandum being too recent to pass judicial muster. The laws ratifying the memoranda, along with the laws implementing them,[12] provided for a scheme of holistic reform of the Greek economy, administration and welfare state, hence the ensemble of the Greek legal order (especially fiscal law, tax law, social security law and labour law). Practically nothing went unchanged; but it was especially the pensions, salary and allowances cuts that provoked the popular ire and therefore were mostly challenged in the courts. The result of this has been a particularly rich constitutional case law, coming mostly from the CoS, as most individual and almost all social rights have been affected by legislative measures adopted during the crisis.

It is obvious from all the above that the economic crisis has been by far the most important factor affecting constitutional adjudication and doctrine. Moreover, since 2010 and up to now, the crisis has embraced all fields of social, political and economic activity in a way that everything cannot be interpreted but in its light. Therefore, it is mainly the pressure exercised by the economic crisis in constitutional adjudication that will be examined. Having said that, I will not omit to mention one specific judgment of the CoS regarding migration and in particular the conditions of nationalisation for children of migrants.

For methodological reasons, the following analysis focuses mainly on the case law of a single Court – the Council of State – so as to be able to examine thoroughly the course of its judgments and the nuances of its legal reasoning. I will defend the thesis that the CoS, through the five years of the crisis, acting as a *de facto* constitutional court, has always tried to shield its case law from the effects of the crisis – at least as far as this is possible. In fact, it has not hesitated in many instances to qualify the crisis as a passing moment, refusing to take into consideration the permanent marks it has left, and was doomed to leave, in the Greek legal landscape. This, of course, does not mean that its overall stance towards the legislator has remained unchanged. On the contrary, it will be argued that from the attitude of submission towards crisis-led legislative initiatives, it has recently crossed the path of reaction to the legislator's choices, hence to the crisis itself. However, by focusing on the crisis as an external pressure factor instead of drawing on the inherent adaptability and flexibility of the Constitution, it has always treated the crisis as an exception and has persistently sought to return to constitutional normality, even though the brute facts of socio-economic reality point to another direction.

Certainly, as the first part of the following analysis will hopefully show, some new key concepts have been indeed developed, while also the scope of substantive control of legislative measures – especially socio-economic ones – has been extended and its intensity amplified. However, in most landmark cases the Court has oscillated between, on the one hand, reaffirming well established doctrines as though nothing had changed, and, on the other hand, introducing in its legal reasoning the concept of 'emergency situation', hence adopting a problematic approach from a rule of law standpoint. In this context, I will proceed to evaluate critically, in the second part of the analysis, the overall attitude of the Court. Finally, in the third part, I will try to explain and eventually justify this attitude, both from a legal/institutional and from a political point of view.

1. The novelties of the crisis

The sudden outburst of the economic crisis and the review of numerous statutory acts passed in order to ratify and implement the agreements with Greece's lenders provided for an excellent opportunity to revise and reshape existing constitutional doctrines, overrule long-standing precedents and invent new rights and concepts. It would be in fact impossible for any Court to stand passive against this almost frenzy of legislative production and not try to internalise the external stimulus of the crisis by producing new constitutional stories.[13] Moreover, it is a common fact that austerity measures have been increasingly challenged constitutionally before courts, mostly on the basis of social rights protection in light of the principle of proportionality.[14]

First of all, it does not come as a surprise that the CoS developed in many of its judgments the concept of 'decent living standard'[15] considered as the extreme limit of any legislative measure cutting salaries or pensions. Drawing on the relevant jurisprudence of the European Court of Human Rights (ECtHR) with respect to the value of the human being,[16] the CoS engages in a fruitful dialogue with the Court in Strasbourg and does not omit to refer explicitly and constantly to its case law especially on article 1 of the 1st Additional Protocol to the ECHR guaranteeing the right to property. The CoS derives the above-mentioned concept from article 2 para. 1 of the Constitution.[17] In its most recent judgments regarding pension cuts, the Court went even further and adopted a social approach to the subsistence minimum concept[18] inspired by the relevant case law of the German Constitutional Court.[19] It declared emphatically that pensions granted by the State should allow pensioners

> [t]o live with dignity, providing them not only the means for their physical subsistence (food, clothing, housing, basic household goods, heating, hygiene and full healthcare), but also the means for their participation in social life in a

> way that does not in any case dissemble essentially from the correspondent conditions of their work life.[20]

In another case involving a law providing for the privatisation of the water company of Athens, the CoS struck it down because the privatisation in question violated the right to health,[21] conceived by the Constitution both as an individual[22] and as a social right.[23] Through a particularly innovative and creative construction of Art. 5 para. 5 of the Constitution – an article which had never before been invoked in order to declare a law unconstitutional – the Court invalidated the transfer of a large share of the water company to private individuals. It was specifically held that such a transaction and the subsequent alienation of the Greek state from the majority of the share capital could in fact be perceived as a threat to public health.[24]

In another series of cases, the CoS elaborated on the concept of the functions belonging to the 'core of the State'. So far this concept had been used in cases involving privatisations,[25] where it is constantly held that a public function belonging inseparably to the 'core of the State' as an expression of sovereignty can only be exercised by the State or a public body.[26] In its judgment regarding salary cuts of the military, police and coastal guard personnel, the CoS accorded to them, along with judges, the status of a special category of public sector employees belonging to the 'hard core of the State'.[27] The legal basis for the unconstitutionality of the law in question was triple:[28] First, the special salary treatment of military personnel accorded to them due to their special mission (belonging to the hard core of the State) and the special conditions and dangerousness of their profession (Art. 45, 23 para. 2 and 29 para. 3);[29] second, the principle of proportionality (Art. 25 para 1);[30] and last but not least, the constitutional provisions guaranteeing equal burden-sharing (Art. 4 para. 5)[31] and social and national solidarity (Art. 25 para. 4).[32] Thus, interpreting holistically several articles of the Constitution, the Court inferred an obligation of special wage treatment and stressed the need to avoid salary cuts that would undermine the efficiency of the forces of order and national security.

In its judgment (Plenary) 460/2013 regarding the constitutionality of the Nationality Act of 2010, the CoS revived an old – and, in my opinion, historically unfortunate – distinction between the people and the nation. It held in particular that the legislator is not completely free to determine the composition of the people as a legal entity but he/she is bound by the provisions of the Constitution and the need to preserve the national homogeneity of the Greek state.[33] This shows that the CoS relied on a romantic conception of the nation,[34] viewed as a transcendental and intergenerational entity which cannot be altered arbitrarily by an ephemeral authority such as the party in power. As a result of this reasoning, nationality cannot be accorded to people who are not but 'slightly or not at all integrated' into Greek society. The CoS thus declared unconstitutional several provisions of law 3838/2010 which accorded a right to nationality to children of immigrants who were born in Greece (based on the *jus soli*) or had completed six years at school, demanding more stringent conditions. It is important to note that in the preamble of the Act it was explicitly stated that the law was passed in order to deal with the burning issue of integration of migrants and their children in Greek society, but this consideration did not seem to weigh in the judges' reasoning.[35]

Finally, one of the most important features of the jurisprudence of crisis is that the CoS has made an extended use of the concept of 'general interest' having recourse to 'novel constructions of the public interest under the prism of the financial crisis'.[36] Concretely, this notion has served as an implicit general clause allowing a narrow interpretation of constitutional provisions conferring rights or, vice versa, of provisions imposing limits to the legislator's powers, such as Art. 78 para. 2 (limiting the power to impose taxes retroactively),[37] as well as the basis for overruling long-standing precedents.[38] Consequently, a brand new notion has emerged, that of 'budgetary interest' conceived as a special form of general public interest (as opposed to pure 'treasury interest').[39] In other words, the broad and vague notion of general public interest has been interpreted recently as including the so called 'budgetary interest', meaning all measures pertaining to the goals of balanced budget, fiscal discipline, financial stability and also collection of public revenues.[40] Pushed to its extreme the notion of budgetary interest can take the form of the sole 'treasury interest' of the State in its effort to consolidate its budget (i.e. plain revenue collection).

The reasons explaining the rise of the notion are that the balance of public finance of the Greek State has been shaken; that public deficit and debt have sharply risen to unprecedented heights; and that dealing with the danger of default is now considered as a matter of national interest given that the financial crisis has turned into a national crisis. The reasoning of the judges in judgment 1620/2011 clearly shows this interrelatedness. The differentiation (in favor of the State) between private individuals and the State regarding the interest rate owed for overdue debts has been justified in terms of its contribution 'to the realization of a major national goal, initially that of safeguarding a balanced budget, and then that of preventing the economic breakdown of the country'.[41] As for the goals to be attained there is the need to cover the financial needs of the country; to improve the future financial and economic situation; and to fulfill the European goal of budgetary discipline and safeguard the stability of the euro zone.[42] In this sense, even the treasury interest, when intertwined with general public interest considerations, is perceived as an interest crucial, necessary and vital for the survival of the state.[43]

Several commentators have stigmatised the frequent and extended recourse to this notion which brings to mind the creation of a state of emergency law, i.e. a law applied under extraordinary circumstances.[44] In a similar way, others point that it is being invoked like in the past decade terrorism and other means of endangerment of national and social security as a way to seriously curb not only social but also individual rights.[45] The Court's attitude in this realm has even been described as reverse budgetary activism, given that in some cases it does not hesitate to step in and (re)constitute the legislator's line of reasoning by inventing new arguments based on public interest considerations in order to uphold the laws in question.[46] The result of this has been that the CoS has failed to protect adequately certain rights, such as the right to property[47] or that to equal treatment,[48] and has been severely criticised for its reluctance to check on the legislature. In this context a 'shrinkage' of fundamental rights occurs due to the financial emergency constructed as an 'overriding public interest'.[49] It would not be an overstatement to argue that the notion of 'general interest' has become during the crisis a super-notion which trumps every right, especially if there is a budgetary aspect, and has served in many respects as a blank cheque that justifies almost every legislative restriction on rights.

Recently, however, the CoS has inaugurated an era of a strong form of judicial review of socio-economic legislative measures, extending the scope and increasing the intensity of the control exercised. Through a comprehensive use of the principle of proportionality enshrined in Art. 25 para. 1 of the Constitution, the CoS has not shown its habitual reluctance to step in and control important measures crucial to the implementation of the government's economic policy. It does not content itself anymore with a plain reasonableness test meaning that it will not hesitate to examine the grounds on which a measure was taken, its impact and efficiency. By amplifying the intensity of the substantive control, the CoS has reaffirmed, even more emphatically, its role as a *de facto* negative legislator, though it always pretends exercising a minimum control that respects the legislature's margin of appreciation. The nature of its role is better understood in light of two recent developments.

First, lately the CoS, being aware of the fiscal impact of its judgments, has made a very loose and highly constructive interpretation of law 4274/2014[50] determining the effects of its judgments in time. It seems to have been inspired on this point by judgment 413/2014 of the Portuguese Constitutional Court ruling that pay cuts in the public sector, as well as cuts to pensions and welfare benefits are unconstitutional, but the judgment is not to be applied retrospectively. It follows that when the Court rules on an issue having a massive impact on the state budget and is about to declare a law unconstitutional, as was the seminal case of the remuneration of university professors[51] or the recent landmark case on pension cuts,[52] it shows its caution by applying its ruling only in the future. The rejection of retroactive force is a way to moderate the effects of judicial law-making without in any case denying justice to the plaintiffs, although recourse to this technique seems to contravene on its face the diffused character of judicial review exercised by the Court.[53]

Second, the CoS has explicitly imposed on the legislator the obligation to provide (appropriate) justification of measures restrictive of social rights, as several dissenting opinions had already asked before.[54] This means justification on the basis of a 'special, in-depth and scientifically documented study',[55] which can then allow a stronger form of proportionality control, since available alternatives will be present and assessed. According to former President of the CoS, S. Rizos, judgment (Plen) 668/2012, which upheld the 1st Memorandum, marks an exception from the rule that actuarial studies are demanded periodically so as to maintain budgetary discipline of social security funds.[56] It is for this reason that through an intervention which he made just a few months before the pension cuts' constitutionality was actually decided before the Court, he stressed the need for a full study which would note exactly the revenues and expenses of social security bodies, but most of all would depict with honesty the goals set out; only by means of such a study, the legislator's arbitrariness could be effectively controlled, hence avoided.[57] Otherwise, legislative choices would run the risk to seem hasty or based on arbitrary considerations and consequently fail to convince courts as to their constitutionality.[58]

2. A critical evaluation of the overall attitude of the CoS

Regarding the novelties of the crisis, it is true that the jurisprudence of the CoS has touched almost every important aspect of constitutional law. The Court has been called to respond to an unprecedented storm of legislative measures which affected all constitutional rights, bearing in mind that what was at stake was the survival of the Greek state. The concept of 'decent standard of living' is thus a pure concept of the crisis. However, the use of the concept of the 'core of the State' has been heavily criticised, when employed in wage cases, because of its inherent vagueness.[59] Indeed, the CoS has not offered any coherent theory of the state in order to back its casuistic approach and shed light to this obscure notion. Likewise, the reference to the individual right to health in the case of the privatization of the Athens water company, cannot hide the fragmentary approach of the CoS in this field,[60] since it has not elaborated on a sophisticated distinction between private/public which could set the constitutional limits of privatizations. Last but not least, the reemergence of the old distinction that has plagued the political history of Greece between people/nation marks a traditionalist and, most of all, outdated approach to the contemporary issue of migration. In general, it is my belief that some of these new elements have not always been successful examples of judicial inventiveness. Equally, they have not always contributed to adjusting existing constitutional doctrine by further elaborating on it in a consistent and coherent way.

Furthermore, despite several innovative and path-breaking judgments, mostly having to do with salary and pension cuts,[61] one cannot but observe the Court's hesitation to break with existing case law and overrule precedents with regard to the scope of the control it exercises. Most illustrating is the fact that it has repeatedly refused to engage in the review of acts of legislative content, i.e. a form of presidential decree enjoying legislative status according to Art. 44 para. 1.[62] This form of executive *fiat* has been on the rise since 2010 and has acquired normality through constant use despite the constitutional dictate that they must only be employed under extraordinary circumstances of urgent and unforeseeable need.[63] In the same manner, the Court has steadily refused to control the *interna corporis*, i.e. the internal procedures leading to the adoption of a legislative bill by Parliament, although, as Contiades and Fotiadou rightly point out, in Greece the Constitution has been openly – and repeatedly, one could add – circumvented with regard to procedural rules.[64] It has thus legitimated indirectly the strengthening of the executive through the constant and gradual diminishment of the role of the legislature.[65] As a conclusion, the CoS has reinforced its power of control in substantive matters, but has remained silent or a passive spectator before the increasing phenomenon of legislative acts that are not voted in Parliament; or equally of laws voted through extremely urgent and/or sloppy procedures.

Another important feature of the jurisprudence of crisis is the absence of the notion of changed circumstances in the legal reasoning of the judges. This notion could in fact justify the Court's judgments in the same way that the Supreme Court of the US upheld emergency measures during the Great Depression and finally achieved the constitutionalisation of the New Deal.[66] Instead, the CoS has chosen to have recourse to the highly problematic notion of 'emergency situation'. The Court has repeatedly used the terms 'acute financial crisis',[67] 'threat of an immediate collapse of the national economy'[68] or 'danger of default and collapse of the national economy'[69] in order to uphold legislative measures and safeguard the country's effort of fiscal consolidation, especially during the initial period 2010–2012. Its line of reasoning usually follows the pattern:

> [T]hese measures, taken under the above explained completely extraordinary circumstances, i.e. the danger of default and collapse of the national economy with unforeseeable economic and social consequences, do not appear, within the context of the marginal control of constitutionality of the correspondent provisions ... as inappropriate or unnecessary for the achievement of the above mentioned, constitutionally legitimate, goal.[70]

As former President of the CoS P. Pikrammenos explained in an important intervention of his, these citations are linked to the emergency doctrine developed by the *Conseil d'État* and the US Supreme Court. The conditions that need to be filled for applying this doctrine are: presence of an imminent danger whose consequences affect the whole society and pose a threat to the continuity of its organized life, while the danger has to be so extraordinary that habitual measures/ restrictions do not suffice to combat it. Finally, the measures taken have to respect the principle of proportionality: they need to be appropriate, provisional, proportional (*stricto sensu*) and also safety valves have to exist in order to avoid misuse. In no way, however, can emergency create new powers or extend existing ones nor can it lead to the violation of the plain letter of the Constitution or statutes. In his opinion, judgment (Plenary) 668/2012, where he himself presided, contains elements of the doctrine but also sets explicit limits.[71]

It follows that by refusing to treat constitutional provisions as inherently flexible and adaptable, the Court has been obliged to turn to century-old doctrines about emergency powers and emergency situations. In other words, the only way it has found to justify harsh legislative measures has been to refer to the concept of 'general interest' and internalise in its reasoning the ancient doctrine of *raison d'État*.[72] This attitude becomes even more clear in the dissenting opinion of three judges in judgment 693/2011 concerning the constitutionality of an extraordinary income tax for the rich which had retroactive force, where essentially the 'danger of an eventual total budgetary derailment'[73] was evoked as a state of emergency *praeter constitutionem*. The arguments presented, under an – undoubtedly – radical form of invocation of the crisis,[74] could even work *contra constitutionem*[75] and eventually lead to the violation of the letter of the constitutional text.[76] According to the approach favoured by the dissenting opinion, 'emergency' becomes the ultimate standard for evaluating the constitutionality of the crisis legislation, because declaring directly a state of emergency pursuant to Art. 48 of the Constitution is a tool ill-suited for achieving the kind of adaptability which financial disasters demand.[77] Likewise, the key notion and only available tool used thanks to its flexibility is proportionality, which ends up applying a balancing test between emergency/reality and individual/social rights.[78]

By choosing to rely on the emergency doctrine – explicitly or implicitly – the Court succeeds in carrying out two separate goals: On the one hand, not to challenge certain basic legislative measures taken in order to ensure the survival of the state; on the other hand, to be able to claim, at any time, the return to 'normality' if the threat to the national economy is not considered imminent (of course based on the Court's assessment itself). In the latter case, frequent denial of the crisis sometimes even takes the form of defiance to the political and economic realities of this period. However, ignoring these realities is not a judicial strategy capable to accommodate the effects of the crisis. Furthermore, and more importantly, although not expressed in such a radical form as in the dissenting opinion mentioned above (which otherwise characterises the overall strategy of the Court pushing it simply to its extremes), constant evocation of emergency doctrine arguments is not a satisfying approach from a rule of law point of view. Even when used moderately and while it might not lead to the violation of the plain letter of the Constitution, it is still incompatible with the role of the Court as defender of individual rights against the legislator's arbitrariness.

3. Shedding light on the Court's attitude

From a legal point of view, one cannot but highlight the restraints from the type of judicial review practiced in Greece. First of all, it should not be forgotten that the CoS is formally the Supreme Administrative Court. It is certainly true that the CoS, encouraged by the legislature to a certain degree,[79] has assumed – in practice – the responsibility of being the country's constitutional court. However, the gap between form and reality proves itself decisive and influences in many respects the content of the judgments as well as the quality of the CoS's reasoning. First, the Court often seems unable to get rid of a legalistic approach rooted in Greek administrative law. This approach is particularly evident in the way its judgments are formulated and justified: they contain highly legalistic arguments and put almost no emphasis on facts, data, and statistics (with the exception of certain dissenting or concurring opinions). Moreover, the incidental character of the review often results in a superficial approach of the issues at hand. The CoS does not seem willing to dig deep in issues such as the relation between national austerity measures and European Union law,[80] the theory of State and the limits of privatizations, or the binding force and the content of socio-economic rights in the context of a bankrupt state. Certainly, the Court cannot avoid reviewing legislative measures, but it can be argued that it has not offered so far solid justifications for its most important judgments nor has it contributed to the renewing of constitutional doctrines.

Moreover, from an institutional point of view, the Court's initial judgments received a sometimes harsh critique from scholars who insisted on the relativisation of the principle of proportionality by the Court and disapproved of the weak form of control exercised until then.[81] To prove this point, the majority opinion in judgment (Plenary) 668/2012 is cited. According to this judgment only 'measures not seen in principle as evidently inappropriate' (instead of simply inappropriate) would be invalidated. This attitude of maximum self-restraint and extreme deference to the legislature accompanied with the reference to the notion of emergency raised for many scholars the danger of establishing 'a permanent state of emergency law'[82] which in truth would be no 'law' at all, especially when linked to imprecise and unclear economic goals;[83] hence the need to reexamine legislative measures periodically in order to assess their efficiency and their constitutionality, precisely because circumstances change and emergency law demands increased justification and consequently stronger judicial review.[84] Faced with these arguments, the Court had to react in order not only to safeguard the binding nature of constitutional provisions, but also to save its institutional prestige. The – manifest in several of its most recent judgments – voluntarism of the Court, cannot but be explained as a reaction to and reversal of the initial frustration and deference towards the choices of the elected branch of government.[85]

From a political standpoint, it could be argued that the CoS has gone along with the political tide. In fact, the Court ratified most of the measures in the beginning,[86] with small exceptions of lesser importance.[87] It adopted a pragmatist approach, especially with respect to social rights,[88] leading inevitably to an attitude of self-restraint.[89] Worth noting is the fact that by that time the idea of reform was still echoing in political and public discourse and the initial shock of the crisis was still present. The emblematic judgment of the Court upholding the first memorandum[90] clearly shows this point: The Court is fearful of the disastrous consequences of not upholding the law in question, but also trusts the legislator that he/she will succeed in consolidating the state budget.

However, when popular opinion starts to swing and becomes more hostile to budgetary and fiscal reforms, the Court's judgments begin to 'bite' more and more. The first judgments during the crisis to declare budget and salary cuts unconstitutional are the ones dealing with the remuneration of military personnel[91] and university professors.[92] In these judgments, for the first time, the CoS does not apply a plain reasonableness test (examining simply if a measure is evidently inappropriate or unnecessary), but exercises a stronger form of control.[93] As a result, the CoS becomes openly hostile to austerity measures, so long as the surrounding discourse stresses their failure to achieve the goals initially set out. Its attitude could now be even described as a resistance to the crisis.[94] This is evidenced clearly by the recent judgments on pensions (issued in June 2015) which found all cuts until 2012 constitutional, i.e. respectful of constitutional provisions and proportional, and all those afterwards unconstitutional.

This analysis is further reinforced by the fact that dissenting opinions have become a common feature of the crisis case law. Their frequent appearance, the force and the persistence of the arguments presented, as well as the number of judges dissenting each time show a major divide within the Court – which is usually split in two lines – reflecting also a similar divide within society and the political spectrum itself. On the one side are those who, in the spirit of former President of the CoS S. Rizos, see the crisis and the subsequent legislative response as a major and largely unnecessary or unjustified – hence unconstitutional – blow to the welfare state. Consequently, they do not wish that the Constitution gives way to the force of reality, although they recognise indeed that the Supreme Law is not a parchment detached from it.[95] On the other side are those who, in the spirit of the dissenting judges in the recent pensions' cuts cases,[96] do not put emphasis on the cuts themselves, but tend to look at the bigger picture. As a result, they treat the laws in question as an attempt – sometimes flawed or even sometimes sloppy, but still necessary and long-awaited – to fix longstanding problems and reform, at last, the Greek economy.

4. Conclusion

Briefly stated, the CoS has undoubtedly produced in the past few years a very important and interesting body of decisions. New concepts have been developed and new rights have been created. At the same time, older doctrines have been reconfigured and reshaped in order to be applied in radically different circumstances. The Court has deepened its control in substantive matters, especially in view of protecting socio-economic rights, but has hesitated to extend it to procedural matters, such as the review of acts of legislative content. As far as its overall judicial strategy is concerned, the Court has chosen to rely on the emergency doctrine, thus treating the effects of the crisis as short-lasting and ephemeral. This strategy has facilitated at first upholding some basic legislative measures taken in the beginning of the crisis in order to avert the bankruptcy of the Greek state. However, as time went by and popular opinion started being more and more hostile to these measures the Court's attitude also switched. It would not be an overstatement to argue that its recent judgments can be interpreted as a form of resistance against the continuing impact of the crisis.

As a conclusion, I believe that the Court was taken by surprise by the crisis, in the same way of course as the Greek society as a whole. Initially reluctant and cautious, it slowly regained its institutional self-confidence and tried to set some limits to the legislative policies imposed by the memoranda. Its methodological choice to rely exclusively on the emergency doctrine proved however problematic to a point, since the crisis was not entirely a passing moment, i.e. an 'emergency', but in many respects a new reality there to stay. Some measures were indeed one-off but others, such as the multiple reforms of the pension scheme, seem to constitute structural reforms which will stand even when (or if?) the crisis is over. It follows that the Court has not always used the proper conceptual tools in order to adjust its judgments to the moving realities. Such a tool would be in fact the changed circumstances doctrine, as it has been suggested by some dissenting opinions.[97] The result is that the Court has not treated the Greek Constitution as a living constitution able to adapt to the changed circumstances. It has thus failed to produce a paradigm shift in Greek constitutional law and guarantee, by affirming the flexibility of the Constitution, a smooth transition to the post-crisis era.

Notes

1 Manitakis (1988) 40.
2 AP 23/1897.
3 Drosos (1996) 200.
4 The power of judicial review is now explicitly recognized by Art. 87 para. 2 and Art. 93 para. 4 of the existing Constitution of 1975. Art. 87 para. 2 states that: 'In the discharge of their duties, judges shall be subject only to the Constitution and the laws; in no case whatsoever shall they be obliged to comply with provisions enacted in violation of the Constitution'. Art. 93 para. 4 is even more explicit: 'The courts shall be bound not to apply a statute whose content is contrary to the Constitution'.
5 Para. 1: 'A Special Supreme Court shall be established, the jurisdiction of which shall comprise [...] e) Settlement of controversies on whether the content of a statute enacted by Parliament is contrary to the Constitution, or on the interpretation of provisions of such statute when conflicting judgments have been pronounced by the Supreme Administrative Court, the Supreme Civil and Criminal Court or the Court of Audit'. Para. 4: 'Provisions of a statute declared unconstitutional shall be invalid as of the date of publication of the respective judgment, or as of the date specified by the ruling'.
6 Contiades and Fotiadou (2015) 4.
7 Pikrammenos (2012) 98.
8 Pikrammenos (2012) 97.
9 In the Greek crisis jargon, memoranda (a.k.a. Memorandum of Understanding) are the legal texts which ratify the accords signed between Greece and the troika of its lenders, i.e. the ECB (European Central Bank), the IMF (International Monetary Fund) and the EU Commission.
10 Law 3845/2010 (Gov Gazette No A′ 65/6.5.2010) entitled 'Measures for the application of the support mechanism for the Greek economy by euro area Member States and the International Monetary Fund'.
11 Law 4046/2012 (Gov Gazette No A′ 28/14.2.2012).
12 Just to mention a few: law 3863/2010 'New social security system and relevant provisions, regulation of labour' (Gov Gazette No A′ 115/15.7.2010); law 3985/2011 'Medium-term Fiscal Strategy Framework 2012–2015' (Gov Gazette No A′ 151/1.7.2011); law 3986/2011 'Urgent Measures Implementing the Medium-term Fiscal Strategy Framework 2012–2015' (Gov Gazette No A′ 152/1.7.2011); law 4024/2011 'Pension provisions, unified salary and hierarchy grid, labour reserve and other provisions implementing the Medium-term Fiscal Strategy Framework 2012–2015' (Gov Gazette No A′ 226/27.10.2011); law 4051/2012 'Pensions-related provisions and other urgent provisions implementing the Memorandum of Understanding of law 4046/2012' (Gov Gazette No A′ 40/29.2.2012); law 4093/2012 'Approval of Medium-term Fiscal Strategy Framework 2013–2016 – Urgent measures implementing law 4046/2012 and the Medium-term Fiscal Strategy Framework 2013–2016' (Gov Gazette No A′ 222/12.11.2012).
13 Contiades (2013) 1.
14 Contiades and Fotiadou (2012) 661.

15 CoS Plen 668/2012 [35]; Plen 1283/2012 [31]; Plen 2288/2015 [7].

16 See *Koufaki and ADEDY v Greece* App. no 57665/12 and 57657/12 (ECHR 7 May 2013) [46]: 'The Court considers that the extent of the reduction in the first applicant's salary was not such as to place her at risk of having insufficient means to live on and thus to constitute a breach of Article 1 of Protocol No. 1'.

17 'Respect and protection of the value of the human being constitute the primary obligations of the State'.

18 Giannakopoulos (2015) 427.

19 See for instance Judgment of the First Senate of 09 February 2010–1 BvL 1/09, 1 BvL 3/09, 1 BvL 4/09 [135], [157] and [166]. Through this judgment, it is apparent that the subsistence minimum is upgraded to the material conditions indispensable not only for a person's physical existence, but also for 'a minimum of participation in social, cultural and political life'. [Contiades and Fotiadou (2012) 681].

20 CoS Plen 2288/2015 [7].

21 CoS Plen 1906/2014 [22].

22 Art. 5 para. 5: 'All persons have the right to the protection of their health and of their genetic identity. Matters relating to the protection of every person against biomedical interventions shall be specified by law'.

23 Art. 21 para. 3: 'The State shall care for the health of citizens and shall adopt special measures for the protection of youth, old age, disability and for the relief of the needy'.

24 CoS Plen 1906/2014 [22].

25 See landmark case Plen 1934/1998 (the concession to a private company of the management of parking meters in the municipality of Athens and the subsequent power to impose fines violates the principles of popular sovereignty and separation of powers).

26 See judgments CoS 866/2002 (privatisation of the Organisation of Public Material Management); 1511/2002 (privatisation of the Organisation of Central Markets and Fisheries); 2165/2002 (privatisation of the Organisation for School Buildings).

27 CoS Plen 2192/2014 [11] and [12].

28 Mouzouraki (2015) 276–77.

29 Art. 45: 'The President of the Republic is the commander in chief of the Nation's Armed Forces, the command of which shall be exercised by the Government, as specified by law. The President shall also confer ranks on those serving therein, as specified by law.'

Art. 23 para. 2: 'Strike constitutes a right to be exercised by lawfully established trade unions in order to protect and promote the financial and the general labour interests of working people. Strikes of any nature whatsoever are prohibited in the case of judicial functionaries and those serving in the security corps.'

Art. 29 para. 3: 'Manifestations of any nature whatsoever in favour of or against a political party by magistrates and by those serving in the armed forces and the security corps, are absolutely prohibited. In the exercise of their duties, manifestations of any nature whatsoever in favour of or against a political party by public servants, employees of local government agencies, of other public law legal persons or of public enterprises or of enterprises of local government agencies or of enterprises whose management is directly or indirectly appointed by the State, by administrative act or by virtue of its capacity as shareholder, are absolutely prohibited'.

30 'Restrictions of any kind which, according to the Constitution, may be imposed upon these rights, should be provided either directly by the Constitution or by statute, should a reservation exist in the latter's favour, and should respect the principle of proportionality'.

31 'Greek citizens contribute without distinction to public charges in proportion to their means'.

32 'The State has the right to claim of all citizens to fulfil the duty of social and national solidarity'.

33 CoS Plen 460/2013 [6].

34 Koutsoukos (2011) 78.
35 With the exception of the dissenting opinion by Councillor M. Pikramenos (see [6]).
36 Contiades and Fotiadou (2015) 16.
37 CoS 693/2011 (ruling in favour of the constitutionality of an extraordinary income tax for the rich).
38 CoS 1620/2011 (ruling in favour of the constitutionality of the privileged interest rate paid by the State – see below note 48). – Mathioudakis (2011) 480.
39 Lazaratos (2013) 686.
40 Giannakopoulos (2012) 101.
41 CoS 1620/2011 [8].
42 Lazaratos (2013) 686.
43 Mathioudakis (2011) 485.
44 Lazaratos (2013) 686.
45 Giannakopoulos (2012) 102.
46 Giannakopoulos (2015) 436–37.
47 See especially CoS Plen 1116–1117/2014 (constitutionality of the haircut imposed on state bonds held by private investors – the so called PSI).
48 In its judgments 1620/2011(constitutionality of the privileged interest rate paid by the State), and Plen 2115/2014 (constitutionality of the privileged interest rate paid by public bodies), which were followed later by judgment 25/2012 of the SSC, the CoS overruled a recent precedent (judgment Plen 1663/2009) based on ECtHR judgments *Meidanis v Greece* App. no. 33977/06 (ECHR 22 August 2008) and *Zouboulidis v Greece* App. no. 36963/6 (ECHR 25 June 2009). Concretely, the CoS upheld, for public interest reasons, a law that established a preferential treatment of the State and other public bodies concerning the interest rate owed to private individuals for overdue debts.
49 Contiades and Fotiadou (2015) 15.
50 See Art. 22 para. 1 of law 4274/2014, adding a para. 3b to Art. 50 of the Presidential Decree 18/1989 fixing the CoS statute.
51 CoS Plen 4741/2014 [26].
52 CoS Plen 2288/2015 [25].
53 Mouzouraki (2015) 294.
54 See judgments CoS Plen 668/2012 [33] and [36]; Plen 1285/2012 [11]; Plen 2307/2014 [23]; 3410/2014 [7]; 3177/2014 [10].
55 CoS Plen 2288/2015 [7].
56 Rizos (2015) 290.
57 Rizos (2015) 292–93.
58 Contiades and Fotiadou (2012) 674.
59 Furthermore, it has been noted that the CoS has not applied this doctrine consistently, since salary cuts imposed to employees of the Ministry of Finance and of the Legal Service of the State were not equally invalidated, although the functions exercised by them undoubtedly belong to the core of the State [Mouzouraki (2015) 278–79, citing judgment Plen 3177/2014].
60 Karavokyris (2015) 176.
61 Recent judgments of the CoS Plen 2287–2290/2015 seem to have been inspired – although no explicit mention is made – by judgments no. 187/2013 (declaring the reduction of vacation allowances due to public servants and pensioners unconstitutional) and no. 413/2014 (declaring pay cuts in the public sector, as well as cuts to pensions and welfare benefits, unconstitutional) of the Constitutional Court of Portugal.
62 'Under extraordinary circumstances of an urgent and unforeseeable need, the President of the Republic may, upon the proposal of the Cabinet, issue acts of legislative content. Such acts shall be submitted to Parliament for ratification, as specified in the provisions of article 72 paragraph 1, within forty days of their issuance or within forty days from

the convocation of a parliamentary session. Should such acts not be submitted to Parliament within the above time-limits or if they should not be ratified by Parliament within three months of their submission, they will henceforth cease to be in force'.

63 Contiades and Fotiadou (2015) 14.
64 Contiades and Fotiadou (2015) 18.
65 Karavokyris (2014) 152.
66 See for instance *Home Building and Loan Association v Blaisdell*, 290 U.S. 398 (1934) (upholding Minnesota's mortgage moratorium because of the emergency conditions created by the Great Depression); West Coast Hotel Co. v Parrish, 300 U.S. 379 (1937) [upholding minimum wage legislation enacted by the State of Washington and overturning *Adkins v Children's Hospital*, 261 US 525 (1923) because of 'the economic conditions which have supervened'].
67 CoS Plen 668/2012 [35].
68 CoS Plen 2288/2015 [7].
69 CoS Plen 1116–1117/2014 [24].
70 CoS Plen 2307/2014 [23] (ruling that the Common Ministerial Decision 6/2012 reforming the existing labour and collective bargaining regulation is, but for a minor issue, constitutional).
71 Pikrammenos (2012) 99–100.
72 Karavokyris (2014) 200–01.
73 [7].
74 Vlahopoulos (2014) 107.
75 Giannakopoulos (2012) 109.
76 In this precise case, Art. 78 para. 2 which states: 'A tax or any other financial charge may not be imposed by a retroactive statute effective prior to the fiscal year preceding the imposition of the tax'.
77 Contiades and Fotiadou (2015) 4.
78 Lazaratos (2013) 687.
79 See for instance law 3900/2010 (Gov Gazette No A′ 213/17.12.2010) providing for a system of 'pivotal trial' allowing lower administrative courts to refer a case to the CoS when a matter of general interest arises.
80 For instance, the CoS has repeatedly refrained from addressing a prejudicial question to the CJEU regarding the compatibility of austerity measures with European Union law.
81 Lazaratos (2013) 688.
82 See for instance judgment 25/2012 of the Special Supreme Court (ruling that the privileged interest rate of 6 per cent for the State is constitutional). In [10], the Court stated, interestingly enough: 'Because establishing and keeping in force for so long (namely since 1877) a provision, according to which the interest rate for overdue debts paid by the State is smaller than that which private individuals have to pay, is justified by the fact that, as a consequence of those [reasons] mentioned in the above paragraph, during all this time the Greek state has undergone subsequent serious financial crises, which have lasted for long periods of time and whose effects extend in periods during which the economic situation is improved and circumstances are ripe for the country's economy to grow'.
83 Lazaratos (2013) 688.
84 Lazaratos (2013) 691.
85 Giannakopoulos (2015) 439.
86 Contiades and Fotiadou qualify this attitude as constitutional inertia claiming that 'the original reactions of Greece and Portugal towards the crisis were submissive' [Contiades and Fotiadou (2015) 12].
87 CoS Plen 1972/2012 (declaring that the interruption of the power supply for not paying a special property tax incorporated in the electricity bill constitutes a constitutionally impermissible interference in the contractual relationship between the consumer and the electricity supplier); Plen 3354/2013 (declaring unconstitutional the

measure of pre-retirement suspension regime); Plen 1906/2014 (declaring unconstitutional the transfer from the State to the Hellenic Republic Asset Development Fund of shares corresponding to 34,033% of the share capital of Athens Water Supply and Sewerage Company); Plen 2307/2014 (declaring that the provisions of Art. 3 paras. 1, 2 and 4 of the Ministerial Council Act 6/2012 abolishing the right to unilaterally resort to arbitration in case of a standoff between the two sides during the process of collective bargaining are contrary to Art. 22 para. 2 of the Constitution). [See Statement of the Greek National Commission for Human Rights (GNCHR) on the impact of the continuing austerity measures on human rights (15.7.2015), Annex II, available at: http://www.nchr.gr/.]

88 Contiades and Fotiadou (2012) 683.

89 Mouzouraki (2015) 275, citing judgments CoS 1620/2011, Plen 668/2012, Plen 1116–1117/2014 and Plen 2307/2014.

90 CoS Plen 668/2012.

91 CoS Plen 2192/2014.

92 CoS Plen 4741/2014.

93 Mouzouraki (2015) 283.

94 Contiades and Fotiadou describe this as a passage from submission to adjustment, through which the original puzzlement and acceptance of the measures, hinting a reluctance to interfere with mega-politics, were soon followed by realism and a 'business as usual' attitude towards adjudication, signalling a recovery phase for fundamental rights which does not however completely ignores the still existing financial emergency [Contiades and Fotiadou (2015) 17–19].

95 Rizos (2015) 293; Giannakopoulos (2015) 421.

96 Plen 2287–2290/2015 [24].

97 See note 96 above.

Bibliography

Contiades, Xenophon, 'Introduction: The Global Financial Crisis and the Constitution', in Xenophon Contiades (ed.), *Constitutions in the Global Financial Crisis. A Comparative Analysis* (Ashgate 2013).

Contiades, Xenophon and Fotiadou, Alkmene, 'On Resilience of Constitutions. What Makes Constitutions Resistant to External Shocks?' (2015). 9 *ICL Journal* 3–26.

Contiades, Xenophon and Fotiadou, Alkmene, 'Social Rights in the Age of Proportionality: Global Economic Crisis and Constitutional Litigation' (2012). 10 *ICON* 660–686.

Drosos, Georgios, *Δοκίμιο ελληνικής συνταγματικής θεωρίας* [*Essay on Greek Constitutional History*] (N. Sakkoulas 1996).

Giannakopoulos, Constantinos, 'Το ελληνικό Σύνταγμα και η επιφύλαξη του εφικτού της προστασίας των κοινωνικών δικαιωμάτων: "να είστε ρεαλιστές, να ζητάτε το αδύνατο"' ['The Hellenic Constitution and the Reserve of Possible Regarding the Protection of Social Rights: "Be Realist, Ask for the Impossible"'] (2015). 4 *Journal of Administrative Law* 417–442.

Giannakopoulos, Constantinos, 'Το δημόσιο συμφέρον υπό το πρίσμα της οικονομικής κρίσης. Σκέψεις με αφορμή τις αποφάσεις ΣτΕ Β΄ *693/2011*, ΣτΕ ΣΤ΄ 1620/2011 και ΣτΕ Α΄ 2094/2011' ['Public Interest in Light of the Economic Crisis: Thoughts on Judgments 693/2011 (2nd chamber), 1620/2011 (6th chamber) and 2094/2011 (1st chamber) of the Council of State'] (2012). 1 *Journal of Administrative Law* 100–112.

Karavokyris, Georgios, 'Τα συνταγματικά όρια στις ιδιωτικοποιήσεις των δημοσίων επιχειρήσεων κοινής ωφέλειας. Σχόλιο στην απόφαση ΣτΕ 1906/2014 (Ολομ.)' ['The Constitutional Limits of Privatizations of Public Utility Companies: Commentary on

Judgment 1906/2014 of the Council of State (Plen.)'] (2015). 63 *Hellenic Review of Human Rights* 161–176.

Karavokyris, Georgios, *Το Σύνταγμα και η κρίση: Από το δίκαιο της ανάγκης στην αναγκαιότητα του δικαίου* [*The Constitution and the Crisis: From Emergency Law to the Necessity of Law*] (Kritiki 2014).

Koutsoukos, Ioannis, 'Η ιθαγένεια, το Έθνος και το κράτος δικαίου' ['Nationality, the Nation and the Rule of Law'] (2011). 1 *Journal of Administrative Law* 77–84.

Lazaratos, Panos, 'Δημοσιονομικό συμφέρον και δίκαιο της ανάγκης' ['Budgetary Interest and Emergency Law'] (2013). 8/9 *Theory and Practice of Administrative Law* 686–692.

Manitakis, Antonios, 'Fondement et légalité du contrôle juridictionnel des lois en Grèce' (1988). 40 *RIDC* 39–55.

Mathioudakis, Iakovos, 'Μετασχηματισμοί του ταμειακού συμφέροντος του Δημοσίου σε περίοδο έντονης οικονομικής κρίσης. Με αφορμή τις πρόσφατες αποφάσεις 693/2011 (κατά μειοψ.) και 1620/2011 (κατά πλειοψ.) του ΣΤ΄ Τμ. του ΣτΕ' ['Transformations of the Treasury Interest of the State in a Period of Intense Economic Crisis: Thoughts on Recent Judgments 693/2011 (diss. opinion) and 1620/2011 (opinion of the Court) of the 6th Chamber of the Council of State'] (2011). 4 *Journal of Administrative Law* 478–488.

Mouzouraki, Paraskevi, 'Τα ειδικά μισθολόγια στο Συμβούλιο της Επικρατείας: μία νέα φάση ή – περισσότερες από μία – αντιφάσεις στη σχετική με την οικονομική κρίση νομολογία του Ανώτατου Διοικητικού Δικαστηρίου; Σκέψεις με αφορμή τις αποφάσεις (Ολ.) 2192/2014 και 4741/2014' ['Special Salaries before the Council of State: A New Phase or – more than one – Contradictions of the Case Law of the Supreme Administrative Court Related to the Economic Crisis? Thoughts on Judgments (Plen.) 2192/2014 and 4741/2014'] (2015). 3 *Journal of Administrative Law* 275–294.

Pikrammenos, Panagiotis, 'Δημόσιο δίκαιο σε έκτακτες συνθήκες από την οπτική της ακυρωτικής διοικητικής διαδικασίας' ['Public Law in Extraordinary Circumstances Within the Context of the Action for Annulment Process'] (2012). 2 *Theory and Practice of Administrative Law* 97–100.

Rizos, Sotirios, 'Το Συμβούλιο της Επικρατείας μεταξύ του συνταγματικού προτύπου του Κοινωνικού Κράτους και της πολιτικής ενστάσεως "Ουκ αν λάβοις παρά του μη έχοντος"' ['The Council of State between the Constitutional Model of Welfare State and the Political Objection "You Cannot Take From the One That Does Not Have"'] (2015). 4 *Theory and Practice of Administrative Law* 289–293.

Vlahopoulos, Spyridon, *Η δυναμική ερμηνεία του Συντάγματος. Η προσαρμογή του συνταγματικού κειμένου στις μεταβαλλόμενες συνθήκες* [*The Dynamic Interpretation of the Constitution: The Adaptation of the Constitutional Text to Changing Circumstances*] (Evrasia 2014).

7 Judicial deference or political loyalty? The Hungarian Constitutional Court's role in tackling crisis situations

Zoltán Szente and Fruzsina Gárdos-Orosz

Introduction

Our basic presumption for this research is that some events and developments of recent years, such as the world financial crisis, terrorism or mass migration, may have affected the national legal systems in Europe, including the constitutional jurisprudence of the various countries. In the case of Hungary, we can say that both assumptions have been realised; that is, some general European tendencies have had deep impacts on Hungary's legal system and the constitutional practice of its Constitutional Court has also changed significantly. Hence, this country seems ideal to be studied for our purposes. The question is whether these challenges really have triggered the most important changes of constitutional jurisprudence, and what have been the internal dynamics of the very recent developments in the interpretive practice of the Hungarian Constitutional Court.

1. The system of constitutional adjudication in Hungary

The institution of the constitutional court does not have a long tradition in Hungary. In fact, a centralised Constitutional Court was one of the new institutions established during the country's transition to democracy, when it was founded by the constitutional amendment in 1989. The Court more or less was founded on the pattern of the German *Bundesverfassungsgericht*,[1] establishing a 'European' or 'Kelsenian' model of constitutional review. In the period of the 'system change', when the Communist rule came to end in Hungary, and the country became a Western-like constitutional democracy through peaceful political negotiations between the representatives of the old political leadership and the new opposition movements, the distrust between the negotiating parties led to the establishment of an independent Constitutional Court with wide-ranging responsibilities.

The Court was provided with an exclusionary power to examine the constitutionality of legal acts through abstract judicial review. Because everybody could submit any statutory act to the court for review (*actio popularis*), virtually, sooner or later, all important laws landed before the body. In certain areas, *ex ante* examination of the constitutionality of legal acts (e.g. international treaties or parliamentary standing orders) fell also within the competence of the Court, which was also empowered to investigate conflicts between international treaties and the national law. The Court decided on individual constitutional complaints too, but in fact it was more an indirect judicial review of the statutes on which the individual judicial decisions were based. Another responsibility was (and is also today) to decide on the conflicts of competence between state organs. The function by which the Court could interpret the provisions of the Constitution without any individual legal dispute granted the Constitutional Court a primary political role because, in this respect, the Court appeared to be the final arbiter of discussions that usually have direct political implications.

The Court was established as a quasi-judicial organ; though it bore some characteristics of judicial tribunals (such as the structural independence or the irremovable status of the judges), other classical judicial principles and guarantees were missing in its procedure (there is no adversarial procedure, for example).[2] The body consisted of 11 members, who were elected by a two-thirds majority of MPs for nine years, and could be re-elected once. The original objective of the condition of qualified majority was to enforce a consensus between the government and the opposition parties of the day, thus eliminating in this way the partisan membership within the Court. This expectation, however, was only moderately realised; although the majority requirement was coupled with strict incompatibility rules, the objective of which was to keep party politics separate from the Court, the way its members were selected (i.e. parliamentary nomination and election) brought the body close to the party politics.

From 1990 onwards, the Constitutional Court established a rich and extensive jurisprudence; virtually, it has dealt with almost all classical issues as is usual in those Western countries that have much longer constitutional traditions. Undoubtedly, the Court reached a pre-eminent position in the Hungarian constitutional system, and it had great success in elaborating and standardising the living constitutional law. It is a commonly shared view among scholars that the Court, in the first nine years of its operation (the period is generally called Sólyom Court after its first president) followed a strongly 'activist' practice[3] relating both to its jurisdiction and to interpretive practice.[4] This activism based on a dispute resolution approach of constitutional review required the Court to decide all constitutional controversies that were submitted to it, rather than to escape from the responsibility of the ultimate decision. Accordingly, the Court not only decided on the most essential constitutional controversies, but, because every attempt to make a new Constitution between 1990 and 2011 proved to be unsuccessful, in a sense the Court undertook a quasi-constitution-making role. Although the body was frequently criticised for its jurisdictional and interpretive activism, this approach seemed to be widely accepted, partly due to the antagonistic relations between the rightist and leftist parties, which excluded any consensus on constitutional issues.

In the general elections of 2010 the former rightist opposition party, the Fidesz, and its satellite Christian Democratic Party won a landslide victory, and owing to the disproportionate election system, the new government acquired a two-thirds majority. In the spring of 2011, the Parliament, in the absence of the two democratic opposition parties (which, protesting against the 'destruction of the rule of law', boycotted the whole constitution-making process), approved a new Fundamental Law of Hungary.

The new Constitution, effective from 1 January 2012, has introduced some explicit principles and methods of constitutional interpretation. The original standards of constitutional review were established by the Constitutional Court in the 1990s. The most important interpretive tool was the so-called 'necessity-proportionality test', by which the Court constantly reviewed the constitutionality of rights-limitations based more or less on the pattern of the jurisdiction of the German *Bundesverfassungsgericht*. This manner was codified by the Fundamental Law in Art. 1.[5] Another major general rule on constitutional interpretation can be found in Art. R para (3) of the Fundamental Law: '[t]he provisions of the Fundamental Law shall be interpreted in accordance with their purposes, with the Avowal of National Faith contained therein, and with the achievements of our historical constitution'. The new Constitution set up further rules of interpretation, partly related to economic considerations.[6]

The Fundamental Law significantly modified the competencies of the Constitutional Court. Thus, the *actio popularis* procedure was abolished, even though it had been the most effective tool to launch a judicial review procedure in constitutionally controversial cases for a long time. Instead, since 2013 only the Government, one-fourth of the members of Parliament, the President of the Curia (the supreme court), the Prosecutor General and the Commissioner for Fundamental Rights have had the right to initiate the *ex post facto* abstract review of legislative acts. In addition, the Court was deprived of its power to review and annul budgetary laws and acts on taxes, duties, pensions, customs or any kind of financial contributions to the state, unless they violated the right to life and human dignity; the right to the protection of personal data; freedom of thought, conscience and religion; and the rights related to Hungarian citizenship. In theory, this limitation has been only provisional, as it would cease when the level of state debt goes below 50 per cent of the GDP. In reality, since then the Constitutional Court has not reviewed the public finance laws. Nevertheless, the Constitutional Court has been compensated to a degree for the loss of its fundamental power; the new constitution, on the German pattern, introduced the politically neutral institution of individual constitutional complaint. While the abstract constitutional review of legal acts has reduced since 2012 and has been a more or less irrelevant competence with regard to its measure, the individual constitutional complaint procedure has become the most viable opportunity for constitutional adjudication. However, the overall assessment of the case load shows that the control function over normative, mostly legislative acts has decreased significantly.[7]

The composition of the Constitutional Court was completely changed as well. Just a few months after its formation in 2010, the new coalition government using its two-thirds majority transformed the process of nominating the judges of the Constitutional Court. Since then, the membership of the parliamentary committee responsible for the nomination has no longer been based on parity, but has instead reflected the party-strength in the Parliament. Besides that, Art. 24 of the Fundamental Law introduced a new design with 15 judges instead of the former 11. The new constitution also empowered Parliament to elect the head of the Court (before that, he or she was elected by the justices themselves).

2. The changing role and jurisprudence of the Constitutional Court in the era of the 'unorthodox economic policy' of Government

2.1 Changing constitutional landscape of national economy and public finance

As it has already been said, Hungary has been deeply affected by some of the challenges about which we talked in the Introduction. First, Hungary is a small, open economic system, highly dependent on the trends of the world economy. The country has been a Member State of the European Union since 2004 where it belongs to the economic periphery with its GDP amounting to about 65 per cent of the average gross national product of the EU countries. Although its rate of economic growth was above the EU average between 1997 and 2006, the results of the economic catching up policy have never been clear as the country has had financial accounting problems since her accession. Before the world economic crisis, since 2004, the European Commission proceeded with an excessive deficit procedure against Hungary because of its longstanding unbalanced budget. The crisis brought about serious economic depression almost immediately after its outbreak in the autumn of 2008, and increased sharply the financial risks of the country. The economic performance turned into a recession, as the loss of GDP was almost 7 per cent in 2009.

As a response to the rising financial risks, the Orbán Government after 2010 discontinued the policy lines of the former government, and started a so-called 'unorthodox' economic policy instead of the traditional and well-admitted instruments of economic recovery.[8] This means the application of unexpected and unusual policy measures such as extending the economic role of the state and limiting market competition; centralising state economic resources; keeping 'strategic enterprises' in Government hands and widening the range of the exclusive economic activity of state (e.g. establishing new monopolies); restructuring the ownership relations in a number of areas of the market economy (enhancing the influence of the 'national owners'); pursuing a protectionist economic policy (e.g. preferring Hungarian companies in public procurements); imposing sectoral special taxes (in banking, telecommunication, energy and retail sectors); rearranging foreign trade relations ('opening to the East'); or launching intensive public work projects (pursuing full employment).

Many pieces of this policy have had constitutional implications. Thus, the constitutional landscape of the economy was changed by the Fundamental Law of 2011. Most importantly, the change of jurisprudence was encouraged by the principles of constitutional interpretation laid down by the Fundamental Law requiring the Constitutional Court to respect extra-legal interests and objectives. Hence, the new Constitution not only prescribes that the constitutional provisions must be interpreted 'in accordance with their purposes', the preamble and the 'achievements' of the historical constitution,[9] but also requires – among others – the Constitutional Court to respect the principles of the 'balanced, transparent and sustainable budget management' in the course of performing its tasks.[10]

The new constitution has also clarified the constitutional nature of the social and economic rights as state aims, instead of recognising them as basic rights. Although this might seem to be a decrease of protection, it brings the regulation closer to practice; the old constitution, for example, declared simply the right to work (as a remnant of its original text, dated in 1949), without any enforceable right. The Fundamental Law emphasises the importance of national assets and the empowerment of the legislature to determine the range of exclusive economic activities of the state. It refers also to the principles of social responsibility of the property right and the right to enterprise.

Moreover, as already mentioned, by restricting the review power of the Constitutional Court, the new basic law has pulled the public finance legislation out of constitutional control. Since then, there have not been any constitutional hurdles to the Government's economic, finance and tax policy. Another meaningful innovation was to create and place debt-brake rules in the Constitution. These provisions have restricted the budgetary power of Parliament, which may not adopt such a state budget 'as a result of which state debt would exceed half of the Gross Domestic Product', and, as long as the national debt exceeds half of the GDP, Parliament may only adopt a central budget that provides the reduction of the state debt.[11]

2.2 Changing constitutional jurisprudence in economic and financial matters

Despite (or precisely because of) the meaningful limitation of the Constitutional Court's review power in economic and financial issues, the jurisprudence of the Court has significantly changed in the past few years. However, at the very beginning after the general election of 2010, when the old judges were still in majority within the Court, the body tried to continue its earlier case-law. When the Orbán Government came to power in 2010, one of its first measures was to get a new legislation through the Parliament that imposed retroactively a 98 per cent tax on the so-called extreme severance payments paid in the public sector from the beginning of that year. The major argument was that these payments, even if they had been lawfully paid, had violated the 'good morals' (*contra bonos mores*) and therefore must be withdrawn. Because the retroactive taxation was expected to be found unconstitutional as it violates the principle of the rule of law,[12] the Government majority modified the old Constitution (of 1949/1989) allowing *ex post facto* tax-imposing legislation in the case of incomes acquired against good morals.[13] The Constitutional Court found that while the modified constitution allowed the retroactive tax-imposing legislation, the new law incorrectly defined severance payment as being against good morals, once it had been paid according to law.[14] As an immediate reaction to this ruling, the Government majority curtailed the review power of the Court in a way discussed above and adopted a modified version of the law on the 98 per cent tax on severance payments. This law was also sent to the Constitutional Court, and the Court, within its recently restricted jurisdiction, and under the political pressure upon it, found a compromise; while it declared unconstitutional that the law sanctioned the severance payment paid since 2005, it upheld retroactive taxation if it extended only to the beginning of the current tax year.[15,16]

One of the most important changes in constitutional jurisprudence was the reduction of the level of the protection of property rights. In 2012, for example, the Government decided to acquire a private savings bank that had a nationwide network of affiliations and had many small shareholders. For this purpose, it first obtained a share in this bank. However, when the other shareholders refused to allow the Government to gain full control over the bank, the Government majority passed a special legislation that effectively handed control of this bank to the national government. This law changed the ownership ratios and limited shareholders' rights (e.g. certain measures, such as issuing of bonds, reduction or increase of its capital are subject to the previous approval of the Savings Bank). The Hungarian Post was entitled to subscribe for the common shares at par value, which is considerably less than the reasonable value based on the Savings Bank's equity situation, and which made it impossible for the previous shareholders to pass resolutions. The constitutional complaints submitted by many shareholders were denied by the Constitutional Court.[17] The Court argued that the contested measures had been taken for the benefit of the earlier owners, as they strengthened the market position of the network of savings banks. Compared with the standards of protection of property rights developed in the 1990s, this was a serious change in jurisprudence. The property rights of the shareholders of the Savings Bank were taken away, which led to the quasi-nationalisation of the Savings Bank. Act CXXXV (135) 2013 on the integration of savings cooperatives created an integration which took away the legal, financial and operational independence of its members. The Hungarian Development Bank, with a call option to the shares of the Savings Bank, was put in an extremely strong position, by which it could pass whatever resolution it wished, thus giving the State a strong controlling position.

The economic crisis of 2008 and especially the rapid exchange rate depreciation of the Hungarian forint resulted in a significantly worsened situation of debtors.[18] Legislative acts aiming to help the situation and related judicial decisions were reviewed by the Constitutional Court continuously. Novel constitutional ideas, unconventional constitutional measures and new doctrinal solutions were born in foreign currency loan-related decisions. In its decision 34/2014. (XI. 14.) the Constitutional Court examined the constitutionality of the legislative act regulating basically two questions: namely, the nullity of exchange rate margins in foreign currency loan contracts and the presumed unfairness of provisions enabling banks to unilateral amendment of interests, fees and costs in foreign-currency consumer loan contracts.[19] According to the Constitutional Court the rules did not attain the level of unconstitutionality either in the details or as a whole. The Court acknowledged that the Act did have a restrictive effect on the fundamental rights in question such as on the freedom to contract, the right to property, the right to fair trial and, furthermore, the Act might raise concerns with regard to its *ex tunc*, retroactive effect, which is against the rule of law, but the Act was not considered unconstitutional as the legislative solution was proportionate with the aim to protect the citizens in desperate financial situations. Giving priority to substantive justice before procedural justice is a new phenomenon in the Hungarian constitutional jurisprudence. The Court in this case argued with the responsibility of the state to provide help for people in desperate situations, and the legitimate aim to help people and do justice for them overruled former principles developed by the Constitutional Court related to the constitutional relevance of procedural fairness, legal stability, predictability and the ban on retroactive legislation (rule of law). This is why it could happen that although the Constitutional Court acknowledged many arguments that have been raised, it still rejected the claims. The Court noted that although this time it accepts the constitutionality of these problematic provisions, the legislative power should use these kinds of instruments in extraordinary cases and only in a narrow sense.[20] In the case of the review of the very same 2014 legislation, the second instance judges who dealt with these cases also turned to the Constitutional Court in judicial referrals, claiming that the law is unconstitutional due to breach of the principle of separation of powers, right to fair trial, rule of law and the legal certainty. In decision 2/2015. (II. 2.)[21] the Constitutional Court rejected all judicial referrals in this round as well. The Constitutional Court emphasised that the reasons explained in the earlier decision justify the restrictions referred to by the judges; therefore, on the basis of proportionality, these rules as well were found to be constitutional.

Yet, the protection of private persons, and the *ex post* risk sharing proved to trump these values. The changing approach of the Court is well characterised by another decision in which it declared that

> in the emergency situation of public finance deepened by the economic situation as well as the financial and economic crisis, it was inevitable to set as a long-term governmental goal, the reduction of public debt. A number of fair and legitimate demands and efforts had to be subject to this goal.[22]

Later, the Constitutional Court concluded a great number of decisions based on the same foreign currency loan crisis legislation. These judicial decisions applied this law. All claims were rejected,[23] although the Court itself acknowledged that the extraordinary emergency solutions were problematic from the rule of law point of view. The legislation imposed unreasonable burden on financial institutions with retroactive effect and furthermore did not allow for a fair trial.[24] Without going into the very rich details of the assessment of the case[25] we must summarise that before 2008, it was unimaginable that such an interpretation would be accepted by the majority of the Constitutional Court with regard to the classic rule of law values. Although it is not unprecedented that the Constitutional Court refers to unfavourable changes of the economic situation in its argumentation, this was very rare in the case-law of the Constitutional Court. Reference to the emergency crises was also very different from the one in decision 34/2014 (IX. 14.) or 2/2015 (II. 2.).

At the very beginning of the 1990s, in its decision no. 26/1992. (IV. 30.) the Constitutional Court stated that

> [a]s a special, one-time circumstance of the change of the regime, in this social phenomenon, the trade union assets accumulated were put in a 'crisis situation' due to cessations and transformations without being settled legally. In this crisis situation the legislator shall secure the protection, the use, the usability and availability of trade union assets guaranteeing the constitutional freedom of the interest group until the terms of financial situation are not settled. The constitutionality of exceptional and one-off interventions is linked to the utmost importance of trade unions and the accomplished transition of trade unions. This, however, does not mean that the transition of other social organisations and settling the financial situation shall be conducted by subsequent legislation.

To contrast with this decision, in the Constitutional Court decision 23/2013. (IX. 25.) the Court declared that the abolishment of the possibility of the early retirement for certain state employees, such as for the policemen or for the members of the army,[26] is constitutional although the change was introduced with retroactive effect. The decision pointed out, that

> in the emergency situation of public finance deepened by the economic situation as well as the financial and economic crisis, it was inevitable to set as a long-term governmental goal, the reduction of public debt. A number of fair and legitimate demands and efforts had to be subject to this goal.[27]

This statement seems to be quite general and means that at any time when special and hard circumstances occur, it is legitimate to deviate from the original rules.

We argue, however, that according to the former jurisprudence of the Court, in case the state of emergency with its special rules has not been declared by the constitutionally dedicated bodies, no specific standards can be applied. The rule of law cannot be protected against the rule of law according to the famous wording of the Court.[28] Although there are very few decisions when the Constitutional Court had altered from regular standards in its former jurisprudence as well, the alterations were indicated as unique ones. What we find, however, in the new financial crisis related jurisprudence, is that special solutions become ordinary rules, because the Constitutional Court claims that whenever these difficulties or challenges occur (which is quite regular in the twenty-first century even if there is a normally operating state), the Constitutional Court can justify the alteration from settled constitutional standards. Although the constitutional framework is partly invented for the sake of providing stability for law and jurisprudence, according to the recent financial crisis related case-law, there is diminished rule of law protection when the state is in trouble.

In another decision, the Constitutional Court upheld the extremely controversial law[29] that had completely restructured the tobacco retail trade market, withdrawing the state concessions from previous tobacconists, and redistributing the government approvals through a highly debated application system. The Court argued that the earlier licences had not established a vested right for the tobacco sellers to continue their activity without limitation. Furthermore, it spectacularly turned away from its earlier practice when it declared that the tobacco seller's licence does not fall within the scope of the property rights. Since the early 1990s, the permanent practice of the Constitutional Court was to extend the protection of property rights to private financial savings, concessions, licenses and similar rights (representing pecuniary interests) on the basis that these rights have the same function as the property (i.e. 'the provision of the material basis of personal autonomy').[30] Notably, in contrast with this decision, the European Court of Human Rights held that the withdrawal of the prior licences by law without compensation was such a breach of property rights that was a violation of Art. 1 of the Protocol No. 1 of the European Convention of Human Rights.[31]

Nonetheless, it must be taken into consideration that because of the reduction of review powers of the Constitutional Court, the most important public finance cases have not been brought before the Court, or if there was a proper petition, referring to this limitation, the body did not undertake to decide the case. Probably, the activist Court of the early 1990s, on the basis of its rich jurisprudence on the right to human dignity, would dare to adjudicate such cases, especially when such important constitutional issues were at stake, for example, the constitutionality of the extraordinary sectoral taxes, the nationalisation of private pension savings without compensation, or withdrawal of vested rights.

3. Migration

Hungary was deeply affected by the migration influx to Europe in 2015. In that year, more than 400,000 migrants arrived in the country,[32] and most of them moved on to Austria and Germany. The country was not able to provide effective border guards to register all migrants and to control their movement. Under such circumstances, the Hungarian Government took a harsh anti-immigration stance from the very beginning of the migrant crisis, and heavily criticised the EU institutions for the way in which they managed the European migration crisis. It initiated a national referendum against the controversial quota system proposed by the EU for the resettlement of migrants among the Member States.[33] According to this plan, the member countries should share the burden of the migrant crisis relocating the asylum seekers from the front-line states (Greece and Italy) among all Member States. Under this plan, Hungary should admit 1,294 people from the total of 160,000. The government refused to accept any refugees under this programme, and filed a case at the European Court of Justice arguing that the EU institutions did not have the power to compel the Member States to allow migrants to settle therein. In addition, at the end of 2015, the Hungarian Government decided to build a border barrier (fence) on its border with Serbia and Croatia in order to prevent immigrants from entering the country illegally.

The Constitutional Court was involved in the fight against 'illegal migration'. First, it refused the petitions asking the Court to invalidate the resolution of Parliament to call the so-called 'quota-referendum'.[34] This popular vote was initiated by the Government in 2016 with the apparent purpose to refuse the refugee relocation policy of the European Union. Although the referendum was obviously unconstitutional for several reasons,[35] the Court interpreted its own scope of authority in a narrow way, arguing that it has the competence to examine only the procedural fairness of the relevant parliamentary resolution.[36] Albeit the law on the Constitutional Court really restricts the scope of constitutional review in such cases, it is to be noted that the jurisprudence of the Court in the 1990s and – occasionally also in the 2000s – was frequently characterised as 'activist' relating to its jurisdiction[37] and self-identity. Also for procedural reasons, without any substantive examination, the Court rejected the constitutional complaints challenging the supreme court's (*Kúria*) decision having approved the question of the referendum as legal.[38] According to the Court, the petitioners had no standing positions as they had not been addressed personally by this judicial decision.

Another decision of the Court was more important, because in this case its competence was not restricted at all. In December 2015 the Commissioner for Fundamental Rights submitted a petition to the Court requesting an abstract constitutional interpretation of two provisions of the Fundamental Law. One provision prohibits the 'collective expulsion' from the territory of Hungary of any Hungarian or foreign citizens. In this regard, the petition put the question whether this prohibition is valid also if another state expels people collectively. Apparently, the background consideration of this question was to encourage the Constitutional Court to declare that relocating 1,294 refugees to Hungary under the auspices of the EU relocation programme is unconstitutional according to Hungarian Fundamental Law (and as such, Hungary can not be obliged to accept and accommodate them). The petitioner explicitly argued that the transfer of these people to Hungary in a procedure 'implemented without the comprehensive examination on the merits of the individual situations of the applicants' is apparently a collective expulsion. The other relevant provision of the Fundamental Law was its Art. E para (2) which provides the constitutional mandate for Hungary's EU membership. This clause determines conditions for transferring competences to the EU institutions and for the joint exercise of powers deriving the Hungarian Constitution.[39] The interpretive questions of the Commissioner's petition was whether the Hungarian authorities are obliged to execute such measures of the EU law that are in contrast with the provisions of the Hungarian Fundamental Law, and if not, which Hungarian institution may declare that. It is worth noting that the Commissioner's questions are clearly based on the political position of the Hungarian Government that the EU Council exceeded its scope of competence when it decided on the relocation program, as this legal act of the EU was not based on a competence transferred by Hungary to the European Union. The Commissioner suggested that the Hungarian institutions are not constitutionally obliged to obey the *ultra vires* EU regulations and it is unconstitutional when the European

Union exercises a competence by going beyond the 'necessary extent' of the competences vested in the Union.

The Constitutional Court, referring to the 'National Avowal' (preamble) of the Fundamental Law and its 'EU-clause', stated that the joint exercising of any competence by the national authorities and the EU institutions may not violate Hungary's sovereignty, and, on the other hand, it cannot lead to the violation of 'constitutional identity'.[40] Both limitations reflected the Government's position attacking the cited EUC Decision 2015/1601. The Court stressed that with the EU accession, Hungary 'has not surrendered its sovereignty', and the national sovereignty 'should be presumed when judging upon the joint exercising of further competences additional to the rights and obligations provided in the Founding Treaties of the European Union'. In addition to this, the Court declared also that it reserves the power to interpret 'the concept of constitutional identity as Hungary's self-identity and it unfolds the content of this concept from case to case'.

Although the Constitutional Court underlined that it does not 'comment on the validity, invalidity or the primacy of application' of the EU legal acts, the whole ruling refutes this statement, as the Court declared itself the 'principal organ' of the protection and safeguarding of the sovereignty of Hungary and its constitutional identity.

The decision is in sharp contrast with the earlier jurisprudence of the Court which had never before claimed the power to review whether the EU legal acts are in harmony with the national sovereignty and the constitutional identity of Hungary. Instead, the Court always respected the division of review power between the European Court of Justice and itself and the primacy and direct applicability of the EU law.[41] According to the ruling approach and the unbroken practice of constitutional interpretation – based on a more or less identical constitutional text – the Constitutional Court does not have competence to review the legality of the EU legal norms.[42]

Before this, the Constitutional Court never developed arguments authorising itself to review the potentially *ultra vires* EU legislation or EU law infringing certain fundamental constitutional provisions.[43] The only reference to the constitutional boundaries of EU law is found in the Lisbon Decision. In this ruling,[44] the Constitutional Court offered the most comprehensive interpretation of the extent of the transfer of sovereignty and the role of the Constitutional Court in reviewing the constitutionality of the division of competence between Hungary and the EU. The petitioner requested the *a posteriori* examination of the unconstitutionality and also the annulment of the Act of Parliament implementing the Treaty of Lisbon. In the petitioner's opinion, certain rules of the Treaty of Lisbon restricted Hungary's sovereignty to an extent that, if their binding nature was recognised, the Republic of Hungary 'would no longer qualify as an independent state governed under the rule of law'. In this case, the Constitutional Court conducted a substantive constitutionality review, whose final conclusion was that the law promulgating the Treaty of Lisbon was not unconstitutional because the constitutions of Member States could still exercise control over the operation of the EU. The principles of subsidiarity and proportionality would remain valid, and they ensure that the national parliaments would still have the power to review draft legislation. Also, Member States would have the right to initiate an action for annulment, citizens could turn to the institutions of the EU through a Citizens' Initiative, and the Charter of Fundamental Rights, which safeguards basic rights, now has the same value as the treaties.[45]

Summing up, it is clear that the Constitutional Court has substantially changed its position towards the relationship between the domestic and the EU law and its own concerning competence. As a judge in his concurring opinion explicitly supposed, 'the Constitutional Court should reconsider its judicial practice related to establishing the place of EU law in the legal system of Hungary'.[46]

Although in one respect the recent interpretive practice of the Court has approached the constitutional text (the Constitutional Court today seems to consider the EU Founding Treaties as international treaties, while in the past it emphasised that the EU law is a *sui generis* legal system), the reference to the constitutional identity is also an unprecedented (and unelaborate) innovation, while its identification with the national sovereignty which can be contrasted with the primacy of the EU law seems to be unfounded reasoning. What is noticeable, however, is its concurrence with the political argumentation of the governing coalition which insistently emphasises the importance of the protection of national sovereignty from the illegitimate influence of 'Brussels' as a symbol of the European Union.

4. Terrorism and inland security

Compared with France, Britain or Germany, Hungary has not been directly affected by terrorism. Indeed, since 2010 only two cases have occurred. The roots of the first case go back to the 2000s, when, according to the charges, the secretly operating extreme-right group 'Arrows of the Hungarians' National Liberating Army' committed a number of violent actions against Hungarian politicians and other public figures, and against Roma and Jewish people and communities. The trial has been running since 2011, and it does not have links to international terrorism. The second relevant case is the trial of 'Ahmed H.' for terrorism, which was launched at the height of the 'migrant crisis' in Hungary and generated wide-ranging international attention and condemnation. According to the official charges, this migrant of Syrian origin incited the crowd waiting for admission at the Hungarian–Serbian border to violence, and then joined the turbulent events and disturbances that took place in September 2015.

Although neither of these two cases have been closed so far, the latter case served as a justification for the Government to submit a new constitutional amendment (its sixth since its entry on 1 January 2012) on the 'crisis situation caused by a terrorist threat', which was adopted by Parliament. The constitutionalisation of 'terrorist danger' has eliminated the constitutional control over the Government's special empowerment in emergency situation announced by the Parliament on account of a terrorist attack or any risk of terrorism.

Yet, the Constitutional Court has preserved its power to judge the constitutionality of any legal acts without this sort of crisis situation. In the exercise of this power, the new practice of the Court can be characterised by a much more deferential behaviour, or, in other words, a much less strict jurisprudence compared with previous times.

Notwithstanding that the terrorist threat has been given great emphasis in Government communication since the migrant flow of 2015, only a few legal acts have been adopted over last years related to domestic security, and even less have reached the Constitutional Court.

One of these was a legislative act amending the law on national security services in 2011. This law authorised the Minister of Justice to approve the application of secret information gathering (i.e. interception or surveillance) to the Counter Terrorism Centre. The Court, refusing the concerning constitutional complaints, upheld the new legislation.[47] Reasoning its decision, the Constitutional Court started off from the view that the way of preventing national security risks needs a political decision that justifies the empowerment of the Minister of Justice to permit secret information gathering. The Court considered it a sufficient guarantee that the Parliament's National Security Committee would exercise oversight over the Minister's authorization procedure. In this way, the Court upheld a general legal authorisation of the counter-terrorism agency without judicial oversight. It was a complete break with the previous case-law in which the Court always insisted on the safeguard of judicial review in such cases, having regard to the extent of the restriction of the right to privacy.[48]

> Since the use of secret tools and methods is a serious intervention in the life of the individuals, they can only be used as an exception, temporary, ultimate solution.[49]

However, the Court on this occasion read from the former decisions only the recognition that the use of secret surveillance, under certain circumstances, can be a necessary and proportionate limitation of basic rights. Surprisingly, the Constitutional Court also cited the jurisprudence of the ECtHR, even if the practice of the Strasbourg Court considers the use of such tools legitimate only if it is under a constant and compulsory control exercised by bodies which are independent of the executive power.[50] Interestingly, the legal case ended up in Strasbourg, where the ECtHR found that Art. 8. of the Convention rights were violated by the Hungarian legislation and the Hungarian Constitutional Court therefore did not provide sufficient remedy in the case.[51]

In light of this rupture with the earlier case-law, which has significantly reduced the level of protection of the right to privacy, it was quite surprising that the Court invalidated another new legislation extending the use of secret surveillance of public officials (making it permanent instead of one-time national security screening).[52]

In the context of domestic security issues, it is worth referring to the increasing limitation on political communication rights that has also been found constitutional by the Constitutional Court. Freedom of assembly, as other political rights, may legitimately be limited for security reasons, but more restrictions of this nature have been imposed in recent times. According to the very liberal statutory regulation, adopted still in the times of the 'system change' in 1989, a street demonstration may be prohibited by public authorities only in two cases: if the police finds that it would seriously endanger the proper functioning of the representative institutions or courts, or if the circulation of the traffic cannot be secured by another route. Any other problem that might emerge during the event (such as the violation of rights of others or the risk of a crime) can result only in the dispersing of the event. In a recent decision, however, the Constitutional Court held that the police acted lawfully and constitutionally when they used a new, non-codified reason to the prior interdiction of a demonstration in front of the home of the prime minister (the reason was the assumed violation of the privacy of the inhabitants in the neighbouring district).[53] The Court also argued that there was an unconstitutional omission in the sense that the Parliament should amend the act on the freedom of assembly in order to regulate the cases when the freedom of assembly and the right to privacy are in collision. The new legislation has not been adopted yet, but it is quite likely that a stricter regulation will be agreed than the present one as a consequence of the decision of the Constitutional Court.

5. Explaining the changing constitutional jurisprudence

The Hungarian Constitutional Court was for two decades the most effective counterbalance of the Executive.[54] It was often considered as one of the strongest among similar courts, and an exemplar of the 'activist' judicial bodies. One could rationally presume that it had to play an important role in maintaining constitutionalism in turbulent times, when, as have seen, the country had to face serious challenges. In point of fact, the recent history of Hungarian constitutionalism suggests that certain crises, especially the economic depression and mass migration, have brought about considerable constitutional changes. In 2011, a new constitution was adopted, and a series of laws has renewed the whole legal system.[55] As we saw, the jurisprudence of the Constitutional Court has significantly changed, which is far from being attributed to the changed constitutional text.

However, a deeper analysis of the recent past of the constitutional review shows that there is hardly any connection between the transformation of the Constitutional Court's case-law and the real need to give responses to the present-day challenges. Put simply, even if some of the modern global crises have profoundly affected the country, these pressures were not the real reasons as to why the Court has altered its jurisprudence.

Although the negative effects and the risks of the world economic crisis, mass migration or the terrorist threat have been frequently referred to in political communication in the last few years, these circumstances did not play an important role in law-making processes, except in cases of the new constitutional and legal provisions relating to the relevant special legal orders. Thus, the Orbán Government declared already in the early 2010s that Hungary had recovered from the economic depression, and when the excessive deficit procedure against the country was abolished in 2013, it was presented by the Government as a clear evidence that Hungary was beyond the crisis. Since then the so-called 'unorthodox economic policy' has not been communicated as a specific crisis management tool but instead as a special Hungarian way for stabilisation and economic growth. Similarly, though government propaganda has continuously laid stress upon the threat of mass migration and international terrorism, since the border fence was built, the migration pressure has practically ceased, and, as we saw, there has not been any violent act that could be linked to international terrorism. Even the restrictive laws were not justified by the crisis, or if this reason had been used, such kinds of references to it were later dropped.[56] In fact, crisis management was conducted mainly by political tools (like the national referendum on the EU 'migrant-quota') rather than by intensive or targeted law-making.

Paradoxically, the Constitutional Court, albeit only in words, tried to use the crisis-argument. Thus, it was a memorable and astonishing manifestation when a member of the Court, Barnabás Lenkovics, shortly before the parliamentary majority elected him to be the President of the Constitutional Court, said in an interview:

> Constitutional adjudication is not independent of time and space. It must keep the pace with the changing conditions. The same standards that were developed and used for law-making by the Constitutional Court under stable [...] circumstances, cannot be invariably applied to different historical conditions. Otherwise, some measures could become dogmas, which would paralyze the operation of the legislature, the government, or even the system of rule of law, and it would make it impossible to handle the [economic] crisis.[57]

These words probably expressed the attitude of the new judges who had been selected and elected one-sidedly by the Government parties; namely, that extraordinary conditions provoked extraordinary solutions, including the reduction in the level of rights-protection or the weakening of constitutional review compared within previous periods. This was a really new approach, as a reverse logic would have followed from the previous practice of the Constitutional Court: In times of crises there is a growing need for constitutional guarantees of fundamental rights and for the strengthening of the rule of law.

In practice, however, the Constitutional Court referred only rarely to the constraints arising from the crisis situations in reasoning its own decisions. When the Court so resolutely upheld the legislative acts of the Government majority, and endorsed the unprecedented extension of the executive power, usually it did not allude to any predicament or emergency situation as a legitimacy basis for its approval.

When this was not the case, the Court's references to the economic crisis 'as a context' served only for a general and loose justification for revising the previously formulated standards without any further legal reasoning, or as a legal ornament concealing the lack of real arguments.

Thus, the Constitutional Court decision 8/2014 (III. 20.) highlighted – in the case of early repayment scheme in mortgage loan cases – that

> a significant, exceptional and serious situation occurred in Hungary in the middle of an international crises which led to an intervention by law.[58]

The reference made to the economic crisis appears in Constitutional Court decisions of 34/2014 (XI 14.) and 2/2015 (II. 2.) as well. The reasoning of the previous one suggested that

> it is commonly known that following the economic crisis of 2008–2009, hundreds of thousands of loan contracts persistently appeared and caused enormous difficulties. A mass of households had to face difficult situations; tens of thousands of families were threatened with eviction. Negative effects of the problem are borne by the society, the whole of the national economy. These problems could have not been resolved by judicial way (as part of individual judicial protection).[59]

A further argument supporting our claim that the changes of constitutional adjudications which have taken place since 2010 cannot be explained by a legal crisis management scenario, is that the jurisprudence of the Court has been deeply transformed in some other areas of law that had not been affected either by the economic crisis or the migration or other global challenges at all. The level of rights-protection was drastically reduced by the Constitutional Court in the case of some other civil liberties, as the Court was not able to prevent the guarantees of the rule of law being weakened, or in some cases undermined. In short, the changes of the Court's case-law were far from being confined to the legal areas affected by crisis or major challenges.

But if it is true that the considerable changes in constitutional jurisprudence cannot be attributed to an adaptation process, in which the major constitutional doctrines and the interpretive practices are adjusted to the changing needs of the changing times, the question remains: For what reasons have the mainstream and outcomes of the Constitutional Court's case-law changed to such a great extent?

We think that the unquestionable changes can only be understood by taking into account their wider context and the developments that formed them. The Hungarian constitutional changes that have taken place since 2010,[60] when the general elections brought about an overwhelming victory for the former opposition parties, and a new conservative Government coalition, based on a two-thirds (i.e. constitution-making) parliamentary majority, started to change the constitutional landscape of the country. Exploiting this overwhelming majority, the Government parties got their own political will through the Parliament, and voted for the new constitution without the consent or even the cooperation of the opposition parties. The adoption of the Fundamental Law of 2011 was followed by a period of intensive law-making activity, which significantly transformed almost all branches of law and legal areas. Both the constitution-making process and the following legislative activity led not only to fierce debates in the country but also caused a stir on an international level as well. The reason for this attention and the heavy criticism was that the measures of the two consecutive terms of Orbán Government after 2010 systematically dismantled the principles of the separation of powers and the rule of law.[61] These developments and events aroused a lot of criticism in international forums, and induced the EU institutions to establish a mechanism of controlling the state of the rule of law, democracy and fundamental rights in the Member States.

The prime minister Viktor Orbán, in a speech in July 2014 openly expressed his views about the policy objectives of the Government. While praising Singapore, China, India, Turkey, Russia as 'making [their] nations successful', and as the new 'stars of international analyses', he stated that 'the new state that we are building is an illiberal state, a non-liberal state'.[62]

The new constitution and the following legislative acts have fundamentally affected also the constitutional adjudication, not only for the newly introduced, constitutionally binding interpretive principles, but also because they have reduced the level of rights-protection: For example, social rights became 'state goals' instead of their former position as fundamental rights deserving elevated protection, or the Fundamental Law enables the legislature to make differences between religious communities, regulates hate speech against the previous constitutional doctrine and restricts political advertisements.

Since the Constitutional Court had been from its very beginnings a powerful counterbalance to executive power, it is not surprising that the body was involved in constitutional changes. As we have discussed above, just a few months after its formation, the new coalition government, using its two-thirds majority transformed the process of nominating the justices of the Constitutional Court. Since then, the membership of the parliamentary committee responsible for the nomination has no longer been based on parity, but reflects the party-strength in the Parliament. Whereas the earlier regulation required a compromise between the parties to nominate justices, under the new conditions, the government parties were able to pack the Court, and the newly elected members of the Court were all elected by the new two-thirds majority of the Parliament given by the governing Fidesz–Christian-Democratic party coalition [later in 2016 the agreement of the green party (LMP) became necessary to elect the four new judges]. By 2016 all judges of the Constitutional Court were elected for 12 years instead of the former 9-year term and all of them are consented to if not appointed by the ruling majority.

The Fourth Amendment to the Fundamental Law in March 2013, with the apparent purpose to force the body to change its interpretive practice, repealed all rulings of the Constitutional Court made prior to the entry into force of the Fundamental Law (1st January 2012).[63] By inscribing the controversial provisions into the text of the Fundamental Law, the same amendment created a hostile environment by openly overruling many former Constitutional Court decisions that had declared important legislative acts of the government majority in Parliament to be unconstitutional.

In effect, in the light of the successful court-packing, it is slightly surprising that the government majority curtailed the review power of a friendly Court in a way as we have seen already, as the repeal of the old decisions can be considered as a precautionary measure with the hope of long-term effects. The underlying reason could be that a strong and independent constitutional review cannot be compatible with parliamentary supremacy[64] in a country where the government parties enjoy a huge popular support, and a constitution-making majority in Parliament.

The Constitutional Court, in its new composition, did not disappoint for those who had designed and accomplished the changes in the institutional setting and the membership of the Court. Both the available qualitative[65] and quantitative[66] research show that in controversial political issues the Court usually makes a decision favourable for the Government, and that the new judges more or less follow their own political orientations.

If we analyse the reasons for the changes in the constitutional environment and especially of the practice of the Constitutional Court since 2010, we can conclude that the world financial crisis, the terrorist danger, the flow of migrants or any other new challenges do not provide plausible explanations for all these fundamental changes that have occurred not only in crisis-led cases but in other areas too. Most changes of constitutional jurisprudence have been brought about by the unquestionable authoritarian tendencies building up a so-called 'illiberal democracy', declining all institutional counterbalances against the executive power.

Of course, even a 'new authoritarianism' might be considered as a special response to the modern challenges of our world. However, if one considers this a realistic option, it must be made clear that this kind of political discourse is outside the dimension of constitutional democracies.

Notes

1 Halmai 2007, 693.
2 Sólyom (2001), 114–115; Sólyom and Brunner (2000), Szente (2013b), 1594.
3 Halmai (2002), 189–211; Schwartz (2000).
4 In Hungarian literature, the term 'jurisdictional activism' refers to the efforts of the Court to extend its powers, whereas 'interpretive activism' means the practice that relies on extraconstitutional sources in its reasoning. For a comprehensive analysis of the interpretive practice of the Constitutional Court, see Szente (2013a) and Jakab and Fröhlich (2017).
5 'The rules relating to fundamental rights and obligations shall be laid down in Acts. A fundamental right may only be restricted in order to allow the exercise of another fundamental right or to protect a constitutional value, to the extent that is absolutely necessary, proportionately to the objective pursued, and respecting the essential content of such fundamental right'. Art. I. para (3) of the Fundamental Law.
6 According to Art. N. para (1) 'In the course of performing their duties, the Constitutional Court, courts, local governments and other state organs shall be bound to respect the principle that Hungary shall enforce the principle of balanced, transparent and sustainable budget management'.
7 For a further and detailed analyses of the recent case-law in numbers see Gárdos-Orosz (2016) 345–390. A short summary is given in Gárdos-Orosz (2012) and Gárdos-Orosz (2017).

8 See the operation of this argument for constitutional changes in Pap (2018) 40–44.
9 This stipulation refers to the unwritten, and, according to the national mythology, the 'one-thousand-year' constitution before the Second World War.
10 Arts. N paras (1) and (3) and R para (3) of the Fundamental Law.
11 Art. 36 paras (4)–(5) of the Fundamental Law.
12 903/B/1990. AB határozat.
13 See also Kovács and Tóth (2011) 192–193.
14 184/2010. (X. 28.) AB határozat.
15 37/2011. (V. 10.) AB határozat.
16 Szente (2013b) 256–257.
17 20/2014. (VII. 3.) AB határozat.
18 Kolozsi, Banai, and Vonnák (2015) 60–87.
19 Act XXXVIII of 2014 on the Resolution of Questions Relating to the Uniformity Decision of the Curia Regarding Consumer Loan Agreements of Financial Institutions.
20 34/2014. (XI. 14.) AB határozat.
21 See also Act XL on the Rules of Settlement Provided for in Act XXXVIII of 2014 on the Resolution of Questions Relating to the Uniformity Decision of the Curia Regarding Consumer Loan Agreements of Financial Institutions and on Other Related Provisions.
22 23/2013. (IX. 25.) AB határozat.
23 According to statistics of the Constitutional Court, in 2015 630 motions were submitted to the Constitutional Court in the same subject and 1,300 constitutional complaints with essentially identical texts were submitted in the same period. Seven hundred foreign currency loan cases were active on 31 December 2015. Source: Alkotmánybíróság, 'Statisztika', http://alkotmanybirosag.hu/dokumentumok/statisztika/2015, accessed 14 February 2017.
24 3103/2016. (V. 24.) AB határozat, 3098/2016. (V. 24.) AB határozat, 3167/2016. (VII. 1.) AB határozat, 3222/2016. (XI. 14.) AB határozat, 3272/2016. (XII. 20.) AB határozat.
25 Gárdos-Orosz (2017).
26 Act CLXVII. of 2011 on retirement benefits, Art. 14. para (1) and (2).
27 23/2013. (IX. 25.) AB határozat.
28 11/1995. (III. 5.) AB határozat.
29 3194/2014. (VII. 14.) AB határozat.
30 See e.g. 17/1992. (III. 30.) AB határozat, 64/1993. (VI. 3.) AB határozat, 1138/B/1995. AB határozat, 51/2001. (IX. 15.) AB határozat, 109/2008. (IX. 26.) AB határozat, 867/B/1997. AB határozat.
31 Vékony v. Hungary, Judgement of 13 January 2015, no. 65681/13.
32 Source: Immigration and Asylum Office and www.police.hu.
33 Council Decision (EU) 2015/1601 of 22 September 2015.
34 12/2016. (VI. 22.) AB határozat.
35 See in details Szente (2016a) and Halmai (2016).
36 According to the Law No CLI of 2011 on the Constitutional Court, the Court reviews the decision of Parliament on rejecting or ordering a national referendum with respect to its consistency with the Fundamental Law and its legality. Art. 33 para (1). The next paragraph allows a merit review only in extraordinary conditions.
37 Halmai (2002) and Schwartz (2000).
38 3130/2016. (VI. 29) AB határozat, 3150/2016. (VII. 22.) AB határozat, 3151/2016. (VII. 22.) AB határozat.
39 'With a view to participating in the European Union as a member state, Hungary may exercise some of its competences arising from the Fundamental Law jointly with other member states through the institutions of the European Union under an international agreement, to the extent required for the exercise of the rights and the fulfilment of the obligations arising from the Founding Treaties'. Art. E para (2) of the Fundamental Law.

40 22/2016. (XII. 5.) AB határozat.
41 1053/E/2004. AB határozat; 72/2006. (XII. 15.) AB határozat; 9/2007. (III. 7.) AB határozat; 143/2010. (VII. 14.) AB határozat, 32/2008. (III. 12.) AB határozat.
42 See e.g. 61/B/2005. AB határozat; 66/2006. (XI. 29.) AB határozat; 87/2008. (VI. 18.) AB határozat.
43 Fazekas (2014) 59.
44 143/2010. (VII. 14.) AB határozat.
45 Ibid.
46 Ibid. See István Stumpf's concurring opinion.
47 32/2013. (XI. 22.) AB határozat.
48 36/2005. (X. 5.) AB határozat, 2/2007. (I. 24.) AB határozat.
49 2/2007. (I. 24.) AB határozat.
50 *Klass and others v Germany* 5029/71 (1978); *Malone v United Kingdom* 8691/79 (1984), *Leander v Sweden* 9248/81 (1987).
51 *Szabó and Vissy v. Hungary* 37138/14 (2016).
52 9/2014. (III. 21.) AB határozat.
53 13/2016. (VII. 18.) AB határozat.
54 See e.g. Schwartz (2000) 87–108; Sólyom and Brunner (2000); and Halmai (2002) 189–211.
55 Read more details in Chronowski and Varju (2015).
56 The extraordinary sectoral taxes in the first years of the Orbán Government have been introduced as only provisional measures referring to the difficult financial situation of the country. However, these arguments were dropped when these taxes were postponed, or imposed again.
57 Jogi Fórum, 2014. május 19. http://www.jogiforum.hu/interju/122.
58 8/2014. (III. 20.) AB határozat.
59 34/2014. (XI. 14.) AB határozat.
60 Vörös (2014) 1–20; Zeller (2013) 307–325; and Vincze (2013) 86–97.
61 For a more detailed description of this process, see Kovács and Tóth (2011) 183–203; Bánkuti, Halmai and Scheppele (2012a) 138–146; Pogány (2013) 341–367; Bánkuti, Halmai and Scheppele (2012b) 237–268. On international level, the European Parliament and the Venice Commission of the Council of Europe have adopted a number of resolutions and opinions criticising the backsliding of the rule of law in Hungary. See in details Szente (2017).
62 The whole speech can be found at http://hungarianspectrum.wordpress.com/2014/07/31/viktor-orbans-speech-at-the-xxv-balvanyos-free-summer-university-and-youth-camp-july-26-2014-baile-tusnad-tusnadfurdo/.
63 Sonnevend, Jakab and Csink (2015) 68; Uitz (2016) 396.
64 Sólyom (2015) 22.
65 Halmai (2014).
66 Szente (2016b).

Bibliography

Bánkuti, Miklós, Halmai, Gábor and Scheppele, Kim Lane, 'Disabling the Constitution' (2012a). 23 *Journal of Democracy*, 3138–146.

Bánkuti, Miklós, Halmai, Gábor and Scheppele, Kim Lane, 'From Separation of Powers to a Government Without Checks: Hungary's Old and New Constitutions', in Gábor Attila Tóth (ed.), *Constitution for a Disunited Nation. On Hungary's 2011 Fundamental Law* (Central University Press 2012b) 237–268.

Chronowski, Nóra and Varju, Márton, 'Two Eras of Hungarian Constitutionalism: From the Rule of Law to Rule by Law' (2016). 8 *Hague Journal on the Rule of Law* 271–289.

Chronowski, Nóra and Varju Márton, 'Constitutional Backsliding in Hungary' (2015). *Tijdschrift voor Constitutioneel Recht*, No. 3.

Fazekas, Flóra, 'EU Law and Hungarian Constitutional Court', in Márton Varju and Ernő Várnay (eds), *European Union Law in Hungary: Institutions, Processes and the Law* (HVG-Orac 2014).

Gárdos-Orosz, Fruzsina, 'The Hungarian Constitutional Court in Transition: From Actio Popularis to Constitutional Complaint' (2012). 53 *Acta Juridica Hungarica, The Hungarian Journal of Legal Studies,* 4302–315.

Gárdos-Orosz, Fruzsina, 'Alkotmánybíróság', in András Jakab and yörgy Gajduschek (eds), *A magyar jogrendszer állapota 2015* (MTA TK 2016).

Gárdos-Orosz, Fruzsina, 'The Hungarian Constitutional Adjudication in Transition', in Péter Paczolay and Fanni Mandak (eds), *Hungarian and Italian Constitutional Change* (Dialog Campus 2017) (forthcoming).

Halmai, Gábor, 'The Hungarian Approach to Constitutional Review: The End of Activism? The First Decade of the Hungarian Constitutional Court', in Wojciek Sadurski (ed.), *Constitutional Justice, East and West. Democratic Legitimacy and Constitutional Courts in Post-Communist Europe in a Comparative Perspective* (Kluwer International Law 2002).

Halmai, Gábor, 'Grundlagen und Grundzüge staatlichen Verfassungsrecht: Ungarn', in Armin von Bogdandy, Pedro Cruz Villalón, and Peter M. Huber (eds), *Handbuch Ius Publicum Europaeum, Band I.* (C. F. Müller 2007).

Halmai, Gábor, 'In memoriam magyar alkotmánybíráskodás. A pártos alkotmánybíráskodás első éve' (2014). 18 *Fundamentum* 1–2, 36–64.

Halmai, Gábor, *The Invalid Anti-Migrant Referendum in Hungary* (2016); http://verfassungsblog.de/hungarys-anti-european-immigration-laws/.

Jakab, András and Fröhlich, Johanna, 'The Constitutional Court of Hungary', in András Jakab, Arthur Dyevre and Giulio Itzcovich (eds), *Comparative Constitutional Reasoning* (Cambridge University Press 2017).

Jogi Fórum, (2014) május 19. http://www.jogiforum.hu/interju/122.

Kolozsi, Péter, Banai, Ádám and Vonnák, Balázs, 'Phasing Out Household Foreign Currency Loans: Schedule and Framework' (2015). 14 *Financial and Economic Review* 60–87.

Kovács, Kriszta and Tóth, Gábor Attila, 'Hungary's Constitutional Transformation' (2011). 7 *European Constitutional Law Review* 2, 183–203.

Pap, L. András, *Democratic Decline in Hungary, Law and Society in an Illiberal Democracy* (Routledge 2018).

Pogány, István, 'The Crisis of Democracy in East Central Europe: The "New Constitutionalism"' (2013). 19 *European Public Law* 2, 341–367.

Schwartz, Herman, *The Struggle for Constitutional Justice in Post-Communist Europe* (The University of Chicago Press 2000).

Sonnevend, Pál, Jakab, András and Csink, Lóránt, 'The Constitution as an Instrument of Everyday Party Politics: The Basic Law of Hungary', in Armin von Bogdandy and Pál Sonnevend (eds), *Constitutional Crises in the European Constitutional Area. Theory, Law and Politics in Hungary and Romania* (Hart 2015).

Sólyom, László and Brunner, Georg, *Constitutional Judiciary in a New Democracy: The Hungarian Constitutional Court* (University of Michigan Press 2000).

Sólyom, László, *Az alkotmánybíráskodás kezdetei Magyarországon* (Osiris 2001).

Sólyom, László, 'The Rise and Decline of Constitutional Culture of Hungary', in Armin von Bogdandy and Pál Sonnevend (eds), *Constitutional Crises in the European Constitutional Area. Theory, Law and Politics in Hungary and Romania* (Hart 2015).

Szente, Zoltán, 'Breaking and Making Constitutional Rules – The Constitutional Effects of Financial Crisis in Hungary', in Xenophon Contiades (ed.), *Constitution in the Global Financial Crisis – A Comparative Analysis* (Ashgate 2013a).

Szente, Zoltán, 'The Interpretive Practice of the Hungarian Constitutional Court: A Critical View' (2013b). 14 *German Law Journal* 8, 1591–1614.

Szente, Zoltán, *The Controversial Anti-Migrant Referendum in Hungary is Invalid* (2016a); http://constitutional-change.com/the-controversial-anti-migrant-referendum-in-hungary-is-invalid/

Szente, Zoltán, 'The Political Orientation of Constitutional Judges in Hungary' (2016b). 1 *Constitutional Studies* 123–149.

Szente, Zoltán, 'Challenging the Basic Values – The Problems of the Rule of Law in Hungary and the Failure of the European Union to Tackle Them', in András Jakab and Dimitry Kochenov (eds), *The Enforcement of EU Law and Values. Ensuring Member States' Compliance* (Oxford University Press 2017).

Uitz, Renáta, 'The Illusion of a Constitution in Europe: The Hungarian Constitutional Court after the Fifth Amendment of the Fundamental Law', in John Bell and Marie-Luce Paris (eds), *Rights-Based Constitutional Review. Constitutional Courts in a Changing Landscape* (Edward Elgar 2016).

Vincze, Attila, 'Wrestling with Constitutionalism: The Supermajority and the Hungarian Constitutional Court' (2013). 8 *ICL Journal – Vienna Journal on International Constitutional Law* 1, 86–97.

Vörös, Imre, 'The Constitutional Landscape after the Fourth and Fifth Amendments of Hungarian Fundamental Law' (2014). 55 *Acta Juridica Hungarica* 1, 1–20.

Zeller, Judit, 'Nichts ist so beständig… Die jüngsten Novellen des Grundgesetzes Ungarns im Kontext der Entscheidungen des Verfassungsgerichts' (2013). 59 *Osteuropa-Recht* 3, 307–325.

8 Global markets, terrorism and immigration

Italy between a troubled economy and a Constitutional crisis

Ines Ciolli

1. The economic crisis and Italian democracy

Over the past decade, the Italian constitutional system has been impacted by considerable economic and financial crisis, associated with a deeper political one, mainly the result of a crisis of representation in Parliament. Many and varied in nature, the causes of this political crisis include a malfunctioning representation model now unable to express the different values and principles existing in a pluralistic society.

In fact, the Italian Assembly suffers from an inability to produce a satisfactory form of mediation of different needs in so fragmented society.[1] It is unclear whether this is a classic crisis of representation or, rather, a crisis of the 'represented' – that is, a crisis of identity relating to common democratic and social values that can no longer be easily traced after the collapse of nation states, and above all after the rise of global economic (and perhaps) political systems breaking up all political unity.

This constitutional crisis has impacted all modern democracies called upon to respond quickly to technological and scientific evolution and to the consequently hasty and rapid change in human conditions.[2] For this reason, managing new conflicts that are upsetting political societies throughout the world is particularly strenuous, and not only for Italy. As Bruce Ackerman asserts in his 'diagnosis' of the diseases of contemporary democracies, these democracies are under continuous attack. The roots of the most recent dysfunctions can be found in a 'change in the relationship of the State, the market and technologies of the destruction'[3] – and with this term he meant terrorism. I am not sure we ought to speak of 'diseases'; democracy is able to accept the challenge of its transformation, because, as Italian philosopher Alessandro Ferrara argues, the essence of this form of government is to be open.[4] In the current democratic government, he traces three challenges to be overcome: a new reading of the principle of separation of powers; an expansion of deliberative democracy; and control over emergency through democratic categories.[5] In my opinion, one may also add control over pluralism that must not become hyper-pluralism, which plays against unity and against the persistence of democratic models.

These are the new challenges to which European democracies, too, are called upon to respond: A new juridical world, partly globalised and partly still tied to nation states, that must renew its categories without betraying the primacy of democracy and, above all, of its constitutions. Terrorism, financial crisis and migration rules have put European constitutions to the test as they try to bypass the democratic principles contained therein; but these principles seem to be maintained in all constitutional charters thanks to the role of the guardians of the constitutions played both by parliaments and by constitutional courts in each country to a different extent.

Italy's particular situation is marked by chronic political and financial issues dating back to earlier periods of the most recent crisis: A historically lacking sense of unity has made our country unable to produce common values and shared political choices; this in turn is the cause and effect of a polarised system of political parties[6] and the result is a weak parliament and a non-cohesive parliamentary majority, so neither parliament nor the government has the strength or authority to impose long-term vision, but are exposed to populism and hasty decisions. This is especially evident in migration.

The lack of long-term political programs is also one of the reasons leading to a high degree of indebtedness: Such a system makes it possible only to squander resources in myriad ways; real investments for the long term, aimed at improving the overall quality of life of society as a whole, cannot be made.[7]

One of the most important constitutional transformations focuses on the economic and financial crises[8] that have impacted and transformed several Italian institutions: The national parliament's legislative power and its control over financial deliberations is called into question;[9] the Government has increased its exceptional regulatory power because of what is mistakenly considered a period of economic emergency and not a permanent transformation.[10] We are also witnessing a 'presidentialisation' of politics and of executive power[11] that a fragmented parliamentary majority encourages because decision-making by a single leader can help avoid long and often unsuccessful bargaining in Parliament or even within the executive; although not very democratic, the leader's resolution comes quickly and, above all, there is certainty as to the amount of time that will be needed – an important element when having to follow (sudden) market trends. This also explains the real abuse of the emergency rules by the Government during the economic crisis.[12] A whole transformation going to the Constitution's very core[13] also involved the Constitutional Court, called upon to interpret the text of the Constitution in light of the new situation.

The Constitutional judges' role in economic fields has changed and is at times transfigured: Sometimes the Constitutional Court replaces the Court of Auditors and becomes an accounting judge;[14] at other times – and of far greater concern – it replaces Parliament in its role as political negotiator. In these cases, its decisions involve a high level of discretion because it is called upon in the absence of the Parliamentary assembly. The Court balances the rights contained in the Constitution with one another and with other fundamental principles, and does not always strictly follow the principles of proportionality or of graduated, appropriate measures.[15]

2. The 'emergency' of new incoming migration flows and constitutional guarantees in a time of stress

Italy and the European Union continue to consider the migratory phenomenon as an exceptional moment, to be solved with exceptional tools. It is now clear to all scholars who have dealt with this issue that only an ordinary regulatory framework can find solutions that can simultaneously take into account the security needs of countries that receive the flows – especially at a time of particular alert for global terrorism and the protection of migrants' rights. Failure to reconcile interests may lead to a breach in one of these constitutional principles.

In recent times, a rupture of constitutional values and principles, and violations of constitutional rights, were avoided mostly due to the great and arduous work of the Constitutional Court, which has intervened several times to protect the freedoms of non-citizens and the stateless. Instead, Parliament has been repeatedly led by demagogic forces and has availed itself of emergency sources for solving what is in fact a structural matter. In Italy, the recent Decree law no. 13/2017 was converted by Parliament into law no. 46/2017 under the pressure of the new migration flows arriving in Southern Italy, with the goal of identifying migrants' needs[16] in greater detail. The Italian Constitution tolerates no violation of civil liberties and personal freedoms, so this law might be declared unconstitutional because it appears to conflict with the Constitutional guarantees of due process of law: The new rules set up a special process that does not include first instance and appeal to reject the Decree of expulsion from national territory (Art. 17); specific and dedicated tribunals are provided for migration affairs (Art. 16); the first and only instance does not ensure the principle of the adversarial process or the guarantees contained in Articles 24 and 111 of the Italian Constitution (Art. 16).[17] In this case, a generic need for security cannot be considered a fundamental principle, nor must it be balanced with personal freedom and other fundamental rights. Vigorously reaffirmed is what was already stated in several previous judgments, in which constitutional judges declared unconstitutional some parts of the Bossi–Fini law.[18]

In criminal law, too, defendant's guarantees are being unconstitutionally set aside. One example of this concerns alternative detention measures, which are not sufficiently protected for immigrants because it is difficult to guarantee home-based detention when residence itself is a requirement rarely met by these people – although, theoretically, these measures should also be granted to irregular immigrants and those without residence permits.[19] For everybody, it provides the guarantee of not being repatriated to the country escaped from and where the person would face persecution; this means that in these cases, expulsion cannot be applied as a substitute sanction or alternative measure of detention.[20] Respect for constitutional rights is at risk when asylum seekers, upon arrival on Italian territory, are deprived of personal freedom because they are accompanied to closed centres, and thus into situations of substantial detention, without having committed a crime and in the absence of the guarantees reserved for prisoners, mostly under inhuman and degrading detention conditions that were censured by the European Court of Human Rights in *Khlaifia v. Italy*.[21]

The permanent state of fear and the economic crisis make it difficult for Parliaments to recognise social rights for immigrants as well, even though domestic and European immigration regulations establish that social rights could be an instrument of integration; however, above all, the principle of equality under Art. 3 of the Constitution does not allow a distinction to be made between needy citizens and needy non-citizens if the latter have entered the country legally.[22] EU legislation follows the same vein.[23] In addition, the provision of social benefits also involves the Italian regions.[24] Therefore, the picture becomes even more complicated by the multilevel government, which legitimises a substantial 'graduated scale' in the provision of rights and services to non-citizens as well.[25] Some social rights are only granted to foreigners who are long-time residents in the same place, even though the Constitutional Court has specified that the residence requirement should not weigh excessively on the delivery of services[26] and is not to be considered in the case of application of the principle of equity to a fundamental right that affects all human beings.[27]

The right to public housing has often been an overestimated requirement.[28] Even if the Constitutional Court has considered it an 'inviolable human right'[29] provided for by Art. 2 of Italian Constitution,[30] regional law does not extend to illegal aliens' access to publicly funded housing, because the Immigration Law (Art. 40, paragraph 6) provides for such measures only for legal aliens.[31]

In the protection of the right to health as well, the difference between legal and illegal aliens persists, even though it is a fundamental right that should be guaranteed to all. Illegal immigrants are entitled to life-saving care alone; other health benefits are solely for legal aliens and citizens. The recurring reason for violating rights – including those of immigrants – is always that of saving economic resources, especially in times of crisis, which deprives the regions of their legislative autonomy. It should be a regional responsibility to activate the rights to participation in local life[32] and the question of the social inclusion of foreign citizens,[33] but these are considered rights that come at an economic cost and that are not in line with first aid. Even when the state wants to set up funds to foster a specific purpose, such as implementing foreign education, it cannot do so because regional autonomy does not allow the central institution to finance the territories for precise purposes,[34] as these must be chosen by local politicians. Often, however, the regions cannot justify to their electorates such courageous (and expensive) choices, nor do they have sufficient funds to do so.

The issue of immigration is rather complex and it should be pointed out that the legislation and the decisions of constitutional courts have long established a system of a graduated scale of rights for non-citizens; However, not only the principle of equality pursuant to Art. 3 of the Italian Constitution, but also the respect for equal social dignity included in it, excludes this hypothesis:[35] Even in cases of scarce resources, a choice in the matter of redistribution must be reasonable, and discrimination could never be considered to conform with the Supreme Law as regards either freedoms or social rights. In addition, a ceiling of common guarantees is needed to avoid discrepancies between the different categories of non-citizens, which include all foreigners, European citizens, non-EU citizens, those with or without residence permits, stateless persons and asylum seekers.[36] Such differences cannot affect the guarantees that the Court has rightly based on the human person and not on his or her differentiated legal status.

Even the most recent debate, in which financial issues have become a supra-constitutional principle,[37] the spending limit is fixed not only by law but by the Constitution as well. Legislators can decide to exclude some categories of people for public benefits, but without distinguishing between immigrants and citizens, because the principle of equality does not allow for different treatment in equal situations: All the needy are in the same condition; a certain differentiation may be assumed for those who have no residence permit. Constitutional judges recognised and extended most social benefits to immigrants and non-citizens when immigrants needed them or were in situations of social discomfort, and if these benefits were closely related to a human being's needs.[38] The debate becomes more heated when it comes to rights not linked to the bare necessities for survival. In several cases, the Constitutional Court also extended benefits to legal non-citizens. In this case, the Constitutional Court won the challenge by managing to maintain the level of rights protection without drawing a distinction between citizens and non-citizens, taking pains not to give up the guarantees of the rule of law, even for immigrants.[39]

3. Terrorism, emergency and suspension of constitutional guarantees

Italy has had a long history of political terrorism. During the 1970s, political terrorism emerged and a balance between security and rights already saw the attention of lawmakers and the Constitutional Court. The government adopted some Legislative Decrees (59/78 and 625/1979) establishing new and vague offences, with lesser guarantees both in police custody and in body or home searches, as well as in interception. The Government adopted the emergency measures, which were ratified by Parliament without hesitation (Laws no. 191/78 and no. 15/80). The Constitutional Court was called upon to control the constitutionality of the question of the maximum length of detention *ante judicium* for some terrorists, and its judges ruled that the Constitution had not been violated because it was an emergency situation that demanded emergency tools.[40] They strongly underlined that

> if it is to be admitted that a general situation in which terrorism is causing death leads to a state of emergency, it must be agreed that the emergency, in its most specific sense, is certainly an abnormal and serious condition, but also by essence 'temporary'. Consequently, it legitimizes unusual measures, but these would lose any legitimacy if they were unjustifiably protracted over time.[41]

This condition of temporariness is not included in the recent emergency condition that has become a permanent condition.[42] Nevertheless, many measures of limitation of personal freedom were also considered to be in line with the Constitution by anti-terrorism laws after 9/11, although they are not limited in time. This is the first and most obvious break with the Constitution.[43]

However, the phenomenon of international terrorism that began with the attack on the World Trade Center is another matter, and demands new tools and new strategies that are relevant to a globalised and interactive world. Furthermore, terrorism and emergency in migration flows are often seen as only a matter of public order requiring exceptional measures, despite being long-term conditions and therefore not limited in time and space, which are the requirements distinguishing emergency sources.[44] Terrorism laws and judicial remedies are always so homogenous because the tools are similar: the government exercises the legislative emergency power; the principle of legality is respected only formally, because parliament simply ratifies the government decisiveness. It is not just a tyranny of the majority as many authors have argued, but a tyranny that the ordinary legislator exercises over the founding fathers and the rule of law: Even for strong constitutions, parliaments modify the rules that represent the heart of constitutions, such as their fundamental principles, thus shattering the deeper meaning of the constitutional pact with no limitation in time – and therefore, in theory, permanently. The law's terrorism measures are not so different in different countries: everywhere they consist of placing limitations on court guarantees and on the right to privacy, and of preventive detention, including terrorist suspects, foreign terrorists and those suspected of terrorism, with no special procedural guarantees, and with easier searches.

Scholars' reactions differ: Some authors have tried to defend the hard core of freedoms[45] whereas others believe that the suspension of some fundamental rights, outside Constitutional provisions, is natural, and that special emergency powers have to be provided for; it is merely because emergencies cannot be anticipated.[46] And if in Italy, in 2006, Paolo Bonetti believed that the Italian system, like other democratic systems, allows derogations from the Constitution only during a state of war, but provides for ordinary instruments to safeguard security needs without sacrificing the protection of liberties[47], Giovanna De Minico,[48] in 2015, when the special emergency legislation had already yielded its effects, raised the most burning issue, asking what were the limits on the compression of fundamental freedoms to ensure preventive control of the terrorism phenomenon. In other words, today's terrorism prevention policies call for renouncing the protection of our rights to be safeguarded against a 'future and uncertain' threat that we cannot quantify.[49] Among the Constitutional changes that this involves is a new way of understanding balance, which necessarily becomes uneven. In the most recent period of terrorism or of economic crisis, political decisions or constitutional controls have often been adopted by evaluating in an unequal way the principles, values and rights contained in the Constitution. The principle of proportionality has become the central tool of Constitutional affairs. When considering the generic protection of 'future generations', which is always taken into account in balancing social costs, the phenomenon becomes clearer. We attempt to protect a category of subjects to whom to transfer a protection we do not know will be commensurate with future times and needs; we renounce protecting some (social) rights for today, betting on a better future.[50] The same reflection may be made with regard to the precautionary principle, which arises in international law (hence with more flexible and non-national rules) and then in European law with the Maastricht Treaty, in particular to defend people against unknown dangers concerning the protection of the environment, and which has expanded until the legislative power and the court's decisions are increasingly discretionary and are spreading unequal balance.[51] Reflection, principles of proportionality and precaution exist alongside another limit that traditionally has to be balanced with rights of liberty in exceptional situations: public order. The proliferation of ancient and modern limits makes the exercise of rights more difficult. In this context, it is easy to contain freedom of speech or privacy and mobile communication interceptions before a threat of terrorism.[52]

As for Italian anti-terrorism measures, Legislative Decree no. 7/2015 was adopted and converted into law no. 43/2015. It takes into consideration the new figure of the international terrorist and of terrorism; a general de-territorialisation of the structure of these organisations; and the purpose of this new form of terrorism designed to undermine the founding values of democracies. The transformation of these new terror organisations is noticeable: These are structures based on flexible, light and horizontal associations, sometimes composed of few members, or even only of a single member, and their attacks on innocent victims are entirely unpredictable, committed for the sole purpose of spreading terror in the population. Therefore, the State's response is also special – some speak of an 'emergency criminal law':[53] As in other legal systems, it punishes the intent; that is, it anticipates the punishment for a crime yet to be committed, and there is a vagueness and uncertainty in the offense.[54] 'Training for activities with purpose of international terrorism' (Article 270 *quinquies* of the Italian criminal code) that is, preparatory acts: the law would hence punish the intent and not the act, thus distorting the sense of criminal law. In this complex picture, not only national but also European law has led to the emergence of exceptions from and breaks in the rules set out in the Treaties.[55]

4. The economic crisis: the hardest challenge to the Constitution rules

As Balaguer Callejón argues,[56] the economic crisis has literally overturned constitutional principles from a number of different standpoints: The crisis changes the way to interpret the economic constitution; it introduces permanent emergency powers that for constitutionalists represent an oxymoron, a contradiction in terms, because emergencies ought to be limited in time; it imposes a different relationship between government and parliament that is not caused by the crisis but has become more evident with it; and it has transformed the constitutionally enshrined division of competence between the State and the Regions by effecting a new centralisation in the state.[57]

The introduction of the budget rule into the Italian Constitution overturned the placement of the economic constitution in the constitutional principle.

Constitutional amendment no. 1/2012, modifying Art. 81, introduced strong new relationships within the Constitution. The original intent of the Constitution's founding fathers was to guarantee a social state through a political mediation of different interests; while they regulate economic freedoms, they found contemplation and limits in social purposes, in social functions and human dignity, or other interests as well (Arts. 41, 42, 43). The introduction of the new Art. 81 to the Constitution placed rights and expenditure on the same rank as the social state. The inevitable consequence of this equal recognition in the Constitution of rights and costs introduces an indirect and hidden idea where rights can be limited or balanced with costs even when that right is constitutionally protected and therefore its enforcement is binding it.

Containing public expenditure has become the beacon and guide for the Constitutional Court, Parliament, and Government in its regulatory power; the Constitutional Court has even disregarded the principle of the retroactive effect of its decisions on containing costs.[58]

The relationship between Parliament and Government has been transformed over these past years. This has not been caused by the crisis, but has put the predominance of the executive into relief and legitimises this anomaly. During the crisis, the fundamental reforms are regulated by Decree Law and by Legislative Decree, and Parliament intervenes only to rouse the delegation or, at the end of the legislative process, to convert the decrees into law. Parliamentary debates are almost absent because the Government intervenes during the conversion with a vote of confidence on its text, which prevents any discussion or amendments by Parliament. This behaviour is functional to the crisis that calls for quick decisions, but expels the parliament in favour of the executive, creating a phenomenon of virtualisation of the well-known political institutions all over the world. In other words, it goes towards leadership without counterweights.

Concerning the Constitutional Court's position with regard to the most recent crisis, in my view it swings from strict compliance with constitutional regimes even when recognising the existence of an economic emergency, to a reversal of the rules, as in the case of judgment no. 10/2015. Also relevant is its general 'juridical policy', which consists of taking the crisis into consideration but without creating its own personal position, its own doctrine of the crisis.[59] However, it is undeniable that many of its decisions were oriented during those periods towards prioritising lower public spending among the interests involved but without renouncing its confirmation of guarantees on social rights or other constitutional rights and powers (for example, concerning State–Region relations). The first result is a sort of concurrence with the role of the Parliament in choosing the best interests of stakeholders.[60] For these reasons, its decisions swing from an absolute prevalence of the principle of equality on budget rules, to a mere minimum (and formal) content of the right to housing in order to contain public expenditures in a time of crisis.[61] Clearly, there are more differences, and the Supreme judges must follow such principles as proportionality and reasonableness, but these are the open clauses that provide for a certain amount of discretion as judgment no. 10/2015 shows or, to the contrary, could be used to defend the social right to an adequate wage (Art. 36 Const.) and an adequate retirement pension (Art. 38) as judgment no. 70 points out.

Sometimes, the Supreme Court seems to adhere to the theory of a graduated access to the rights and conditioned rights, which have their basis in the German theory of *Vorbehalt des Möglichen* (reserve of the possible: only if and when social rights that are possible are satisfied). This occurs when it declares that in periods of scarce resources, only the core of rights that cost money should be protected.[62] This could affect the prescriptive nature of constitutional rights, which would be conditioned by available resources and thus deferred in their implementation.

Globalisation today is more aggressive and sophisticated. It has found a way to reinforce that it is 'entering' into the domain of States. This globalisation process is the ability to dictate global norms on a local scale. In order to prevent or counteract this, the state can, among other solutions, activate that of guaranteeing its own local scale, which is for Italy the regional state. Instead, in this last decade, the Constitutional Court has preferred to legitimate a re-centralisation of the legislative competence in the State, even when the Constitution entrusts concurrent competence shared between State and Regions, or in rare cases re-centralisation removes competences conferred by the Constitution to the Regions alone.[63] The constitutional judges, through the use of such technical tools as the 'clause of the prevalence' of State competence, or the 'coordination of public finance', are tending inexorably towards a new and solid return to the central State for implementing an economy of scale where the State can better control the use of the public resources. The challenge to maintain the territorial set-up imposed by the 2001 constitutional reform appears to be lost.

5. Final considerations

The changes and events impacting constitutional law and its institutions are now global in scope – the responses to them, at least as regards Western democracies, are quite homogeneous. In particular, all of Europe has suffered from and continues to grapple with what is now a cyclical economic and financial crisis – a crisis that has imposed prompt and exceptional measures aimed at filling the gaps and following the markets' trends, both in European Union law and in the national states.

This 'exceptionality' and 'promptness' are two new and challenging developments that constitutions have to face when entering the global world. The challenge for the constitutional courts is an insidious and unnatural one: they were born to govern, with certain and predictable rules, moments that are at times exceptional:[64] The relationship with continuous exceptionality and emergency shines the spotlight on their inadequacy. Moreover, there is also a continuous and palpable tension between constitutions – which are designed to last, theoretically, for all eternity so as to be immortal and in force indefinitely – and the precarious nature of the fast time frames and contracts now demanded of state institutions in order to regulate increasingly fleeting and fluid current phenomena.

The time factor has made its impact by demanding faster and faster decisions aimed at circumventing complex ones – decisions that require more time for debate and approval than those adopted by a single person, or by the Government. This is the reason for the increasingly frequent recourse to urgent legislations – not so much, or not only, because the decision is taken without having to bargain with parliamentary minorities, but also because it proves faster and more prepared to follow the markets' own timing, and to reassure markets in order to keep them from considering the States as unreliable. But in this way, constitutions are navigating by 'dead reckoning', losing their ability to guide events and to plan and foresee behaviour. It need hardly be mentioned that this also impacts the arrangements of the form of government, and the relationship between constitutional bodies: The relationship that exists between the Government and Parliament is increasingly skewed towards the former, and the role of the latter is becoming that of 'ratifying' the political choices imposed by the majority. But within the Government, too, relationships are changing: There is no more time for bargaining within the council of ministers; the 'presidentialisation' of the executives is a phenomenon impacting Italy and other democracies. I am thinking of the personal and not strictly party-linked rise of France's President Macron; but I am also thinking of the Italian executive, where collegiality was sacrificed in the name of a more marked leadership by the Prime Minister.

The speed has also brought its effects on the rules of constitutional review: The norm that introduced the balanced budget into the Italian Constitution[65] was approved in accordance with the times imposed by Art. 138 of the Constitution (a three-month interval between the first and second vote on the revision law), but under duress, with some inconvenience and without waiting one day more than required. The Constitution was thus respected in form but not in substance: The parliamentary debate needed for constitutional review was lacking; public opinion was not involved; and the very meaning of the review as an opportunity for reflection was therefore overturned.

On the other hand, the rules to contain the deficit and the public debt were adopted in a regime of emergency that was imposed upon the normal juridical rules of both the Union and of its Member States. This has meant that the relationship between the law and the economy was overturned: It is no longer the constitutions that dictate the rules – within the framework of their own principles and values – within which the economic constitution can function, but it is the latter, as a part now detached from everything the constitutional pact is, that is the model within which rights must be played out, and in light of which constitutional principles must be interpreted. The social state, which has for some time undergone the attacks of the doctrine closest to ordoliberalism, was given greater vigour by the crisis. Although representing the true new development and the very essence of the post-War constitutions, in recent years it has been seen as an expensive accessory, and has been strongly conditioned by the central importance of controlling spending.[66] The Italian Constitutional Court, after the entry into force of Constitutional Law no. 1/2012 which introduced the balanced budget into the Constitution, yielded oscillating decisions, often protecting social rights but on one occasion in such a way as to transfigure the very system of seeking redress in court, in decision no. 10 of 2015.[67] But it cannot be said to have renounced the rights of the weakest; in fact, in this field, it attempted to interpret national legislation favourably to them, without distinguishing among the needy parties to be given benefits, whether they were immigrants or citizens in conditions of economic and social precariousness.[68] However, after decision no. 10, some perplexities with regard to striking a balance between rights and the need to contain expenses have appeared on the horizon. Part of the doctrine deemed that it could represent the first step for a subsequent restriction of rights, especially of all those demanding a benefit from the State so that these rights might be effectively enjoyed. However, subsequent decisions showed the Court's ability to adjust its aim and to demonstrate that the Constitution held firm when it came to protecting rights. Therefore, more than a *revirement*, subsequent decisions clarified how Art. 81 can impact the Constitution, but without excessively restricting rights, and without affecting their essential nucleus. Clearly, it is for lawmakers and the Court itself to quantify and assess how much protection may be included in the essential nucleus. Certainly, not even budget requirements can legitimate a violation of articles 36 and 38 of the Constitution, which regard the right to fair pay and a fair pension. Similarly, it held as unconstitutional the freeze, repeated over time and now almost permanent, of wages for workers in the public sector, and not even the constitutional principle of balancing the budget inserted into Art. 81 of the Constitution could legitimate this right.

In other words, the Court found that constitutionally guaranteed rights should continue to be so, that every restriction must always be in proportion to the end to be achieved, and, above all, that every restriction of rights must be limited in time, thereby re-establishing the concept of temporariness in emergency regulatory measures. This concept was stressed by the constitutional judges in decision no. 275 of 2016, in which, even where there are particular and serious spending requirements, the rights of the weakest, in this case the disabled's right to education, must at any rate be protected, in spite of the strict budgetary limits imposed by the Region. The Court holds that it must be politics to choose how to employ resources, but in compliance with the Constitution and with protection of rights.[69]

It is however in Italian regionalism that the crisis deployed all its (bad) influence. Italy's decentralised system was put to a difficult test by the economic crisis, since in times of scarce resources, a centralisation within the State of both political decisions and of spending is classically proposed. In this case, the same constitutional norms on sharing jurisdiction were bent by lawmakers as a result of the crisis's exceptional nature, and this was endorsed by the Constitutional Court which, for example, 'rewrote' the financial rules governing the delicate relationships between the State and the Regions, by 'inventing', in the matter of coordinating public finances, an exclusive State jurisdiction not present in the Constitution. It recognised the exceptional nature of the situation, and even admitted that some competences could be modified to combat the crisis and guarantee protection to the weakest parties.[70] It similarly found that the special Regions, too, albeit not in deficit conditions, should also reduce healthcare benefits if they were not deemed strictly necessary;[71] continuing to remain with the theme of containing public spending in compliance with Art. 81 of the Constitution, it also found that the Regions in deficit could not guarantee care, even if directed towards citizens with serious pathologies, which was not considered essential in the Court's assessment.[72]

On a number of occasions, the Court used the issue of the economic crisis, mentioning it as if it were an element that could actually modify constitutional norms by the very fact of its existence. That is, it has been taken for granted that it could modify the spirit of the Constitution and could in some way condition it. The question takes on all its importance when we consider that one of our country's points of pride is that of not having turned our back on the Constitution, even to overcome the bloodiest terrorism of the 1970s.

It is precisely in the matter of terrorism that the challenge to the guarantees offered by rigid Constitutions is most insidious: The need to prevent a centralization of powers and to ensure, in every situation, the constitutional guarantees of the rights of freedom, was put to a hard test by the legislation adopted after the attacks on the World Trade Center and above all after the recent acts of terrorism affecting every part of the world. Western democracies have reacted with emergency legislation and with the use of such instruments as wiretapping that have limited their citizens' private lives. As always takes place, the phenomena were intertwined, and thus the economic crisis, along with intense flows of migration and with international terrorism, has produced an age-old phenomenon – the fear of others[73] – and a new phenomenon: attempting to prevent these ills, to conceive a principle of precaution to be applied to social facts and not merely to those involving health and the environment. The distinctive juridical element to be grappled with is the limitation of historically established rights, such as for example the secrecy of communications, in favour of a 'possible' terror attack; therefore, 'certain' historical guarantees of the rights of freedom are renounced in exchange for an 'uncertain' greater security. In the name of this uncertain protection, the consequences of a rapid process are accepted, without such jurisdictional guarantees as the right to appeal or respect for the principle of the adversarial system, thus losing sight of the fact that the proper function of the trial process is a guarantee not only for the individual accused, but for society as a whole when speaking of democratic societies. The same considerations apply for the challenge the immigration phenomenon poses for Western democracies. No extraordinary exodus will ever be able to legitimate degrading conditions for persons fleeing famine, war, and persecution. On this point, the European Court of Human Rights, national lawmakers, and the Constitutional Court itself have thus far taken action to remedy situations of greatest violation of such universally recognised rights as respect for human dignity and for personal freedoms. More difficult, and entirely within the state, is the protection of social rights, for which the Italian Parliament has provided for a graduated scale of protections, in accordance with the legal condition of the foreign national residing or spending time in our territory. The Constitutional Court has attempted to extend the social guarantees whenever it has found itself protecting the weakest parties, but in this case the real solution might also lie in a simpler granting of citizenship, first and foremost to those resident aliens now belonging to the second generation, born in Italy, who are citizens *de facto* but not under Italian law.

Notes

1 Many authors have analysed the crisis of political representation, which is the first of the problems facing contemporary Parliaments and the crisis of democracy. The relationship between representation, political parties and pluralism has been examined by Crouch (2004), Offe (2011) and Luciani (2001). For an overview of the issues related to today's crisis, see Drigo (2017) 6 and Renner (2011) 93–112.
2 We are witnessing the deepest and most intense transformation of contemporary democracies, as argued by Rosanvallon (2000) 426–434, where sovereignty, viewed as the expression of a collective will, no longer exists. There remain the 'two illusions' of a restoration of the collective will through nationalism and strict control of the boundaries, or through the management of globalisation.
3 Ackerman (2006) 14.
4 Ferrara (2011) especially 47 ff., where the author illustrates democracy's passion for openness, consisting of an open attitude towards the new.
5 Ferrara (2011) 84 ff.
6 Luciani (2011b) 1–16.
7 Ignazi (2014) 160–169.
8 For a broad comparison on crisis in the European countries, see Contiades (2013) 1 and Teubner (2011). For an analysis of the relationship with political globalisation and the Constitutional crisis, see Ciolli (2015) 1–22.
9 Fasone (2015), who analyses some transformations taking place in parliamentary decisions, such as those on transparency, on relationships in the bicameral system, and on the scrutiny of the Chamber in executive power in light of the new budget procedures; see also Tuori and Tuori (2014), 194–206 as regards the loss of autonomy of national parliaments in budget procedures.
10 Agamben (2003) speaks about a 'permanent' state of exception; Ackerman (2004) recalled that the emergency should not endanger the fundamental principles of democratic order and should instead be constitutionally provided for and disavowed.
11 Poguntke and Webb (2007) 1 ff. who take into consideration different forms of the concentration of power – even in parliamentary regimes – which consists not only of a polarisation of the decision in the Executive power, but precisely of a progressive form of concentration of power around a leader in a democratic political system.
12 This is well explained in Calvano (2013), 1–24, who casts light on the marginalisation of parliamentary debate, 6 ff., Rivosecchi (2015) 119–154, who speaks of the 'twisting imposed on constitutional norms by the use of the decree laws' and Bilancia (2015) 219–236, who illustrates how the decree law is also an instrument entrusted to domestic EU law implementation.
13 As argued, Drigo (2017) 2.
14 Especially in judgment no. 70/2012, where the Italian Constitutional Court performed a direct audit of the budget of the Campania region and declared unconstitutional the regional law that provided this budget because it also included funds that were not reliable and not yet available in regional funds. See, on this point Morgante (2012) 1–39.
15 Although the use of this principle is also a problem, because it might overturn the relationship between lawmaker and judge in favour of the latter. The strict proportionality scrutiny stated from the outset that the judge also assessed the impact and effects of his judgment, which is a predominantly political activity, and suggested replacing the latter with a more reassuring rule of the judges. The debate focusing on the relationship between judge and legislator, now strongly skewed towards the judges, is examined by Hirschl (2007); for the principle of proportionality see Barak (2012). In Italy, the Constitutional Court's judgments do not apply the principle of strict proportionality and therefore the relationship between judges and legislators is balanced, but nevertheless a progressive assertion of jurisprudential activity on legislation, because of its absence, is examined by Chessa (2014). For the transformation of constitutional

law and the relationship between proportionality and the doctrine of neo-constitutionalism, see Stone Sweet and Matthews (2008).

16 This is the latest regulatory framework on the subject, which only partially modifies Law no. 122/2016 and Legislative Decree no. 203/2016, as well as the corpus of the immigration's legislation embodied in Law no. 189/2002, called the Bossi–Fini Law.

17 The Constitutional Court had declared unconstitutional a similar question contained in the Bossi–Fini Law for the violation of the principle of adversarial process in judgment no. 222/2004; see the comment by Bascherini (2004).

18 The Constitutional Court intervened several times to defend the rights of migrants as human beings: In judgment no. 105/2001, it declared unconstitutional any restriction, for anyone, of personal freedom (citizens and non-citizens alike) without respect for jurisdictional guarantees. In judgments no. 222/2004 and no. 223/2004, it intervened because Legislative Decree no. 286/1998 did not respect the limits and guarantees contained in art. 13 of the Italian Constitution (judgment no. 222) and the principle of the due process of law (judgment no. 223)

19 Judgment no. 299/2010. The Constitutional Court maintained the proper interpretation of the Constitution and proposed considering 'domicile' to include 'housing accommodations' at 'reception centres' for people without accommodations (judgment no. 61/2011).

20 Art. 16, paragraph 9, Immigration Law.

21 *Khlaifia and others v. Italy* App. no.16483/12 (ECHR 15 December 2016), where Italy was condemned for violation of Article 5, paragraph 1 (and consequently of Articles 5, par. 2 and 5, par. 4), on account of a lack of legal basis for the deprivation of the applicants' liberty. Their de facto detention without any formal decision had deprived them of the constitutional habeas corpus guarantees afforded to individuals held in a removal centre and, even in the context of a migration crisis, this could not be compatible with the aim of Article 5 of the Convention taken together with Article 3, in respect of the conditions of detention. See, on this point, Rinaldi (2016).

22 Corsi (2014) 1–30.

23 Biondi Dal Monte (2008).

24 Article 117 Const., para. 2 attributes to the State legislative competence for a) asylum and legal status of citizens of non-EU states; b) immigration. The Constitutional Court specifies that State legislation must be limited to 'programming policy of the immigration flow in the national territory' (judgment no. 134/2010) and the policy of regularisation of irregular foreigners (judgment no. 201/2005). Therefore, the Italian Constitution and immigration legislation does not exclude the competence of the Regions, called upon to regulate others aspects of the life of non-citizens, like health, social assistance and education, which includes all public service facilities (judgments no. 156/2006, no. 300/2005, no. 299/2010). Legislative Decree no. 286/1998, referred to as the Immigration Law, is the framework with which Regions can adopt broader norms in line with state prescriptions, except in social welfare, where the Regions have full competence (judgment no. 10/2010). Article 3, paragraph 5 of the Immigration Law requires Regions and other local authorities to 'take the necessary measures to remove obstacles to the full recognition of the rights and interests recognized for foreigners in the territory of the State, in particular the right to housing, social integration, the study of the Italian language, with respect for the fundamental rights of the human being'. In practice, this model of sharing competence between the State and Regions is not so clear and undisputed; on this point, see Corsi (2013) 229–251, Ronchetti (2014), and Sciortino (2013).

25 As stated in Art. 41 of the Immigration Law; see Salazar (2011) 3237–3274.

26 In the field of social assistance and social services, the Constitutional Court has stated that social provisions do not tolerate distinctions based either on citizenship or on particular types of residence, because any requirement regarding residence or domicile excludes, paradoxically, precisely the needy and troubled persons that this assistance model aims to address in the pursuit of social purposes (judgment no. 40/2011). In its judgment no. 269/2010, the Constitutional Court recognised that Tuscany's regional

law no. 29/2009 (rules on the reception, participatory integration, and protection of foreign nationals in the Tuscany Region) stated that extending to non-citizens, even without a valid residence permit, an irreducible core of the protection of the right to health protected by the Constitution as an inviolable domain of human dignity, is not contrary to the principle and spirit of the Constitution. For an analysis of regional policies for foreigners, see Carrozza (2016) 86 ff. and Grosso (2007).

27 Constitutional Court judgments no. 10/1993, no. 198/2000, no. 105/2001, no. 252/2001, no. 222/2004, no. 224/2005, no. 432/2005. Some of these decisions are alongside – and others before – the constitutional amendments of 2001, when regionalism was strengthened. As regards the recognition of fundamental rights for all people in order to protect human dignity, see Constitutional Court judgment no. 148/2008.

28 Constitutional Court judgment no. 432/2005. For a comprehensive picture of the security and social rights of the weakest, see Ruotolo (2012) 1–276. On the requirement of a qualified residence in order to access regional welfare, see Monticelli (2016)

29 The Constitutional Court, in judgement no. 404/1988, declares that all personal and some social rights must be recognised for human beings. For a point of view regarding the right to housing and its recognition for all human beings with no distinction made between citizens, qualified residents and immigrants, including illegal ones, see Pallante (2016) 135–155.

30 Judgment no. 209/2009; Order no. 76 of 2010.

31 Judgment no. 61/2011.

32 Judgments no. 372 and 379/2004.

33 Judgments no. 300/2005.

34 Judgment no. 50/2008.

35 Ciervo (2011) 367–388, Benvenuti (2011) 59–92.

36 For the different juridical treatment of asylum seekers and refugees, see Benvenuti (2007) 11 ff; Guarnier (2014).

37 Ciolli (2015).

38 The Constitutional Court extended benefits to non-citizens (but with a regular residence permit) when unable to work (judgments no. 11/2009, 187/2010, 22/2015, 230/2015) and requiring assistance by means of economic resources (judgments no. 306/2008, 329/2011, 40/2013). Such aid may not, moreover, be subject to the condition of long-term residence (judgment no. 2/2013). See Cartabia (2016), 3 ff.

39 For example, free access to regional transport for the disabled, although a benefit that could not be included in the essential levels of assistance, is extended to all people in this condition, without considering the citizenship requirement (Constitutional Court, judgment no. 432/2005).

40 They reaffirmed that the principle of the inviolability of personal freedom is the rule and limitation an exception.

41 Judgment no. 15/1982, point 7.

42 Ciolli (2015).

43 Groppi (2010).

44 For an idea of the 'ordinary emergency', see Groppi (2010) 8 and De Minico (2016) 7; but see also Bonetti (2009) 95–116.

45 Ackerman (2004) 1029–1091, at 1030 had guessed, as early as the attack on the Twin Towers, that democracy was at stake because the emergency powers that tried to steer the crisis suspended too many liberties and guarantees.

46 But De Minico (2015) 1 raises the most burning issue as to what are the limits of the compression of fundamental freedoms to ensure preventive control of the terrorism phenomenon. When speaking of prevention, the extent of gravity can only be assumed; so much depends on the state of alert that is created and the state of fear that is generated in public opinion. Gross (2000) 1825–1868 speaks of a dichotomy between norm and exception, which cannot be overcome with a constitutional legal provision of state of exception: the response to emergency could be undemocratic. Gross (2003), at

1021–1026, and at 1058–1081, after the attack on the Twin Towers, explains that: 'the Business as usual model is based on notions of constitutional absolutism and perfection. According to this model, ordinary legal rules and norms continue to follow strictly with no substantive change even in times of emergency and crisis. Other models of emergency power may be grouped together under the general category of "model of dis-accommodation" insofar as they attempt to accommodate, within the existing normative structure, intact as much as possible, some exceptional adjustments introduced to accommodate exigency. […] I suggest that these traditional models may not always to be adequate: both as a matter of theory and practice.' Gross criticises this model because it is naive and hypocritical in the sense that it disregards the reality of governmental exercise of emergency that is hidden by the ordinary system, and especially because this model is likely to make the emergency permanent. Tribe and Gudridge (2004) 1801–1870, at 1803 are also critical of Ackerman's thought and they consider his scheme with 'the vaguest contours'. The emergency clauses seem to be 'improvised' and conferred 'unspecified institutions and at unspecified times'. See, also Groppi (2010) dedicate to the role of judges and especially of the constitutional court in the defence of the rights and freedom in a time of terrorism emergency.

47 Bonetti (2006), as recalled by Legislative Decree no. 144/2005 (converted into law no. 15/2005), which extended the anti-Mafia law to the fight against terrorism, and also includes some measures concerning the juridical condition of foreigners.

48 De Minico (2015) 1.

49 Ivi, 4.

50 Luciani (2008), who refuses this idea of a juridical category of future generation because it refers to an abstract person that has not yet existed and cannot be a holder of rights.

51 A global vision of this phenomenon, and in particular an accurate examination of the Precautionary Principle, is contained in Sunstein (2005) 109–174.

52 Fabbrini and Jackson (2016) 1–20.

53 See Bartoli (2017) 4.

54 Wenin (2016) 108 and 117 argues on 'international policies regarding the issue of training for the purpose of terrorism. This study provides an opportunity to reflect upon the strains faced by "classic" criminal law against the desired anticipation of punishability for purely premonitory conduct, in which the risk of taking on excessive consequences as opposed to actual intent arises. The severity of the threat has prompted the legislature to increasingly anticipate punishments with the risk of affecting socially neutral conduct and the consequential loss of the selective capability of the criminal law'.

55 I am referring here to the 'new Schengen rules' contained in particular in Regulation no. 399/2016 of the European Parliament and of the Council of 9 March 2016 'on a Union Code on the rules governing the movement of persons across borders (Schengen Borders Code)'; on their conflict with the goal of freedom of movement, see Rinaldi (2016) 336 ff.

56 Balaguer Callejón (2013) 449–450. For an interpretation of the crisis as a new model of constitutionalism see also Cantaro (2012).

57 For the constitutional process see Groppi, Spigno and Vizioli (2013) 102 and Ciolli (2014); as regards the impact of the insertion of this amendment in the Italian Constitution, see Groppi (2012).

58 As Bergonzini (2016) 181 stated, this judgement 'represents the Court's first attempt to limit the retroactive effects of a ruling of unconstitutionality to protect budgetary equilibrium'; in fact, Constitutional court declares unconstitutional the rule containing the Robin Tax for oil companies and the consequence of the retroactive effects of the Court's decisions should have been to refund the tax, for past years as well. This would have represented a serious budgetary problem, so the Court provided only for a future refund. This, however, is a breach of the Italian constitutional model as regards seeking redress at the Constitutional Court. See Bergonzini (2016) 181.

59 Benvenuti (2013) 969 ff.
60 Ibidem.
61 In judgment no. 121/2010, the right to housing is considered to be satisfied not by obtaining housing but by being included on waiting lists until public resources are available for the purpose.
62 As in judgment no. 316/2010, when the Supreme Court judges did not apply the principle of pegging public wages to the cost of living as the Constitution prescribes, basically to speed its return.
63 Judgments no. 10/2010 and no. 62/2013.
64 I am referring to Articles 77 and 78 of the Italian Constitution.
65 Constitutional law no. 1/2012.
66 Lo Surdo (2016) 155 ff. illustrated the transformations, including profound ones, of European and national rules in the matter of the social state, casting light on how the rules on balancing the budget, from the fiscal compact to Italian constitutional review, have literally bent the fundamental norms of the EU treaties and of the Italian Constitution.
67 Even though the Court itself appears to explain that it takes so innovative a decision in the matter of complying with art. 81 Const. precisely because the balancing is not between a social right and the needs for containing expenditure contained in art. 81 Const. In fact, the decision – by preventing a considerable outlay by the State – makes it indirectly possible to use, at a moment of profound economic crisis, the sum saved for public interventions, and even those social in nature: In point 8 of the 'considered in law' clause, the Court maintains that the overall consequences of the decision's retroactive effect would end up requiring, in a period of persisting economic and financial crisis weighing upon the weaker segments of society, an unreasonable distribution of wealth in favour of those economic operators that may instead have benefited from a favourable economic trend. This would thus irremediably prejudice the requirements of social solidarity, gravely violating articles 2 and 3 of the Constitution.
68 Most recently, order no. 95/2017 in the matter of also granting maternity benefits to women applying for asylum and holding a humanitarian residence permit but not a long-term residence permit, in which the Court declared the question inadmissible because the judge a quo could have recognised that right on the strength of art. 34, paragraph 5, of Legislative Decree no. 251/2007. For the most recent Constitutional Court approach of social rights see Massa (2017), 73–93.
69 It is in this decision that the Court states "It is the guarantee of non-restrictable rights that impacts the budget, and not its balancing that conditions its necessary distribution."
70 In judgment no. 10/2010, the Court dealt with the 'social card' – a card allowing the poor to purchase food. It found that for reasons of extraordinary need and urgency, although the assignment of the social card was included among the matters under the region's purview, it could be considered, on an entirely exceptional basis, a State matter for the purpose of maintaining the law and guaranteeing, through this instrument, a protection of the primary right to access food.
71 Constitutional Court, judgement no. 115 of 2012, with comment by Lupo and Rivosecchi (2012), 1–13.
72 Constitutional Court, judgement no. 192 of 2012 where the Court says that 'The principle of prior coverage of the expenditure in the legislative setting, provided for by art. 81 Const., is imperative'.
73 Bilancia, Di Sciullo and Rimoli (2008) 1–335.

Bibliography

Ackerman, Bruce, *Before the Next Attack: Preserving Civil Liberties in an Age of Terrorism* (Yale University Press 2006).

Ackerman, Bruce, 'The Emergency Constitution' (2004). *The Yale Law Journal*, 113, 1029–1091.

Agamben, Giorgio, *Stato di eccezione* (Bollati Boringhieri 2003) (Eng. Trans.: *State of Exception*, University of Chicago Press, 2005).

Balaguer Callejón, Francisco, 'Una interpretación constitucional de la crisis económica' (2013). *Revista de Derecho Constitucional Europeo*, 19, 449–454.

Barak, Aharon, *Proportionality* (CUP 2012).

Bartoli, Roberto, 'Legislazione e prassi in tema di contrasto al terrorismo internazionale: un nuovo paradigma emergenziale?' (2017). *Diritto penale contemporaneo*, 4 (30 marzo 2017).

Bascherini, Gianluca, La Corte costituzionale dichiara l'illegittimità costituzionale di alcune disposizioni della legge Bossi-Fini' (2004). *Costituzionalismo.it* (20/004); http://www.costituzionalismo.it/notizie/158/, last accessed 20 May 2017.

Benvenuti, Marco, *Il diritto di asilo nell'ordinamento costituzionale italiano* (CEDAM 2007).

Benvenuti, Marco, 'La protezione internazionale degli stranieri tra polarità vecchie e nuove', in Francesca Angelini, Marco Benvenuti and Angelo Schillaci (eds), *Le nuove frontiere del diritto dell'immigrazione: integrazione, diritti, sicurezza* (Atti del convegno di Roma 2–3 febbraio 2011; Jovene, 2011) 59–92.

Benvenuti, Marco, 'Brevi considerazioni intorno al ricorso all'argomento della crisi economica nella più recente giurisprudenza costituzionale' (2013). *Giurisprudenza Costituzionale*, 2, 969–979.

Bergonzini, Chiara, 'The Italian Constitutional Court and Balancing the Budget' (2016). *European Constitutional Law Review*, 12, 177–191.

Bilancia, Francesco, 'Il decreto-legge come strumento di attuazione del diritto UE dell'emergenza finanziaria. Riflessioni conclusive', in Roberta Calvano (ed.), *'Legislazione governativa d'urgenza' e crisi* (Editoriale Scientifica 2015) 219–236.

Bilancia, Francesco, Di Sciullo, Franco M. and Rimoli, Franceso, *Paura dell'Altro. Identità occidentale e cittadinanza* (Carocci 2008).

Biondi Dal Monte, Francesca, 'I diritti sociali degli stranieri tra frammentazione e non discriminazione. Alcune questioni problematiche' (2008). *Le istituzioni del federalism*, 5, 557–595.

Bonetti, Paolo, *Terrorismo, emergenza e Costituzioni democratiche* (Mulino 2006).

Bonetti, Paolo, 'Problemi e prospettive costituzionali nella lotta al terrorismo', in Massimo Cavino, Losano G. Marco and Chiara Tripodina (eds), *Lotta al terrorismo e tutela dei diritti costituzionali. Atti del convegno dell'Associazione di Diritto Pubblico Comparato ed Europeo. Alessandria, Università degli Studi, 9 maggio 2008* (Giappichelli 2009) 95–116.

Calvano, Roberta, 'La crisi e la produzione normativa del governo nel periodo 2011–2013. Riflessioni critiche' (2013). *Osservatorio sulle fonti*, 3, 1–24.

Calvano, Roberta (ed.), *Legislazione governativa d'urgenza' e crisi* (Editoriale Scientifica 2015).

Cantaro, Antonio, 'Crisi costituzionale europea e diritto della crisi', in Fausto Del Vecchio and Biagio Andò (eds), *Costituzione, globalizzazione e tradizione giuridica europea* (CEDAM 2012) 353–371.

Carrozza, Paolo, 'Diritti degli stranieri e politiche regionali e locali', in Claudio Panzera, Alessio Rauti, Carmela Salazar and Antonino Spataro (eds), *Metamorfosi della cittadinanza e diritti degli stranieri. Atti del Convegno Internazionale di Studi, Reggio Calabria, 26–27 marzo 2015* (Editoriale Scientifica 2016) 57–141.

Cartabia, Marta, 'Gli "immigrati" nella giurisprudenza costituzionale: titolari di diritti e protagonisti della solidarietà', in Claudio Panzera, Alessio Rauti, Carmela Salazar and Antonino Spataro (eds), *Quattro lezioni sugli stranieri* (Jovene 2016) 3–21.

Ciolli, Ines, 'The Balanced Budget Rule in the Italian Constitution: It Ain't Necessarily So… Useful?' (2014). *Rivista AIC*, 4.

Ciolli, Ines, 'The Constitutional Consequences of Financial Crisis and the Use of Emergency Powers: Flexibility and Emergency Sources' (2015). *Rivista AIC*, 1.

Chessa, Omar, *I giudici del diritto. Problemi teorici della giustizia costituzionale* (Franco Angeli 2014).

Ciervo, Antonello, 'I diritti sociali degli stranieri: un difficile equilibrio tra principio di non discriminazione e pari dignità sociale', in Francesca Angelini, Marco Benvenuti, Angelo Schillaci (eds), *Le nuove frontiere del diritto dell'immigrazione: integrazione, diritti, sicurezza* (Jovene 2011) 367–388.

Contiades, Xenophon (ed.), *Constitutions in the Global Financial Crisis: A Comparative Analysis* (Routledge 2013).

Corsi, Cecilia, 'Immigrazione e diritti sociali: il nodo irrisolto del riparto di competenza tra Stato e Regioni', in Emanule Rossi, Francesca Biondi Dal Monte and Massimiliano Vrenna (eds), *La governance dell'immigrazione. Diritti, politiche e competenze* (Il Mulino 2013) 229–251.

Corsi, Cecilia, 'Stranieri, diritti sociali e principio di eguaglianza nella giurisprudenza della Corte costituzionale' (2014). *Federalismi.it*, 3, 1–30.

Crouch, Colin, *Post-Democracy* (Polity Press 2004).

De Minico, di Giovana, 'Le libertà fondamentali in tempo di ordinario terrorismo' (2015). *Federalismi.it*, 10, 1–28.

De Minico, di Giovana, *Costituzione, emergenza e terrorismo* (Jovene 2016).

Drigo, Caterina, 'Interpretation and Use of Principles in Constitutional Reasoning. Some Remarks on the Challenges Stemming from the Recent Italian "Constitutional Case Law of Crisis"' (2017). *Federalismi.it*, 19 April.

Fabbrini, Frederico and Jackson, Vicki C. (eds), *Constitutionalism Across the Borders in the Struggle Against Terrorism* (Edward Elgar Publishing 2016).

Fasone, Cristina, 'National Parliaments in the Eurozone Crisis: Challenges and Opportunities' (2015). *Toruskie Studia Polsko-Woskie*, 11, 7–27.

Ferrara, Alessandro, *Democrazia e apertura* (Bruno Mondadori 2011) (Eng. Trans.: *The Democratic Horizon: Hyper Pluralism and the Renewal of Political Liberalism*) (Cambridge University Press, 2014).

Groppi, Tania, '"Business as Usual". Le dialogue judiciaire sur les affaires antiterroristes après le 11 septembre 2001', in Julia Iliopoulos-Strangas, Oliver Diggelman and Hartmut Bauer (eds), *Etat de droit, Sécurité et Liberté en Europe* (Sakkoulas, Bruylant, NOMOS Verlagsgesellschaft 2010) 325 ff.

Groppi, Tania, 'The Impact of the Financial Crisis on the Italian Written Constitution' (2012). *Italian Journal of Public Law*, 2, 1–14.

Groppi, Tania, Spigno, Irene and Vizioli, N., 'The Constitutional Consequences of the Financial Crisis in Italy', in Xenophon Contiades (ed.), *Constitutions in the Global Financial Crisis. A Comparative Analysis* (Ashgate 2013) 3–88.

Gross, Oren, 'Chaos and Rules: Should Responses to Violent Crises Always Be Constitutional?' (2003). *The Yale Law Journal*, 112, 1011–1134.

Gross, Oren, 'The Normless and Exceptionless Exception: Carl Schmitt's Theory of Emergency Powers and the "Norm-Exception" Dichotomy' (2000). *Cardozo Law Review*, 21, 1825–1868.

Grosso, Enrico, 'Stranieri irregolari e diritto alla salute. L'esperienza giurisprudenziale', in R. Balduzzi (ed.), *Cittadinanza, Corti, Salute* (CEDAM 2007) 157–170.

Guarnier, Tatiana, 'La cittadinanza e la condizione giuridica degli stranieri nell'ordinamento italiano', in Maria Pia Paternò (ed.), *Questioni di confine. Riflessioni sulla convivenza giuridico-politica in una prospettiva multidisciplinare* (Editoriale Scientifica 2014) 131–156.

Hirschl, Ran, *Towards Juristocracy. The Origins and Consequences of the New Constitutionalism* (Harvard University Press 2007).

Ignazi, Piero, 'Power and the (Il)legitimacy of Political Parties: An Unavoidable Paradox of Contemporary Democracy?' (2014). *Party Politics*, 20, 160–169.

Losurdo, Federico, *Lo Stato sociale condizionato. Stabilità e crescita nell'ordinamento costituzionale* (Giappichelli 2016).

Luciani, Massimo, 'Costituzione, istituzioni e processi di costruzione dell'unità nazionale' (2011b). *Rivista AIC*, 2, 1–16.

Luciani, Massimo, 'Il paradigma della rappresentanza di fronte alla crisi del rappresentato', in Nicoló Zanon and Francesca Biondi (eds), *Percorsi e vicende attuali della rappresentanza e della responsabilità politica. Atti del convegno, 16–17 marzo 2000; introduzione di G. Zagrebelsky* (Giuffrè 2001) 109–117.

Luciani, Massimo, 'Generazioni future, distribuzione temporale della spesa pubblica e vincoli costituzionali', in Rafaele Bifulco, Antonio D'Aloia (eds), *Un diritto per il futuro. Teorie e modelli dello sviluppo sostenibile e della responsabilità intergenerazionale* (Jovene 2008) 425.

Luciani, Massimo, 'Unità nazionale e struttura economica. La prospettiva della Costituzione repubblicana' (2011a). *Diritto e Società*, 2, 636–719.

Lupo, Nicola and Rivosecchi, Guido, 'Quando l'equilibrio di bilancio prevale sulle politiche sanitarie regionali' (2012). *Regioni*, 5–6, 1062–1075.

Massa, Michele, 'Discrezionalità, sostenibilità, responsabilità nella giurisprudenza costituzionale sui diritti sociali' (2017). *Quaderni costituzionali*, 1, 73–93.

Monticelli, Elena, 'La giurisprudenza costituzionale italiana in materia di residenza qualificata e accesso al welfare regionale' (2016). *Osservatorio AIC*, 2.

Morgante, Daniela, 'La costituzionalizzazione del pareggio di bilancio' (2012). *Federalismi.it*, 11 July, 2–42.

Offe, Claus, 'Crisis and Innovation of Liberal Democracy: Can Deliberation Be Institutionalised?' (2011). *Czech Sociological Review*, 47, 447–472.

Pallante, Francesco, 'Gli stranieri e il diritto all'abitazione' (2016). *Costituzionalismo*.it, 3, 135–155.

Poguntke, Thomas and Webb, Paul, *The Presidentialization of Politics: A Comparative Study of Modern Democracies* (Oxford University Press 2007).

Renner, Moritz, 'Death of Complexity. The Financial Crisis and the Crisis of Law in the World Society', in Poul F. Kjaer, Günter Teubner and Alberto Febbrajo (eds), *The Financial Crisis in Constitutional Perspective: The Dark Side of Functional Differentiation* (Hart Publishing 2011) 93–111.

Rinaldi, Eleonora, 'L'Unione europea e le deroghe alla libertà di circolazione in funzione di governo dei flussi migratori' (2016). *Costituzionalismo.it*, 3, 325–354.

Rivosecchi, Guido, 'Decretazione d'urgenza e governo dell'economia', in Roberta Calvano (ed.), *Legislazione governativa d'urgenza e crisi* (Editoriale Scientifica 2015) 119–154.

Ronchetti, Laura (ed.), *La Repubblica e le migrazioni* (Giuffrè 2014).

Rosanvallon, Pierre, *La démocratie inachevée* (Gallimard 2000).

Ruotolo, Marco, *Sicurezza, dignità e lotta alla povertà. Dal 'diritto alla sicurezza' alla 'sicurezza dei diritti'* (Editoriale Scientifica 2012).

Salazar, Carmela, 'Leggi statali, leggi regionali e politiche per gli immigrati: i diritti dei 'clandestini' e degli 'irregolari' in due recenti decisioni della Corte costituzionale (Sentenze. n. 134 e 269/2010)', in *Studi in onore di Franco Modugno* (Edizioni Scientifiche Italiane 2011) 3237–3274.

Sunstein, Cass R., *Laws of Fear Beyond the Precautionary Principle* (Cambridge University Press 2005).

Stone, Sweet Alec and Mathews, Jud, 'Proportionality Balancing and Global Constitutionalism' (2008). *Yale Law School Faculty Scholarship Series*, 14, 72–164.

Teubner, Günter, 'A Constitutional Moment? The Logics of "Hitting the Bottom"', in Poul F. Kjaer, Günter Teubner and Alberto Febbrajo (eds), *The Financial Crisis in Constitutional Perspective: The Dark Side of Functional Differentiation* (Hart Publishing 2011) 3–42.

Tribe, Laurence H. and Gudridge, Patrick O., 'The Anti-emergency Constitution' (2004). *The Yale Law Journal*, 113, 1801–1870.

Tuori, Kaarlo and Tuori, Klaus, *The Eurozone Crisis. A Constitutional Analysis* (Cambridge University Press 2014).

Wenin, Roberto, 'Una riflessione comparata sulle norme in materia di addestramento per finalità di terrorismo, Comparative Law Observations on the Rules and Regulations Concerning Terrorism Training' (2016). *Diritto penale contemporaneo*, 4, 108–140.

9 Constitutional judiciary in crisis

The case of Poland

Mirosław Granat

The Constitutional Tribunal has played a key role in shaping the democratic rule of law and in protecting human rights in Poland. Over the 30 years of its activity (1986–2016) it has developed significant jurisprudence. In the autumn of 2015, a crisis of the judicial review of the constitutionality of the law in Poland began, whose development led to a slowdown and, eventually, to stopping the activity of the Tribunal.

In section 1 of this chapter I outline the origins of the constitutional judiciary in Poland and the status of the Tribunal under the Constitution of 1997. Section 2 is devoted to a discussion of selected cases from the Tribunal's jurisprudence related to a sensitive constitutional principle, especially in the period of the world financial crisis, namely the principle of budget balance. The cited judgements demonstrate the tension between the financial cuts made by the government in the name of maintaining budget balance and the necessity of protecting the social rights of citizens by the Tribunal. Section 3, of necessity unfinished, concerns the crisis of the Tribunal and its activity.

1 The origins and development of the Polish Constitutional Tribunal

1.1 The origins of the constitutional judiciary in Poland

The Constitutional Tribunal was established in Poland at a politically very bad moment.[1] It was founded in the early 1980s still in the period of the so-called real socialism. The introduction of the judicial review of the constitutionality of the law was a concession made by the communists, whose power was declining, to society, which demanded respect for their subjective rights. The moment of the establishment of the Tribunal, which derives from the previous system, but is based on the idea of the judicial review of the constitutionality of the law according to Kelsen's model, is not perceived as a burden on its current status. Thanks to its jurisprudence, the Tribunal has certainly thrown off the burden of 'an illegitimate origin'. If the judicial review of the constitutionality of the law is sometimes questioned today in Poland, it is for reasons other than the circumstances of the Tribunal's establishment. Even in the 1980s, in an essentially communist country, the Tribunal's judgements contributed to defending citizens against extreme abuses of the government. As the system of real socialism was decomposing, the importance of the constitutional judiciary was growing. In the early 1990s the Tribunal became an independent constitutional court.

The specificity of 'the Polish way' to the constitutional judiciary is also manifested in the fact that Poland did not adopt a ready-made institutional model of judicial review from Western Europe. For the majority of countries of Central and Eastern Europe, the German Federal Constitutional Court served as a model. In Poland, the Constitutional Tribunal has developed on the basis of domestic doctrine of law as well as some solutions of Kelsen's model of judicial review. Until 1992 the Tribunal's jurisdiction was limited, e.g. international agreements could not be the subject of review. Distrust towards the emerging constitutional court also manifested itself in the fact that the judgements on the unconstitutionality of laws could be rejected by the Sejm (Lower House of the Polish Parliament) by a two-thirds majority of votes. These 'fuses' were completely removed in the Constitution of 1997. The Tribunal became a constitutional court par excellence.

1.2 The Constitutional Tribunal in the Constitution of 1997

In the Constitution of 1997 the Tribunal is an independent constitutional court. It belongs to the judiciary.[2] It consists of 15 judges elected by the Sejm for a term of office of 9 years from amongst 'persons distinguished by their knowledge of the law'. Re-election to the Tribunal is prohibited.[3] Judges are elected by an absolute majority of votes in the presence of at least half of the total number of deputies. Candidates for judges are proposed in the Sejm by at least 50 deputies or the Presidium of the Sejm. The majority required for the election of judges was thus far a statutory matter.[4] The current law on the status of judges of the Constitutional Tribunal of 30 November 2016 (entered into force on 4 January 2017) moved this matter to the Rules of the Sejm,[5] which have the form of a resolution, i.e. only an internal act of the Sejm.

The President and Vice-President of the Constitutional Tribunal are appointed by the President of the Republic from amongst candidates proposed by the General Assembly of the Judges of the Constitutional Tribunal.[6] The current law on the organisation and functioning of the Constitutional Tribunal of 30 November 2016[7] (entered into force on 4 January 2017) states that it is enough for a judge to receive five votes to stand as a candidate for the post of the President of the Constitutional Tribunal.[8]

The jurisdiction of the Tribunal is typical of 'the court of the law'. The Tribunal examines the conformity of normative acts to the Constitution. It also has the authority to settle disputes between some organs of the state as well as to adjudicate on the conformity to the Constitution of the purposes or activities of political parties. Judgements of the Tribunal are universally binding and final.[9] They are required to be 'immediately published' in the official publication in which the original normative act was promulgated.[10] All these provisions underwent a difficult test in the course of the crisis of the Tribunal which began in the autumn of 2015.

The Tribunal's jurisprudence developed on the basis of the Constitution played a key role in the establishment of the constitutional democracy system in Poland.[11] The Tribunal's judgements gave meaning to the fundamental principles of the Constitution. They developed the substance of the Constitution. The Tribunal fulfilled the role of the guardian of the Constitution. It enjoyed very high social prestige (also among politicians and political parties).[12] It can be argued that it marked 'the centre of gravity' in the system based on the Constitution of 1997.

2 The jurisprudence of the Polish Constitutional Tribunal

2.1 Presentation of selected judgements of the Constitutional Tribunal

The Tribunal occupied a position typical of a constitutional court until the outbreak of the crisis concerning its staffing in 2015. Its jurisprudence indicated that it was 'the court of the law' in a deeper sense than only Kelsenian. In its judgements it went beyond the positivist interpretation of the law. It seems that such non-Kelsenian understanding of the Tribunal as 'the court of the law' has been gaining importance in recent years. The Tribunal treated the Constitution of 1997 primarily as a set of principles of law rather than as a collection of individual provisions, which enabled it to reach a number of constitutional values. Of course, the Tribunal did not adjudicate on the basis of values as they are not constitutive elements in adjudication. The point is that the principles of law enshrined in the Constitution allowed the Tribunal to reach numerous constitutional values. In adjudication, the Tribunal invoked values such as human dignity and the common good or justice. It perceived and applied the Constitution as a set of principles of law that interact with each other.

As has already been mentioned, the selected cases relate to a sensitive matter of the tension between the State's public finances and the social rights of citizens. The first one is the judgement of 28 October 2015 on the so-called tax-free amount (Section 1.1). The Tribunal pointed out the relationship between a tax-free amount and human dignity. It seems that this is an example of a judgement in which the protection of human dignity prevailed over the discipline imposed by the principle of budget balance. On the other hand, the judgement of 19 December 2012 on pension adjustment (Section 1.2) illustrates the clash between the principle of social justice of Article 2 of the Constitution (a truly 'revolutionary' principle) and the principle of justice in its classical Aristotelian sense ('one should receive what he rightfully deserves') expressed in the Preamble.

The provisions of the Law on Personal Income Tax of 1991 stipulated that the so-called tax-free amount (i.e. the amount decreasing the total tax) was 3091 zloty per person per year (i.e. approximately 250 zloty per month). It had not been adjusted by the legislator since 2004 despite an increase in salaries. The Ombudsman argued before the Tribunal that the legislator should leave a citizen a minimum income, which he or she can dispose of freely.[13] This income should be sufficient to satisfy the basic needs of a taxpayer. A low, not adjusted tax-free amount is irrational in the case of those who receive low income (not exceeding the poverty line). It leads the low-income taxpayers to depend on the social assistance system. In 2014, the amount of money at the subsistence level was approximately 6500 zloty. The subsistence minimum was therefore twice as much as the tax-free amount.

In the judgement of 28 October 2015, the Constitutional Tribunal acknowledged that the imposition of taxes and public levies as well as determining the way in which they are collected remains within the scope of the legislator's discretion. The legislator's discretion in the field of taxation is limited on the one hand by the legislative correctness of regulations and on the other hand by the constitutional principles and values prohibiting regulations which are unjust and unduly restrict the rights of the taxpayer. As a result, it is not allowed to introduce tax law solutions forcing the taxpayer to rely on social welfare benefits.[14] At the same time, from the citizen's point of view, the obligation to pay taxes has a constitutional basis (Article 84).

The legislator defended the existing regulation on a tax-free amount with three arguments. Firstly, the Constitution does not contain the obligation to introduce a tax-free amount. Admittedly, this amount is low, but it might as well not exist. Besides, tax law provides for other solutions beneficial to the taxpayer that compensate for the low tax-free amount. Secondly, the principle of a balanced state budget and the requirement to maintain the stability of the public finances have priority in relation to a tax-free amount. Shaping the provisions of the Law on Personal Income Tax, the legislator must take into account the principle of a balanced budget.[15] It is not a coincidence that the primary function of a tax in tax law is the fiscal function. And finally, even if a tax-free amount is low (and has not been adjusted for several years), the taxpayer may receive social welfare benefits after paying a tax. This would suggest that the legislator is allowed to move citizens from the group of taxpayers to those relying on social welfare benefits.

The Tribunal ruled that since the legislator had already introduced a tax-free amount (which was not its constitutional obligation) and had maintained it since 1991, it should meet constitutional standards. These standards concern not only the formal aspect of the regulation. The non-conformity of Article 27 of the Law on Personal Income Tax to the principle of social justice resulted from the fact that the legislator had not linked the ability of citizens to pay taxes to the provisions concerning the subsistence minimum. The Tribunal emphasised that a tax-free amount belongs to the citizen. It is a manifestation of his or her rights and freedoms in the state. It is a kind of his or her basic property. The legislator's approach to a tax-free amount is based on a certain vision of the State and its attitude to the citizen.[16]

In the case under discussion, the Tribunal demonstrated the relationship between social justice of Art. 2 and human dignity of Art. 30 of the Constitution. A tax obligation imposed by the State must take into account leaving an individual the means 'necessary to satisfy basic needs', enabling him or her to lead an independent life in society. Leaving an individual the means corresponding to the minimum subsistence level stems from his or her right to dignity. The design of the tax scale must take into account the taxpayer's standard of living so as to prevent them from falling into poverty. It must ensure that everyone, even the poor, participate in the tax system by paying personal income tax. In doing so, they contribute to the common good without being pushed below the poverty line.[17]

The cited judgement has been executed by the Sejm, at least partially. Tax law has been amended in such a way that a tax-free amount has been raised for low income earners. The legislator also announced increasing a tax-free amount for all taxpayers to ensure maintaining its relation to the cost of living.

In 2012, the legislator resigned from percentage adjustment of pensions in favour of a quota adjustment on a one-off basis. Each pensioner received the same amount of adjustment (71 zloty per month) regardless of the amount of his or her pension. The new method of pension adjustment aroused the interest of the beneficiaries (their number exceeds 10 million) and the issue became a political problem.

In the proceedings before the Constitutional Tribunal (case no. K 9/12),[18] the Ombudsman claimed that a quota adjustment violated the principle of social justice (Article 2 of the Constitution) and a related principle of citizen's trust in the state and its law as well as the constitutional right to social security (Article 67 of the Constitution). The mechanism in question ensured that the real value of pensions was maintained only in the case of some pensioners, i.e. those whose pensions were relatively low (did not exceed 1480 zloty). In my opinion, the applicant rightly complained that this inequality, expressed in the same amount of adjustment for all pensioners, would influence the future level of pensions. The return to percentage adjustment would be based on the level of pensions already established as a result of unjust adjustment.[19]

In the judgement of 19 December 2012, the Tribunal ruled that a quota adjustment of pensions was consistent with the Constitution. Such an action of the legislator was deemed necessary from the point of view of maintaining the public finance balance. The amendment to the Law on Pensions was part of 'a wider programme of balancing public finances'.[20] The Tribunal also invoked social solidarity and the need to protect a minimum level of social security guaranteed by the Constitution in Article 67. It acknowledged that the legislator treated differently similar entities with the same relevant feature, i.e. being entitled to a pension. Such differentiation, however, was proportionate and justified in the light of constitutional principles and values.

If this judgement is examined from the point of view of social justice principle, then it must be concluded that adjustment for 2012 was carried out according to the principle 'equally for all'. The Tribunal worked on an assumption, which seems to be characteristic of the financial crisis period, that the relevant feature of each of the beneficiaries was 'an ability to make ends meet,' i.e. that public authority should ensure that everyone supports himself or herself until he or she receives the next salary. Undoubtedly, all pensioners are equal in this respect. Every person should have the means to survive until the end of the month. The Tribunal took the view that if the state budget funds are limited, then each person entitled to benefits must be provided with the subsistence minimum. The mechanism in question was unfavourable to pensioners with high pensions (over 1480 zloty).[21] According to the Tribunal, if the legislator applied percentage adjustment (as called for by the

Ombudsman), 'the poorest would be even poorer'. Their pensions would have increased only slightly.

In the case concerning pension adjustment, there was a clash between 'justice' (appears in the Preamble) and 'social justice' of Article 2 of the Constitution. Article 2 of the Constitution states that the Republic of Poland shall be a democratic state ruled by law and implementing the principles of social justice. In this provision, social justice serves to direct Poland as a democratic state ruled by law. In the jurisprudence, social justice is instantiated by the principle of equality. Both principles are close to each other in the jurisprudence of the Constitutional Tribunal. In my opinion, the Tribunal rightly states that to some extent they overlap. One principle should not be considered without a reference to the other, but that does not mean that the Tribunal identifies equality with social justice. In addition, according to the Tribunal, the principle of social justice also has 'a substantive aspect', manifested in an imperative to protect certain constitutional principles and values by the law. In this regard, the principle of social justice is independent from the principle of equality. An infringement of one principle does not entail an infringement of the other. It is therefore possible to satisfy the principle of social justice at the expense of equality, provided that the legislator maintains constitutional standards, such as those following from the principle of proportionality. This substantive aspect of understanding the principle of social justice may justify an increase in inequality among subjects of law. Granting equal amount of adjustment to each pensioner may be perhaps regarded as inequality, but it satisfies social justice. It is necessary to point out after the Tribunal that this kind of inequality consistent with social justice must have a strong basis in other constitutional principles and values.

To sum up, the conflict between justice and social justice in the reasoning of the Tribunal concerning the legislator's treatment of pensioners was resolved in favour of the latter. During the financial crisis, social justice fulfilled the function of the principle of law, in a sense, correcting equality before the law. The principle of social justice justified granting the same amount of adjustment to all pensioners despite their diversity in terms of material status. A large group of them not only received a small amount (disproportionate to the level of their pensions), but it turned out to be consistent with the principle of social justice. The Tribunal acknowledged the priority of social justice, but it is clear that it did so at the expense of the principle of citizen's trust in the state and its law. It applied the principle of social justice in such a way as to give purpose to justice. Using this principle, it corrected the situation in which pensioners are equal before the law, i.e. that they should be treated according to the criterion of merit, that is according to the amount of contributions they brought into their future pension. It seems that the Tribunal shared the assumption of the legislator that during the financial crisis there should not be 'equal and more equal in poverty'. The essence of the judgement of December 2012 can be paraphrased in such a way that as a result of a quota adjustment 'the rich will make ends meet anyway', but 'the poor cannot be even poorer', because they will not be able to make ends meet. In short, the Tribunal acknowledged that the principle of social justice was more important than justice.

What seems disturbing in the Tribunal's stance in the abovementioned case is that it assumed here a particular vision of social relations. My understanding of it is that the legislator's goal, at least during the crisis, should be to reduce income differences between people. The Tribunal emphasised that it had taken into account 'social and economic facts', i.e. that it had noticed growing economic disparities among pensioners and had decided to correct these phenomena in accordance with constitutional principles and values.[22] The legislator's interference into the pension system was unfavourable to the better-off, but justified from the perspective of 'values co-creating the principle of social justice'.[23]

An overall analysis of the jurisprudence of the Tribunal during the financial crisis demonstrates that it seems rather uncontroversial that the Tribunal took the side of the state budget balance. In spite of the disputability of the judgement on pension adjustment and possibly other judgments, the rulings were accepted as issued by an independent court and independent judges. They did not reflect the criterion of the political 'origin' of the judges who made them.

3 Disempowerment of the Constitutional Tribunal

3.1 The crisis of the Tribunal related to the election of judges

The crisis of the Tribunal began in the autumn of 2015. It led to the destruction of the authority of the Tribunal and its judges.

The crisis developed against the background of the conflict concerning the choice of constitutional judges. In November and December 2015, the terms of office of five judges elected back in 2006 expired. Three of them ended their terms of office in November 2015 and two in December 2015. The major political forces sought to influence the filling of these vacancies. They assumed that they would impact in this way the direction of the Tribunal's jurisprudence.

On 8 October 2015, the Sejm of the seventh term (2011–2015) elected a total of five judges, including three judges to replace those whose terms of office expired on 7 November 2015. It was a right solution given that the Sejm's term of office ended on 11 November 2015. Therefore, the vacancies in question appeared still during the seventh term of the Sejm. However, the Sejm elected two additional judges to replace those whose terms of office were to expire in December 2015, i.e. during the Sejm's eighth term of office, which started on 12 November 2015. In total, the outgoing Sejm of the seventh term elected five judges, even though it was obvious that only three vacancies would appear during its term of office. Two vacancies were filled in advance, which tied the hands of the next Sejm.

In the Sejm of the eighth term the majority was won by the opposition (elections were held on 25 October 2015). The Sejm passed a resolution on 'the lack of legal force' of the election of all five judges by the Sejm of the previous term. The election of three judges on 8 October 2015 was also declared null and void. Next, on 2 December 2015, new five judges were elected by the Sejm.

In case no. K 34/15 (judgement of 3 December 2015), the Constitutional Tribunal examined the statutory basis for the election of judges. The judgement stated that the choice made on 8 October 2015 of three judges who were to take office on 7 November 2015 was carried out in accordance with the law. However, the election in advance of two judges who were to take office in December 2015 was illegal. The Tribunal held that it was the President's obligation to swear in three legally elected judges immediately.[24] The judgement of 3 December 2015, despite some delay, was published by the Prime Minister, so it is binding. To the present day, however, the Head of State has not sworn in the said three judges.

The description of the facts presented above might not be exhaustive. What is more important, however, is that the Sejm of the seventh as well as of the eighth term made 'double' choice of judges for vacancies appearing in November and December 2015. The Sejm of the seventh term elected five judges, with two elected illegally. The Sejm of the eighth term also elected five judges, with three, according to the Tribunal's judgement of 3 December 2015, to fill the vacancies already filled. The election of three judges made on 8 October 2015 was declared by the Tribunal to have been carried out on the basis of constitutional regulations. These judges, de jure, are still waiting to be sworn in by the President.

3.2 The crisis of the Constitutional Tribunal's activity

According to the Tribunal's judgement of 3 December 2015, there were 12 judges of unquestionable legal status in the Tribunal. The remaining three seats should be filled by the judges chosen by the Sejm of the seventh term on 8 October 2015. According to the Sejm's resolution, these seats should be filled by the judges chosen by the Sejm of the eighth term on 2 December 2015. From the formal point of view, the conflict on the staffing of the Tribunal ended on 20 December 2016 when the newly appointed President of the Constitutional Tribunal included three judges elected on 2 December 2015 in the bench, based on the new law on the Constitutional Tribunal of December 2016. So far (February 2017), the Constitutional Tribunal staffed in December 2016 has not issued any ruling. It might be then concluded that the crisis related to the election of judges has turned into the crisis of the Tribunal's activity.

There has been a noticeable decrease in the number of applications, constitutional complaints and questions of law submitted to the Tribunal. One gets the impression that the entities entitled to initiating proceedings before the Tribunal are gradually losing trust in this institution.

Between November 2015 and December 2016, the Sejm passed a series of seven laws on the organization and functioning of the Tribunal, called 'remedy laws'. The declared purpose was to improve the Tribunal's functioning (despite the incompleteness of its bench) as well as to strengthen the legitimacy of its decisions. In spite of the name, many implemented solutions, in fact, deepened the paralysis of the Tribunal's activity. Numerous key provisions of these laws were of an ad hoc character. They served the legislator as temporary solutions of the problems related to the activity of the Tribunal. They contained provisions of a specific and individual character, which contradicted the purpose of a statute. There is no need to analyse the provisions of individual acts as they proved to be episodic (they are no longer binding). Nevertheless, two things should be pointed out.

First of all, the laws passed in November 2015, December 2015 and July 2016 were immediately challenged before the Constitutional Tribunal, in some cases by several subjects at a time. The Constitutional Tribunal was still able to examine them and to decide on their constitutionality or unconstitutionality. On the other hand, currently binding three consecutive laws passed in November and December 2016 have not been challenged before the Tribunal even though they contain legal solutions dubious from the point of view of their constitutionality. Presumably, this stems from the applicants' disbelief that the Tribunal will be able to adjudicate in this matter.[25]

Secondly, it is important how 'remedy laws' relate to the Constitution. This is because some legal regulations were clearly unconstitutional. I would like to demonstrate this with an example of the 'remedy law' of 22 December 2015.

The amendment of 22 December 2015 to the Law on the Constitutional Tribunal introduced significant modifications in the principles of the Constitution, shifting the position of the Constitutional Tribunal within the system of separation and balance of powers. The amendment provided for changes in the Tribunal's functioning undermining the balance of powers. It was not an incidental legislative action which violated the provisions of the Constitution (these are usual cases of unconstitutionality). In fact, it sought to modify the Constitution by marginalising the Tribunal in the system of powers.

The amendment resulted in a situation whereby the legislator introduced some changes to the system of constitutional bodies by means of 'procedural' amendments. The following mechanisms were introduced: a) an obligation to examine cases in the order in which they were submitted; b) a requirement of a two-thirds majority of votes for judgements made by the full bench; c) changes in the disciplinary proceedings against judges (by virtue of which the executive could initiate disciplinary proceedings and the legislative branch could terminate them). For example, an obligation to examine cases in the order in which they were submitted was not and is not a procedural matter, but interferes with the independence and autonomy of the Tribunal, depriving the chair of the adjudicating panel of the right to submit cases to hearing. Similarly, the requirement of a qualified majority in cases examined by the full bench would mean that the more difficult a case, the lower the chances of reaching a verdict. These solutions changed the relationship between the legislative branch and the judiciary.

At the same time, the legislator 'impregnated' the amendment against review by the Tribunal through an intentional removal of vacatio legis (so that its provisions could enter into force immediately after passing by the Sejm). Immediate entry into force exposed the Tribunal to the risk of 'circularity of reasoning' in review, i.e. the review of the amendment would have to be carried out on the basis of that amendment. In fact, if the Tribunal issued a ruling on the unconstitutionality of the amendment based on that amendment, it would contradict itself since such a decision would be based on the law declared unconstitutional. In such a situation, the only logical ruling would be one on the constitutionality of the amendment.

By depriving the Tribunal of an opportunity to declare the unconstitutionality of a lower-order legal act through its immediate entry into force, the legislator undermined the principle of the supremacy of the Constitution, because a law would be binding whose constitutionality could not be reviewed.

Obviously, the legislator cannot be deprived of the legitimacy to make changes in the organization and functioning of the Constitutional Tribunal.[26] However, such changes must be introduced within the framework of the Constitution (a statute cannot change constitutional concepts), they cannot destroy the balance of powers (through the lack of ability to review the law) and they cannot make radical changes without vacatio legis. The specificity of the position of a constitutional court in the system of government is part of the essence of the rule of law. Otherwise, the unconstitutionality of the legislator's activity is assumed by default. An intentionally different interpretation of such a sensitive principle as the principle of separation and balance of powers could lead to a change in the constitutional identity.

My purpose is not to analyse all existing legislation concerning the Tribunal (passed in the years 2015–2016), nevertheless, it is difficult to mention only the amendment of December 2015 as an instance of a regulation undermining the Constitution. I would like to present one more example. Another 'remedy law' of July 2016 introduced the principle that the legality of certain judgements of the Tribunal could be determined by the Prime Minister.[27] The fact that the executive decided on the publication of rulings deprived the Tribunal of the ability to review the constitutionality of the law. The executive would assume a control function with regard to the court. Such a change of the relationship between powers would interfere with the independence of the judiciary and, undoubtedly, it would endanger the identity of the Constitution.

3.3 What is the future of the Constitutional Tribunal?

On 20 December 2016 the President of the Republic appointed the new President of the Constitutional Tribunal.[28] The new President included three judges elected on 2 December 2015 in the bench. The Tribunal is thus seated with 15 judges, although the following reservations must be kept in mind: a) the status of three judges included in the bench on 20 December is debatable in the light of the Tribunal's judgement of 3 December 2015; b) three judges elected by the Sejm of the seventh term, who were not sworn in by the President, but, in the light of the Tribunal's judgement of 3 December 2015, were elected in accordance with the law, are not included in the bench. As already mentioned, the present bench seems to hinder or prevent the functioning of the Tribunal.

At the moment, the future of the judicial review of the constitutionality of the law in Poland is unknown. Surely, different visions of the constitutional court are possible, including various mechanisms of electing judges or the Tribunal's functioning. Almost every political party has a certain idea with regard to the Tribunal. Questions arose whether the Constitutional Tribunal is necessary in Poland – what is the Constitutional Tribunal for? Some politicians and lawyers pointed out that there are countries in which there is no constitutional court, yet they are also democratic.[29] It seems that Poland's political system is undergoing a change in that constitutional democracy (where the Constitution is the supreme law whose guardian is the Constitutional Tribunal) is turning into representative democracy (where the majority decides).[30]

The most negative aspect of the conflict concerning the staffing of the Tribunal is, in my opinion, the fact that a division between 'our judges' and 'your judges' developed. Such a division is deadly in that it destroys the Tribunal's ability to function. It also devastates the position of the Constitutional Tribunal. It undermined trust in this institution. It is a consequence of the rejection of the idea of the Tribunal as an independent entity, an independent body of the judiciary. Politicians also rejected a sort of democratic myth which the Tribunal represents in countries with established democracy. Such an approach to the Tribunal has been replaced by perceiving it as a political body dependent on the ruling majority. It is a paradoxical situation whereby elected judges do not exercise their office and those elected for seats already filled do. The attack on the Constitutional Tribunal and its judges has caused irreversible damage to the legal culture. A 'positive' aspect of the conflict is, however, very relative. It is the fact that citizens have been made aware of the existence of the constitutional judiciary and of its role in the protection of their constitutional rights.

It is difficult to predict how the degradation of the Tribunal and its judges could be overcome in the future. Proposals to introduce a two thirds majority of votes as a condition for the election of a judge by the Sejm would require a consensus of political forces concerning the change in the Constitution. An agreement among politicians with regard to a constitutional amendment seems difficult to achieve, given a high degree of mistrust towards each other. The question also arises whether such a majority would dismiss allegations against constitutional judges being politically motivated? So far, the judges have been treated as having political views, but in spite of this, they were seen as independent.

In my opinion, the Tribunal obviously does not have to exist. Some countries indeed do without a constitutional court. However, if there were no Constitutional Tribunal, Poland would become an arena of completely arbitrary legislative activity. And the continuity and permanence of law are one of the greatest values of the rule of law.

Notes

1 The Constitutional Tribunal was introduced into the Constitution of the People's Republic of Poland in 1982, still in the period of martial law. Three years later, in 1985, the Parliament adopted the Law on the Constitutional Tribunal. The Tribunal began functioning on 1 January 1986. For more about the origins of the judicial review of the constitutionality of the law in Poland see Granat (2003) 23.
2 Cf. Art. 173 of the Constitution.
3 Cf. Art. 194 of the Constitution.
4 Cf. Journal of Laws of 2016, item 2073.
5 Cf. Art. 30 and 31 of the Rules of the Sejm.

6 Cf. Art. 190(1) of the Constitution.
7 Cf. Journal of Laws of 2016, item 2072.
8 Cf. Art. 11(10) of this law.
9 Cf. Art. 190(4) of the Constitution.
10 Cf. Art. 190(1) of the Constitution.
11 Between May 1986 and May 2016, the Tribunal issued more than 10,000 decisions, including more than 1,300 judgements, many of which were essential for human rights and democratic rule of law.
12 It was manifested in politicians' statements, such as 'let the matter be decided by the Constitutional Tribunal' or 'we will challenge the legislation before the Tribunal and wait for the verdict'.
13 Cf. judgement of 28 October 2015, no. K 21/14, OTK ZU, no. 9/A/2015, item 152, 1974.
14 Ibid. 1969.
15 Ibid.1964.
16 Ibid.1976.
17 Granat (2016).
18 Cf. judgement of 19 December 2012, no. K 9/12, OTK ZU no. 11/A/2012, item 136.
19 Cf. OTK ZU no. 11/A/2012, item 136, 1792–1795.
20 Cf. 6.2.6 and 6.2.8 in the statement of reasons for the judgement in this case.
21 This is still a modest amount compared with the cost of living.
22 Cf. K 9/12, OTK ZU no. 11/A/2012, item 136, 1814.
23 Cf. K 9/12, OTK ZU no. 11/A/2012, item 136, 1812.
24 Cf. judgement of 3 December 2015, no. K 34/15, OTK ZU no. 11A, item 185.
25 The application in this case was submitted on 27 January 2017 by the Ombudsman.
26 Cf. Art. 197 of the Constitution which gives the legislator authority to pass a law on the organisation and functioning of the Constitutional Tribunal.
27 Under Article 80(4) of this law, the President of the Constitutional Court had to make a request to the Prime Minister to publish the judgement of the Tribunal.
28 On 19 December 2016 the term of office of the previous President expired.
29 Stawrowski (2016).
30 As regards the background of political and constitutional changes in Poland (and Hungary) as well as the EU's stance, cf. Halmai (2016).

Bibliography

Granat, Mirosław, 'Trybunał Konstytucyjny. Osiągnięcie czy zadanie?', in A. Szmnyt (ed.), *Trzecia władza. Sądy i Trybunały w Polsce* (Gdańsk University Press 2003).

Granat, Mirosław, 'Ile sprawiedliwości w sprawiedliwości społecznej?', in W. Arndt and S. Bober (eds.), *Sprawiedliwość społeczna w polityce polskiej* (Akademia Ignatianum 2016).

Halmai, Gábor, Second-grade Constitutionalism? Hungary and Poland: How the EU Can and Should Cope with Illiberal Member State', Working Paper, EUI Law Department, Faculty Seminar (2016).

Stawrowski, Zbiniew, 'Kto jest w Polsce suwerenem' (2016). *Rzeczpospolita*, 20 February.

10 Constitutional law and crisis

The Portuguese Constitutional Court under pressure?

Mariana Canotilho

Introduction

The Portuguese mechanism of judicial review was instituted by the Constitution of the Portuguese Republic of 1976, approved after the military and democratic Revolution of 1974. Its current features, however, were enshrined in the Constitution after the 1982 amendment process. It is a mixed system, as it contains elements that are typical of concentrated, Kelsen-type review and others that are usually found in common law, judicial review countries.

The Constitutional Court has specific competence to judge matters of a constitutional nature. It has exclusive competences in cases of preventive (*a priori*) and abstract (*a posteriori*) review of constitutionality and unconstitutionality by omission, as well as in a set of matters related to other constitutional organs of the State. As for concrete judicial review of legislation, the Constitutional Court functions as an appeals' court, reviewing the decisions of ordinary courts in matters of constitutionality. In fact, unlike most European systems, in Portugal all judges have what is known as direct access to the Constitution and may review norms that are to be applied in judicial cases.

During the recent economic crisis, especially in the period between 2010 and 2015, the Portuguese Constitutional Court has been called upon to review the constitutionality (mostly in *a posteriori* abstract review proceedings) of several pieces of legislation that implemented or transposed into the national legal order so-called 'austerity measures', agreed with EU authorities and the IMF, in exchange for economic support. Some of the Court's decisions, especially the ones declaring the unconstitutionality of State Budget's norms, have led to strong criticism and to a vivid (and sometimes harsh) public debate.[1] The Court was accused by some authors and politicians of unprecedented judicial activism, and acclaimed by others as the 'last defender' of fundamental rights and of the Constitution.[2] This chapter will analyse such jurisprudence and the role of the Constitutional Court, and try to explain why I think the critics are fundamentally unfair, as the Court has mainly followed jurisprudential paths it had previously tried.

1. Economic and social crisis and its legal consequences

The outbursts of the economic crisis in 2008, and, later on, the impact of the Eurozone sovereign debt crisis have had particularly severe effects in Portugal. The data speak for themselves: Between 2008 and 2015, public debt went up (from 71.7 per cent to 129 per cent of the GDP); during the same period, investment fell almost 40 per cent in nominal terms. In a country with approximately 10 million people, between 2010 and 2013 almost 500,000 jobs were destroyed, which led to a huge rise in unemployment (from 7.6 per cent in 2008 to 16.2 per cent in 2013, which still remained at 12.4 per cent in 2015), especially among young people. Emigration reached impressive numbers as well. More than 100,000 people have left the country, definitively or temporarily, every year since 2011, with a record of 134,000 emigrants in 2014.[3]

The Portuguese Government soon felt the need to design a strategy to endorse solid budgetary consolidation aimed at the reduction of the general government deficit, and to control the growth of the general government debt, in order to reduce its proportion of the GDP. The first Stability and Growth Programme, which contained several austerity measures including retroactive taxation and reductions in public workers' salaries, adopted in order to decrease the budget deficit, dates back to March 2010.

One year later, in May 2011, the Government negotiated a bailout programme with the European Commission (EC), the European Central Bank (ECB) and the International Monetary Fund (IMF). The bailout took the form of an agreement on an Economic and Financial Adjustment Programme[4] with the *Troika* (composed of the ECB, the Commission and the IMF) whereby the Portuguese Republic undertook several commitments in exchange for a financial loan of 78 billion Euro at lower rates than the ones offered by the markets.[5] Two opposition parties also signed the agreement.

From a legal and constitutional point of view, the Memoranda are atypical instruments, approved by a Government resolution.[6] This specific approval method, without the intervention of the Parliament in such a sensitive matter, would seem to indicate the clear political nature of the documents, but such classification is not followed by many national authors, nor by the Constitutional Court. In fact, the Court has stated[7] that the Memoranda are legally binding for the Portuguese State, insofar as they are based on the international law treaties that have created the entities that take part in them, and of which Portugal is a member. The Court has, thus, acknowledged the situation of financial distress and accepted the country's legal obligations under international and European Union law, which have been seen as a relevant element of constitutional interpretation.

As for legal doctrine, there is no agreement about the legal classification of the Memoranda. Some argue that they are international contracts; a few state that they are treaties – with the consequent legal status foreseen in the national constitution. Finally, others, following the position of the IMF itself, think that the Memorandum signed with the Fund is formed by two distinct, unilateral acts (one act of the IMF and the other act of the Portuguese State) whereas the Memorandum signed with the European Commission and the ECB is a European law instrument with simple political – not legal – obligations.[8]

This uncertainty regarding the legal status of the Adjustment Programme clearly shows how the whole process is an example of a worrying trend[9] of escape from the traditional mechanisms of constitutional law, thus avoiding the legal demands and obligations imposed by it. That is the reason that justifies the intent – quite clear in the case of the Memorandum signed with the IMF – of maintaining the agreements with the *Troika* in a merely political plan. At the same time, most authors defend the legally binding character of the Memoranda, stating that there are legal consequences in case of non-compliance; however, most academics also sustain a view according to which the intervention of the Parliament in the negotiation and signing process is not necessary, it being sufficient the approval by the Government and the signature of the President.[10]

Despite the arguments favouring it, the lack of intervention of the Parliament in the adoption of the Memoranda raises doubts from a constitutional point of view. It is actually arguable that some of the matters regulated in the bailout agreement are included in the reserve of competence of the Parliament (Art. 165 of the Portuguese Constitution), which has already intervened, in the past, in the adoption of other instruments concerning public finances, debt and deficit.[11]

The Economic and Financial Adjustment Programme specified yearly fiscal objectives but also commitments to implement certain public policies and to reform legislation in specific matters, especially in areas concerning economic and social rights (education, health, social security, working conditions), which, according to the Portuguese Constitution, are considered full-fledged fundamental rights, and not mere government objectives or guidelines. Therefore, the Economic and Financial Adjustment functioned as a catalyst of national legislation adopted in order to transpose the commitments to the national legal order, as well as a political and legal argument to justify profound and contested changes to social policies.

Representatives of the *Troika* closely monitored the implementation of the Programme and the delivery of the subsequent tranches of the loan depended on a positive evaluation by the monitoring committee, conducted on a regular basis.

A significant part of this legislation establishes austerity measures that have been challenged by unconstitutionality claims before the Constitutional Court. The review proceedings have earned the Portuguese Constitutional Court unprecedented attention not only nationally but also internationally. The focus on the Portuguese Constitutional Court and its case law on austerity legislation have re-ignited the national debate on the problem of the guardian of the Constitution and who should be the last interpreter of the fundamental law.

The implementation of the austerity measures has had economic, social and fiscal consequences that raise several constitutional issues. The vast majority of these measures have been challenged in procedures of abstract review of constitutionality. Such abstract reviews have been filed both in *a priori* (preventive) and *a posteriori* (successive) proceedings, i.e. before the bill has been ratified by the President of the Republic, or after the legislative procedure has been duly concluded and the legislative act has entered into force. The next section of this work describes some of the most important case law and analyses the grounds of the Court's decisions.

2. The Constitutional Court under pressure?

During the crisis period, and up to 2014, the Constitutional Court delivered a significant number of decisions regarding austerity measures. Most of these decisions are rather long for the normal standards of the Court and argumentatively complex, so their analysis is not easy. If we centre the attention on the abstract review of constitutionality, we will find around 12 decisions divided in accordance with three main subjects: (1) legislation concerning (i) public sector workers concerning pay-cuts (2011/2012/2013/2014/2015), (ii) extra work and working time, (iii) requalification of public workers; (2) legislation concerning retired citizens that deals with (i) pay-cuts and special solidarity contribution, (ii) convergence of pension systems, (iii) special sustainability contribution; and (3) legislation concerning taxes and other sources of tax revenue that deals with (i) surtax on personal income tax, (ii) personal income tax brackets reduction, (iii) additional solidarity tax, reduction of itemised deductions, (iv) contribution imposed upon sick and unemployment benefits.[12]

2.1 Legislation concerning public sector workers

Pay-cuts of public sector workers were one of the most contested and repeated austerity measures, having remained partially in place up until 2015. They were adopted both by the socialist Government in 2011 and by the conservative coalition in 2012, 2013, 2014 and 2015. The rules imposing the cuts have been brought before the Constitutional Court on several occasions, and analysed in Decisions 396/11 (*State Budget 2011*),[13] 353/12 (*State Budget 2012*),[14] 187/13 (*State Budget 2013*),[15] 413/2014 (*State Budget 2014*)[16] and 574/2014 (*Pay-cuts 2014–2018*).[17]

In its first decision in 2011 – regarding pay-cuts that varied between 3.5 per cent and 10 per cent progressively – the Court reviewed a number of norms of the State Budget Law for 2011 upon request by the opposition's Members of Parliament. The first remark it made – one that was repeated in many judgments afterwards – was that provisions such as the those regarding pay-cuts should be deemed to be temporary, a conclusion drawn from the Government's Report on the State Budget.[18]

In the Court's words:

> these measures will last for several years, but that does not allow us to question their transitory character, bearing in mind the nature and objectives pursued, which consist in a normative answer to an exceptional situation that is supposed to be corrected, urgent and briefly, back to normal standards.[19]

The Court then recognised that the right to pay is a fundamental right enshrined in the Portuguese Constitution and that it enjoys the special protection conferred upon liberty rights (*direitos, liberdades e garantias*). However, it stressed that there is an important difference between the right to be paid and the right to receive a specific amount of money, not reducible by law, however the circumstances and the economic and financial variables influencing it.[20]

The Constitutional Court finally analysed if the imposition of sacrifices only to public workers, to ensure the fulfilment of a public goal that benefits the whole political community, violated fundamental constitutional principles, such as the principle of equality. The Court declared that it is not within its powers to enter into the debate over the equivalence of effects between measures that reduce the State's expenses (such as pay-cuts) and others that increase the State's gains (such as raising taxes). Therefore, in the absence of a definitive answer, the Constitutional Court decided that the measures under appreciation should be considered admissible and constitutional, especially if one recalls the urgency of the measures.

The following year, 2012, the newly-elected Government not only maintained the 2011 pay-cuts but also added a new austerity measure: the partial or total suspension of Christmas and holiday pay[21] for all public sector employees with salaries between 600 and 1,100 Euros, or over 1,100 Euros per month, respectively.

Opposition Members of Parliament asked the Constitutional Court once again to review the constitutionality of these new measures. This time, however, the Court considered that it was necessary to prove that, more than one year later, additional pay-cuts were the best and/or only measure at the Government's disposal to reach public objectives related to public deficit and debt. Although admitting that the legislature's choice was particularly effective and produced quick results, the Court ruled that even in a context of crisis there must be a limit to the possibility of discrimination against public workers, by cutting their wages. The Court concluded that in this case the sacrifices imposed upon public workers had no equivalent to what was demanded from their fellow citizens, even from those receiving high incomes from other sources. Therefore, it declared the unconstitutionality of the additional pay-cuts.

Nevertheless, in a very contested decision, the Court decided to suspend the effects of its ruling, causing, in practice, that the unconstitutional measures were effectively applied during 2012, and only forbidden from then on.

The Government then decided to redraw the austerity measures adopted to reduce the deficit and public debt. The State Budget Law for 2013 enacted one of the biggest tax raises the country has ever seen, especially as regards the personal annual income tax (IRS); measures that were reviewed by the Constitutional Court and considered constitutionally valid. However, added to this, another pay-cut was imposed on public workers – this time the suspension of the additional holiday pay (the Christmas pay was not suspended). The 2011 pay-cuts, previously approved by the Constitutional Court, as was mentioned earlier, also remained in place.

This time, the Court's intervention was requested both by the Head of State, President Cavaco Silva, by two groups of opposition Members of Parliament and by the Ombudsman. In its judgment, the Court recalled that the right to pay enshrined in the Constitution does not imply that it is impossible, under any circumstance, to apply pay-cuts, and therefore that Article 59 of the Fundamental Law cannot ground a ruling of unconstitutionality in this case. Therefore, the

Court relied heavily on its 2011 and 2012 decisions, affirming that the question was to assess whether the sacrifice the restrictive measures implied for public workers could be considered valid and in accordance with the principles of equality, proportionality and the protection of legitimate expectations, which it was not. This time, however, the Court did not moderate any of the consequences of the unconstitutionality ruling, so the Government was forced to pay the full amount of the holiday pay to all public employees.

Finally, in 2014, yet again two opposition groups of the Parliament demanded the constitutional review of several norms of the State Budget Law for 2014. Among the contested norms was the one that introduced new pay-cuts designed to overcome the previous declarations of unconstitutionality of the suspension of the holiday and Christmas pay. Following these guidelines, a new pay-cut varying from 2.5 per cent to 12 per cent was to be applied to public sector workers with wages greater than 675 Euros. These cuts should replace the 2011 cuts (which ranged between 3.5 per cent and 10 per cent to wages greater than 1,500 Euros) that had been enforced since then up to the end of 2013.

The Constitutional Court recalled its 2011, 2012 and 2013 decisions, stressing that it had already admitted a certain degree of difference in treatment between public and private workers, provided that the difference in question was proportional and justified. The Court then stated that the degree of sacrifice demanded of public workers with the new law was significantly greater. Some of the wages affected, the Court said,

> are so low in the first place that any reduction has a strong negative impact and produces a sacrifice much greater than its objective quantification.[22]

Therefore, the Court once again declared the pay-cuts unconstitutional due to the violation of the principle of equality, especially of equality regarding public burdens. However, it decided to repeat the limitation of effects of its decision and ruled that they would only be applied *ex nunc*, that is, from the moment of the sentence on. Since the decision was enacted at the end of May, this limitation meant that, in practice, the cuts were kept in force for five months.

After this judgment, a new bill reinstated the 2011 pay-cuts and established a timeframe for the reduction of those cuts; they were supposed to diminish by 20 per cent in 2015 and then more in the remaining years, up to 2018, when the full wage should be reinstated to all public workers. Called upon to review the new measures, the Court's reasoning[23] is again centred on the principles of equality and of the protection of legitimate expectations. Following previous case-law, in particular the *State Budget 2014*[24] decision, the Court admitted the possibility of pay-cuts for the remainder of the year 2014 and 2015, bearing in mind that the country was still subject to an excessive deficit procedure by European authorities and that the whole economic and financial situation could not yet be considered normal. To reach this judgment, it was considered highly relevant that the pay-cuts for 2015 would be 20 per cent lower. However, for the period 2016–2018, the Constitutional Court affirmed that one could no longer consider the cuts to be a temporary measure, and therefore declared the pay-cuts for the years 2016–2018 to be unconstitutional for violating the principle of equality. The Court also remembered that it is not constitutionally admissible to base the whole strategy for balanced public finances on the reduction of expenses focused on a continuous sacrifice of public workers.

The Court's rulings in the cases described above have been highly criticised. G. A. Ribeiro accused it of unpredictability and illegitimacy.[25] Other authors have said the Court did not distinguish fundamental constitutional rights from legal rights, and did not understand that different constitutional problems demand different intensities of scrutiny from its part.[26] In their dissenting vote in the 2013 decision,[27] five Judges, including the Vice-President M. L. Amaral, supported these criticisms, stating that in situations like the one analysed – pay-cuts for public workers to meet the country's extraordinary financial demands – the Constitutional Court can only declare the unconstitutionality of measures that are evidently unreasonable, but it cannot substitute the legislator to choose the best solution for any given problem.

I do not agree with the criticism. It is obviously possible to disagree with the Court's decisions, both from the political and the legal points of view. That will often be an opinion directly connected to the way in which each author regards the interpretation of constitutional norms and the role of the Constitutional Court in the national political system, as well as their vision about the solutions chosen to tackle the crisis during the last decade. However, I do not think the Court was illegitimate or unpredictable. First of all, the Court did not declare the unconstitutionality of all the austerity measures under review. As we will see below, in matters such as labour and tax law, it gave a wide margin of appreciation to the legislator, letting many of the measures stay in place. To affirm the Court's judgement in the cases of pay-cuts was illegitimate really implies that it could not strike down almost any legislative initiative in times of financial crisis – a kind of financial state of exception whose existence is not supported, in any way, by the Constitution. The Court's position was perfectly acceptable within the Portuguese constitutional system, and it did not surpass or abuse its powers. On the contrary, I believe it performed exactly according to its role, which is to uphold constitutional norms.[28]

On the other hand, it is my opinion that the perception of the Court's decisions as unpredictable derives from a lack of understanding of its reasoning and arguments. From the very beginning, as has been shown, the Constitutional Court has insisted in the transitory character of the austerity measures as a fundamental element of their constitutional admissibility. As time goes by, this argument becomes progressively weaker, and it should be expected that the Court would add additional layers of scrutiny, namely a more thorough analysis of fundamental principles such as equality and proportionality, which are recurrent grounds for its decisions.

The legislation regarding overtime and working time provides good examples of the self-restraint of the Court and its respect for the legislator. This legislation was subject to important changes during the period of economic crisis, justified by the Government with the need to reduce salaries (the amount of an hour's work) and to increase productivity. The reduction of overtime pay was one of the measures the Government agreed with the *Troika*. It was first put in practice with the amendments to the Labour Code (*Código do Trabalho*) approved in 2012, which reduced the payment of extra hours by 50 per cent and eliminated the period of rest that was given to the worker as compensation for doing extra work. The opposition parties asked the Court to review these changes. In its decision,[29] the Court stressed that despite the strong reduction of compensation for extra working hours, there was still a more favourable treatment of that kind of work as far as payment is concerned. For this reason, the norms were considered in accordance with the Constitution. Similar but even higher cuts concerning overtime pay were imposed upon public workers both in the State Budget Law for 2012 and the State Budget Law for 2013. The Constitutional Court reviewed the measure upon request filed by a minority group of Members of Parliament. It stated that the additional payment of overtime could not be technically considered as salary, unlike the holidays and Christmas pay, because it did not have the regularity that is the latter's characteristic feature.[30] Since overtime is not included in the concept of salary, at least in a direct and necessary way, the constitutional protection of the right to pay cannot be invoked as a ground of unconstitutionality. There are no legitimate expectations to an additional compensation for extra work that deserve constitutional protection. Therefore, the Constitutional Court did not declare the norms under scrutiny unconstitutional.

Regarding working time, the Parliament approved legislation proposed by the Government, increasing the normal working time of public employees from 7 hours a day and 35 hours a week to 8 hours a day and 40 hours a week. This measure was highly contested by trade unions and the entire political opposition, who immediately used their Members of Parliament groups to ask the Constitutional Court to review the new norms. However, the Court considered[31] that the new law and 40 hours per week working time corresponded to a free and fundamental choice of the legislature, that should be understood in the context of a reform of public administration, in order to make its legal regime closer to that of private workers. The Constitutional Court recognised that the 5 hour increase in working time implied a big sacrifice for public workers, making it more difficult to harmonise their private and family lives with their working lives, and even causing additional public expenses and admitted that the new working time entrenched a real pay-cut by raising the working time without equally increasing the salary. But such loss of salary was considered similar to the decrease in overtime pay, which the Court had already ruled constitutionally admissible. Even the cases, also foreseen by the new norms, in which a public worker can now be demanded to work more than 40 hours a week were not judged unconstitutional by the Court, because the 40 hour limit can only be overcome by the legal flexibility mechanisms. These mechanisms, identical to the ones that exist for private working relations, had already been reviewed by the Court and considered allowed by the Constitution, as a legitimate restriction to the worker's right to rest and to leisure time.[32] Furthermore, the Court considered that the new working time of public workers had some advantages to the general public, as it allowed for expansion to the opening hours of public services, which had a positive effect on every individual user and in broader terms, on the whole of the society. It also complied with one of the demands of the European Commission, the European Central Bank and the International Monetary Fund to decrease the expenses with public workers' pay through the reduction in overtime compensation and the restrictions to new hires. For these reasons, the Constitutional Court declared that the norms under review were constitutionally valid.

Finally, as to what regards austerity measures that affect public workers, it is important to mention Decision 474/2013[33] (*Public Workers Requalification*) adopted following an *a priori* review request by the President of the Republic. The Constitutional Court was asked to review draft legislation approved by the Parliament, upon Government's initiative, that set up a new system of reduction of the number of public workers. That system effectively allowed for the dismissal of public workers under a set number of conditions. Since the Portuguese Constitution expressly forbids firing a worker without due cause (Art. 53) the reasons to justify the dismissal, in this case, were all presented as having an objective ground, which both the law and constitutional jurisprudence had already admitted could be applied both to private and public workers. In fact, the Constitutional Court had said several times that the Constitution does not guarantee an absolute protection against dismissal· The Court also reminded that there have been several reforms that made the legal regime of public workers quite similar to the private workers' statute. However, there is a dimension of job security applicable to public workers with tenure that has not really been affected by those reforms. The workers' expectations on this issue were also reinforced by many of the austerity measures imposed upon them to reduce public expenses and public deficit. Moreover, the Constitutional Court explained, the legislature did not explain the public interest reasons that could possibly justify yet another unfavourable change of the public workers' status, especially one that clearly goes against the expectations created by previous State's actions. For this reason, the norms under review were considered unconstitutional. This decision was almost unanimous and draws extensively on previous jurisprudence, both on the decisions about austerity measures and others regarding the statute of public workers.[34]

Almost all these decisions about pay-cuts and public workers develop quite extensively the jurisprudential interpretation of the equality principle. They do not however, in my opinion, create an entirely new understanding of such principle, nor does the Court abandon its previous jurisprudence on equality. Even authors with a critical view of these rulings admit that the Court does not seem to abandon its former understanding of equality as prohibition of arbitrary decisions.[35] It has merely intensified its scrutiny, according to a more demanding formula of 'proportional equality', similar to the one adopted by the German Constitutional Court, combining both dimensions of the principle in other decisions that have nothing to do with austerity measures.[36]

2.2 Legislation applied to retired citizens

Retired citizens were another category highly affected by the sacrifices demanded in order to achieve the goal of reducing public deficit and public debt. In fact, they have suffered pay-cuts very similar to the ones imposed upon the public sector workers, although not always through the same legislative measures.

One common cut was the suspension of the extra holiday and Christmas pay in 2012 and the suspension of the payment of 90 per cent of the holiday pay in 2013. These norms were brought before the Constitutional Court and analysed in the *State Budget 2012* and *State Budget 2013* decisions. The Court affirmed in both decisions that all the arguments presented to justify the rulings on the public workers' pay-cuts were also relevant as regards retired citizens', especially what had been stressed about the principle of equality regarding public burdens and the principle of proportionality. Moreover, the Court added that there were also specific grounds of unconstitutionality that only concerned retired citizens, such as the principle of the protection of legitimate expectations. This principle had a high relevance because, in most cases, these citizens cannot choose an alternative source of income or change their life plans; unlike workers, who at least in theory may seek a better job, enhance their qualifications or even try emigration – for retired citizens the fundamental life choices have already been made. For this reason, the Court stated, for retired citizens the suspension of Christmas and holidays pay might mean 'the utter impossibility of adapting their life plan to a new scenario', and declared them unconstitutional both in 2012 and 2013 (applying the same restriction of its decision's effects, in 2012, as was stated above).

In order to impose another pay-cut on retired citizens similar to the one applied from 2011 to 2013 to public workers, a Special Solidarity Contribution (CES) was approved. The measure was first applied in 2011 by imposing a 10 per cent contribution on pensions above 5,000 Euros per month before taxes and other contributions. In 2012 and 2013 these rules were aggravated and revised and a much greater number of pensioners were affected. The contribution paid by the pensioners was destined for the different branches of the social security system responsible for paying their retirement allowances, so it was an intra-systemic measure. Such a measure was highly contested, both from the political and constitutional points of view, and its declaration of unconstitutionality was taken for granted by many commentators following the review requests made by the President of the Republic, the Ombudsman and opposition Members of Parliament in 2013. However, that was not the conclusion reached by the Constitutional Court. Although it recognised that this kind of obligation was a deviation to the normal functioning of social security, the Court stated that the possibility of using other sources of financing is within the margin of appreciation of the legislature. Furthermore, the Constitutional Court stressed that this was a temporary measure, created in times of severe economic and financial crisis to ensure that the social security system is able to fulfil all the obligations taken on by the State. Bearing in mind the specific relationship of the retired citizens with that system, the Court found that the special contribution imposed upon them could be considered proportional and justified.

At the end of 2013, the Government proposed the Parliament a reform of the legal regime of former public workers' pensions that established a unilateral and definitive 10 per cent cut in the total amount of former public workers' pensions and imposed that a part of those pensions should be recalculated according to the formula used for the general social security system. The Government considered that the public system had had more favourable rules in the past, and that it was neither fair nor sustainable, and should be more similar to the general social security system. The President challenged the measures and sent them to the Constitutional Court for prior review. In a unanimous decision, the Court ruled this legislation unconstitutional on grounds of the violation of the principle of the protection of legitimate expectations.[37] The Court noted that both public and private systems are much more complex than one would see only by looking at the formulas used to calculate pensions, and both have an intricate set of rules some of which are less favourable in the CGA (Caixa Geral de Aposentações) than in the general social security system, and explained that to allow a cut in pensions already being paid, a measure that entails a very strong violation of the confidence that its beneficiaries have in the system and in the State itself, could only be justified if it was integrated in a general, structural and well-studied reform that took into account several different factors. This was not the case. The Constitutional Court considered the norms under review as an isolated measure with the sole purpose of immediately reducing expenses, and sustained that it could do nothing else than judge the norms under review to be unconstitutional.

Following this decision, the Special Solidarity Contribution was yet again redesigned and once more brought to the Constitutional Court for review by Members of Parliament of the opposition. In its Decision 572/2014,[38] the Constitutional Court maintained its 2013 reasoning, stating that the importance of the contribution's purpose (the balance and short-term sustainability of the social security system) justified its prevalence over the rights of pensioners. Two main arguments were crucial to this position: the fact that the Court still considered the special solidarity contribution to be temporary and exceptional; and, secondly, the fact that the contribution still was, to some degree, a redistributive measure, due to its different and progressive rates, which was in harmony with the principle of self-financing of the social security system and in accordance with the principle of proportionality.

Finally, one should notice the Constitutional Court's decision on the Special Sustainability Contribution.[39] This contribution was designed to replace the Special Solidarity Contribution applied to retired citizens between 2011 and 2014, and it basically consisted of a contribution very similar to its predecessor but with lower applicable rates. Unlike its predecessor, the new contribution was to be permanent and it did not include the amounts paid by private pension schemes, outside the general public social security system. In the legislative proposal, the Government alleged that it was of vital importance to the long-term sustainability of social security and that this measure was a special contribution to social security, similar to the one applied in 2013 and 2014 that had been characterised as such by the Constitutional Court. The Court, however, did not agree. It stressed that by excluding private pension schemes, the legislature had transformed the measure in a simple and straightforward cut.[40] The Court explained that the simple and isolated reduction of the rates could not transform a typical austerity measure – meant to allow immediate savings and the decrease of public expenses – into a structural measure, able to guarantee the medium and long term sustainability of the public pensions' system. For this reason, it decided to declare the unconstitutionality of the Special Sustainability Contribution.

This jurisprudence is understandably grounded on a review of the proportionality of the measures, as well as in the protection of legitimate expectations, which acquires added importance in situations that have been steady over a long period of time. This principle has been thoroughly developed by the Constitutional Court for many years, with the Court establishing a strict test to determine whether or not it has been violated.[41] Again, I believe it is unfair to affirm that the Court's decision was unexpected or unusual, as it represents a recurrent argument that has been used again since these decisions.[42]

2.3 Taxes and other sources of tax revenue

In Decision 399/2010[43] the Constitutional Court ruled on the constitutionality of a law establishing a surtax on the IRS enacted in June 2010 (therefore, even prior to the bailout). Since the surtax was established in June (and increased in July) but was applicable to all of the 2010 personal annual income, the question brought before the Constitutional Court was focused on the retroactive character of the measure.[44] The Court decided that it is possible to enact legal provisions on a given tax, during their tax periods, which are designed to produce effects for the entire period. This possibility, however, must pass the test of the principle of the protection of legitimate expectations. The Constitutional Court, in applying this test, concluded that, on the one hand, given the socio-economic situation and the political discourse around it, the taxpayers could reasonably and objectively expect a tax increase in the short-term. On the other hand, the relative importance of the public interest at stake – the soundness of the State's public finances – was considered to be sufficient to justify the measure when the Court balanced it against the public's expectations. It concluded that the law could not be considered intolerable or unbearable to the taxpayers.

The Budget Law of 2013 established yet another surtax on the personal annual income tax. The question of constitutionality brought before the Constitutional Court was the compatibility of this surtax with two constitutional principles that must be followed in terms of personal income tax law: there must be a single tax and it must be progressive.

In line with the previous case law, the Constitutional Court, in Decision 187/2013 (*State Budget 2013*), considered the 2013 surtax not unconstitutional. It considered that the tax incidence of both taxes was the same – on the same income – which is the 'essential dimension of the constitutional requirement of unity' of the personal income tax. For the Court, the differences between regimes existed only in secondary aspects of tax law and were 'exceptions' which represented the 'temporary' and 'exceptional' adaptation of the personal income tax system to relevant public interests, well within the 'margin of appreciation' of the legislature.

The margin of appreciation was repeatedly invoked in the review of other pieces of tax law, namely the one establishing reduction of the number of tax brackets from the previous 8 to 5 and generally increasing the tax rates applicable to each specific range of taxable income. The constitutionality of these amendments was challenged once more on the basis of Article 104(1) of the Constitution – more specifically the requirement of progressiveness of the personal income tax, and that it must 'pay due regard to the needs and incomes of households'. The Court regarded the requirement of progressiveness of the personal income tax as undetermined and susceptible to various degrees of implementation by the legislature.[45] Hence, the constitutionally imposed progressiveness is only such that should bear the potential to reduce income inequality. This means, for instance, that a flat rate tax is forbidden by the Constitution, even if it does not cover a minimum subsistence level of per capita income. Again, and giving the legislator a large margin to define tax policies, the Court considered the amendments to the Personal Income Tax Code to be consistent with the Constitution, despite the reduction of the general level of progressiveness.

The same line of reasoning was followed in the analysis of other fiscal measures, such as the reduction of itemised deductions (expenses that reduce an individual's taxable income). The Constitutional Court accepted that this amendment to the tax code signified the increase of the tax due and a decrease of the correspondence between taxable income and real personal income, thus disregarding the ability-to-pay of families and households. However, the Court took into consideration the context of the amendments to the tax code – the general rise of taxation and a higher tax-paying effort demanded to all tax-payers, especially the ones with higher incomes. The ability-to-pay constitutional principle was regarded as a general principle and standard of the tax system, which does not justify a declaration of unconstitutionality of these measures.

2.4 The contribution imposed on sick and unemployment benefits

Finally, the 2013 Budget Law also imposed a 'contribution' of 5 per cent on sick benefits and of 6 per cent on unemployment benefits. The Constitutional Court was asked if the 'contribution' was in accordance with the Constitution – especially with the equality principle (because of the vulnerability of the beneficiaries) and the constitutional provisions that guarantee every worker's right to material assistance (Arts. 59(1(e)(f)), 63(3), of the Constitution).

The Court qualified this 'contribution' as a parafiscal tax equivalent to social security contributions – but levied on the beneficiaries of the benefits. Therefore, it considered that it did not have to comply with the constitutional rules governing taxes. However, the Court stated it had to determine whether the new rules, which burdened social security beneficiaries who were in a vulnerable position, were consistent with the principle of proportionality. Once again – as it affirmed in the case of salaries – the Court found that the constitutional right to social security, established in Article 63, does not cover the quantitative amount of the benefit in question. Nevertheless, the Constitutional Court judged the 'contribution' unconstitutional because of the absence of a protective clause that could safeguard the lower benefits. The Constitutional Court found that

> While one may not doubt the reversibility of concrete rights and subjectively grounded expectations, one cannot fail to recognize that, even in a state of economic emergency, there should always be a caveat regarding the essential core of minimum guarantees already put into effect by the general legislation governing entitlement to benefits in the contingencies of sickness or unemployment, so it [the contribution] may be considered contrary to the constitutional protection of a decent existence.[46]

The measures were re-enacted in 2014, although a safeguard of a minimum amount of income was added to the legislation. However, it was once again declared unconstitutional by the Court in the *State Budget 2014* Decision. The Constitutional Court stressed that it does not deem reasonable, even in a context of economic crisis, the imposition of further burdens on the life conditions of citizens already affected by disease or unemployment. It is my view that this concern with the constitutional protection of vulnerable citizens and their right to a decent existence is very much in line with the jurisprudence of the Court, both prior and posterior to this specific decision. Other good examples of this view are the Court's sentences regarding the right to a minimum income,[47] characterised as a positive dimension of the constitutional right to a decent existence, which derives from human dignity, a principle foreseen in Article 1 of the Constitution.

3. Conclusions and lessons from the Portuguese experience

The case law of the Portuguese Constitutional Court during the crisis period is a vivid (but not unique) example of the role that some courts have been forced to play in what is essentially a very complex political problem. In fact, in many cases, they were asked to rule on the compatibility between austerity measures and fundamental rights.

While the Portuguese Court's fundamental part during the crisis is usually either accused or praised for what is perceived as a firm intervention in the defence of individual rights, a closer analysis of the so-called 'crisis jurisprudence' allows me to affirm that the truth is less straightforward. Far from the judicial activism for which it is famous,[48] the Court has – as the examples above demonstrate, especially in what regards labour and tax law – adopted a notable degree of self-restraint in its decisions, and has given the margin of discretion of the legislature a significant role on its reasoning, by way of deferring to the legislature's choices. Consequently, a significant part of austerity legislation allegedly affecting fundamental rights has been considered to be according to the Constitution.

Furthermore, as has been previously noted, the Court has grounded its rulings on the breach of well-established constitutional principles such as equality, legal certainty and the protection of confidence and legitimate expectations. The decisions do not recognise the violation of specific fundamental rights *per se*, much less of social and economic rights, whose justiciability (and respective limits) is still discussed. This fact has several important consequences. It is true, on one hand, that this undermines the demands for judicial enforcing of social rights, as well as the long fight for the recognition of their equal status with traditional civic and political rights. However, unlike individual rights, whose modification through a reform of the Constitution could be easily achieved (upon consensus between the two major political parties), fundamental principles are not changeable, nor dischargeable, as they are the core of any democratic and constitutional state. This is not even a question of being part of the eternal clauses, stated in Art. 288 of the Constitution. It is more than that: a constitution is not democratic if it does not contain fundamental principles such as equality, proportionality and the rule of law. No matter what its specific content is, these will always have to be present. Consequently, it is virtually impossible to modify the constitutional framework that was used to uphold the Court's decisions, hence making them, somewhat surprisingly, more resistant to contingency.

Additionally, the protection of fundamental rights through general principles may be the easiest way to reach a majority decision, as it allows accommodating the conflicting views of the judges. It should be recalled that the Constitutional Court's judgments were usually not unanimous rulings (except in rare cases, such as the *Pensions' Convergence* decision), but a choice of the majority, where dissenting and concurrent opinions are always allowed. There are very different opinions regarding the legal status of social and economic rights, and the obligations that may impend upon the legislator due to such rights, for example. Therefore, some judges might find it problematic to ground a declaration of unconstitutionality solely on those norms; it is easier to agree upon a common reasoning and arguments based on principles.

It is arguable that some of the arguments used by the Constitutional Court to justify its rulings are quite interesting, in particular the ones related to a broad understanding of the principle of equality. In fact, as it has been seen above, the Court has upheld the need to provide special protection to the unemployed and the sick, due to their vulnerability; it has also taken into consideration the redistributive nature of certain fiscal measures to accept their compatibility with the Constitution. However, in general terms, the Portuguese constitutional jurisprudence has allowed for a greater margin of appreciation of the legislator, in order to give response to the problems caused by the economic crisis. The Court's decisions regarding the reforms of labour law, which have changed the balance of power within the working relationship in favour of the employers, are particularly representative of this fact, having in mind that the vast majority of the measures have not been deemed unconstitutional, although they include, for example, significant changes to collective labour agreements. This kind of reasoning is actually quite typical in matters of labour law, such as older rulings of the Court may demonstrate.[49]

The role of the Court during the crisis thus shows, on one hand, its undeniable importance as a mechanism of guarantee of fundamental rights and limit to the exercise of power. The Court was, for a brief period of time, the most important balance to the activities of the executive, upholding citizens' rights against it, as the decisions about pay-cuts and pensions demonstrate. It is true that, for many citizens, the Court has been the sole mechanism of the social and democratic state that has worked to their benefit, ensuring the protection and the public provisions that the constitutional pact had attributed them until the beginning of the crisis.

On the other hand, the Court's role also highlights the contradictions and limitations inherent to constitutional decisions. In fact, an objective analysis of the 'crisis jurisprudence' also shows some critical points and deficiencies.

First of all, one should remember that the Court is strongly limited in its action, which depends of concrete requests presented to it. Regarding this aspect, it is worth noting that minority Members of Parliament, in Portugal, have played a fundamental role by initiating the process of abstract judicial review of legislation of several measures, adopted to give response to the crises, which affected individuals' rights. That was the case of the pay-cuts of salaries and pensions in 2012 and 2013, as well as that of the special contribution imposed upon unemployment and sick benefits. This is actually a very interesting dimension of the possible dialogue between courts and parliaments, and an important mechanism of control of the legislative power exercised by the Government.

Secondly, there is a significant amount of legislation that has been considered to comply with constitutional demands, as well as an even bigger number of norms and measures that have not been challenged at all, such as many of the reforms concerning social security benefits, access to health and access to education.[50] Although in the legal and political discourse the discussion is usually about the declarations of unconstitutionality, these have been quite rare, if we take the total universe of austerity measures into consideration. Furthermore, the Court has sometimes limited the effects of its decisions, in order not to affect the balance of the State's Budget, pursued by the executive and legislative powers. The best example of these worries is the *State Budget 2012* decision, in which the effects of the declaration of unconstitutionality of the suspension of the Christmas and Holiday pays were limited by the Constitutional Court, in such a way that the unconstitutional measures were fully applied, in practise.

Thirdly, the 'crisis jurisprudence' was repeatedly accused of being manipulated by political minorities and groups of activists, in order to displace a normal political fight to the arena of judicial activism. Critics have stated that in the framework of a democratic political regime, political divergence should remain as such, and that its transference to the courts bears risks of contamination to both the political and the judicial fields.[51]

It is my view that the Constitutional Court is quite well protected against the risks of manipulation by all the guarantees of independence of the judiciary, having in mind all the constitutional and legal guarantees of independence given to the judges. Nevertheless, being a Court, it is not structurally prepared to solve large scale problems, only concrete ones; for that reason, political and ideological confrontation should not have the Constitutional Court as its primary scenario. Therefore, the ups and downs of some norms that guarantee social rights and benefits are a very good example of the way in which an individualistic and protective jurisprudence rapidly retreats – for understandable reasons – when confronted with general problems, potentially generators of financial unbalances. The resolution of such questions demands a wide set of competences that do not belong to the sphere of the judiciary; the latter may only function as a limit to the enactment of norms that violate constitutional obligations, but never as the promoter of a true social development, in accordance to the constitutional project and provisions.

Finally, an interesting note: a recent study on the role of the Constitutional Court between 2002 and 2016 found no evidence of any increased activism of the judges in dealing with austerity policies, meaning there was no increased propensity to block such measures on different grounds of unconstitutionality. This sustains the argument according to which the Court mainly followed its previous paths and methods, as well as some of its most important jurisprudential lines.

What the study did find was a clear manifestation of diverse ideological preferences, but this fact is well known to the public, and it is neither new nor unexpected on the basis of the institutional rules of appointments to the Court. It seems to be true that judges appointed by left-wing parties were more likely to conclude that financially restrictive measures were unconstitutional, but this was similar to other policies passed before that period. The study is consistent with previous work on the matter and it only confirms that political parties try to nominate like-minded judges and academics, which may bring their worldview to the discussions within the Court.[52] This is actually an intentional element of the Portuguese system of Constitutional review, and a consequence (and safeguard) of political pluralism and democracy.

Notes

1 The Court's decisions have even led to an amendment to the Economic and Financial Assistance Programme, with a new item on 'legal safeguards' being added to the 'Memorandum of Economic and Financial Policies' (available at http://ec.europa.eu/economy_finance/publications/occasional_paper/2011/pdf/ocp79_en.pdf), on its revision of 12 June 2013, stating the following: '9. Legal safeguards. We will take a number of steps aimed at mitigating legal risks from future potential Constitutional Court rulings. First, expenditure reforms will be designed with the principle of public/private sector and intergenerational equity in mind as well as the need to address the sustainability of social security systems. Second, legislation underpinning the expenditure reforms will be duly justified on compliance with the fiscal sustainability rules in the recently ratified European Fiscal Compact, which now ranks higher than ordinary legislation. Third, the government will rely as much as possible on general laws – rather than on one-year budget laws – consistent with the structural nature of the reforms. This also opens the possibility of prior constitutional review of said laws, thus allowing early reaction on the part of the government in case these reforms raise constitutional issues' (see https://www.imf.org/external/np/loi/2013/prt/061213.pdf).

2 About this debate, check, for example Novais (2014), Ribeiro and Coutinho (2014), Ribeiro (2013), Coutinho, Torre and Smith (2015), Kilpatrick and de Witte (2014).

3 All the numbers can be found at the following websites: www.ine.pt and www.pordata.pt.

4 Which comprises three documents: the Memorandum of Economic and Financial Policies, the Technical Memorandum of Understanding, and the Memorandum of Understanding on Specific Economic Policy Conditionality.
5 The financial loan was provided by the European Financial Stabilisation Mechanism (EFSM), the European Financial Stability Facility and the IMF.
6 See *Resolução do Conselho de Ministros* n.° 8/2011, 5th May 2011.
7 See Portuguese Constitutional Court Decision no. 353/2012.
8 The myriad different opinions about the Memoranda can be found, for example, in Ferreira (2013). See also Baptista (2011) and Coutinho (2013).
9 Other examples of such a trend are the institutional fragmentation and the growing importance of informal mechanisms of decision-making within the EU, as well as the need to use intergovernmental instruments such as the *Treaty on Stability, Coordination and Governance in the Economic and Monetary Union* to develop fundamental policies. For an excellent analysis of the problem, check Balaguer Callejón (2012).
10 Baptista (2011).
11 See. e.g., Hanek and Gallo (2015).
12 For a comprehensive view of the legislation concerned and of Court's decisions, see Canotilho, Violante and Lanceiro (2015), which I will closely follow in this chapter.
13 Portuguese Constitutional Court Decision no. 396/2011.
14 Portuguese Constitutional Court Decision no. 353/2012.
15 Portuguese Constitutional Court Decision no. 187/2013.
16 Portuguese Constitutional Court Decision no. 413/2014.
17 Portuguese Constitutional Court Decision no. 574/2014.
18 See, again, Portuguese Constitutional Court Decision no. 396/2011, point 5, in fine.
19 See Portuguese Constitutional Court Decision no. 396/2011, point 5, in fine.
20 Again, Portuguese Constitutional Court Decision no. 396/2011, point 7.
21 Christmas and holidays pays, also known as 13th and 14th months, correspond to additional monthly pays, usually due in June/July and November. They are part of the yearly wage, both under public and private law.
22 Portuguese Constitutional Court Decision no. 413/2014, point 42.
23 Portuguese Constitutional Court Decision no. 574/2014.
24 Portuguese Constitutional Court Decision no. 413/2014.
25 Ribeiro (2013).
26 Alexandrino (2014).
27 Portuguese Constitutional Court Decision no. 187/2013.
28 In this sense, see Novais (2014).
29 Portuguese Constitutional Court Decision no. 602/2013.
30 Portuguese Constitutional Court Decision no. 187/2013.
31 Portuguese Constitutional Court Decision no. 794/2013.
32 Portuguese Constitutional Court Decision no. 602/2013.
33 Portuguese Constitutional Court Decision no. 474/2013.
34 Such as Portuguese Constitutional Court Decision no. 154/2010, and Portuguese Constitutional Court Decision no. 683/1999.
35 Pereira (2013).
36 See Portuguese Constitutional Court Decision no. 594/2012.
37 Portuguese Constitutional Court Decision no. 862/2013.
38 Portuguese Constitutional Court Decision no. 572/2014.
39 Portuguese Constitutional Court Decision no. 575/2014,
40 Portuguese Constitutional Court Decision no. 575/2014.
41 For example, Portuguese Constitutional Court Decision no. 287/1990; Portuguese Constitutional Court Decision no. 188/2009.
42 Portuguese Constitutional Court Decision no. 3/2016.
43 Portuguese Constitutional Court Decision no. 399/2010.

44 Article 103(3) of the Portuguese Constitution establishes that 'No one shall be obliged to pay taxes that are not created in accordance with this Constitution, are retroactive in nature, or are not charged or collected as laid down by law'.
45 Portuguese Constitutional Court Decision no. 187/2013, point 98.
46 Portuguese Constitutional Court Decision no. 187/2013, point 94.
47 Portuguese Constitutional Court Decision no. 509/2002; Portuguese Constitutional Court Decision no. 141/2015; Portuguese Constitutional Court Decision no. 296/2015.
48 As has been stated, several authors have accused the Portuguese Constitutional Court of 'activism'. See, for example, Ribeiro and Coutinho (2014).
49 Portuguese Constitutional Court Decision no. 306/2003, and Portuguese Constitutional Court Decision no. 338/2010.
50 Canotilho (2016).
51 See Ribeiro and Coutinho (2014).
52 Amaral-Garcia, Garoupa and Grembi (2009) and Coroado, Garoupa and Magalhaes (2017).

Bibliography

Alexandrino, José de Melo, 'Jurisprudência da Crise. Das questões prévias às perplexidades', in Gonçalo de Almeida Ribeiro and Luís Pereira Coutinho (eds), *O Tribunal Constitucional e a Crise – Ensaios Críticos* (Almedina, 2014).

Amaral-Garcia, Sofia, Garoupa, Nuno and Grembi, Veronica, 'Judicial Independence and Party Politics in the Kelsenian Constitutional Courts: The Case of Portugal' (2009). *Journal of Empirical Legal Studies*, 6(2), 381–404.

Balaguer Callejón, Francisco, 'El final de una época dorada. Una reflexión sobre la crisis económica y el declive del Derecho constitucional nacional', in Fernando Alves Correia, Jonatas Eduardo Mendes Machado and João Carlos Loureiro (eds), *Estudos em Homenagem ao Prof. Doutor José Joaquim Gomes Canotilho* (Coimbra Editora 2012).

Baptista, Eduardo Correia, 'Natureza Jurídica dos memorandos de FMI e a UE' (2011). *Revista da Ordem dos Advogados*, 71(2), 477–488.

Canotilho, Mariana, 'Austeridad y derecho constitucional: el ejemplo portugués' (2016). *Democrazia e Sicurezza-Democracy and Security Review*, 1; http://www.democraziaesicurezza.it/Saggi/Austeridad-y-derecho-constitucional-el-ejemplo-portugues, last accessed 18 July 2017.

Canotilho, Mariana, Violante, Teresa and Lanceiro, Rui, 'Austerity Measures Under Judicial Scrutiny: The Portuguese Constitutional Case-law' (2015). *European Constitutional Law Review*, 11, 155–183.

Coroado, Susana, Garoupa, Nuno and Magalhaes, Pedro C., 'Judicial Behavior Under Austerity: An Empirical Analysis of Behavioral Changes in the Portuguese Constitutional Court, 2002–2016', forthcoming in *Journal of Law and Courts*; https://ssrn.com/abstract=2928196, last accessed on 5 March 2017.

Coutinho, Luis Pereira, 'A natureza jurídica dos memorandos da "troika"' (2013). *Themis*, XIII(24/25), 147–179.

Coutinho, Luis Pereira, La La Torre, Massimo and Smith, Steven D. (eds), *Judicial Activism: An Interdisciplinary Approach to the American and European Experiences* (Springer 2015).

Ferreira, Eduardo Paz (ed.), *Troika Ano II. Uma avaliação de 66 cidadãos* (Edições 70 2013).

Hanek, Rita De Brito Gião and Gallo, Daniele, 'Constitutional Change Through Euro Crisis Law: "Portugal"' (2015). Law Department Project funded by The Research

Council of the EUI; http://eurocrisislaw.eui.eu/portugal/, last accessed on 1 May 2017.

Kilpatrick, Claire and De Witte, Bruno, 'Social Rights in Times of Crisis in the Eurozone: The Role of Fundamental Rights Challenges' (2014). EUI Working Paper LAW 2014/05.

Pereira, Ravi A., 'Igualdade e proporcionalidade: um comentário às decisões do Tribunal Constitucional de Portugal sobre cortes salariais no sector público' (2013). *Revista española de derecho constitucional*, No. 98, 317–370.

Novais, Jorge Reis, *Em Defesa do Tribunal Constitucional* (Almedina, 2014).

Ribeiro, Gonçalo de Almeida and Coutinho, Luis Pereira (eds), *O Tribunal Constitucional e a Crise – Ensaios Críticos* (Almedina, 2014).

Ribeiro, Gonçalo de Almeida, 'Judicial Activism Against Austerity in Portugal' (*I-CONnect Blog*, 3 December 2013); www.iconnectblog.com/2013/12/judicial-activism-against-austerity-in-portugal/, last accessed on 1 May 2017.

11 Constitutional courts under pressure – New challenges to constitutional adjudication

The Case of Spain

Francisco Balaguer Callejón

1. Main areas of constitutional tension

Spain is a country with a considerably advanced normative and democratic Constitution, which was approved in 1978, following the end of the Franco dictatorship, having only been reformed on two occasions up to the present day. The first reform took place in 1992 to adapt the constitutional text to the Treaty on the European Union and was limited to incorporating the addition of 'and passive' to the right to suffrage that article 13.2 recognises for foreigners in municipal elections.[1] The second revision had a greater reach and occurred in 2011, incorporating the principle of budgetary equilibrium into article 135 of the Constitution,[2] being a precursor to others that would have to follow other European countries in application of the subsequent Treaty on Stability, Coordination and Governance in the Economic and Monetary Union,[3] to 'calm' the markets in the context of the financial crisis.[4]

This absence of reforms in almost 40 years has been possible thanks to the great flexibility that diverse mechanisms granted to the Constitution for later development, which have made possible, amongst other things, the configuration of a specific model of territorial pluralism and the opening up to the process of European integration. The territorial model depends to a large extent on the Statutes of Autonomy; rules subjected to the Constitution that have given rise to what is known as the 'Autonomous State'. It involves a type of State that is materially federal, to which it refers to the extent of the competencies held by the territories, but lacks some of the institutions of the Federal State, which has led to problems in its practical functioning and also generated tensions in constitutional jurisprudence. These tensions have increased in the present day as a result of the recent claim for sovereignty in Catalonia.

Spanish constitutional history has been conflictive and problematic since the beginning of the nineteenth century. Periods of democratic stability have been very brief and it can be said that, beyond the experience of the Second Republic, which ended tragically with the military uprising and the civil war, Spain has only enjoyed democratic normality in the years following the political transition, with the elections of 15 June 1977, which have given rise to a period of 40 years of pacific coexistence in Spanish society. However, the Franco dictatorship also lasted some 40 years and its effects have been noticed in the problems it created and enhanced, and which have been present for a long time.

The first of these, and the most dramatic – although fortunately now overcome – was the terrorism of ETA that arose during the Franco dictatorship and existed throughout the democratic period, with a terrible inertia that not only produced irreparable personal damage to hundreds of human lives but also affected the political system and the moral foundations of coexistence. The pressure of terrorism has inevitably affected legislative measures and has also had its effect on constitutional jurisprudence. Although fortunately this is a question that can be today considered as overcome, the threat of 'jihadist' terrorism, which manifested itself in a particularly tragic manner in our country with the attacks of 11 March 2004 and 17 August 2017, continues to exist.

Disassociated from the terrorism of ETA but also conditioned by the repression of the Franco regime, the question of the incorporation of the Basque Country into Spain must be considered, which has presented a number of problematic profiles of adaptability from the moment of the drawing up and passing of the Constitution. For many years the Basque Nationalist Party has been the main actor in negotiations with the government of the State as it has been the party that has controlled the autonomous government for the longest time. Attention must also be drawn to a number of tensions arising as a consequence of a temporary sovereignist drift that gave rise to the failed 'Ibarretxe Plan', and which has been to some extent reflected in constitutional jurisprudence.

Although it cannot be said that the Catalan independence movement has developed as a result of the repression of Franco regime, it is nevertheless possible to perceive a double incidence in its evolution: On the one hand, the traces left by the repression of the dictatorship in relation to the Catalan identity and language. On the other hand, the persistence of a centralist political culture inherited from Francoism as well as cultural patterns that favour antidemocratic approaches due to an anachronistic perception of the political struggle that is situated in the logic of anti-Francoism, are totally inappropriate for a constitutional and democratic system.

The persistence of cultural patterns inherited from Francoism in our political class is perceptible, first of all, in conservative sectors. Perhaps this explains the regrouping of all the right-wing sectors, which is a particular characteristic of our political system, as there is no relevant extreme right party. All parliamentary representation of the right-wing sectors (except that referred to nationalist parties in some Autonomous Regions) is concentrated in the *Partido Popular* (People's Party, PP). However, beyond the survival that Francoism could have in conservative sectors, there also exists a reflection of guidelines and values in Spanish society that are not very democratic. This survival manifests itself in many areas, from the scarce capacity for dialogue and consensus from the political agents, to the widespread centralist mentality and, of course, in that referring to the level that political corruption has reached in our country. A political culture that is not yet completely democratic would inevitably have some kind of impact on institutions such as the Constitutional Court (*Tribunal Constitucional*) as we have had occasion to see recently with the challenge that the Catalan separatists have raised through frontal and direct disobedience of Constitutional Court resolutions. This attitude can also be explained as a manifestation of the cultural patterns inherited from the Franco regime, in this case through a specific 'anti-Francoist' mentality of lack of respect for the law, which although it was justified in the struggle against the dictatorship half a century ago, lacks foundation in a democratic system like the current one, in which respect for the Constitution and laws is the basis of peaceful coexistence.

Beyond the 'internal' questions of a national State, the context of globalisation and supranational integration has also influenced the work of constitutional jurisdiction in two spheres. On the one hand, that of European integration, which has required an adjustment in the relationships between legal orders not always well resolved by the Constitutional Court although respectful, in general terms, of the principle of primacy and the preferential application of European law. The preventative control mechanism of the International Treaties has been activated as much for what is referred to as the Treaty on the European Union as for the Constitutional Treaty project, giving rise to a relevant doctrine in matters of relations between European and domestic law.

Furthermore, if Spain has traditionally been a country of emigrants, which is reflected in the only constitutional provisions relating to immigration dedicated to the protection of the rights of Spanish emigrants abroad and the promotion of their return to Spain,[5] during the years prior to the crisis there was an extraordinary increase in immigration that manifested itself in an ever higher percentage of the immigrant population in Spain. Tensions over the question of immigration also reached the Constitutional Court, which had to pronounce on the status of non-Spanish citizens and their constitutional rights. In general, the pronouncements emanating from the Court have maintained a coherent line respectful to constitutional principles, although with some occasional rupture.

Lastly, the area that most needed the corrective intervention of the Constitutional Court – the measures related to the financial crisis – has been where it was more absent, with a completely permissive attitude that has led to it uncritically validating those measures.

2. The Spanish Constitutional Court

In the Spanish constitutional system the Constitutional Court has a fundamental role. Our country has a model of concentrated jurisdiction, with a Court that has a monopoly on the control of the constitutionality of the laws (with the exception of the *ultra vires* control of legislative delegation, which is explained by historical reasons)[6] and that also carries out an important function in the protection of Fundamental Rights via *recurso de amparo* (appeal for constitutional protection filed by citizens). The Constitutional Court is also responsible for the solution of conflicts of powers that can arise between the State and the Autonomous Communities or between the Autonomous Communities themselves and also the conflicts between the constitutional bodies of the State. Likewise, control of the constitutionality of International Treaties also falls to the Constitutional Court, which can also be activated as a preventive control.

Control of the constitutionality of laws can come about through two channels. First, there can be direct control (action of unconstitutionality) at the instance of the President of the Government, the Ombudsman, 50 Deputies or 50 Senators. Likewise, referring to the Autonomous Communities, the legitimacy in putting forward an appeal of unconstitutionality against State laws, provisions or enactments having the force of law that may affect their own area of autonomy, falls on the executive collegiate bodies and Autonomous Parliaments. The jurisprudence of the Constitutional Court reveals a flexible interpretation of the requirement that these laws 'may affect their own area of autonomy' which, furthermore, is a condition imposed in the Organic Law on the Constitutional Court but does not appear in the Constitution itself.

The other channel provided for the control of the constitutionality of laws is the question of unconstitutionality. On this regard, where a judge or a court, *motu proprio* or at the request of a party, considers that an enactment having the force of law which is applicable to a case and on which the validity of the ruling depends may be contrary to the Constitution, the judge or court shall raise the question before the Constitutional Court. The legal process is then suspended until the Constitutional Court pronounces on the question of unconstitutionality. It must be taken into account that, although the action of unconstitutionality is subject to a limited period, the question of unconstitutionality can be filed at any time, as long as the required procedural conditions are given. For this reason, the question of unconstitutionality allows for the control of the constitutionality of laws to be left open where the period for the action of unconstitutionality has ended.

The Spanish Constitutional Court has carried out a very important function of interpretation and development of a constitutional system of fundamental rights, the guarantee of constitutional provisions and principles and the construction of the Autonomous State. In that which refers to the spheres of constitutional tension we can say that it has been a body of great prestige at the time of its founding and that it carried out its functions showing a considerable independence from the political parties and, especially, the parliamentary majority. This prestige has been weakened over time, unfortunately, as political parties have occupied positions in the institutions of our constitutional system. The Court's decisions have been increasingly predictable as well as the votes of the judges, which certainly does nothing to promote the image of independence.

3. Immigrants' rights

The Spanish Constitution did not attempt to carry out a regulation of the rights of immigrants that confronted the needs deriving from the increase in immigration. This growth was not foreseeable in 1978 when Spain was still a country of emigrants and there was mention in the Constitution of concern for the treatment to which Spanish workers abroad could be subject.[7] Despite this, if the constitutional formulation is still appropriate it is because of the degree of openness and lack of definition that it finally assumed. This relatively open constitutional framework leaves the basic configuration of the legal system of immigrants' rights in the hands of the Constitutional Court. Initially, the Constitutional Court gave a very wide interpretation to the faculties of the legislator and a very narrow one to the constitutional conditioning of these faculties. This doctrine has been progressively corrected, however, establishing a direct relationship between the rights of foreigners and the Constitution, which limits the possibilities of the legislator and tends to formulate a similar legal status between the constitutional rights of foreigners and those of Spaniards.

In its first jurisprudential pronouncements, in effect, although the Constitutional Court understands that there is not a de-constitutionalisation of foreigners' rights, it adheres to the specifying of these rights to the legislator understanding that they all, without exception, have a legal configuration.[8] Notwithstanding, it is necessary to point out that, in these first pronouncements, the Court also establishes a connection between specific foreigners' rights and the principle of the dignity of the person, which converts them into holders of these rights in complete equality with Spanish citizens.[9] From this connection with the principle of dignity, the Constitutional Court establishes a triple differentiation in matters relating to foreigners' rights:

> The problem with the holding and exercising of rights and, more specifically, the problem of equality in the exercising of rights, which is the question posed here, thus depends on the right affected. There are rights that correspond equally to Spanish and foreign citizens and whose regulation must be the same for both; there are rights that do not apply to foreigners at all (those recognised in Art. 23 of the Constitution, according to the stipulations of Art 13.2 and with the provision it contains); there are others that will or will not belong to foreigners according to the stipulations of treaties and laws.[10]

This doctrine is going to evolve in a more restrictive sense than the possibilities of configuration from the legislator, admitting that determined fundamental rights of foreigners derive directly from the Constitution, insofar as its constitutional recognition is equally applicable to Spanish and foreign citizens.[11] This proposal, by which it is recognised that foreigners are holders of constitutional rights that derive directly from the Constitution and for whose regulation the legislator is limited by the guarantee of essential content (the minimum content of the right protected against the legislator), would be confirmed in the jurisprudence of the Court, becoming consolidated doctrine[12] – a doctrine that reaffirms the direct holding of rights connected to the guarantee of human dignity and limits the capacity for configuration by the legislator who must respect 'the content delimited by the Constitution' for the fundamental right[13] which means appealing again to the essential content as a limit.[14]

In short, constitutional jurisprudence has made an interpretation of the Constitution that goes beyond the initial openness and lack of definition with which article 13.1 had been contemplated (whose development relied, excessively, on the legislator) and is progressively oriented towards equal constitutional rights between Spanish and foreign citizens. To this end, constitutional jurisprudence has used different interpretation criteria, amongst which those that can be considered as especially relevant are the connection of rights with the principle of the dignity of the person, and the appeal to the guarantee of the essential content of rights. The linking of rights to the principle of the dignity of the person allows us to define an intangible nucleus of rights that are inherent to the person and of which foreigners cannot be dispossessed. For its part, the appeal to the guarantee of essential content allows a limit to be established on the legislator for the regulation of foreigners' rights, which obliges it to respect the essential content of those rights. In this manner, the differences regarding the rights of Spanish citizens that the legislator wishes to introduce must be situated outside the essential content of those rights, which must be equally respected for Spanish and foreign citizens.

Despite this being the constant jurisprudence of the Constitutional Court, a certain rupture can be seen in STC 236/2007, which gives a response to the challenges against Organic Law 8/200 in relation to the rights of foreigners in an irregular situation.[15] Although the Constitutional Court declares the unconstitutionality and nullity of the legal precepts that limited the rights of immigrants in an irregular situation to education, legal aid[16] and the right to strike,[17] the Court understands that the declaration of unconstitutionality does not have to be connected to the nullity of the precepts relating to the rights to assembly, association and to join trade unions,[18] or the nullity of the subparagraph that links the exercise of these constitutional rights to immigrants obtaining authorisation to stay or reside in Spain. The Court understands that if it declares the nullity of this subparagraph in the event of these rights this would suppose an alteration of the will of the legislator as in this way it would fully equated to all foreigners, regardless of their administrative situation, the ability to exercise the rights in question.

This formulation breaks the coherence of the arguments followed by the Court itself in application of the preceding doctrine, as it enables the legislator to establish a different legal system for immigrants in an irregular situation, despite the previously established link between the rights affected and the dignity of the person and the essential content of the rights that the Constitution directly attributes. The application of these criteria should have led the Constitutional Court to apply the same legal system to all rights affected without making any distinction between them. In any event, this occasional rupture in constitutional doctrine in matters of immigration should not prevent an overall positive assessment of the jurisprudence of the Constitutional Court although it could be considered a sign of possible extra-juridical conditioning in a topic that is so subject to political debate, if we take into account that this Organic Law was passed by the *Partido Popular* and its declaration of unconstitutionality, despite coming about under the mandate of another (PSOE) government of a different sign supposed a rejection of the policy of that party in matters of immigration.

4. The fight against terrorism

Terrorism has had a constant presence in Spain since the Franco dictatorship, with various organisations, amongst which the terrorist group ETA, active until 20 October 2011, particularly stands out. Its criminal actions were produced over a period of 43 years, killing over 800 people and causing many more non-mortal victims. The other terrorist organisations had been previously dissolving, although Spain suffered two terrible attacks by radical Muslims on 11 March 2004 and 17 August 2017. Following the France attacks in January 2015 the so-called 'anti-jihadist' pact was signed between the PP and the PSOE and has been subsequently adhered to by other political parties.

Regarding constitutional jurisprudence, it can be said that a very tense 'social climate' has existed, which has influenced the doctrine of the Constitutional Court. This tension has manifested itself to a lesser extent in relation to the instruments destined to investigating and pursuing terrorists – notwithstanding the fact that anti-terrorist legislation in this matter has also been examined by the Constitutional Court[19] – and to a greater extent by subsequent repression via prison measures or the debate on the illegalisation of the 'political wing' of ETA. Thus, specific doctrines have been accepted, that will later be declared contrary to the European Convention on Human Rights by the European Court of Human Rights, such is the case of the Parot Doctrine, by virtue of which penitentiary benefits began to be applied to each one of the penalties imposed on the convict and not on the legal maximum permitted, thus provoking a prolongation of the criminal conviction, which was carried out via a retrospective interpretation of criminal matters. This doctrine does not come from the Constitutional Court, but the Supreme Court, which established it in Judgment 197/2006, but the Constitutional Court did not invalidate it[20] even if it occasionally concedes the *amparo* for reasons different from those that would derive from the challenge of the Parot doctrine.[21] The European Court of Human Rights condemned Spain for this doctrine in the *Del Río Prada v Spain* case (10 July 2012), confirmed by the Grand Chamber of the ECHR on 21 October 2013.

Furthermore, the fact that the terrorism of ETA had a 'political wing' that coincided with electoral processes via specific political parties, gave rise to legislation situated in the 'militant democracy' logic, expressed in Organic Law 6/2002 of 27 June, on Political Parties, considered to be in line with the Constitution by STC 48/2003 of 12 March. As José Antonio Montilla points out, STC 48/2003 established a model in the Spanish legal system, although attenuated, of militant democracy, incorporating evident restrictions on the right to form parties and other fundamental rights linked to the legal-constitutional regime of political parties, furthermore being a judgment that was passed in very specific circumstances, amongst other reasons because it was resolved in under six months when the average duration of appeals for unconstitutionality at that time stood at seven years (thus highlighting the political pressure that the Constitutional Court was subject to).[22] In application of the aforementioned Organic Law 6/2002, the political wing of ETA was made illegal, which would also be declared constitutional by the Constitutional Court in STCs 5 and 6/2004 of 16 January that rejected the corresponding appeals for *amparo*. Finally, the European Court of Human Rights upheld the decisions of the Constitutional Court in 2009.[23]

The Constitutional Court ruled on a wide range of sentences on the occasion of several appeals for *amparo* about the proclamation of candidates for electoral processes in terms of their relationship to the previously dissolved parties, granting or denying *amparo* depending on the circumstances of fact.[24] STC 126/2009 of 21 May (FJ 9), in which the *amparo* is granted, recognises the risk attached to this work of the Constitutional Court:

> It is necessary to maximise exactitude when accepting as proven the reality of the fraud in a Judgment dissolving political parties in order to dissipate the risk of harming the ideological plurality that the Constitution promotes and protects with a fundamental value of the legal system. The risk, in short, in confounding the ideology professed by a party and the means defended or used to promote it, of ending up harming those who share the same ideology even where it cannot be demonstrated that they defend it through violent means, or that it is used as an instrument purely against those whose modus operandi is terrorist violence. You incur in this risk in this case when the connections appreciated are established with a single reference to the Abertzale left. There is no room for excluding any type of ideology in our legal system, either because of its content or foundations, or because of the means by which it is defended. These means, however, if violent, will be unacceptable as such, but without any prejudice whatsoever to the ideology that they attempt to serve.

Finally, in STC 62/2011 of 5 May (FJ13), on the same lines, the Court states that:

> [m]ere suspicion cannot constitute a legally acceptable argument for excluding anybody from the full exercise of their fundamental right to political participation. It could be that the suspicion is later confirmed, but for the current trial, it could not lead to a limiting result, under the danger of leaving the free exercise of the rights to political participation guaranteed in Article 23 SC uncertain and, with it, the value of political pluralism on which the constitutional legal system of the democratic State is grounded. The objective of guaranteeing the security of the constitutional State at any cost, via preventative controls, puts the constitutional State itself seriously at risk.

The change of tone in these latest judgments from the Court is clearly perceptible; revealing the tension to which it has been subject in relation to proceedings whose constitutional placement is problematic. The permanent pressure from the media must be taken into account. Some media have placed the question of terrorism at the heart of a political strategy that is more than dubious from the constitutional point of view, promoting the idea that any defence of constitutional guarantees must be relativised in the anti-terrorist cause.

This change of tone would have its epilogue in STC 138/2012 of 20 June, in which the Court grants the *amparo* and declares the formation of the political party 'Sortu' as appropriate, recognising the right of the appellants to their inscription. For the Court (FJ 12):

> [t]he suspicion that the political party whose inscription in the Registry of political parties has been rejected could attempt to continue or follow the activity of political parties judicially illegalised and dissolved eight years previously cannot constitute a legally sufficient argument to condition the full exercise of a fundamental right, in this case, the right to association, in the scope of the right to the creation of political parties (Art. 22 SC, in relation to Art. 6). No suspicion can lead to a result that limits the free exercise of the right to association and, with it, of the value of political pluralism upon which the constitutional legal system of the democratic State is grounded.

In general terms it can be said that there has not existed in Spain a limitation of freedoms in the fight against terrorism similar to what has occurred in other countries following the attacks of 11 September in New York.[25] A paradigmatic example of the different way of addressing this problem can be observed in the reaction following the attack of 11 March 2004 in Madrid. Police measures were sufficient and it was not considered necessary to promote an additional limitation to constitutional rights as an instrument of anti-terrorist policy. It is certain that there was already, sadly, a very extensive experience of the anti-terrorist fight, with specific legislation based on constitutional provisions. There was, as we have indicated, a very strong social and political tension in relation to the penal treatment of terrorists and regarding the political environment of ETA. Furthermore, an increase can also be appreciated in recent times in legal actions related to crimes of opinion under the accusation of 'justifying terrorism', which usually occur within the space of political antagonism, with an unwarranted resource of criminal intervention.

5. Territorial conflicts

Within the tensions that the Constitutional Court has been suffering, especially noteworthy is that which has occurred within the sphere of the autonomous regions in recent years with specific proposals for reforming the Statutes of Autonomy, in particular in the case of the Basque Country and Catalonia, as well as the drift towards pro-sovereignty that has taken place in Catalonia that has ended up generating a democratic involution in Catalonia with decisions manifestly contrary to the constitutional and statutory order by autonomous authorities that represent only a minority of the Catalan population (less than 48 per cent) even though they have a majority –certainly meagre – in Parliament, due to the distortions of the electoral system.

Concerning the Basque Country, it involved a failed reform, formulated as a 'Proposal for reform of the political statute of the autonomous region of the

Basque Country', which was roundly rejected by the Chamber of Deputies on 1 February 2005 following a long political and doctrinal controversy in which the complete unsuitability of the proposal to the Constitution in many of its aspects was revealed. Both because of its philosophy and the reach of many of its provisions, the 'Ibarretxe Plan' (named after the President of the Basque Government who launched it) was unacceptable and would not have been approved under its terms by Parliament without producing a large rupture in the constitutional system. Furthermore, political negotiation was ruled out from the beginning, given the evident difficulty in finding formulas for consensus that could eliminate the serious problems of constitutionality presented by the Plan.

The later attempt of a popular consultation can be considered as an epilogue to this failed Plan, via Basque Parliament Law 9/2008, of 27 June, declared unconstitutional and void by STC 103/2008 of 11 September. This law authorised the President of the Basque Government (the *Lehendakari*) to put two questions to a non-binding consultation of the citizens of the Basque Country, amongst which was the beginning of a process of negotiation to reach 'a Democratic Agreement on the exercise of the right to decide of the Basque people' – an agreement that would have to be put to referendum before the end of 2010. The Constitutional Court considered that the holding of a referendum was a competence of the state and, as such, the Law violated the stipulations of Article 149.1.32 of the Constitution. As far as the 'right to decide' of the Basque people is concerned, the Court declared that the identification of a subject equipped with a right of such a nature is impossible without a prior reform of the Constitution.[26] As we will see, in the subsequent jurisprudence relating to Catalonia this argument will be reiterated but with a more elaborated doctrine that contains some differentiating aspects of interest.

The failed Ibarretxe Plan will be followed by other statutory reforms, already within the constitutional framework, headed by the Statute of Catalonia, the object of a great political controversy and of a claim before the Constitutional Court, lodged by the *Partido Popular*. Of the eight statutes reformed in the last period of statutory reform concluded to date (which affect the majority of the population and territory of Spain, although not the majority of the 17 Autonomous Regions), five were the object of challenge before the Constitutional Court, a challenge that was accepted in three cases, affecting one complete article of the Statute of Andalusia and another of the Statute of Catalonia, a paragraph of an article of the Statute of Castile and Leon and another three specific paragraphs of articles or specific sections of the Statute of Catalonia. Taking into account the hundreds of articles that have not been affected by any declaration of unconstitutionality, it could be said that the Constitutional Court has validated the fundamental lines of the statutory reforms. Notwithstanding, this cannot prevent us from recognising that some of the declarations of unconstitutionality have affected aspects that had a great symbolic and political value, which has generated an extremely negative feeling regarding the pronouncements of the Court.[27]

In effect, Constitutional Court Judgment 31/2010 of 28 June, relating to the Statute of Catalonia, declared that just one complete Article of the Statute was unconstitutional together with another three specific paragraphs of Articles or specific clauses that do not affect relevant legal issues related to the reform. However, its political impact was very negative as it unnecessarily affected questions of identity and because of the circumstances under which the pronouncement of the Constitutional Court was made. The result of the challenge to the Statute of Catalonia has had a very damaging effect on the Autonomous State. In general, we can say that the Autonomous State as we currently know it would not have been possible without the impressive jurisprudential efforts of the Constitutional Court. However, STC 31/2010, in relation to the Statute of Catalonia, has fostered a large drive towards pro-independence positions and an evolution towards these positions on the part of the main nationalist party, which has been the governing party throughout almost the entire existence of the Autonomous Region.

It could even be said that the most important tension towards the Constitutional Court began with the appeal against the Statute of Catalonia (until reaching the open challenge that was subsequently raised by the Catalan separatist sectors), generating important changes in aspects fundamental to the conception of the Autonomous State (for example, in relation to the position of the Statutes of Autonomy in the Spanish constitutional system). From a political point of view, the most obvious consequence of the pronouncement of the Constitutional Court on the Statute of Catalonia has been a pro-independence drift, which has found a motive in the judgment for promoting disaffection for the 1978 Constitution and the State itself.

This evolution has been reinforced by a feeling of discontent that is also related to the financial crisis and with the funding of this Autonomous Region. The total absence of dialogue to attempt to solve this problem adequately, via a new constitutional consensus that makes possible – through a reform of the Constitution – the integration of the Catalan specificity within a common project, led towards the increase of the political conflict. The latest jurisprudential developments in this conflict extend from 2014 to 2017. In Judgment 42/2014 of 25 March, the Constitutional Court partially upheld the challenge filed by the Government of the Nation against Resolution 5/X of the Parliament of Catalonia, which approved the 'Declaration of sovereignty and the right to decide of the people of Catalonia', considering as 'unconstitutional and void the so-called first principle entitled *Sovereignty* of the Declaration approved by Resolution 5/X of the Parliament of Catalonia'.

At the same time, the Court affirms in the same Judgment 42/2014 that

> the references to the 'right to decide of the citizens of Catalonia' contained in the title, initial part, and in the second, third, seventh and ninth principles, second paragraph, of the Declaration approved by Resolution 5/X of the Parliament of Catalonia are not unconstitutional if they are interpreted in the sense expounded in legal grounds 3 and 4 of this Judgment.

For the constitutional Court (FJ 4):

> the proposal of conceptions that attempt to modify the foundations of the constitutional system itself have a place in our legal system, as long as it is not

> prepared or defended through an activity that breaches democratic principles, fundamental rights or any other constitutional mandates, and the attempt at its effective attainment is carried out within the scope of constitutional reform procedures, as respect for these is always, in any event, mandatory.

It involves a significant jurisprudential evolution, with a more adjusted and open interpretation than STC 103/2008 of 11 September, which we alluded to when talking about the Basque Country.

The jurisprudential pronouncements of 2015 are largely related to the popular consultation promoted by the Government of Catalonia on 9 November 2014, carried out under non-legal conditions, without its result (with an otherwise relevant participation but minority in terms of the number of voters) can be considered valid: Constitutional Court Judgments 31/2015 of 25 February (which annuls some of the precepts of the Law of the Parliament of Catalonia 10/2014 of 26 September on non-referendum popular consultations and other forms of citizen participation); 24/2015 of 25 February (which annuls Decree 129/2014 of 27 September on the holding of a non-referendum popular consultation on the political future of Catalonia) and the STC 138/2015 of 11 June 2015 (which declares the actions of the *Generalitat* of Catalonia in relation to the holding of the consultation as unconstitutional).

A new challenge was presented with the aim of holding 'plebiscite' elections in Catalonia on 27 September 2015. On the one hand, the pro-independence parties lost the 'plebiscite' in these elections by not obtaining more than 48 per cent of the votes of the electorate. However, due to the electoral system, they gained a sufficient majority of seats to form a new government and propel new measures oriented towards a possible declaration of independence, which is incompatible with a minimum respect for democratic rules, since a minority cannot impose independence on the majority of society.[28] For its part, the Government of the Nation has continued to lodging appeals to the Constitutional Court as a brake, challenging the Parliament of Catalonia[29] and promoting a reform of the Organic Law of the Constitutional Court to grant it direct sanctioning powers against those who fail to comply with its decisions.[30]

The last jurisprudential pronouncement of the year 2015 is related to the result of the 'plebiscitary' elections. STC 259/2015 of 2 December declares the unconstitutionality and nullity of Resolution 1/XI of the parliament of Catalonia, adopted on 9 November 2015, 'on the beginning of the political process in Catalonia as a result of the election results of 27 September 2015'. The Constitutional Court indicates clearly in the FJ 7 of that sentence 'the autonomic chamber can not be erected as a source of legal and political legitimacy reaching to arrogate the power to violate the constitutional order that sustains its own authority'.

In 2016 several orders are issued by the Constitutional Court related to Catalonia in execution of the STC 259/2015 of 2 December, in particular the AATC 141/2016 of 19 July and 170/2016 of 6 October. In 2017, in addition to the Constitutional Court order 24/2017 of 14 February, also issued in execution of the STC 259/2015, we have to mention SSTC 51/2017 of 10 May on the law of popular consultations Catalan and 52/2017 of the same date, relative to the commissioner for the National Transition of Catalonia, as well as the STC 90/2017 of 5 July, relative to the unconstitutionality of the budgetary forecasts of the Generalitat of Catalonia related to the convocation of the referendum. Again, we must insist that, beyond the accuracy of the Constitutional Court's pronouncements in this area, the solution to the problem will never be jurisprudential and would have required dialogue and political negotiation, as the Constitutional Court itself has stated.

The conflict would be aggravated extraordinarily in September 2017 when, with the narrow majority that had separatists in the Parliament of Catalonia, they decided to start the absolute break with the constitutional order through laws that were approved in an irregular manner, without respecting the rights of minorities and with the opposition also of the legal services of the Chamber and the reproach of the Catalonian highest organ of guarantees, the Council of Statutory Guarantees. It is necessary to take into account to understand the dimension of the problem, that not only the Constitutional Court but the Catalan guarantee institutions (whose members had been appointed by the separatists themselves) were against these laws. In spite of this, a 'referendum' was convened for 1 October that lacked minimum legal guarantees and in which, for instance, were counted more votes in favour in 71 districts than the real census (in some of them for three times). The so-called 'referendum' was boycotted by the constitutionalist parties (which represent the majority of voters but not the majority of the seats in Parliament) and participation reached only 42 per cent of the census.

Although the separatists continued without having the majority of the citizen vote, they maintained their intention to declare independence. This led to a massive flight of companies to other places in Spain. In October, almost two thousand companies (1982) moved out of Catalonia to other places in Spain; a very important reaction not only because of the number but especially because they are large companies representing a great portion of the GDP in Catalonia, and concerning employment they represent more than 50 per cent of the companies with more than two thousand workers. If to this is added the unanimous rejection of the European Union to independence, it was clear that all the elements that could have made it possible were lacking: neither democratic or constitutional legitimacy, nor international support nor consensus among social and economic agents. Faced with this situation, the pro independence movement began to hesitate, declaring independence but immediately suspending it. The Government of the Nation, for its part, initiated the measures of protection of the constitutional order envisaged in article 155 Spanish Constitution (which are similar to those of the article that inspires it, article 37 of the German Constitution) with the previous complaint lodged to the President of the Generalitat, who did not attend to any of the two deadlines that were given to him and who refused to call autonomic elections even though he had previously announced that he would do so. Finally, the Senate authorised the Government of the Nation to adopt the necessary measures to restore the constitutional order and the President of the Government, in use of these powers, convened elections in Catalonia for 21 December, ceasing in office the President of the Generalitat and the regional councillors.

Meanwhile, the Constitutional Court has had several occasions to rule on the laws and resolutions adopted by the Parliament of Catalonia in September and October 2016. The last, the STC of 17 October 2017, declared unconstitutionality and nullity of the Law of Catalonia 19/2017, of 6 September, on 'the referendum of self-determination'. In that judgment the Court says rightly by reference to the Parliament of Catalonia that 'A power that expressly denies the Law refuses itself as an authority worthy of respect' as well as that 'In the constitutional state can not be dissociated the democratic principle of the unconditional primacy of the Constitution [STC 259/2015, FJ 4.b)]; which also does not allow any constituted power to adopt decisions that are intended irreversible or without return for the political community' also remembering that 'each and every one of the constitutional rules are subject to modification' provided that such modification be made following the procedures established.

In general it could be said that the doctrine of the Constitutional Court in autonomy matters experienced a certain regression starting with the STC 31/2010 towards a less integrating and less flexible approach than the one that had been produced in the construction of the Autonomous State, precisely at the most delicate moment of the evolution of territorial questions and when a doctrine that followed the previous line of integration was most necessary. The reasons must be searched for in the increase in political tension in relation to the demands that were firstly related to autonomy and then pro-independence from Catalan nationalist sectors, and in the strategies of the main political parties (PP and PSOE), excessively reflected in the position of the Constitutional Court. In any case, in what refers specifically to Catalonia, this orientation of the jurisprudence of the Constitutional Court has always been respectful of the possibilities of constitutional reform to face the demands of the Catalan nationalist sectors, which unfortunately, never tried to promote the constitutional reform and chose an absolutely inadequate strategy in a democratic and constitutional system such as Spain, trying to give an absurd image of 'oppressed people' by the Spanish State that contrasts with the fact that Catalonia is the most rich community of Spain (or was it, at least, until the recent flight of companies motivated by the declaration of independence) and with an autonomy and own political power comparable and in many cases superior to that of any member state of a federation such as the United States or Germany, for instance.

6. The financial crisis

Surprisingly, the doctrine of the Constitutional Court has upheld practically all of the measures adopted in relation to the financial crisis as much in terms of formal questions as the mass use of Decrees-Laws (emergency legislation issued by the government) as material ones. In contrast to what has occurred in relation to the territorial conflicts, which have generated the greatest tension to which the Constitutional Court has been subject in its history, in relation to the laws relating to the financial crisis there has been a lack of social pressure towards the Court. This is surely explained by the fact that the two big parties (up to the 20 December

2015 election, when the Spanish political system substantially changed with the end of the bi-party system) that have alternated in government (PP and PSOE) have assumed, to a greater or lesser extent, the 'economic interpretation of the Constitution' that has been imposed on our constitutional system, as in other European countries.

This does not mean that there has been no internal debate in the Constitutional Court, as shown by the dissenting votes cast in relation to many judgments in recent years. But this internal debate has been more a consequence of the personal conviction of the dissident judges than a social and media tension on the Court projected by the big parties. The surprising thing about this political 'consensus' is that the financial crisis has generated a massive attack on the foundations of the Constitution to which it appears that it is this area where the greatest tension in relation to the Constitutional Court and its doctrine should have produced.

In effect, since it began to manifest the current economic crisis we have witnessed a progressive limitation of the formal and material conditions that have defined up to now pluralist democracy along with a weakening of the normativity of the Constitution. This affectation of pluralist democracy and the constitutional order is linked to an economic interpretation of the Constitution that is being imposed in the European public debate. The essential characteristics of this 'economic interpretation of the Constitution' could be summarised thus:

1 Firstly, this economic interpretation is not limited to inserting the economic aspect into the social order, rather it is attempting, on the contrary, to be the backbone for the entire social order and the Constitution itself from this economic aspect, in such a manner that aspires to an overall conception of the entire constitutional system based on the economy.
2 The economic interpretation of the Constitution is not limited to interacting, as one more factor, with other constitutional principles or rights, rather it attempts to subject these principles and rights not just to the economy but rather to a specific economic orientation, which is presented as the only one possible – the only viable way – out to solve the crises and rationally regulate the economy.
3 The result of this intention is an alteration of the constitutional meaning of constitutional principles and rights. Thus, for example, democracy is no longer presented as a process, but as a product, with a functional sense. The idea of democracy as a product has been driven by the financial crisis, in the sense that decisions are adopted independently of the result of electoral processes (be it by non-application of electoral programmes in the design of government policies, or via a change in governments in itself).
4 This economic approach of democracy is equally applied to other constitutional principles and rights. For example, to the principle of territorial autonomy, which is perceived with distrust as increasing public expenditure. Needless to say, social rights are also now just interpreted from the perspective of the need to limit spending. The entire system of constitutional interpretation of these principles and rights, which has been incorporated into European

constitutional culture for decades, is now displaced and subject to economic and functional criteria.

5 From a constitutional point of view this economic interpretation of the Constitution tends to reject social and political conflict, thus impeding the Constitution from fulfilling one of its essential functions, which is to articulate and channel social and political conflicts, and it is also generating a historical regression from this perspective.[31]

These features can be found in the political and constitutional debate on the crisis in Spain and other countries, and also to some degree in the doctrine of the Constitutional Court related to the financial crisis, which has been limited to validate the policies of the governing majority, without carrying out an effective control of constitutionality that establishes the constitutional limits that should be taken into consideration in the development of European policies.[32] In the face of this economic interpretation of the Constitution that has been finally imposed, it would have been desirable for the Constitutional Court to assume (as some of the dissenting votes that have opposed the majority doctrine have done, in some way) a 'constitutional interpretation of the economic crisis' that serves to recover pluralist democracy and revitalise the normativity of the Constitution.

The Constitutional Court has lost many opportunities to assert a constitutional interpretation of the crisis and, on the contrary, has assumed the basic features of this economic interpretation of the Constitution that is producing so much damage to European constitutional heritage in general, and to some member States of the European Union. There has been an acceptance of formal infringements on the Constitution[33] and alterations to the balance of power between legislative and executive,[34] with few corrective pronouncements[35] beyond completely obvious cases.[36] There has also been a validation, via STC 215/2014 of 18 December, of the damage to the autonomy of the Autonomous Regions and the recentralisation generated by Organic Law 2/2012 of 27 April on Budgetary Stability and Financial Sustainability.[37] It is a decision from the Constitutional Court, based on a purely rhetorical argument,[38] which not only affects the Autonomous State but also limits the competences of the Autonomous Communities to implement policies that guarantee constitutional rights such as education and health, linked to autonomous competencies. The same can be said in relation to the right to housing, regarding which the Constitutional Court has intervened in the promotional measures adopted by some Autonomous Communities, accepting the claim of the state.[39] We could say that, to a large extent, the doctrine of the Constitutional Court prior to the crisis has taken refuge in the numerous dissenting votes cast in relation to the judgments.[40]

7. Conclusions

The Spanish Constitutional Court has been subject to strong tensions in relation to the territorial questions that could affect the integrity of the State, initially regarding the Basque Country (including here terrorism in the different sides in which this problem has manifested itself), and then regarding Catalonia. Constitutional Court doctrine experienced a certain regression with the STC 31//2010 if its previous potential for integration is taken into consideration, which served to make the construction of the Autonomous State possible. Current challenges surpass the possibilities of the Constitutional Court because of the fact that political tension has shifted from statutory reforms to the Constitution itself with a very significant progress of the pro-independence positions in Catalonia. We are, therefore, facing a political problem that demands negotiation and agreements such as what happened in the United Kingdom in relation to Scotland. Unfortunately, the Catalan separatists, despite representing a minority with respect to the population as a whole and losing the plebiscite elections they called (even if they formed government due to the characteristics of the electoral system in fact they obtained less than 48 per cent of the popular vote) opted for a unilateral declaration of independence in October 2017 to which the Government of the Nation has responded with the application of Article 155 Spanish Constitution and the call for new Catalonian elections for 21 December 2017. Whatever the outcome of those elections, it must always be remembered that constitutional democracy requires high consensus to adopt decisions that obliges the community as a whole and that the formation of a new State is one of those fundamental decisions that can not be adopted by a simple majority of government but requires a high degree of agreement among all the citizens, at least above the two-thirds that the Statute of Autonomy of Catalonia itself requires for its reform.

Regarding matters relating to immigration, the Constitutional Court has generated a consolidated doctrine of the development of immigrants' rights, in line with constitutional principles and, especially, with the dignity of the person and with the guarantee of the essential content of rights. In its latest pronouncements this doctrine has been subject to the occasional rupture, a possible reflection of the excessive politicisation (in the sense of dependence on the political parties) of the Court, but it cannot be considered as significant compared to the previous doctrine. In any event, this is a question that is subject to the evolution of economic parameters, in such a way that the trend has become inverted in recent years as the consequence of the crisis, with more Spaniards looking for work abroad than the immigrants our country receives.

Regarding terrorism it can be said that, generally speaking, there has not existed a very strong social and political tension related to the measures adopted for the persecution of crimes and terrorist organisations. Notwithstanding, there have been very intense social debates in relation to the criminal measures applicable to terrorists, giving rise to legal interpretations that were not invalidated by the Constitutional Court and were later condemned by the ECHR. There have also been intense political conflicts relating to the illegalisation of the political environment of ETA, which would give rise to a more nuanced jurisprudence of the Constitutional Court, validated by the ECHR.

Lastly, regarding the financial crisis, despite the fact that we find ourselves before a climate in which a progressive dismantling of our constitutional heritage is taking place, due to an 'economic interpretation of the Constitution' that has been imposed on Spain and other European countries, there has not been significant tension aimed at the Constitutional Court which has endorsed, in general terms, the measures adopted by the parliamentary majority. Despite the doctrine of the Court being the object of internal debate, as evidenced by the large number of dissenting votes, the truth is that there has been no social debate in relation to this doctrine, unlike the case for territorial conflicts, where such debate has existed and continues to exist.

Notes

1 The reform of article 13.2 of the Spanish Constitution came into force on 28 August 1992.

2 The reform of article 135 of the Spanish Constitution came into force on 27 September 2011.

3 http://www.consilium.europa.eu/en/european-council/pdf/Treaty-on-Stability-Coordination-and-Governance-TSCG/

4 In the case of Spain the reform is related to the letter from the President of the European Central Bank, Trichet, to President Zapatero, dated 5 August 2011, which would not be published until the end of 2013 in a book of memoires by the then ex-President of the Government. Paradoxically, the letter did not expressly demand a constitutional reform, unlike in the case of Italy.

5 Article 42 of the Constitution: 'The State shall be especially concerned with safeguarding the economic and social rights of Spanish workers abroad, and shall direct its policy towards their return'.

6 The doctrine in Spain already understood, from before the passing of the Constitution, that this control was exercised over a power to make regulations and not a legislative power. The Constitutional Court itself considers that the raising of the question of unconstitutionality on the part of ordinary courts is unnecessary where it involves controlling 'the excesses of legislative delegation', this being an assumption in which the capacity of control 'not only corresponds to the Constitutional Court, but ordinary jurisdiction as well'. Constitutional Court Judgment (hereafter STC) 47/1984, of 4 April, Legal Ground (hereafter FJ) 3.

7 Art. 42 of the Spanish Constitution.

8 Thus, STC 107/1984, of 23 November, FJ 3, 'they are all, without exception, legally configured rights in terms of their content'.

9 In this same Judgment, and referring to the legal configuration of these rights, the Court affirms that 'rights such as the right to life, physical and moral integrity, to privacy, ideological freedom, etc., correspond to foreigners by their own constitutional mandate, and it is not possible to treat them unequally in relation to Spanish citizens'.

10 STC 107/1984 (FJ 4).

11 From STC 99/1985, of 30 September. The Court understands, in this judgment (FJ 2) that one of these rights that corresponds equally to Spanish and foreign citizens alike, and whose regulation must be equal for both, is the right to effective legal protection from Article 24.1 SC, whose essential content must be preserved.

12 Thus, in STC 115/1987, of 7 July, which resolved an appeal for unconstitutionality lodged against Organic Law 7/1985, of 1 July, on Rights and Freedoms of Foreigners in Spain, it is declared (FJs 2 and 3) that foreigners are directly holders of specific constitutional rights, insofar as the Constitution does not specifically reserve them for Spanish citizens. In this manner, constitutional limits are established on the legislator's capacity for configuration.

13 STC 242/1994, of 20 July, in which it is also affirmed that, even though Constitutional Court doctrine admits that Art. 13 SC authorises the legislator to establish

restrictions and limitations on the fundamental rights that foreigners may enjoy in Spain, this possibility is not without condition, as it cannot affect specific rights nor can it not acknowledge the respect for the constitutional content of law or that incorporated into treaties ratified by Spain. Regarding the rights that it cannot affect, they are those relating to the dignity of the person (FJ4).

14 In the same vein, STC 95/2000, of 10 April, reiterates the aforementioned jurisprudence, also extending the ownership of the rights of foreigners to all constitutional rights connected to the realisation of the principle of the dignity of the person.

15 Doctrine reiterated in STC 259 to 265/2007. Referring to the right to legal aid, STC 236/2007 reiterates in turn the doctrine established in STC 95/2003 and declares 'the unconstitutionality of paragraph 2 of Art. 22 (formerly 20) of Organic Law 4/2000, in the wording given by point 16 of the first Article of Organic Law 8/2000 as it goes against Art. 24 SC' (FJ13).

16 The declaration of unconstitutionality is linked to nullity in these cases.

17 This last reach is also provided by the operative part of the judgment in the subsequent STC 259/2007, of 19 December, in which the appeal of unconstitutionality lodged by the Autonomous Government of Andalusia is resolved. The Constitutional Court decides in paragraph 3 of the Ruling of STC 259/2007 'to declare the unconstitutionality and nullity of the insert "when they are authorised to work" of Art. 11.2 of Organic Law 4/2000, of 11 January, in the wording given by Organic Law 8/2000 of 22 December'.

18 For the Court 'it does not proceed to declare the nullity of the articles of Organic Law 8/2000 that guarantee the right to assembly, association and to join trade unions of foreigners who have obtained authorisation to be or reside in Spain because that would produce a legal void that would not be in accordance with the Constitution, as it would lead to the denial of such rights to all foreigners in Spain, regardless of their situation. It does not proceed, either, to only declare the nullity of the insert "and which they may able exercise where they obtain authorisation to be or reside in Spain", which appears in each one of those articles, given that this would entail a clear alteration of the will of the legislator as in this way all foreigners would clearly be equated, regardless of their administrative situation, with the exercise of the indicated rights'. In any case, the LO 2/2009 has modified the articles deemed unconstitutional giving the same treatment to immigrants in an irregular situation and those who are in a regular situation.

19 It is the case, for example, of STC 199/1987, of 16 December, which declared Organic Law 9/1984 of 26 December as partially unconstitutional. Equally, STC 71/1994, of 3 March, which partially upheld the appeal for unconstitutionality against Organic Law 4/1988, of 25 May, on the Reform of the Law of Criminal Procedure.

20 In STC 113/2012, of 24 May (FJ 8), the Constitutional Court affirmed: 'it is not a function of the Court to interpret ordinary legality and, in what interests us here, where it does not correspond to us to make a direct pronouncement on how to interpret and apply Art. 70 to the case in relation to Art. 100 of the 1973 Penal Code, and on which it must be the limit of fulfilment and the method of calculating penalty reductions, as this involves decisions of enforcing judgments which, in accordance with Art. 117 SC correspond exclusively to judicial bodies (STC 147/1988, of 14 July, FJ 2; similarly, 237/1998, of 14 December, FJ 3; and 31/1999, of 8 March, FJ 3). Our function is limited to examine such decisions, from the perspective of the fundamental rights, whose content is the limit to legal proceedings'.

21 cf., in this respect Fernández (2013).

22 Montilla Martos (2002) 585.

23 cf. Foruria (2010).

24 Thus, in SCJs 85/2003, of 8 May, 176/2003, of 10 October, 99/2004, of 27 May, 110/2007, of 10 May, 112/2007, of 10 May, 43/2009, of 12 February, 44/2009, of 12 February and 126/2009, of 21 May, amongst others.

25 cf., on antiterrorist legislation in Spain, Foruria (1994) 61–132.

26 'The procedure that is sought to open, within its own reach, cannot but affect all Spanish citizens, as it would address the redefinition of the order constituted by the sovereign will of the Nation, whose course, constitutionally speaking, is none other than that of the formal revision of the Constitution' (FJ 5).
27 Furthermore, it must also be taken into account that the doctrine of the Court has been particularly confusing in some areas, and it has focused on a potentially regressive sense in relation to matters of great importance for the Autonomous State, such as that relating to the constitutional function of the Statutes of Autonomy.
28 Resolution of the Parliament of Catalonia 1/XI of 9 November 2015, on the beginning of the political process in Catalonia as a consequence of the electoral results of 27 September 2015.
29 STC 259/2015, of 2 December.
30 Organic Law 15/2015 of 16 October on the reform of Organic Law 2/1979 of 3 October of the Constitutional Court, for the enforcement of Constitutional Court Decisions as a guarantee of the Rule of Law.
31 As Enrique Guillén points out: 'Facing the financial crisis that affects the EU hypertrophying the concept of necessity, and devaluing that of choice, leads to the crisis reaching a political dimension in the European project unknown until now. In this sense, if the concepts of politics, legitimacy, popular sovereignty, in short, democracy and choice are not recovered in the sense that of the emergence of an authentic European government subject to the political responsibility of the holders of sovereignty, it will be difficult for us to overcome the political-constitutional and moral crisis (because democracy is an individual and collective project of emancipation) which is damaging the EU and the Member States' López (2013).
32 In the case Spain, in the opinion of Aguilar: 'Unfortunately, the recent attitude of the Constitutional Court has not been one to preserve the social question or citizens' rights. Its discourse seems to hold to the government's mantra of budgetary austerity' Aguilar Calahorro (2015) 161–185.
33 In matters reserved for Organic Laws, for example, in STC 215/2014, of 18 December, as 5 of the 12 Constitutional Court judges express in their dissenting vote: Adela Asua Batarrita, Luis Ortega Álvarez, Encarnación Roca Trías, Fernando Valdés Dal-Ré and Juan Antonio Xiol Ríos.
34 cf., to this regard Ragone (2015) 519–542.
35 With practically no effect, such as the case of STC 211/2015 of 8 October, which declared Article 124 of Royal Decree-Law 8/2014 of 4 July as unconstitutional due to a lack of accreditation of the enabling condition to urgently pass a reform of the regulation of the state tax on deposits in credit entities. The judgment did not affect material regulation as the content of this decree had previously been incorporated into a law, the Law 18/2014 of 15 October.
36 In the case of STC 26/2016 of 18 February, relating to Decree-Law 14/2012. It is a Decree-Law that was remitted to a regulation for its later development and therefore the absence of enabling condition in relation to the urgency was evident. In a similar sense STC of 16 April 2016.
37 In STC 215/2014 of 18 December, which re-reads the areas of competence of the State, which according to the Court 'enables it to adopt the measures necessary to comply with mandates from the European Union, with a view to reducing the public deficit and the attaining of economic stability and the gradual recovery of budgetary equilibrium' (FJ 3b).
38 See, for example, this paragraph of Legal Ground 4b of Constitutional Court Judgment 215/2014: 'We have before us a number of measures that, despite affecting the scope of autonomy of the Autonomous Communities, must be considered legitimate from a constitutional point of view as they are directed at the correction of the deviation produced regarding allowing both the fulfilment of the individually marked objectives and the homogenous action of all of the entities implicated, in terms of the attaining of the collectively accepted objective'.

39 It is the case of STC 93/2015 of 14 May, which partially upholds the claim of unconstitutionality lodged by the Government of the State against Law 1/2010 of 5 March, which regulates the right to housing in Andalusia. Regarding Catalonia, the STC 62/2016 of 17 March has partially upheld the claim by the Government of the State against Decree-Law 6/2013 of the Generalitat of Catalonia on the prohibition of disconnection of electricity supply or gas, in order to protect the vulnerable consumer.

40 Amongst the many examples that could be mentioned, that of the dissenting vote presented by the judges Fernando Valdés Dal-Ré, Luis Ortega Álvarez, Adela Asua Batarrita and Juan Antonio Xiol Ríos, in STC 49/2015 of 15 March 2015, which rejects the claim of unconstitutionality against Article 2.1 of Royal Decree-Law 28/2012, which questions the consideration by the majority of the court towards the updating of pensions as a 'mere expectation of rights' when it is an authentic 'acquired' right when the prior established condition is met.

Bibliography

Aguilar Calahorro, Augusto, 'El impacto de la crisis económica en España: el renacimiento de la política frente a la economía', in Francisco Balaguer Callejón, Miguel Azpitarte Sánchez, Enrique Guillén López and Juan Francisco Sánchez Barrilao (eds), *The Impact of the Economic Crisis on the EU Institutions and Member States* (Thomson Reuters Aranzadi 2015).

Guillén López, Enrique, 'La crisis económica y la dirección política: reflexiones sobre los conceptos de necesidad y de elección en la teoría constitucional' (2013). *Revista de Derecho Constitucional Europeo*, n. 20.

Montilla Martos, Antonio José, 'Algunos cambios en la concepción de los partidos: comentario a la STC 48/ 2003, sobre la Ley Orgánica 6/2002, de partidos políticos' (2004). *Teoría y Realidad Constitucional*, No. 12–13, 559–585.

Nuñez Fernández, José, 'La Doctrina Parot y el fallo del TEDH en el asunto Del Río Prada c. España: el principio del fin de un conflicto sobre el castigo de hechos acaecidos hace más de veinte años' (2013). *Revista de Derecho Penal y Criminología*, 3 *Época* 9, 377–436.

Ragone, Sabrina, 'La incidencia de la crisis en la distribución interna del poder entre parlamentos y gobiernos nacionales', in Francisco Balaguer Callejón, Miguel Azpitarte Sánchez, Enrique Guillén López and Juan Francisco Sánchez Barrilao (eds), *The Impact of the Economic Crisis on the EU Institutions and Member States* (Thomson Reuters Aranzadi 2015).

Vírgala Foruria, Eduardo, 'La suspensión de derechos por terrorismo en el ordenamiento español' (1994). *Revista Española de Derecho Constitucional*, 14(40), Enero–Abril.

Vírgala Foruria, Eduardo, 'El Tribunal Europeo de Derechos Humanos avala la ilegalización de Batasuna (aspectos positivos y algunos pocos negativos de su jurisprudencia)' (2010). *Revista de Derecho Constitucional Europeo*, 7(13), Enero–Junio.

12 National security and the limits of judicial protection

Patrick Birkinshaw

Introduction

This chapter will examine national security and the limits of judicial protection in the United Kingdom (UK).[1] National security is a matter reserved to the Westminster government and Parliament. As we shall see, it is an area subject to the pervasive protection of secrecy, an aspect I have addressed in previous publications.[2] An eminent judge and jurist Sir Stephen Sedley has written that the UK's security establishment has arguably become a fourth power of the state.[3] The democratic and justice ideals of a liberal democratic state such as the UK have to come to terms with institutions which are of long antiquity in British governance but that have escaped any form of democratic and justice oversight until comparatively recently. In a democratic system this posed particular difficulties in a country like the UK which has no written constitution. The overriding symbol of power and legitimacy in the UK is the Crown. The Crown in Parliament is the sovereign law maker. Unlike a written constitution, the 'Crown' does not provide the ultimate source of public powers. Rather '[p]ower in the United Kingdom flows up from the state's component elements, making the Crown its receptacle [and its cover][4], not its source'.[5] I think this chapter will illustrate Sedley's concerns that 'National security furnishes a series of critical instances of the difficulty of reconciling the modern state with the rule of law'.[6]

The most pressing questions that involve the courts and national security are: To what, if any, extent can courts review decisions based on national security? To what extent may courts investigate claims of national security as a justification for executive actions that interfere with individual rights and to what extent can the law offer protection to such individuals? Thirdly, as much of national security litigation is subject to executive demands to conduct litigation in secrecy, or to place severe constraints on what evidence may be heard in open court, what qualifications have been made to the common law fundamental right of 'open justice' in civil actions? Fourthly, are there limits set by the courts to the extent to which executive action can avoid or override the procedural and substantive protection which individuals would have a right to rely on to protect their own individual rights? Lastly, what safeguards are provided by law in the intrusive surveillance practices exercised by security and intelligence bodies to protect the right to privacy?

By way of introduction I should say that, and despite some notable exceptions, English law starts from the basis that individuals are entitled to live their lives in a free and democratic environment in which personal liberty is jealously protected by the ordinary courts of law under the premises of the rule of law that includes protection of human rights. Cases from the Second World War period in which basic principles of liberty and legality were ignored by senior judges are today regarded as deeply flawed (perhaps not quite universally so).[7] In national security judges and natural justice had to take a back seat. It was a matter of uncontrolled executive discretion.[8] The position in the 1970s and 1980s often left much to be desired. The advance of judicial review and judicial protection has made inroads into the general zone of executive immunity. But there are subjects on which the judges are reluctant to speak. Although the common law can sometimes speak the language of legal fundamentalism, a number of special tribunals exist to deal with security matters in the UK and the common law's premium on 'open justice' is heavily qualified. Statutes have also allowed considerable incursions into individuals' liberties and freedoms in the name of national security.

The UK has a long exposure to terrorist activities. From the 1960s this was largely confined to Irish Republicanism, although the Irish 'troubles' go back much further. Secrecy, security, allegations of breaches of Arts 2, 3, and 6 ECHR and detention without trial under Art 5 were familiar fare. More recently the spotlight has moved to Islamic fundamentalism and global terrorism. The assumptions and context of the 1960s–1990s, in which judicial safeguards were less developed, have had to accommodate safeguards contained in the Human Rights Act 1998.

UK judges are currently in high constitutional mode and are sedulously working out the contours of national constitutionalism, common law fundamentalism and human rights protection.[9] I would emphasise at this early point that the Human Rights Act (HRA), which incorporated parts but not all of the ECHR into UK law, has had a profound effect in fortifying judicial protection of individual rights within the UK. The operation of the ECHR by virtue of the HRA and subject to the interpretations of domestic judges has been an enormously rich period in domestic legal development.[10] The HRA is not liked by the present government but plans to replace it with a domestic measure have run into serious difficulties. The effects of the ECHR will be seen throughout this chapter. But one recent example provides a dramatic illustration of its importance.

In *Miranda* the partner of a journalist was stopped under powers contained in the Terrorism Act 2000 Sched 7 at Heathrow airport. This provision allows a person present at a port or in the border area to be detained for up to nine hours in order to establish whether they appear to be a person falling within section 40(1)(b) of the 2000 Act, i.e. a person who is or had been concerned in the commission, preparation or instigation of acts of terrorism. He was suspected of possessing information related to the Edward Snowden disclosures on global surveillance by the USA and UK. His laptop, which contained encrypted material derived from the Snowden leaks, was confiscated by the police. This material was to be used to assist his partner's journalism. According to the witness statement of the Deputy National Security Adviser for Intelligence, Security and Resilience in the Cabinet office, the encrypted data on the external hard drive taken from *M* contained approximately 58,000 highly classified UK intelligence documents, many of which were classified as SECRET or TOP SECRET. The Court of Appeal ruled this was a lawful exercise of power under the 2000 Act but in disagreement with the Divisional Court, the court declared that the stop power conferred by para 2(1) of Schedule 7 is incompatible with article 10 of the Convention in relation to journalistic material in that it is not subject to adequate safeguards against its arbitrary exercise. The court allowed the appeal in relation to that issue. It will be for Parliament to provide such protection. The most obvious safeguard would be some form of judicial or other independent and impartial scrutiny conducted in such a way as to protect the confidentiality in the material, the court believed.[11] In the Investigatory Powers Act 2016 additional protection was provided for journalists' sources and confidential material under the Act's surveillance powers.

1. The UK's national security agencies

The operative agencies, or the major ones, are the security service MI5, the intelligence service MI6 (now SIS) and the General Communications Headquarters (GCHQ). MI5 are responsible for internal security, MI6 for intelligence and they operate overseas. GCHQ is the surveillance centre based at Cheltenham. Security vetting takes place at various levels according to published criteria. Cooperation exists with the 'Five Eyes' group of Anglophonic intelligence services (UK, USA, Canada, Australia and New Zealand) and with the European Counter-Terrorism Group.[12] Brexit has produced uncertainty in future UK/EU relations and this is certainly true in future arrangements for security and intelligence.

The UK agencies (hereafter S&IS) are protected by official secrecy laws and as we shall see have exclusions from the Freedom of Information Act 2000. Until 1989 the services operated under the royal prerogative and not legislation. The age-old aphorism 'salus populi suprema lex' ensured they would operate clandestinely and without interference. This helped fuel mystery and numerous scandalous rumours – some emerging as fact. The agencies have no executive powers as such – they rely upon the police for powers of arrest, detention and other matters. A National Police Agency established in 2013 to replace the Serious Organised Crime Agency is a national agency dealing with serious crime and cyber crime.

Commencing in 1989, MI5 was placed on a statutory basis by the Security Service Act of that year. This defined their objectives. The Intelligence Service Act 1994 introduced legislation for MI6 and GCHQ. The Acts have been added to subsequently. The 1994 Act also introduced the Intelligence and Security Committee (ISC) as a special committee of the UK Parliament that did not sit in Parliament. This Committee, which has been heavily criticised for inadequate supervision, was subject to various reforms under the Justice and Security Act 2013 Part I and Sched I[13] making it a 'committee of Parliament', and increasing its independence from government and extending the ambit of its investigations into security operations under careful qualifications as well as matters of policy, expenditure and administration. Service chiefs are no longer able to refuse evidence – this must be done by the minister who remains accountable to Parliament. The Prime Minister (PM) is given power to censor reports that are otherwise made public although reports may be made only to the PM.

Over recent years the services have been brought more into the glare of public scrutiny[14] and in 2014 the agency chiefs made their first ever public appearance before ISC. In November 2016 the head of MI5 gave the first ever newspaper interview which highlighted the increasing threat from Russia. Increasing scrutiny has been unavoidable given the allegations of wrongdoing by the agencies.

S&IS operate under a Commissioner who is, or was, a senior judge and who investigates the operations of the services including their special investigation powers[15] and bulk data sets. The Commissioner's brief was extended by the 2013 Act. An interception of Communications Commissioner oversees the statutory regime of intercepts and acquisition of data communications laid out in the Regulation of Investigatory Powers Act 2000 (RIPA below). Warrants for special investigation powers and intercepts etc are given by the secretary of state and may be investigated by the Commissioners. Warrants are not required for data communications. Reforms have gone through Parliament (below). The Investigatory Powers Tribunal hears complaints about activities of the services (below).

Finally, an Independent Reviewer of Terrorism Legislation was provided by the Prevention of Terrorism Act 2005, although the office pre-dates that legislation.[16] Reports are presented to Parliament and published. The Counter-Terrorism and Security Act 2015 increased the range of the reviewer's work and established a Civil Liberties and Privacy Board to assist the reviewer. There is an extensive array of terrorist legislation affecting the rights and liberties of citizens and aliens.

2. Maintaining secrecy

It will come as little surprise that the S&IS have been protected by secrecy. S 1 Official Secrets Act 1989 prohibits service personnel and 'designated persons' from making unauthorised disclosures of security and intelligence information. Other officials and third parties are prohibited from making damaging disclosures and in the latter case knowing or having reasonable cause to believe that the information was protected. S 4(3) prohibits unauthorised disclosure of special investigation powers and interception of communications.

In *Shayler* the House of Lords ruled that the breadth of these offences did not mean that they were absolute offences, although they are not far from that, and they were a legitimate requirement of national security.[17] They did not constitute a breach of Art. 10 ECHR.

The Freedom of Information Act 2000 excludes the services (s 23) and the National Crime Agency from their provisions and in the case of public authorities holding such information – for example, the Home, Cabinet or Foreign Offices or police – the information is protected by an absolute exemption.[18] This means that the Information Commissioner cannot determine whether the public interest requires disclosure of such information. Under s 24 national security is a ground for exempting information from disclosure although here, and also under s 23, a challenge may be made against the secretary of state's certificate designating the information as protected by national security or that it relates to S&IS. The appeal lies to the Upper Tribunal against the certificate.

National security litigation invariably raises questions of maintaining the secrecy of the services, their operations and informers, methods etc. Non disclosure has been a serious problem – both in terms of the courts and access to justice and also in relation the Intelligence and Security Committee of Parliament.[19]

Courts have very wide powers under civil law to prevent publication of information whose disclosure would be against the public interest.[20] Members of the S&IS are under a life-long duty of confidence to the Crown.[21] Although special protection for Art. 10 ECHR rights is contained in the HRA s12, arguments based on national security would weigh very heavily in a court's deliberations.[22]

3. Liability

Most of the examples that concern this study involve questions of policy and its implementation through various instruments. But an issue that has featured with growing frequency in the English courts concerns questions of liability and compensation for wrong-doing and civil actions for tortious conduct on behalf of the authorities. The authorities have usually been the secretaries of state for foreign and home affairs, S&IS and the armed forces. A basic principle of English law is that officials, including the services above, are liable for wrong-doing under the ordinary law. They are given no powers of torture, murder, assault, unlawful imprisonment or kidnapping (extraordinary rendition). Statute allows them special investigation powers (including burglary) and interception powers under various safeguards (below). The services and ministers remain liable under the ordinary law, civil or criminal, for wrong-doing.

The absence of a 'sovereign immunity' since 1947 has meant that English courts have witnessed an increasing number of civil actions brought by individuals caught up in anti-terrorist activity. The litigants have often brought claims involving alleged breaches of human rights as well as common law fundamental rights and civil rights. Decisions of the Court of Human Rights have expanded the basis of liability under the Human Rights Act for actions of HM forces and officials overseas. Matters have not been finally resolved in the UK courts.[23] Liability for wrong-doing by HM armed forces and security services is a real issue which it is claimed inhibits the defence and security capabilities of the services. The litigants have been assisted by English civil procedures allowing disclosure and inspection of documents held by defendants – a factor which led to the extension of closed material procedures (below). But the litigation has also brought about a significant reconsideration of various immunities available to domestic and foreign governments whose actions were claimed to be inviolable in domestic courts.

As well as state immunity we have seen re-examination of doctrines such as act of state, and foreign act of state involving a foreign government. The Supreme Court has overruled the Court of Appeal and ruled that an act of state by the UK government which is of 'an inherently governmental nature in the conduct of foreign affairs' is immune from tort actions in domestic courts but this immunity does not include torture or maltreatment of detainees.[24] The Supreme Court upheld the Court of Appeal in cases where foreign acts of state are pleaded as an immunity against allegations of torture, unlawful detention, rendition and breaches of fundamental rights. Actions would be allowed to proceed on a case by case assessment. Consequences for international relations are a factor to consider. In the event, an action was allowed to proceed against a former UK Foreign Secretary involving evidence of alleged breaches of human rights by US intelligence forces.[25]

Rather than face publicity in litigation the government has settled many cases. The actions have added to the executive hostility to the HRA. They also led to the Justice and Security Act 2013 which I examine below. Inquiries and investigations were set in motion to investigate serious allegations of mistreatment by UK forces in Iran and Afghanistan although many investigations were dropped or ended inconsequentially.[26]

4. Policy questions and the courts

> "Let judges also remember that Solomon's throne was supported by lions on both sides; let them be lions, but lions under the throne; being circumspect that they do not check or oppose any points of sovereignty. F. Bacon *Essaies* (1625 ed)".[27]

Britain is not alone in judicial recognition of the respect due for policy decisions. The realm of policy is not inviolable to judicial challenge as the case law exemplifies[28] but respect is shown to executive expertise, experience, knowledge and the safeguards of democratic accountability. In matters of policy weighing of evidence is for the executive. In the absence of manifest or clear error the courts would be reluctant to intervene. This judicial deference to executive expertise in pure policy matters is probably the high watermark of the separation of powers in the UK constitution where there is no formal separation between the executive and Parliament.

The respect due to executive expertise is most pronounced in the area of foreign, defence and security policy. The reasons are straightforward. A decision in these areas could have immense international repercussions endangering the public interest. It is better that such policies are effected through one mouth piece. In the absence of legal error the courts abstain. They do not remain silent. A second home grown reason is that the UK constitution maintains a dualistic approach to the recognition of international law. The separation is not as hermetically sealed as previous generations believed, and we saw above how various immunities have been qualified. The actions of the executive in international relations – of which national security is a primary example – are left to the executive unless a clear breach of law is established.[29]

5. The prerogative and national security

The prerogative is not immune from judicial review. Whether the court will review turns on subject matter, context and the scope of the prerogative.[30] Review is not determined on a basis of a general principle of immunity but turns on 'subject matter and suitability in the particular case'.[31] The courts will not question a decision by the executive to declare war or whether a war was illegal.[32] They will not press a secretary of state to make diplomatic representations to a foreign power on behalf of British nationals or residents imprisoned in a facility controlled by the foreign power – though they may require a secretary to abide by public statements on support for such an individual.[33] The courts have vindicated cessation of an investigation and prosecution into alleged corruption in arms sales because of the involvement of a member of the Saudi Arabian royal family and threats of non cooperation by the Saudi government in intelligence sharing if the investigation was not 'pulled'.[34]

In *Yunus Rahmatullah*[35] the Supreme Court examined an agreement between the US and UK to establish the terms of detention of an alien in Iraq who had been handed over to the Americans by the British. This was not a treaty but a 'diplomatic agreement' incorporating the Geneva Convention the court ruled. It appeared prima facie that the terms of the agreement were not complied with by the US authorities. This was a sufficient basis to issue the writ of habeas corpus on the UK secretary of state to seek a justification for detention from the US. A justification was forthcoming.

Long ago, the Judicial Committee of the Privy Council ruled that although assessment of 'national security' is for the executive alone there has to be evidence of national security[36] – although this has sometimes been expediently applied.[37] Courts give wide berth to a declaration of a state of emergency justifying derogation from the ECHR Art 5 under Art 15.[38] However, this did not prevent the instruments of derogation being ruled disproportionate, irrational and discriminatory and the statutory provision on which detention on national security grounds and suspicion of terrorism was based being declared incompatible with the ECHR. A declaration of incompatibility is a remedy provided for by the HRA but this does not invalidate the offending statutory provision. A declaration invariably leads to reform in the legislation.

Where powers are contained in legislation judges act more like lions under the Parliamentary Mace rather than lions under the Throne. But they are the sole interpreters of Parliament's legislation and have developed long established principles to construe statutes and preserve their jurisdiction. However, legislative subjects differ in sensitivity and may offer limited scope for judicial intervention. At the level of high policy in the general interest, the courts will be reluctant to intervene. This has been a consistent approach. The more a policy impacts upon identifiable individuals, the more inquisitive the courts become. This has become more pronounced in recent years. Where human rights and fundamental freedoms are involved, proportionality may be invoked.[39] These points are best illustrated through some examples.

In *Rehman* an alien Islamic cleric suspected of training terrorists in England to launch attacks on the Indian sub-continent was subject to a deportation order issued by the secretary of state who deemed that his presence in the UK was not conducive to the public interest on the grounds of national security.[40] This was successfully challenged before SIAC (below) on, essentially, the absence of an established question of jurisdictional fact. The House of Lords allowing the secretary of state's appeal left no doubt that this judgment was not a question of fact for the judicial tribunal but was within the secretary of state's sole preserve. While the court might intervene in cases where clear error was shown, the question of judgment was for the secretary alone and his expert knowledge and resources, in matters on which judges were not experienced. Deportation would be subject to Art 3 ECHR considerations.

In *Lord Carlile QC* the question involved a dissident Iranian politician resident in Paris, who had sought entry to the UK to speak at the UK Parliament on democracy, human rights and other policy issues at the invitation of the Parliamentary appellants.[41] The secretary of state excluded her because she thought that her presence in the UK would have a damaging effect on Britain's relations with Iran and may lead to retaliatory action by Iran against British interests abroad. She justified the decision on the grounds that her presence in the UK would 'not be conducive to the public good for reasons of foreign policy and in the light of the need to take a firm stance against terrorism'. Furthermore, admission would be seen as a 'deliberate political move against Iran', which risked destabilising relations between the UK and Iran that in turn would be detrimental to the conduct of foreign policy and the advancement of UK national security interests. The diplomatic and national security evidence relied upon was before the public. However, key aspects of the government's case had not been challenged by cross-examination. Lord Neuberger believed that legal challenges were not limited to rationality, legality or procedural impropriety – classic grounds of review in English law. Lord Sumption opined that whilst the court was required to 'test the adequacy of the factual basis claimed for the decision', and was the 'ultimate arbiter of the appropriate balance between' the Convention rights engaged and the interests of the community, the court was not usually concerned with remaking the decision-maker's assessment of the evidence if it was an assessment reasonably open to her. As Lord Sumption said at [para 46]: 'We have no experience and no material which could justify us in rejecting the Foreign Office assessment in favour of a more optimistic assessment of our own'. Similarly Lord Neuberger said at [para 71] whilst a citizen might question the decision of the secretary of state, a judge has neither the experience nor knowledge to make such a finding, save in exceptional circumstances, which could not be established in the absence of any cross-examination. Three of the Justices (Neuberger, Hale and Clarke) expressly noted that there was room for considerable scepticism about the views reached but that in the absence of cross-examination it would be difficult to challenge them. It should be noted that MI5 officers were questioned in *Zatuliveter v SSHD*[42] and their evidence found unreliable. Lord Kerr delivered a dissenting judgment.

The point has frequently been emphasised that while questions of policy in national security must be treated with great caution by the courts, the courts are more exacting when an individual's rights, especially human rights, are involved. *Carlisle* involved policy and Art 10 rights. In *A* (above) the regime of executive detention of alien terrorist suspects resident in the UK was ruled unlawful as we saw. The law was subsequently modified. In a further iteration of *A* ([2005] UKHL 71) the law lords ruled that evidence obtained by torture overseas (from overseas security services) could not be admitted before a judicial body in the UK. It offended the common law. However, the limitations of this ruling have been exposed (below).[43]

In *Ahmed* the newly established Supreme Court gave a ruling on the implementation of UN Security Council resolutions concerning financial freezing orders. In a long and complex judgment, which had a speedy successor, the Court ruled that the UK legislative provision chosen to implement the measures into domestic law, the United Nations Act 1946, neither justified the measures contained within the delegated legislation on the principle of legality and they amounted to an unlawful interference with common law fundamental rights to property and access to justice.[44] This, along with *Bank Mellat No 2* below, was a high water mark of judicial protection of individual rights in suspected terrorist litigation. Subsequently the government piloted a bill through Parliament nullifying the effects of the two judgments, the second refused to defer the effect of the first judgment, and then legislation at the end of 2010 contained, inter alia, the necessary procedural safeguards to comply with the judgment.

In *Bank Mellat No 2*[45] an Iranian bank had been the subject of orders served by HM Treasury restricting access to UK financial markets. This was because it was alleged to have close connections to the Iranian nuclear weapons programmes. The orders, which had to be approved by Parliament under the relevant legislation, had to be 'proportionate' and were subject to appeal to the High Court. The orders are delegated legislation made under primary legislation (statute) and are subject, unlike statutes, to judicial control. This is so under UK law whether their effect is of an individual or legislative nature. Nonetheless, a majority found that they were arbitrary, irrational, disproportionate and discriminatory. Only this Iranian bank had been singled out; the risk involved was 'inherent in banking' and no different from that posed by other banks who were not subject to orders (orders subsequently involved all Iranian banks). The majority also ruled that *BM* should have been given a hearing before the orders were served notwithstanding the procedural safeguards contained in the orders. Despite the division of judicial opinion in this case it remains a remarkable example of judicial interference in national security affairs. It remains to be seen whether such a robust approach will characterise future case law involving alleged ISIS.

The approach in these cases should be compared with *Youssef*.[46] *Y* was an Egyptian national allowed leave to remain in the UK. The question in *Y* concerned asset freezing orders issued by the UN Sanctions Committee imposed on *Y*. The Committee maintains a list of those subject to freezing orders. The secretary of state had initially agreed in 2005 to listing of the appellant by the Committee, specifically he had lifted the 'hold' he possessed to prevent listing, but then following *Ahmed* had supported de-listing by the Committee. Subsequently, when the UN Ombudsperson reported (with reasons [para 5]) on the grounds for having a reasonable belief that the appellant was a suspected terrorist, the secretary of state refused to support *Y*'s de-listing. Ostensibly, the case of *Y* at first would seem very close to *Ahmed*. In a single judgment given by Lord Carnwath, which basically supported Laws LJ in the Court of Appeal,[47] several points distinguishing *Ahmed* were emphasised. Firstly, the court ruled that although the prerogative of foreign affairs was involved by virtue of the SoS's membership of the UN Committee, decisions were challengeable albeit 'courts proceed with caution'. The object of attack was the SoS decision, not those of the UN Committee. The bases of the SoS's decisions were not tainted by evidence obtained by torture Carnwath believed and the SoS was under no duty to investigate the evidential basis of decisions of other members of the Committee and whether those decisions relied upon torture evidence [para 29]. The provenance of some evidence used by other members seems highly questionable. The phrase used by the measures impugned by the court in *Ahmed* – 'reasonable suspicion of being a terrorist suspect' – was not formed in relation to a UK statute that did not justify in its very broad terms an interference with basic rights as was the situation in *Ahmed*. The phrase was a precautionary one and had been used by the UN Financial Action Task Force in its recommendations on asset freezing and as formulated by the UN Ombudsperson in her report to the UN Security Council and was not imposed under a UK prerogative power but by virtue of EC Regulation 881/2002 Annex I [para 35]. Courts should pay 'very high respect to ministerial security assessments on competence and constitutional grounds' [para 51]. While not disagreeing with the courts' rulings on proportionality in *Carlisle*, proportionality would not lead to a different result and would not allow a merits review in the present context. In some contexts human rights protection will allow something approaching a merits review of a decision which usually is not a subject that can be impeached on judicial review in England and Wales.

There are some troubling aspects to the court's points of distinction from *Ahmed*. In *Ahmed* the court confirmed in dramatic circumstances the overriding importance of legality in the protection of human rights when interpreting a domestic statute – vague or general words do not suffice to override such rights whether their provenance is common law or European law. Does the EC measure provide a clear framework for such interference? The measure had been amended to allow for review of evidence by the Sanctions Committee. Furthermore, the phrase 'reasonable grounds for suspicion' which was deficient in *Ahmed* because of its non compliance with the wording of the Security Council resolution in question and the very punitive effects the decisions had on an individual have just the same consequences in *Youssef*. The effects are the same. The Terrorist Asset-Freezing etc Act 2010 had introduced appeal rights in domestic courts against orders issued by HM Treasury as well as humanitarian exceptions for subsistence. Reliance on 'context is everything' is often used to explain nuances in development of legal principle. On first reading *Youssef* seems just a little too expedient. 'Risk cannot be assessed on a balance of probabilities. It involves a question of degree' [para 50]. *Y* had been 'a strong vocal supporter of Al Qaida and its objectives' and had not refuted the allegations [para 61]. However, 'reasonable cause' is a precautionary term and has to be objectively quantified and rationally supported by evidence one would expect. This was the very point of disagreement between Lord Atkin and the other judges in the 1942 case of *Liversidge v Anderson* which introduced our discussion. Words cannot be twisted to mean whatever the official wants them to mean. They require objective proof and grounds for suspecting terrorist activity.

6. National security and open justice

As far back as 1637 litigation concerning matters of national security were dealt with in open court according to what we now term 'open justice'.[48] 'Open justice' was confirmed as the model of adjudication in English courts by the House of Lords in 1913.[49] Lord Shaw quoting Jeremy Bentham exclaimed 'Publicity is the very soul of Justice'. The same judge sat in a case two years later when the same court approved more secretive procedures for administrative proceedings.[50] Judges should not impose their standards on the administration the later judgments stated. Courts retained the power to prohibit publication of evidence and information by the press and media. They could hold proceedings *in camera* ie privately. This might occur in official secrets prosecutions. A decision of the Court of Appeal (Criminal Division) in 2014 ruled that criminal courts could sit with only accredited members of the press present and with strict safeguards to prevent publication until authorised.[51]

The Crown was immune from civil suit in its own courts until 1947 – not so individual ministers and officials in their personal capacity. When the Crown was subjected to civil liability under civil law it retained privileges in relation to non disclosure and inspection of documents and evidence in litigation where the public interest required secrecy. The nature of the claim and reasons for the claim are well understood but led to routine abuse.[52] The judicial response was for judges eventually to determine for themselves that they might inspect the documents in question to see whether the interests of justice required disclosure and inspection by the plaintiff.[53] The government would claim public interest immunity (PII) for documents or evidence.

However, in terrorist cases the resort to PII presented serious problems for the Crown. While government was usually able to protect sensitive information, successful application for PII meant the Crown could not benefit from the evidence to defend itself in actions against litigants claiming damages for civil wrongs. Neither side could invoke the evidence although clearly the Crown had sight of the materials. Such actions were increasing in number after the invasions of Iraq and Afghanistan and in the wake of allegations of British intelligence and security services' involvement in torture and extraordinary rendition (above).

The litigation is still continuing and has raised and developed common law principles in relation to the jurisdiction of UK courts to hear cases with a marked degree of international involvement (above). The most dramatic illustration of 'open justice' occurred in the *Bin Yam Mohamed* case.[54]

This case involved an application by *BYM* for documents held by the UK secretary of state detailing torture and mistreatment by American security officials. Many documents had been disclosed but although most of the judgments had been given after open proceedings there had been closed (non-public) proceedings with closed judgments.[55] The meaning of these terms will be explained below. Objections to disclosure of information came from the highest source in the USA. Disclosure by the English courts would undermine the US 'control principle' and would jeopardise intelligence sharing in the future between the UK and USA – a claim that was treated with some scepticism by the English courts. The question before the Court of Appeal concerned seven paragraphs of the judgment in the High Court which the Crown requested should not be published. Pending appeal, the High Court ruled these should be published. These had been published in an American judgment by the time the Court of Appeal came to its ruling. But for this it would have suppressed publication. The High Court decision was upheld.

However, it transpired that the court had been prevailed upon to keep three paragraphs of its own judgment (Lord Neuberger's) secret after 'complaints' by counsel for the secretary of state – Jonathan Sumption, who is now a justice of the Supreme Court. This fomented a second judgment after the press became aware of, and publicised, the suppression. The omitted paragraphs were set out in full after publication in the reconvened judgment [paras 168–170].

These placed serious doubt on the veracity of claims by the security services that they respected human rights and that 'coercive interrogation techniques were alien to the services' general ethics, methodology and training'. This further placed in doubt the reliability of the secretary of state's certificates based on witness statements from the security personnel.

The government determined that such public discussion of matters which it had long desired to be protected by complete secrecy had to be brought to quietus. This was achieved by the Justice and Security Act 2013 ss 17–18. These sections prevent a court exercising the 'residual jurisdiction' to allow disclosure of 'sensitive information' ie intelligence and that specified or described by the secretary of state. The secretary of state may issue a certificate on this matter – which is conclusive on the court in relation to intelligence material. The secretary of state may issue a certificate only if s/he considers it would be contrary to the interests of national security or the international relations of the United Kingdom to disclose the information, whether the information exists, or whether the person said to hold the information is in fact in possession of the information. A party to proceedings may apply for a review of the certificate by the court but not in relation to intelligence material.

A final point on open justice should be made about a remarkable episode involving an inquest into the death of former KGB agent Alexander Litvinenko allegedly murdered by polonium administered by soviet agents in a drink in a London hotel. The coroner, a senior judge, requested the Home Secretary to call an inquiry to investigate the circumstances of the death. The question of Russian involvement was one that he wished to pursue. On procedural grounds he was not entitled at an inquest to obtain the evidence he required from the government, a decision upheld by the High Court.[56] He therefore requested that the government establish an inquiry under s1 of the Inquiries Act 2005 which could sit *in camera* (privately) and consider secret evidence. The government refused to accede to this. The Divisional Court ruled on several grounds that the Home Secretary's refusal was unlawful.[57] The secretary of state had not provided a rational basis for not accepting the coroner's request. Better reasons by law were required for a refusal.

When the Inquiry was held the coroner reported of 'probable approval' of the decision to murder by the Russian President himself.[58] This is a remarkable intervention by a judicial body into political affairs with unforeseen international consequences.

7. Special adjudicatory bodies

A variety of judicial bodies deal with security issues. I will deal with the two most important. Both of these can receive evidence that ordinary courts could not; for example, hearsay and intercept. They cannot hear evidence obtained by torture.

7.1 Special Immigration Appeals Commission (SIAC)

SIAC was established in 1997. It was a response to *Chahal v UK* and the pitifully inadequate procedures available prior to SIAC for cases of deportation on grounds of national security.[59] The CHR (Court of Human Rights) ruled that the procedure adopted by the UK was in breach of Article 5(4).[60] We have noted in *Rehman* how the courts circumscribed the challenges they could make to judgments 'in the interests of national security'. SIAC provided a new procedure now known as the closed material procedure (CMP) to attend to the problems caused by security sensitive evidence.[61] This development is so important that it is explained in a following section. As we shall see, the procedure seeks to ensure that evidence against a terrorist suspect may not be shown to the suspect and proceedings in which such evidence is heard will be conducted in the absence of the suspect and his lawyer. A special advocate is appointed to represent the interests of the suspect (below). CMPs were extended to high court procedures dealing with suspected terrorist 'control orders' and their successors and then to civil actions generally.[62]

7.2 The Investigatory Powers Tribunal (IPT)[63]

The IPT was established by RIPA 2000. Much of RIPA is to be recast under the Investigatory Powers Act 2016 which I deal with below. It is chaired by a senior judge who sits with legally qualified personnel. Members are a matter of public record. The tribunal is the only body that can deal with human rights complaints against the services and surveillance complaints. In *R (A) v B* the House of Lords ruled that the tribunal was the only body that could deal with complaints by members or former members of the services who were refused permission to publish material.[64] The tribunal invariably sat in private but more recently it has sat in public and has published its judgments although not sensitive material. The tribunal announces on its site that it is required by law (RIPA section 69(6)(b)) not to disclose material provided to it which would threaten the national interest, national security, operations against serious crime or any functions of the intelligence agencies. However, it has concluded that publication of a ruling on a point of law or on the basis of assumed facts does not compromise these areas or the 'neither confirm nor deny' principle by which the intelligence agencies operate. It seeks where possible to publish its judgments. It also publishes its judgments where a determination of unlawful conduct is made. The tribunal cannot be challenged in court proceedings on appeal or review although the bill above has provisions removing this protection. The procedures of the IPT were given approval by the CHR in *Kennedy v UK*.[65]

The tribunal has been engaged in some highly publicised litigation following the revelations of Chelsea Manning (WikiLeaks) and Edward Snowden re world-wide interception and data retention by the US National Security Agency and GCHQ. While the overall schemes of surveillance and data retention contained in RIPA were ruled compliant with Arts 8 and 10 ECHR, the tribunal found breaches of those provisions in individual cases. The judgments had led to publication of material on surveillance that rendered the surveillance ECHR compliant.[66] The tribunal has ruled that surveillance has breached legal professional privilege.[67] Furthermore the interception of Westminster MPs' communications was not ruled a breach of an undertaking given by a previous prime minister in 1966 in relation to untargeted surveillance, only directed (on an individual) surveillance was covered. But these undertakings did not constitute a legal undertaking because the services had to abide by the law and their own statutory codes which had now been published.[68] The tribunal ruled in a claim brought against the Commissioner of Police of the Metropolis by News Group Newspapers and three journalists employed by *The Sun* newspaper that the 2007 Communications Code did not provide effective safeguards in a case in which the purpose of an authorisation made under s 22 of RIPA was to obtain disclosure of the identity of a journalist's source. Accordingly, the authorisations were not compatible with the Convention rights of the complainants under Article 10.[69]

Bulk surveillance powers have featured in its case law. In *Privacy International v Secretary of State for F&CA etc*[70] the tribunal ruled it was permissible to use s 94 Telecommunications Act 1984 to obtain bulk communications data (BCD). RIPA expressly preserved s 94 in s 80. The bulk personal data system operated by SIS and GCHQ prior to BPDs (bulk personal datasets) avowal (publication) in March 2015 did not satisfy ECHR requirements ie 'in accordance with the law'. The bulk communications data system BCD did not satisfy ECHR principles prior to its avowal in November 2015 and the introduction of a more 'adequate system of supervision' at that date. Both BPD and BCD systems complied with the principles after those respective dates. The tribunal still has to consider the question of proportionality and EU law. The question of data transfer was not included.

8. Closed Material Procedures (CMPs)

CMPs were introduced in 1997 under the SIAC procedures[71] and were influenced to an extent by what was presumed to be the practice in Canadian procedures.[72] SIAC was the first tribunal in the UK to make use of special advocates (SAs).[73] It deals with national security deportations.[74] SAs are experienced and security cleared counsel who test the closed material, by all accounts vigorously, in the deportee's interests. But they are not the deportee's lawyer. The deportee and his lawyer may meet with the SA but may communicate only under strict directions after the closed material has been shown to the SA (CPR 82.11). The CM must not be discussed with them. The deportee therefore cannot give instructions on the material or offer an explanation or denial of what the material contains. The way the system operates raises the most serious of questions about fair procedure or due process. As Chief Justice McLachlin expressed it 'How can one meet a case one does not know?'[75]

SAs were extended by Civil Procedure Rules (CPR) to control order measures which were introduced after the House of Lords ruled that the provisions allowing executive detention for aliens (based on immigration laws) in the Anti-terrorism, Crime and Security Act 2001[76] were unlawful because the measures breached the ECHR.[77] This was under the Prevention of Terrorism Act 2005.[78] These measures were themselves replaced in 2011 by legislation introducing terrorism prevention and investigation measures[79] which rely upon the secretary of state being satisfied, on the balance of probabilities, that the suspect is or has been involved in terrorism related activities. This formulation was added by the Counter Terrorism etc Act 2015 ss 20(1) 52(5) and replaced a 'reasonable belief' test. CMPs are used.

It was reported by Justice in 2009 that 14 statutes had been passed since 1997 authorising use of secret evidence in tribunals as diverse as employment and land use planning.[80]

The extension of SAs and CMPs under common law was allowed by the Court of Appeal and then by the House of Lords without specific statutory authorisation.[81] However, though its use was allowed in employment vetting and suspension procedures[82] the Supreme Court ruled that they were not permissible in common law civil actions[83] although that court could hear appeals in a closed procedure from proceedings involving SAs under a CMP.[84] This of course covered the numerous instances where the UK government was being sued for the actions of its security and armed services which we referred to above.

In the Justice and Security Act 2013[85] the government obtained in legislation powers to authorize ministers to certify that CMPs should be used in any *civil* procedure thereby reversing *Al Rawi*. This now provides a general legislative basis for CMPs and they are subject to limited judicial oversight. The orders have to be Art 6 ECHR compliant so the following case law is relevant on judicial supervision. The judge must first consider whether a Public Interest Immunity certificate (above) has been considered by the Minister. If not appropriate a CMP may be applied for from the judge. CMP declarations may be revoked by the court.[86]

A crucial question for the courts has been what is the defendant before CMPs allowed as of right to know to satisfy the requirements of Art 6 ECHR or Art 47 EU CFR? The UK government's case was that if the evidence was so strong that there was no answer to it, there would be no unfairness in withholding the evidence from the defendant. In the event, the CHR which had ruled that in national security cases not all the evidence had to be revealed[87] determined that basically evidence on which a case fell or prevailed had to be disclosed to the defendant.[88] This approach was adopted, with some reluctance, by the House of Lords in domestic law.[89] The test for detention would be the same for control orders or their successors. As Lord Phillips put the point [para 59]:

> [The CHR] establishes that the controlee must be given sufficient information about the allegations against him to enable him to give effective instructions in relation to those allegations. Provided that this requirement is satisfied there can be a fair trial notwithstanding that the controlee is not provided with the detail or the sources of the evidence forming the basis of the allegations. Where, however, the open material consists purely of general assertions and the case against the controlee is based solely or to a decisive degree on closed materials the requirement of a fair trial will not be satisfied, however cogent the case based on the closed materials may be.

Tariq, which was referred to above, did not accept that the test in *AF* applied in all SA cases. The claimant in *Tariq* was employed as an immigration officer but was suspended when his security clearance was withdrawn. He claimed that he was the victim of discrimination on the grounds of race and religious belief invoking EU law. The Home Office said that it was in the interests of national security that much of the evidence on which it wished to rely should not be disclosed to the claimant or his advisers. The Supreme Court held that the *AF (No.3)* standard of disclosure was not a uniform requirement and that on the particular facts of *Tariq* the disadvantage to the claimant of withholding secret material was outweighed by the paramount need to protect the integrity of the security vetting process.

Summarising the position, Richards LJ in *Bank Mellat* quoted from paragraphs 20–23 of Lord Dyson's judgment in *Kiani* [2015] EWCA Civ 1020:[90]

> 23. In summary, therefore, the requirements of article 6 depend on context and all the circumstances of the case. The particular circumstances in *Tariq* included the fact that (i) it did not involve the liberty of the subject; (ii) the claimant had been provided with a degree of information as to the basis for the decision to withdraw his security vetting: he was not completely in the dark; (iii) there was real scope for the special advocate to test the issue of discrimination without obtaining instructions on the facts from the claimant; and (iv) this was a security vetting case and it was clearly established in the Strasbourg jurisprudence that an individual was not entitled to full article 6 rights if to accord him such rights would jeopardise the efficacy of the vetting regime itself.
>
> [para 159]

The Court of Appeal ruled that the *AF* standard applies to financial prohibition notices as in *Bank Mellat* as they would in freezing orders, and TPIMs (Terrorism Prevention and Investigation Measures), the latter being the replacement for control orders (above).[91] The court further held that the disclosure to Bank Mellat had not been specific enough to satisfy the *AF* test.

On one point the British courts have been adamant. In 2005, the Law Lords ruled that judicial bodies such as SIAC or the IPT could not admit evidence or intelligence obtained by torture overseas. The common law found such a prospect abhorrent.[92] The protection given to this 'constitutional right', which was far more significant than a mere rule of evidence, has to be contextualised by the fact that the person alleging the torture had to prove the allegation – don't forget they are subject to CMPs – and the prohibition only applied to *judicial* proceedings. It had no legal bearing on the use of intelligence obtained overseas by foreign powers by the executive in other circumstances. Detailed guidance is set out on torture. This states the government's policy is clear. 'We do not participate in, solicit, encourage or condone the use of torture or cruel or inhuman or degrading punishment for any purpose.'[93] We saw above how in *Youssef* the secretary of state was not under a duty to examine the evidentiary basis of decision-making by other members of the UN Security Council although the court was satisfied the secretary had not used torture intelligence to make the security assessment.

9. Surveillance

RIPA 2000 regulated surveillance by the S&IS and police. The main point here is that intercept material cannot be used in judicial proceedings – although there are numerous exceptions. The major reason for this is to protect intelligence material. RIPA was amended in 2014 by the Data Retention and Investigatory Powers Act (DRIPA). This Act has effect until December 2016. An Investigatory Powers Bill 2015–16 (now enacted) will amend the provisions dealing with interceptions and data retention (below). In 2015, crucial elements of DRIPA were ruled incompatible by an English court with EU law and the Charter of Fundamental Rights (CFR) following the *Digital Rights* judgment of the ECJ.[94] In particular, the Act does not allow clear and precise rules allowing access to retained data to be strictly restricted to the purposes of prevention/investigation or prosecution of serious crime and access to the data was not dependent on prior judicial or independent administrative authorisation restricting access to what was strictly necessary. S 1 of DRIPA was ruled in breach of EU law. The offending provisions of the Act were subject to a suspended disapplication.

The appeal in *Davis* was heard in November 2015. Basically the Court of Appeal (CA)[95] cast doubt on the Divisional Court's ruling that the ECJ's judgment in *Digital Rights*, which ruled the EC Data Retention Directive (2006/24/EC) disproportionate in its aim of collecting in a mass form communications data for the purposes of investigation, detection and prosecution of serious crime, set down mandatory requirements of EU law for national legislation in relation to access to those data by national authorities. The object of the ECJ's criticism was the EC Directive, not national legislation. The court believed that the ECJ's ruling could affect aspects of data retention and use not covered by EU law, ie outside EU competence such as national security. The Court of Appeal further suggested that EU law according to the ECJ went further than ECHR protection. The CA accepted that Art 8 EUCFR was not limited in scope by Art 8 ECHR. However, the CA doubted whether the ECJ intended to lay down more stringent measures for protection of data than the CHR jurisprudence established [para 111]. This is apparent at para 114 where the CA asked: Did the ECJ go further than the CHR re requiring judicial/independent authorisation for the transfer of the data? The CHR, said the CA, reviewed 'all aspects of the authorisation and oversight regime in existence [in a state] to assess whether it provides overall sufficient protections to democratic freedoms.' In the light of this the court referred the case to the ECJ requesting an expedited hearing. It is interesting that the CA did not take the route of allowing an appeal to the UK Supreme Court. The questions referred to the ECJ under Art 276 TFEU are at para 118 of the CA's judgment and concern access to the data. The Advocate General's opinion was a more stringent judgment insisting on legal protection than the Court of Appeal. The AG saw no need to give an opinion on the ECHR matters raised.[96]

In December 2016 the Grand Chamber of the ECJ gave judgment in the joined case[97] and, differing from the AG in several crucial respects, ruled that national legislation in question (DRIPA 2014 s.1 for the UK) fell within the scope of the relevant EU law (para 81). The right to confidentiality of communications must be strictly interpreted and derogations are limited to those set out in the Directive, for example, national security and investigation of crime. They are exhaustive. They must be interpreted in accordance with the CFR and protection of privacy and freedom of expression as well as relevant EU case law. Derogations must be interpreted as 'necessary, appropriate and proportionate measure within a democratic society' [para 95]. The scope of the retention in the referred cases was a serious interference with privacy and freedom of expression. Only the objective of fighting serious crime would justify such a measure – the court accepted state or national security was outside EU competence but offered various opinions on that subject which will meet with national opposition. General and indiscriminate retention of all traffic and location data would not be justified [para 103]. Even the fight against terrorism 'cannot in itself justify that national legislation providing for the general and indiscriminate retention of all traffic and location data should be considered necessary' [para 103].

Retention must be strictly necessary for the objective of preventing or investigating serious crime and objectively justifiable vis a vis the data retained and the legitimate objective pursued. Article 15(1) of Directive 2002/58, read in the light of Articles 7, 8 and 11 and Article 52(1) of the Charter, does not prevent a Member State from adopting legislation permitting, as a preventive measure, the targeted retention of traffic and location data, for the purpose of fighting serious crime, provided that the retention of data is limited, with respect to the categories of data to be retained, the means of communication affected, the persons concerned and the retention period adopted, to what is strictly necessary [para 108]. The court at this point suggested that geographical profiling based on 'objective evidence' may be permissible, which raises very sensitive questions of racial and social discrimination. With regard to 'bulk' retention as the 2016 UK legislation terms it, Article 15(1) of Directive 2002/58, read in the light of Articles 7, 8 and 11 and Article 52(1) of the Charter, must be interpreted as precluding national legislation which, for the purpose of fighting crime (let alone other objectives), provides for the general and indiscriminate retention of all traffic and location data of all subscribers and registered users relating to all means of electronic communication [para 112].

The court addressed the question of security of data retained for the purposes of serious crime and access by the authorities to those data where that access is not subject to prior review by a court or independent administrative authority, and where there is no requirement that the data concerned should be retained within the EU. Only the objective of fighting serious crime is capable of justifying access to the retained data [para 115]. Safeguards, both procedural i.e. prior review, and substantive, must be laid down in clear and legally binding rules [paras 118–119].

Accordingly, and since general access to all retained data, regardless of whether there is any link, at least indirect, with the intended purpose, cannot be regarded as limited to what is strictly necessary, the national legislation concerned must be based on objective criteria in order to define the circumstances and conditions under which the competent national authorities are to be granted access to the data of subscribers or registered users. In that regard, access can, as a general rule, be granted, in relation to the objective of fighting crime, only to the data of individuals suspected of planning, committing or having committed a serious crime or of being implicated in one way or another in such a crime (*Zakharov v. Russia*, CE:ECHR:2015:1204JUD004714306, § 260 cited). In the war against terrorism, as distinguished from investigating or preventing serious crime, the court suggested:

> access to the data of other persons might also be granted where there is objective evidence from which it can be deduced that that data might, in a specific case, make an effective contribution to combating such activities. [para 119]

Is this not a matter within national competence?

In relation to access to retained data the court ruled that in order to ensure that those conditions are fully respected, it is essential that access of the competent national authorities to retained data should, as a general rule, except in cases of validly established urgency, be subject to a prior review carried out either by a court or by an independent administrative body, and that the decision of that court or body should be made following a reasoned request by those authorities submitted, inter alia, within the framework of procedures for the prevention, detection or prosecution of crime. The court cited the *Digital Rights* judgment, paragraph 62; and in relation to Article 8 of the ECHR *Szabó and Vissy v. Hungary* (ECHR, 2016 §§ 77 and 80).

The court stated that competent national authorities to whom access to the retained data has been granted must notify the persons affected, under the applicable national procedures, as soon as that notification is no longer liable to jeopardise the investigations being undertaken by those authorities. That notification is, in fact, necessary to enable the persons affected to exercise, inter alia, their right to a legal remedy, expressly provided for in Article 15(2) of Directive 2002/58 and relevant EU case law.

The question raised by the Court of Appeal in relation to the ECHR was general and hypothetical on a point of EU law and inadmissible [para 133]. However, that did not prevent the EUECJ referring to judgments of the CHR as seen above. In short, the rulings of the court were: EU law must be interpreted as precluding national legislation which, for the purpose of fighting crime, provides for general and indiscriminate retention of all traffic and location data of all subscribers and registered users relating to all means of electronic communication. And, EU law (the point referred by the Court of Appeal) … must be interpreted as precluding national legislation governing the protection and security of traffic and location data and, in particular, access of the competent national authorities to the retained data, where the objective pursued by that access, in the context of fighting crime, is not restricted solely to fighting serious crime, where access is not subject to prior review by a court or an independent administrative authority, and where there is no requirement that the data concerned should be retained within the European Union.

This judgment, which has to be applied in England and Wales by the Court of Appeal, the referring court, will have enormous implications for the legality of the newly enacted regime of UK surveillance. The ECJ was addressing DRIPA and left little doubt that that Act had serious incompatibilities with EU law including the CFR. However, retention of communications data in the 2016 Act is far more extensive in subject coverage than the ECJ would permit and the 2016 Act has provision for bulk data sets and bulk data retention. The point has been made that EU judges take a stricter approach on privacy protection than would British judges who acknowledge the benefits of surveillance as set out in the 2016 Act for legitimate purposes in the public interest.[98] The judgment is also likely to prompt national judges to examine what the true significance of Art 4(2) TEU is: 'In particular, national security remains the sole responsibility of each Member State.' The ECJ is unclear in setting subject boundaries on this.

10. Investigatory Powers Act 2016

An Investigatory Powers Act recasting surveillance laws has been approved by Parliament and signed into law by the Monarch.[99] The Bill followed a review by the Independent Reviewer of Terrorist Legislation of existing laws of investigatory powers, a review by the Intelligence and Security Committee of Parliament and by the Panel of the Independent Surveillance Review convened by the Royal United Services Institute. All three agreed that current powers remained essential for the UK's security. There were also critical reactions in the media.

The Act brings together powers for interception of communications, obtaining communications and communications data, bulk data and bulk data sets powers and it relates to collection of data in bulk by interception, communications data acquisition and equipment interference – computer hacking – powers and collection of personal information about large numbers of individuals most of whom will be of no interest to the S&IS (only S&IS have the 'bulk' capabilities basically for national security and serious crime objectives), and internet connection records in real time. Communications service providers will be under a duty to assist interceptions and to provide these data.

This Act introduces the requirement for 'double-lock' approval by a minister and a judge (retired) for certain warrants ie interception, equipment and bulk equipment interference, bulk data and bulk data sets' powers. Warrants may only be issued to nine (ten are listed) responsible intercepting bodies under three specified powers: national security, prevention of serious crime and economic well-being in relation to national security. Warrants are not required for targeted communications data. Access to such data will be by authorisations granted by designated senior officers in 'relevant' public authorities with stricter requirements for local authorities. In all cases, and they extend far beyond serious crime (s 61(7) a – j), action must be 'necessary and proportionate'. Powers of the secretary of state to require retention of communications data, which may be for up to twelve months, need the approval of a judicial commissioner.

There is to be oversight by an Investigatory Powers Commissioner, a senior judge. There are to be special safeguards in 'particularly sensitive material' eg involving lawyers, MPs and journalists. There will be 'single point contacts' for communications data and intercept connection records, not warrants. The Bill retains the extra-territorial effect of the 2014 Act. Crucially, a right of appeal from the IP Tribunal's decisions to the Court of Appeal is introduced for the first time. Schedule 6 provides for the making of codes of practice on the operation of the powers. The Act says nothing about use of informers and other forms of human, intrusive and covert surveillance which is governed by the 2000 Act. The Act sets out safeguards on holding data, duration of warrants and the role of the Information Commissioner. A Technical Advisory Board has been established following the report by the Independent Reviewer and will advise on the impact of changes in technology.

The ISC of Parliament issued a critical report on the Bill. Amongst other criticisms it recommended laws on universal privacy protection and that S&IS capabilities in equipment interference, bulk data sets and communications data are too broad and lack clarity.[100] The Bill was revised and introduced in Parliament in March 2016 to take account of some of these criticisms.[101] The Bill was subject to further amendments in Parliament including overarching provisions on privacy protection in s 2, safeguards in the warrant process, protection of trade unions, and enhanced protections for sensitive professions and parliamentarians, including the requirement that a Judicial Commissioner must consider that there is "an overriding public interest" before any request to identify a journalist's source can be approved. The Prime Minister must also personally approve a warrant to obtain the communications of an MP or a member of another relevant legislature. The Independent Reviewer of Terrorism Legislation also conducted a review of bulk powers for the government with a team of experts chosen by him. His report found that such powers are of vital importance to S&IS and alternatives were slower, more intrusive, more expensive and more dangerous.[102] The Bill was enacted in November 2016.

11. Conclusion

On the whole the UK judicial record in national security case law has shown an independence, sometimes robust, from the executive. As I have had occasion to mention previously the courts have travelled a long way since the 1970s and 1980s when they afforded almost *carte blanche* to the executive in such matters. I have no doubt that the courts have been invigorated by the jurisprudence of the CHR and ECHR under the HRA. It is becoming more popular now for judges to seek domestic inspiration for human rights protection. This is a process exemplified by the *Ahmed* judgments where because it was believed that the ECHR did not apply, this was before the CHR judgment in *Al Jedda*, the protection of the common law of fundamental rights would apply. The common law of human rights, so recently developed, would survive the repeal of the HRA and removal of the ECHR. For how long we don't know. The attacks on the HRA have been prolonged and repeal has again been deferred by the UK government. We have to wait and see when, if ever, it is repealed and what replaces it. In evidence to the House of Lords EU sub-committee on Justice on 2 February 2016, the Justice Secretary accepted that any replacement would retain the rights in the ECHR but there may be a 'difference in emphasis'.[103] Under questioning he accepted that any British legislation would be subject to 'European law', a point which needs clarification. But, I would add, the Act's extra territorial dimension is something that the government would certainly wish to see removed as well as prevention of deportees to foreign jurisdictions. Theresa May's new government indicated that the ECHR would not apply in future overseas conflict involving British forces.

The process of secret justice is not confined to terrorism in the UK. Secret justice is becoming a zone of tension between the executive and the judiciary. It raises the most pressing of questions on judicial efficacy. Secrecy is anathema to the rule of law. Secret justice is to remove legal protection built on the rock to one built on sand as Lord Shaw expressed the point emphatically in *Scott v Scott* in 1913.

While there is inevitably a tension between the executive, the legislature and the courts the rights of all of us have to be protected by constructive cooperation between those branches. Although the Investigatory Powers Act, for instance, is a big improvement on what it will replace much surveillance through informers is not included in its reforms and the ISC and other committees have pointed out weaknesses.[104] The judgment of the EUECJ on surveillance will create difficulties for the UK government even post Brexit. There is no doubt that there are major philosophical differences between the EUECJ and British judges on the legitimate role and extent of surveillance.

I think that the UK is a mature enough democracy to ensure that while there may be tension between the executive, the courts and Parliament there should not be hostility. But if Sedley is correct that the intelligence services are a fourth power in the state we will need to develop judicial and legislative powers, and executive duties, to ensure they do not seriously disturb the democratic and justice dynamic. Complacency must be avoided but there is much to build on. One views with some apprehension how the USA will approach the task of balancing security and liberty under a new President.[105] The election of Donald Trump to the presidency in November 2016 would very likely have profound changes in the national security and transparency agenda in American, UK and global public life.

Notes

1 For comparative literature see Ignatieff (2004); Sands (2005, 2008); Dyzenhaus (2006); Posner and Vermeule (2007); Moss (2011); Gearty (2013); and Lazurus et al. (2014). A survey of terrorism law is in Walker (2011, 2014). For the ECHR: National Security and European Case-law CoE (2013) https://rm.coe.int/CoERMPublicCommonSearchServices/DisplayDCTMContent?documentId=090000168067d214 [17/01/2017].

2 Birkinshaw (2010); Birkinshaw (2013).

3 Sedley (2015) ch 9.

4 Added by present author.

5 Ibid 228.

6 Ibid 227.

7 *Liversidge v Anderson* [1942] AC 206. *Liversidge* concerned the use of notoriously broad executive powers of detention under Defence Regulation 18B in wartime against those who were suspected of disloyalty and which was untested by any legal process: Simpson (1992).

8 *Lord Denning in R v Secretary of State for the Home Dept. Ex p Hosenball* [1977] 3 All ER 452 (CA). See Birkinshaw (2013).

9 Birkinshaw and Varney (2016).

10 Birkinshaw (2014); Sales (2013). On use of ECHR jurisprudence by domestic courts see ss 2 and 3 HRA. On declarations of incompatibility, s 4.

11 *R (Miranda) v Secretary of State for the Home Department et al* [2016] EWCA Civ 6. See the report by the Interception Commissioner on journalists' sources and interception http://www.iocco-uk.info/docs/Press%20Release%20IOCCO%20Journalist%20Inquiry.pdf [17/01/2017].

12 https://www.gov.uk/government/speeches/home-secretary-on-the-brussels-terror-attacks [17/01/2017]. See the United Kingdom's exit from and new partnership with the European Union Cm 9417 January 2017 ch. 11.

13 See http://www.legislation.gov.uk/ukpga/2013/18/contents. The annual report for 2015–16 is at https://b1cba9b3-a-5e6631fd-s-sites.googlegroups.com/a/independent.gov.uk/isc/files/2015-2016_ISC_AR.pdf?attachauth=ANoY7crYogOjBob4k0VTUpysTNLN7AnjYdXk6d81BtCUCzwOXJ47uxqMlrCx6nz9GHoDnXnE936uStUyr5975MFXCjuFkJFgBWKw_f5wQ7FKCiqIwFVEimo1IoelfdD3iRwRYrEJJmxzi2bQB-WQeHf84AkhEkbWD92GohzhIJm5o7msvjpl1SQJAktREs6ivP8L_0bojKuzHR6PvvVawKxPuXjtEPPf1m60ZjulICuWJ9yv7et8GlE%3D&attredirects=0 [17/01/2017].

14 See Birkinshaw (2010) ch 2.

15 See the latest annual report http://intelligencecommissioner.com/docs/56892%20HC%20459%20web.pdf [17/01/2017].

16 https://terrorismlegislationreviewer.independent.gov.uk/ D. Anderson (2014) [17/01/2017].

17 *R v Shayler* [2002] UKHL 11. The Law Commission has launched a consultation of reform of official secrecy laws: Protection of Official Data Paper No 230 February

(2017). http://www.lawcom.gov.uk/wp-content/uploads/2017/02/cp230_protection_of_official_data.pdf

18 S 23. See *Corderoy & Ahmed v IC, AG & CO* [2017] UKUT 495 (AAC) for a possible limitation relating to legal advice.

19 See note 54 below. *R (Bancoult No 2) v SoS FA* [2008] UKHL 61 – appealed to UKSC for non-disclosure by the Crown side in the litigation – claimants unsuccessful [2016] UKSC 35.

20 *AG v Guardian Newspapers Ltd (No 2)* [1988] 3 All ER 545. See *Observer and Guardian v UK* [1991] EHRR 153.

21 *Guardian Newspapers* ibid.

22 Birkinshaw and Varney (2011) ch 2, especially at interlocutory stages.

23 The extra territorial effect of the HRA has been a major point of contention: *Al Skeini v UK Secretary of State etc* [2007] UKHL 26 ruled that Art 1 ECHR as interpreted by the ECtHR established the jurisdiction of ECHR rights implemented under the HRA and *Al Skeini v UK* App no 55721/07 (ECHR, 7 July 2011); *R (Al-Jedda) v SoS D* [2007] UKHL 58 http://www.bailii.org/uk/cases/UKHL/2007/58.html; *Al-Jedda v UK* [2011] ECHR 1092 http://www.bailii.org/eu/cases/ECHR/2011/1092.html; *Kay v Lambeth* [2006] UKHL 10 http://www.bailii.org/uk/cases/UKHL/2006/10.html on following rules of precedent under English law and English case law; *Smith v Ministry of Defence* [2013] UKSC 41 http://www.bailii.org/uk/cases/UKSC/2013/41.html on the influence of *Al Skeini* in the CHR on English law. The UK Supreme Court believed that *Hassan v UK* App no 29750/09 (ECHR, 16 September 2014), [2014] ECHR 936 and 1162 modified the *Al Jedda v UK* judgment: *Abd Ali Hameed-Waheed v Ministry of Defence and Serdar Mohammed v Ministry of Defence* [2017] UKSC 2. The UK Defence Secretary announced that the UK would derogate from the ECHR to exclude UK armed forces from the ECHR in future overseas activities. See *Armani da Silva v UK* App no 5878/08 (ECHR, 30 March 2016) on investigatory procedures following the shooting of a suspected (wrongly) suicide bomber in London where no procedural breach of Art. 2 ECHR was established.

24 *Rahmatullah (No 2) v Ministry of Defence* [2017] UKSC 1 [36–37, 72, 81].

25 *Belhaj et al v Straw et al* [2017] UKSC 3; see also *Ministry of Defence v Iraqi Citizens* [2016] UKSC 25.

26 The Gibson Inquiry http://www.detaineeinquiry.org.uk/wp-content/uploads/2013/12/35100_Trafalgar-Text-accessible.pdf [17/01/2017]; the Al Sweady report https://www.gov.uk/government/publications/al-sweady-inquiry-report [17/01/2017]; and the Chilcot inquiry into the Iraq war http://www.iraqinquiry.org.uk/ [17/01/2017]. See the Commons Defence Committee Sixth Report HC 109 (2016–17) Who Guards the Guardians? and the Iraq Historic Allegations Team's termination by the secretary of state in February 2017.

27 Cited by Sedley (2015) 123.

28 *Laker Airways* [1977] 1 QB 643 (CA); *R v Secretary of State for the Home Department ex parte Fire Brigades Union* [1995] 2 AC 513; *Bank Mellat v HM Treasury No 2* [2013] UKSC 39; *R (Miller) v Secretary of State for Exiting the EU etc* [2017] UKSC 5 – on triggering Art 50 TEU for Brexit.

29 See *HM Treasury v Ahmed et al* [2010] UKSC 2 & 5 and *Youssef* note 46 below and *Miller* note 28 above and *Belhaj & An'r v Straw et al* (2017) UKSC 3.

30 *Council of Civil Service Unions v Minister for the Civil Service* [1983] UKHL 6. A significant development took place in *Bancoult No 2 v Secretary of State for Foreign Affairs* [2008] UKHL 61. See *Miller et al* note 28 on arguments about the existence and scope of a prerogative.

31 *R (Abbasi) v Secretary of State for Foreign Affairs* [2002] EWCA Civ 1598 para 85. *Rahmatullah (No 2) and Belhaj* above notes 24 and 29. See Birkinshaw (2015).

32 *R (Gentle) v Prime Minister et al* [2008] UKHL 20.

33 *Abbasi* above, *R (Sandiford) v Secretary of State* [2014] UKSC 44.
34 *R (Corner House Research & Ors) v The Serious Fraud Office* [2008] UKHL 60. The lower court had ruled the decision to stop the investigation unlawful as basically an affront to the rule of law http://www.bailii.org/uk/cases/UKHL/2008/60.html
35 [2012] UKSC 48.
36 *Zamora* [1916] UKPC 24 at p 16 per Lord Parker. He referred to a statement on oath on the urgent need for national security grounds to take action. But he then spelt out how a claimant may vindicate a right against the Crown in judicial proceedings. Sometimes the courts have queried whether national security was actually involved: *R v Secretary of State for the Home Dept. Ex p McQuillan* [1995] 4 All ER 400.
37 *Secretary of State for Defence v Guardian Newspapers* [1984] 3 All ER 601 (HL).
38 *A v Secretary of State HD* [2004] UKHL 56 state of emergency and executive detention.
39 The full extent of proportionality has to be finally established by the Supreme Court: see eg *Kennedy v The Charity Commission* [2014] UKSC 20; *Pham* [2015] UKSC 19; *Keyu* [2015] UKSC 69; *Michalak v GMC* [2017] UKSC 71; *Youssef* note 46 below.
40 *Secretary of State for the Home Dept v Rehman* [2001] UKHL 47.
41 *R (Lord Carlile QC) v SoS HD* [2014] UKSC https://www.supremecourt.uk/cases/uksc-2013-0098.html
42 [2011] UKSIAC 103/2010.
43 Birkinshaw (2009).
44 *HM Treasury v Ahmed No 2* [2010] UKSC 2 & 5. In *Ahmed* the offending measures were ruled ineffective with immediate effect: cf Cases C-402/05 P and C-415/05 P *Kadi v Council and Commission.*
45 *Bank Mellat v HM Treasury No 2* [2013] UKSC 39. https://www.supremecourt.uk/cases/docs/uksc-2011-0040-judgment.pdf
46 *Youssef v Secretary of State for Foreign etc Affairs* [2016] UKSC 3. https://www.supremecourt.uk/ca.ses/docs/uksc-2014-0028-judgment.pdf. *Y* had applied to the EU General Court claiming that he should be de-listed from the relevant EU regulation. The court found that the Commission had not followed correct procedures but nonetheless dismissed his claim that listing was irrational: Case T-306/10 *Yusef v Commission* (sic). Cf. Cases C-584/10 P, C-593/10 P and C-595/10 P *Commission v Kadi.*
47 [2013] EWCA Civ 1302. Carnwath differed on some legal points but agreed on the outcome.
48 *R v Hampden* (1637) 3 St Tr 825 – the famous case of ship money and the Crown's prerogative power of taxation for national defence.
49 *Scott v Scott* [1913] AC 417.
50 *Local Government Board v Arlidge* [1915] 120.
51 *Guardian News and Media Ltd v AB, CD* [2014] EWCA Crim 1861. The decision on closure is for the court: *Guardian News et al v R & E. Incedal* [2016] EWCA Crim 11.
52 Birkinshaw (2010) ch 11.
53 *Conway v Rimmer* [1968] UKHL 2.
54 *Bin Yam Mohamed* [2010] EWCA Civ 65. A non British citizen resident in the UK. http://www.bailii.org/ew/cases/EWCA/Civ/2010/65.html See para 7 for the High Court judgment references [2010] EWCA Civ 158 Lord Neuberger MR http://www.bailii.org/ew/cases/EWCA/Civ/2010/158.html. See *Norwich Pharmacal Co v The Customs and Excise Comrs* [1974] AC 133.
55 The High Court judgment in *BYM* was anxious about the unavailability in the archives of closed judgments and closed proceedings: see Birkinshaw (2014b) ch 4 66–67.
56 *Secretary of State for Foreign and Commonwealth Affairs v Assistant Deputy Coroner for Inner North London* [2013] EWHC 3724 (Admin). See also *Secretary of State for Home Affairs v HM Coroner etc* [2016] EWHC 3001 (Admin).

57 *R (Litvinenko) v Home Secretary et al* [2014] EWHC 194 (Admin). http://www.bailii.org/ew/cases/EWHC/Admin/2014/194.html
58 HC 695 (2015–16): https://www.litvinenkoinquiry.org/files/Litvinenko-Inquiry-Report-web-version.pdf para 10.16 [17/01/2017].
59 *Chahal v UK* App no 22414/93 (ECHR, 15 November 1996).
60 For EU nationals, Cases C–65 & 111/95 *R v Home Secretary ex p Shigara and Radiom* [1997] ECR I-3343.
61 https://www.judiciary.gov.uk/publications/special-immigration-appeals-commission-tribunal-guidance/ [17/01/2017].
62 Under the Justice and Security Act 2013. See generally Ip (2008) and Murphy (2013).
63 http://www.ipt-uk.com/ [17/01/2017] and http://www.ipt-uk.com/section.aspx?pageid=8 [17/01/2017]. On exclusion of judicial review of the IPT see *R (Privacy International) v IPT* [2017] EWHC 114 (Admin).
64 [2009] UKSC 12.
65 (2010) ECHR 682 (18/5/10) interceptions.
66 *Liberty & Others vs. the Security Service, SIS, GCHQ* http://www.ipt-uk.com/docs/IPT_13_168-173_H.pdf [All IPT cases 17/01/2017]. This judgment and related IPT judgments are available at: http://www.ipt-uk.com/judgments.asp
67 *Belhadj & Others vs. the Security Service, SIS, GCHQ, Home Office and FCO* http://www.ipt-uk.com/docs/Belhaj_Determination_final.pdf. http://www.ipt-uk.com/docs/ABDEL_HAKIM_BELHADJ_Final.pdf
68 *Caroline Clucas MP et al v The Security Service*http://www.ipt-uk.com/docs/Caroline_Lucas_JUDGMENT.pdf
69 *News Group Newspapers Ltd v Commissioner of the Metropolitan Police* http://www.ipt-uk.com/docs/IPT_14_176_H.pdf On Art 10 ECHR see *Miranda* note 11.
70 [2016] UKIPTrib 15_110 C-H http://www.ipt-uk.com/docs/Bulk_Data_Judgment.pdf15-110 CH [17/10/16]. See *Human Rights Watch v Secretary of State for F&CA* [2016] UKIPTrib 15_165 C-H. See *Privacy International v Secretary of State for F&CA* [2016] UKIPTrib 14_85 C-H – on Computer Network Exploitation (hacking) by GCHQ.
71 See note 61 above.
72 Sedley (2015) has shown how the understanding of the Canadian position was misinformed p.167. For a comparative study on secret evidence for the European Parliament see http://www.europarl.europa.eu/RegData/etudes/STUD/2014/509991/IPOL_STU%282014%29509991_EN.pdf [17/01/2107].
73 *Special Advocates* House of Commons Constitutional Affairs Committee HC 323-I (2004–05).
74 Such procedures raise the spectre of torture or use of torture evidence in the country to which someone claiming asylum will be returned. See *B (Algeria) etc v Secretary of State for the Home Department* [2009] UKHL 10 and *Othman (Abu Qatada) v UK* [2012] ECHR 56.
75 *Charkaoui v Canada* (2007) 1 SCR 350 para 64. Evidence insulated from challenge may positively mislead, Lord Kerr in *Al Rawi* note 83 para 93.
76 www.opsi.gov.uk/acts/acts2001/20010024.htm
77 *A v Secretary of State HD* [2005] 3 All ER 169 (HL).
78 www.opsi.gov.uk/acts/acts2005/20050002.htm See Kavanagh (2010).
79 Horne and Walker (2014); Fenwick (2015).
80 Justice (2009). Special Advocates: House of Commons Constitutional Affairs Committee HC 323-I (2004–05). Zuckerman (2011). CMPs are not used in criminal trails: *R v H* [2004] UKHL 3 where their use was strongly discouraged. See *Guardian News & Media Ltd v R & E. Incedal* [2016] EWCA Crim 11 para 66 on use of 'independent' lawyers by a criminal trial judge.
81 *Home Secretary v Rehman* [2000] 3 All ER 778; *Roberts v Parole Board* [2005] UKHL 45.

82 *Home Office v Tariq* [2011] UKSC 35.
83 *Al Rawi et al v Security Service et al* [2011] UKSC 34.
84 *Bank Mellat v HM Treasury No 1* [2013] UKSC 38.
85 http://www.legislation.gov.uk/ukpga/2013/18/contents
86 See s 8 Justice and Security Act 2013 on disclosure and Civil Procedure Rules Part 82.13 and 82.14 and *R (Sarkandi) v Secretary of State for Foreign etc Affairs* [2015] EWCA Civ 687; *Rahmatullah v MoD* [2017] EWHC 547 (QB).
87 *Kennedy v UK* App. no 26839/05 (ECHR, 18 May 2010).
88 *A v UK* App. no. 100/1997/884/1096 (ECHR, 23 September 1998) For EU law see *ZZ (France) v Secretary of State Home Department* Case C-300/11 – a deportation case.
89 *Secretary of State v AF* [2009] UKHL 28 doubting *MB v SoS HD* etc. Also on privacy rights *W (Algeria) v SoSHD* [2012] UKSC 8; *Guardian News Media* [2010] UKSC 1.
90 *Bank Mellat v HM Treasury* [2015] EWCA Civ 1052. A successor to the Bank Mellat litigation in the Supreme Court at note 45 above analysing the disclosure requirements of a CMP. *Kiani* [2015] EWCA Civ 776 concerned security vetting and dismissal of an immigration officer. *Tariq* followed.
91 See also *Ali v SoSHD* [2011] EWCA Civ 787; *SoS HD v CD* [2011] EWHC 2087; *Tariq* [2011] UKSC 35 and limits of gisting [67]-[69]; [81]-[83] in cases not dealing with detention, freezing or prohibition notices or TPIMs. See note 85 for the Justice and Security Act 2013.
92 *A et al v Secretary of State HD* [2005] UKHL 71 http://www.bailii.org/uk/cases/UKHL/2005/71.html
93 https://www.gov.uk/government/uploads/system/uploads/attachment_data/file/62632/Consolidated_Guidance_November_2011.pdf [17/01/2017].
94 Case C-293/12 [2014] ECJ.
95 [2015] EWCA Civ 1185.
96 Joined Cases C-203/15 and C-698/15 [2016]. *Tele2 Sverige AB v Post-och telestyrelsen* (Case C-203/15 ECJ [2016]) and *Secretary of State for the Home Department v Tom Watson* (Case C-698/15 ECJ [2016]).
97 EU ECJ C-203/16 [2016] (21 December 2016). See L.Woods http://eulawanalysis.blogspot.co.uk/2016/12/data-retention-and-national-law-ecj.html [17/01/2017].
98 See https://terrorismlegislationreviewer.independent.gov.uk/cjeu-judgment-in-watson/. See also House of Lords EU Committee 7th Report HL 77 (2016–2017) Brexit: Future UK–EU security and police cooperation http://www.publications.parliament.uk/pa/ld201617/ldselect/ldeucom/77/7702.htm [both 17/01/2017]. See Miller (2017) on transatlantic comparisons. A reference to the ECJ was made by the IP Tribunal on bulk data communications and EU law on 8 September and 30 October 2017. *Privacy International v Secretary of State for Foreign Affairs etc* http://www.ipt-uk.com/judgments.asp [31 October 2017].
99 See https://www.gov.uk/government/uploads/system/uploads/attachment_data/file/473770/Draft_Investigatory_Powers_Bill.pdf and http://www.legislation.gov.uk/ukpga/2016/25/pdfs/ukpgaen_20160025_en.pdf [both 17/01/2017] for the Explanatory Notes. *A Question of Trust* (2015) Independent Reviewer of Terrorism Legislation https://terrorismlegislationreviewer.independent.gov.uk/wp-content/uploads/2015/06/IPR-Report-Print-Version.pdf; Intelligence and Security Committee Report: http://isc.independent.gov.uk/news-archive/12march2015; Royal United Services Institute Report: https://rusi.org/rusi-news/rusi-responds-draft-investigatory-powers-bill; The Law Society on legal professional privilege: http://www.lawsociety.org.uk/news/press-releases/lawyers-call-for-statutory-protection-of-lawyer-client-communications/?_hsenc=p2ANqtz-8GWQqqDnM8w9XjWjLmbbUmxMadtMwGc_uQf8m4TPXqz3EnFdCbsJw-hRNo8V-1ivreAcTvcKL9TXlvDg6xI9AuuXbfIQ&_hsm

i=23348694 [all 17/01/2017] The legislation authorising communications surveillance goes back to UK reaction to *Malone v UK* App. no 8691/79 (ECHR, 2 August 1984).

100 HC 795 (2015–16) Report on the Draft Investigatory Powers Bill. See the Commons Science and Technology Committee on the bill's technology HC 573 (2015–16) and the Joint Committee on the Bill HL 93 HC 651 (2015–16). A report on Bulk Data Powers was published in August 2016 by the Independent Reviewer of Terrorism Legislation Sir David Anderson (Cm 9326, 2016) https://terrorismlegislationreviewer.independent.gov.uk/wp-content/uploads/2016/08/Bulk-Powers-Review-final-report.pdf [17/01/2017].

101 http://www.publications.parliament.uk/pa/bills/cbill/2015-2016/0143/cbill_2015-20160143_en_1.htm and https://www.gov.uk/government/collections/investigatory-powers-bill [both 17/01/2017] for draft codes and policy statement. There remained criticism that the Bill was not consistent with the Grand Chamber of the ECJ in Schrems EUECJ C- 362/14 and *R Zakharov v Russia Grand Chamber* CHR 4/12/15. See discussion at note 99 et seq above.

102 Note 100.

103 http://www.parliament.uk/business/committees/committees-a-z/lords-select/eu-justice-subcommittee/inquiries/parliament-2015/potential-impact-of-repealing-the-human-rights-act-on-eu-law/ [17/01/2017].

104 See note 100.

105 See *State of Washington et al v Donald J. Trump President et al* No 17–35105 CA Ninth Circ 9/02/2017 and the courts' suspension of Trump's Executive Order banning immigrants from seven Muslim countries. 'Although courts owe considerable deference to the President's policy determinations with respect to immigration and national security, it is beyond question that the federal judiciary retains the authority to adjudicate constitutional challenges to executive action'. 18. http://cdn.ca9.uscourts.gov/datastore/opinions/2017/02/09/17-35105.pdf (10/02/2017). For judicial orders against modified executive orders, see http://www.vox.com/2017/3/15/14940946/read-full-text-hawaii-court-order-trump-refugee-travel-ban. The US Supreme Court upheld Trump's appeal to the extent that the preliminary injunctions were stayed (ceased to have effect) in relation to foreign nationals with no bona fide relationship with a 'person or entity' in the US: *Trump et al v International Refugee Assistance Project* Nos 16–1436 (26/06/2017) https://www.supremecourt.gov/opinions/16pdf/16-1436_l6hc.pdf. In December 2017, the US Supreme Court allowed the travel bans in modified form to take full effect pending final substantive appeals: *Trump v Hawaii 17A550 and Trump v International Refugee Assistance* (4/12/2017) USSC.

Bibliography

Anderson, David, 'The Independent Review of Terrorist Laws' (2014). *Public Law* 403.

Birkinshaw, Patrick, 'English Law and Evidence Obtained by Torture: Vindication of Basic Principle or Judicial Abnegation? Implications of *A v. Secretary of State for the Home Department*', in Bev Clucas, Gerry Johnstone and Tony Ward (eds), *Torture: Moral Absolutes and Ambiguities* (Nomos 2009) ch 6.

Birkinshaw, Patrick, *Freedom of Information: The Law, the Practice and the Ideal* (4th edn, Cambridge University Press 2010).

Birkinshaw, Patrick, 'Terrorism, Secrecy and Human Rights', in Katja S. Ziegler and Peter M. Huber (eds), *Current Problems in the Protection of Human Rights* (Hart 2013) ch 14.

Birkinshaw, Patrick, *European Public Law: The Achievement and the Challenge* (Wolters Kluwer 2014).

Birkinshaw, Patrick, 'Valuing Transparency in Government and Media', in Nigel Bowles, James T. Hamilton and David A.L. Levy (eds), *Transparency in Politics and Media* (University of Oxford 2014b) ch 4.

Birkinshaw, Patrick, in Aurélien Antoine (ed), *Le Droit public britannique: état des lieux et perspectives Société de Législation Comparée* (Societé de législation comparé 2015).

Birkinshaw, Patrick and Varney, Mike, *Government and Information: The Law Relating to Access, Disclosure and their Regulation* (4th edn, Bloomsbury Professional 2011).

Birkinshaw, Patrick and Varney, Mike, 'Britain Alone Constitutionally: Brexit and Restitutio in Integrum', in Patrick Birkinshaw and Alan Biondi (eds), *Britain Alone! The Implications and Consequences of United Kingdom Withdrawal from the European Union* (Wolters Kluwer 2016).

Council of Europe/European Court of Human Rights*National Security and European Case-law* (2013).

Dyzenhaus, David, *The Constitution of Law: Legality in a Time of Emergency* (CUP 2006).

Fenwick, Helen, 'Redefining the Role of TPIMs in Combating "Home Grown" Terrorism Within the Widening Counter Terrorism Framework' (2015). *European Human Rights Law Review*, no. 1, 41–56.

Gearty, Conor, *Liberty and Security* (Polity Press 2013).

Horne, Alexander and Walker, Clive, 'Lessons Learned from Political Constitutionalism? Comparing the Enactment of Control Orders and Terrorism Prevention and Investigation Measures by the UK Parliament' (2014). *Public Law* 267–288.

Ignatieff, Michael, *The Lesser Evil: Political Ethics in an Age of Terror* (Princeton University Press 2004).

Ip, John, 'The Rise and Spread of the Special Advocate' (2008). *Public Law* 717.

Justice (2009) *Secret Evidence* http://justice.org.uk/secret-evidence/.

Kavanagh, Aileen, 'Special Advocates, Control Orders and the Right to a Fair Trial' (2010). 73 *Modern Law Review* 836–857.

Lazurus, Liora, McCrudden, Christopher and Bowles, Nigel (eds), *Reasoning Rights: Comparative Judicial Engagement* (Hart Publishing 2014).

Miller, Russel A.(ed.), *Privacy and Power: A Transatlantic Dialogue in the Shadow of the NSA-Affair* (CUP 2017).

Moss, Kate, *Balancing Liberty and Security: Human Rights, Human Wrongs* (Palgrave Macmillan 2011)

Murphy, Cian, 'Counter-Terrorism and the Culture of Legality: The Case of Special Advocates' (2013). 24 *King's Law Journal* 19–37.

Posner, Eric A. and Vermeule, Adrian, *Terror in the Balance: Security, Liberty and the Courts* (OUP 2007).

Sales, Patrick, 'Law and Democracy in a Human Rights Framework', in David Feldman (ed.), *Law in Politics, Politics in Law* (Bloomsbury Publishing 2013).

Sands, Philippe, *Lawless World* (Allen Lane 2005).

Sands, Philippe, *Torture Team: Uncovering War Crimes in the Land of the Free* (Penguin/ Palgrave Macmillan 2008).

Sedley, Stephen, *Lions Under the Throne* (CUP 2015).

Simpson, Alfred William Brian, *In the Highest Degree Odious: Detention without Trial in Wartime* (OUP 1992).

Walker, Clive, *Terrorism and the Law* (OUP 2011).

Walker, Clive, *The Anti-Terrorism Legislation* (3rd edn, OUP 2014).

Zuckerman, Adrian, 'Closed Material Procedure – Denial of Natural Justice' (2011). 30 *Civil Justice Quarterly*, 345–359.

13 The UK Supreme Court and Parliament

Judicial and Political Dialogues

John McEldowney

Introduction

The UK offers a distinctive case study of the role of courts and Parliament[1] in a modern parliamentary democracy during a period of rapid change and uncertainty. The pivotal constitutional doctrine is parliamentary sovereignty that defines the basis of the UK's constitutional arrangements. Sovereignty attributes to the UK Parliament unlimited authority in domestic matters by permitting Parliament virtually unfettered power. It also defines the relationship between Parliament and public institutions, prioritises political power[2] and sets the constitutional agenda. Most controversial is the UK's continued membership of the European Union as well as the jurisprudence of the European Convention on Human Rights following the EU referendum decision to leave in June 2016. In general the courts operate within the limits of not being able to hold an Act of Parliament unconstitutional or illegal[3] because of obedience to parliamentary sovereignty. EU law is one of the few exceptions to the doctrine of sovereignty, conceding EU law has priority over UK law. In the case of Brexit and leaving the EU, the most significant constitutional case heard by the Supreme Court[4] relates to the role of Parliament in the decision to trigger Article 50 of the Treaty of European Union to withdraw from the European Union after the June 2016 referendum decision to leave.

The UK's constitutional arrangements are also defined by the rule of law[5] as a means of restraint on arbitrary power. The rule of law expresses the moral constraints on arbitrary power that inform both political and legal worlds.[6] In the UK, political choices of the government of the day, are subject to few constitutional limitations as elected politicians are the final determination of policy making, often overriding legal considerations and propriety. The UK example is illustrative of tensions between judicial decisions in the Supreme Court and political choices of the Government, often between law and politics. Three substantive areas highlight the role of the Supreme Court; namely, cases involving judicial review including human rights; devolution cases and decisions on EU law, including more recently the role of Parliament and Article 50. There is also the question of the funding of judicial challenges before the courts and the political sensitivity of the funding arrangements.

1. The historical context: Defining the role of the courts in the common law tradition; the rule of law and parliamentary sovereignty in the UK

It is over 800 years since Magna Carta (1215) defined legal and political powers in the United Kingdom. It will be recalled that Magna Carta represented the triumph of judicial process and ultimately the rule of law over arbitrary power exercised by the King or other royal authority. It provides a useful point of reference to begin analysis of the role of judges in contemporary times. The common law is justifiably well-known for the case by case approach to the development of judicial review that refers to the procedure whereby there can be judicial scrutiny over the lawfulness of a decision or discretion exercised by a public body. Seldom does this involve the merits of a political policy though the grounds for review are broadly drawn. The grounds for review include illegality where the decision is not in accordance with the relevant law, irrationality where the decision is so unreasonable that no reasonable body could have taken it. Procedural impropriety is where the failure to consult or to act in accordance of natural justice is claimed. There is also proportionality where the decision is not proportionate to the outcome.

The English common law system of judicial review through independent courts has strong medieval origins through a system of remedies, the most famous of which is *habeas corpus*. The development of the common law is distinctive from civil law systems. Judicial review is about adaptation and change as much as the pragmatic style of case by case decisions. The doctrine of parliamentary sovereignty makes it impossible for a UK Act of Parliament to be held to be illegal except where EU law is concerned.[7] After Brexit the role of EU law is likely to diminish, but this will depend on the nature of the negotiated settlement under Article 50. The UK is a unitary, non-federal state, with widely defined legislative powers to Scotland, Wales and N. Ireland. Local government is subservient to central government and is susceptible to judicial review for its decisions and discretion.

2. The role of the Supreme Court – Parliament and the courts

Dawn Oliver identifies the various strands of the relationship between the courts and Parliament in the UK.

> The courts interpret Acts consistently with the UK's Treaty obligations, and with fundamental rights and as the law develops with principles of legality, constitutionalism and the rule of law; if Parliament intends to legislate in breach of these then it should use express and clear language, not general or ambiguous words.[8]

Oliver's overall analysis is that the UK's constitutional system places shared responsibilities across the institutions of government without a Supreme Court to adjudicate on the constitutionality of an Act of Parliament, except in the rare circumstances of conflict with EU law. This leaves open the possibility that politicians or judges may make 'unconstitutional laws', though this is unlikely and has only rarely happened. The doctrine of parliamentary sovereignty retains ultimate political authority rather than a written constitution with a Supreme Court or Constitutional Court with powers of judicial review including the power to strike down legislation that may be interpreted as unconstitutional or illegal. In the UK context democratic accountability is given greater pre-eminence over the perspectives of unelected judges. Prioritising policy making by elected politicians is premised on strong and vibrant political parties that provide electors real choices that are not pre-determined but are part of a five-year electoral cycle.[9]

The democratic legitimacy of government depends on the dynamic interaction between politics and law-making. In *Jackson v Attorney General*[10] a challenge to the validity of the Hunting Act 2004 was considered that raised precisely the political decisions of an elected government with an electoral mandate. The Hunting Act was highly controversial and political. It was introduced by the Labour Government on the basis of an election manifesto promise, banning the hunting of foxes with dogs that initially passed in the House of Commons was on the first attempt not passed by the House of Lords. The Act was re-introduced in the House of Commons and after further debate was passed for the second time in the House of Commons. The second debate in the House of Lords involved the use of the Parliament Act 1949 that resulted in the Act being passed even though the House of Lords opposed the details of the Act. This was a rare use of the Parliament Act which defined the role of the House of Lords as confined to a revising function rather than a power of absolute veto. This confirmed the elected chamber, the House of Commons having overall authority over the unelected House of Lords. In discussing the changing nature of sovereignty, Lord Hope acknowledged the role of the courts and Parliament:

> Our constitution is dominated by the sovereignty of Parliament. But parliamentary sovereignty is no longer, if it ever was, absolute. Step by step, gradually but surely, the English principle of the absolute sovereignty of Parliament which Dicey derived from Coke and Blackstone is being qualified … . The rule of law enforced by the courts is the ultimate controlling factor on which our constitution is based.

What precisely might the rule of law mean? Would it be possible for the courts to overturn an Act of Parliament when the act was considered in conflict with the rule of law? The rule of law provides both normative and evaluative mechanisms to ensure that there is accountability over the government of the day but it is unlikely to be used to overturn an Act of Parliament. Lord Hope's speculation has yet to be fully realised.

While the rule of law may appear weak when compared with the authority of elected government with parliamentary control of the legislative agenda in Parliament, it is important to recognise parliamentary forms of oversight. Despite the ability of Government to pass the vast bulk of its legislation, there are systems of scrutiny and oversight provided by select committees and parliamentary watch-dogs. These are too often overlooked in the discussion of legal and constitutional powers provided by courts as a check on arbitrary power.

3. The UK courts and EU law

There are, two possible exceptions that challenge the UK's constitutional orthodoxy and the simple principle of majority created legislation. The first arises from EU law and the second from the law relating to human rights (discussed in more detail below). In the case of European law, the courts accept its primacy over domestic laws.[11] The UK's decision to leave the EU will require careful calibration and adjustments to the future role of the European Court of Justice. That role is far from clear. This is mainly because of the interpretation afforded to EU law because of the European Community Act 1972 and also because of the jurisprudence of the European Court of Justice on Member States even though the UK will leave. Since 1972, EU law has been interpreted to be an exception to the traditional doctrine of sovereignty of parliament or alternatively a variation on the doctrine itself.[12] Concerns about legal and political sovereignty have been highly influential in the UK. The UK has negotiated a series of opt outs including in the Treaty of Lisbon an 'opt out' though a protocol of the ECHR. The UK is not a member of the Euro and not part of the Schengen agreement allowing citizens of Member States cross boundary access. Currently the UK Government is in discussion with the EU, having triggered Article 50 to leave. Negotiations are expected to be concluded by March 2019 when the UK is expected to leave the EU. Sovereignty is of enormous influence in how the UK has applied principles laid down in the Treaty. The strength of the Anglo-Saxon common law tradition has created a certain resistance to the civil law tradition especially the role of codified rules and EU approaches to problems solving is seen as too bureaucratic in creating regulatory burdens on Government and business. EU law in fact settles many issues where the law defines the areas of EU competences. Beyond this narrow interpretation lies many normative rules and principles that have become influential on the courts and how legal rules should be interpreted. One example is the development of proportionality as a ground of review that has been encouraged by EU law and applied by UK courts. European public law has also proved to be inspirational and grown though a mixture of UK courts interacting with many EU principles. The law of many Member States is intermixed with EU law and adopted and developed by the European Court of Justice in Luxembourg. It is hard not to appreciate the on-going importance and influence of mutual understandings and the coming together of both common law and civil law systems. Cases such as *Francovich*[13] establishing the nature of remedies in damages for state liability are path breaking in establishing the full effectiveness of EU rights that requires Member States to comply with EU law.

Resolving competing competences between national courts and the European Court of Justice is likely to be a matter for some speculation over the next decade as economic and political frictions within the EU between Member States has increased in recent years and the UK's withdrawal will have an impact. There are also the conceptual questions of the reasoning and approach adopted by courts in reaching their decisions and to what extent has the European Court of Justice's teleological approach to interpretation become accepted by British courts. Sir William Wade acknowledged in his *Constitutional Fundamentals* in 1989 that in matters of sovereignty, 'shifts' in judicial loyalty are possible and that this occurred in the seventeenth century in England, in the attitudes of the courts in eighteenth-century America and in the general dissolution of the British Empire. It is possible that new 'generations of judges' will have a different attitude to a new constitutional settlement.[14] Lord Bridge in *Factortame* when discussing the European Communities Act 1972 explained how it should be interpreted on the basis that

> whatever the limitation of its sovereignty Parliament accepted when it enacted the European Communities Act 1972 was entirely voluntary. Under the terms of the 1972 Act it has always been clear that it was the duty of a United Kingdom court, when delivering final judgement to override any rule of national law found to be in conflict with any directly enforceable rule of Community law.[15]

Lord Bingham in his book on the *Rule of Law*[16] commented that:

> This (the Factortame decision) is the best example from the critics' point of view, since the process does involve the invalidation of statutes by the courts. But the courts acts in that way only because Parliament, exercising its legislative authority, has told them to. If Parliament, exercising the same authority, told them not to do so, they would obey that injunction also.[17]

The argument that statutory interpretation provides a satisfactory explanation of the *Factortame* decision on how to construct EU law as part of the national legal system, has some limitations. *Factortame* was the first time that a UK statute was set aside by the courts. Interpreting Parliament's intention is one way the courts may seek to understand legislation. However, the decision goes beyond the courts merely interpreting Parliament's intention alone. The approach taken is more far reaching than the traditional way courts in the UK interpreted Parliament's intention. What appears to be at work is a purposive approach which is commonly used when interpreting EU law allowing for a broad inquiry[18] beyond mere intention. It looks at how EU law has created a special legal regime and this is a radical break with the past and one that is not simply explained by construing a statute alone. Sir William Wade accepts this by arguing that the way in which EU law is construed operates outside the traditional role of the courts and is not explicable by the construction of a statute. Even the express words of a statute could be overridden by EU law. This may be regarded as a 'revolution' or simply a shift in legal reasoning and doctrine.

Paul Craig[19] supported by Trevor Allan[20] suggests another approach beyond the construction argument and also different than Sir William Wade:

> There is however a third way in which to regard the courts' jurisprudence. This is to regard decisions about supremacy as being based on normative arguments of legal principle the content of which can and will vary across time.[21]

This is a welcome and refreshing approach that is subtle and nuanced in the politics of the time and the underpinnings of legal doctrine. It also reaffirms that the UK's relationship with the EU is not fixed in any one point in time but continues to evolve. This is well illustrated by the passage of the European Union Act 2011 predicated on the principle that power resides with the UK Parliament with the addition of a referendum as a 'double lock' against any erosion of that power.[22] There is, however, nothing in the European Union Act 2011 that seeks to entrench the referendum requirement and this may be modified or repealed by a future Act of Parliament. Section 18 of the Act contains a declaratory statement on the status of EU law continuing on a statutory basis. This extends the long standing rule that Treaty obligations require an Act of Parliament for their enforcement but there is the interesting prospect of such a change being rejected by a referendum even if approved by an Act of Parliament. Craig admits that:

> The United Kingdom's relationship with the EU, and the conception of sovereignty that shapes and is shaped by it, will continue to occupy the political terrain.[23]

Dawn Oliver also identifies[24] some of the main reasons for British courts accepting the authority of European law and the doctrine that European law will be given effect even if it conflicts with an Act of the UK Parliament. The most obvious reason is that the doctrine was well developed by the European Court of Justice long before the UK joined; that the courts in other Member States have accepted the role of the European Court and the principle of giving direct effect and primacy to EU law is well established. Section 2(4) of the European Communities Act is also relevant as it provides instructions to British Courts to accept the express intention of Parliament and this is an obligation in UK law as well as in EU law. The last point is that section 18 of the European Union Act 2011 confirms that UK membership under the European Communities Act 1972 Act is the basis for EU law to be 'recognised and available' in law in the UK, and together the two Acts have altered the doctrine of implied repeal. Perhaps the underlying basis for the acceptance of European law is also partly contractual – it was part of the package agreed on accession and the terms of the agreement set out in the European Communities Act 1972 have to be followed.

The importance of the democratic principle is as Oliver[25] admits unconvincing as a rationale for sovereignty. Sovereignty may allow Parliament to pass legislation that is unrepresentative and unfair or discriminatory. In the context of the EU this raises a euro sceptical concern that the courts giving way to the primacy of EU law may enable policy and laws passed within the EU to have sway when their democratic credentials are in doubt. Future directions are difficult to predict. The relationship between the government of the day, Parliament and the courts is always evolving through elements of pragmatism and some degree of self-limitation that has avoided outright conflict. Writing in 1971, de Smith was rather cautious in his prediction and measured in his judgement of the potential impact of membership of the European Community on the UK and cautioned against rash prediction or hasty conclusions. In this well-known analysis de Smith explains the time-less quality of sovereignty as it is defined and re-defined by each generation, often underpinning the overall political realities of where economic and legal powers actually reside:

> If, however, with the passage of time, the Community develops characteristics of a political federation, and if the incongruity of the orthodox doctrine of parliamentary sovereignty becomes increasingly apparent in a context of expanding Community law, then a climate of opinion will doubtless develop in which heterodoxy will thrive and eventually prevail. The legal concept of parliamentary sovereignty may then drift away into the shadowy background from which it emerged.[26]

Professor Sir Francis Jacob in his Hamlyn Lectures, *The Sovereignty of Parliament: The European Way*[27] in 2006 admitted that sovereignty was not always compatible 'both internationally and internally, with another concept which also has a lengthy history, but which today is widely regarded as a paramount value: the rule of law'.[28] The UK's decision to leave the EU will profoundly impact on the question of UK sovereignty and it will remain to be seen what arrangements will be agreed in terms of enforcing EU law in the UK. It is intended to pass a Great Repeal Bill that the Government intends will adopt all EU law into UK law and repeal the European Communities Act 1972.[29] Notwithstanding the UK leaving the EU, the implications of EU law will remain an influence over the UK in how the UK courts have developed legal methodology and approaches to legal reasoning.

4. The UK courts and human rights

Human rights in the UK courts is highly contentious amongst academics and politicians that raise questions about the legitimacy of the European Convention on Human Rights, the jurisprudence of the Strasbourg Court and its application to United Kingdom domestic law.[30] The starting point is the Human Rights Act 1998, passed by the UK government to bring Convention rights into UK law and is an important source of rights. The Act has permitted the Convention to be interpreted and pleaded directly before the UK's national courts. This has given rise to a highly contested discussion about how to place rights within the UK's constitutional arrangements. A rights-based approach to constitutional and administrative law has enormous significance for judicial review. Courts are obliged to interpret legislation, UK Acts of Parliament in so far as it is possible to be compliant with the Convention. If this proves impossible then the court may issue a declaration of incompatibility and based on the declaration, the UK Parliament may decide to pass amending legislation or decide to take no further action. The Human Rights Act has an important significance in creating a rights presumption that public bodies are expected to be rights complicit. This means that all public bodies, including courts are aware of their human rights responsibilities and are expected to comply with the legal requirements under the Convention. However, the Act does not define the term public body and this has been left to judicial interpretation. The exclusion of private bodies is intended. For example, a private care home was held by the House of Lords[31] not to have to apply the Human Rights Act. The presumption that public bodies are compliant also applies to the passage of legislation whereby the relevant Minister has to sign a certificate that the proposed legislation is rights compliant. This leaves the courts with a discretion as to whether or not the legislation is compatible with Convention rights under the Act. The express aim is to avoid judges overturning Acts of Parliament. This makes sense if the government is based on a parliamentary system where the government is answerable to parliament and political choices or policy are regarded as drawn from political choices rather than the imposition of judicial opinions. The pre-eminence given to party political choices is easier to achieve under a parliamentary rather than a presidential system of government.

It is inevitable that a rights-focussed agenda may become enmeshed in the attitude of the courts in interpreting the law and this may create a change in approach to the role of the UK courts and a noticeable shift from political forms of power to judicial influences. One example is the Supreme Court decision in *Pham v Secretary of State for the Home Department*[32] in which the court considered the doctrine of proportionality as a common law ground for judicial review. The facts of the case concerned the question of whether or not it was lawful for the Home Secretary to take away the appellant's British citizenship and deport him to Vietnam. The appellant had acquired British citizenship in 1995 but did not renounce his Vietnamese citizenship based on where he had been born. The Home Secretary's actions were in connection with terrorism and the allegation that he had participated in terrorist activities. There were EU issues but the doctrine of proportionality was not dependant on EU law. Instead the UK courts are enabled to develop their own contextual approach to what is reasonable and a careful consideration of the policy implications as well as the value of judicial discretion on a case by case basis. The Supreme Court were far from convinced that the Home Secretary's decision was a proportionate one. *Pham* is a good example of the evolution of the common law through an understanding of EU influences that is not wholly dependent on interpreting EU law. The UK Supreme Court allowed the Secretary of State the powers to make a decision even though its effects might be to take away British citizenship.

The Human Rights Act 1998 provides a statutory basis for international obligations to be honoured by interpreting the European Convention on Human Rights as part of domestic law. The European Union has also created a complementary set of obligations including rights and legally enforceable rules. In the UK context this has given rise to tensions between the government of the day and the courts that provide the basis for an ongoing conflict that is often presented as conflict between elected politicians and unelected judges.[33]

The interaction between courts and Parliament has become acute in respect of a relatively small number of cases. The Strasbourg Court in *Hirst v UK (No.2)*[34] concluded that the blanket ban on prisoners voting was discriminatory and disproportionate. In the UK, the Government is opposed to the Strasbourg Court's perspective. On this occasion it decided to appeal the original decision and was reluctant to fast-track legislation to implement the incompatibility between UK law and the analysis offered by the Strasbourg Court in 2005. The issue of prisoners' voting remains unresolved even to this day as the UK has persistently failed to remove the ban and the House of Commons voted to retain the ban notwithstanding the decision of the Strasbourg Court. In *Scoppola v Italy (No. 3)*[35] the Grand Chamber affirmed the earlier decision in *Hirst* and concluded that a general and automatic disenfranchisement of all serving prisoners was incompatible with Article 3 of protocol 1 of the Convention. The question of prisoners' voting was debated at various stages of the discussion between the UK Government and the Strasbourg Court.[36] In November 2012 the Government published a draft Bill, the Voting Eligibility (Prisoners) Bill for pre-legislative scrutiny by a Joint Committee of both Houses. The Government published a draft report recommending that all prisoners serving sentences of 12 months or less to vote in all UK parliamentary, local and European elections. The Government has been fairly non-committal about this recommendation. The Strasbourg Court in August 2014 and February 2015 noted that the UK continued to violate the Convention in respect of prisoners' votes but the Court did not award any compensation or legal expenses.[37]

Further complexity arises in cases where prisoners are serving custodial sentences in terms of EU law.[38] In October 2015, the Court of Justice of the European Union (the Luxembourg Court), in an important decision on the rights of EU citizens and the EU Parliament, considered a French law that denied certain categories of prisoners the vote. The Luxembourg Court held that the French law was legal in *Thiery Deligne v Commune de Lesparre-Médoc and Préfet de la Gironde*.[39] The reasoning in the case was that the French law was proportionate under Article 52(1) of the Charter of Fundamental Rights of the European Union. The case might raise the possibility that UK law might be regarded as compatible. The problem is that the UK's position is based on a blanket ban rather than a more targeted response. The French law took account of the nature and gravity of the criminal offence committed and was not a blanket ban. The French case involved the defendant Mr Deligne being convicted of murder and receiving a 12-year sentence. He was not permitted to register to vote and his subsequent complaint was based on arguing that the French law was incompatible with EU law.

The UK Government has not decided how to respond to the Interim Resolution of the Council of Europe's Committee of Ministers calling on the UK to consider its obligations[40]. The UK is currently considering what response to make and is taking time to consider its options.

Resolving potential conflict between the courts and Parliament is almost an inevitable consequence of UK courts having to adapt to influences from international and European sources. The question is how such tensions and potential conflicts be best resolved? The answer involves a mixture of possibilities. Dawn Oliver suggests an evolving comity between 'institutions and workability'.[41] There are other possibilities. Developing priorities and setting boundaries that provide adequate road maps of constitutional propriety and respect for the rule of law is essential. Political policy making is the most difficult where judges are less likely to be able to settle legal debate without the Executive giving way to judicial interpretation.

Some guidance as to what might be involved in defining the future role of the courts came in *Thoburn v Sunderland City Council.*[42] In this case street traders were prosecuted for selling goods using imperial measures rather than metric measures. The UK Government's obligations to apply metric measurement arose from Directives and section 2(2) of the European Communities Act 1972. Lord Justice Laws found that there was no inconsistency between the Directive and the Weights and Measures Act 1985 and therefore no implied repeal of the European Communities Act 1972 arose. Lord Justice Laws recognised the changes in UK sovereignty and this had modified the doctrine of implied repeal when it came to EU law. The doctrine of implied repeal suggests that a later Act of Parliament may overturn an earlier Act. In the case of UK law the 1972 Act is seen as setting out a position where later Acts of Parliament will be read as consistent to the 1972 Act. Of course in the future it is possible for a UK Act of Parliament to expressly repeal the 1972 Act. That would require clear and unambiguous words and repeal would have to be spelt out very clearly. The basis of the UK's relationship was a matter of the common law and the common law was the basis of any resolution. Consequently he reasoned that while ordinary statutes were subject to the implied repeal doctrine what he called 'constitutional statutes' were not. Defining a constitutional statute was one which dealt with fundamental constitutional rights, including the European Communities Act 1972, and the only conditions where such a repeal might be possible arose from express words in the later statute.

Further elaboration is forthcoming in *R (HS2 Action Alliance Ltd.,) and others v Secretary of State for Transport*[43] where the applicants argued that the adoption of a Hybrid Bill procedure was not compatible with the requirements of the Environmental Impact Assessment Directive (Directive 2011/92/EU) requiring effective opportunities for objectors to participate in environmental decision-making procedures. The process of Hybrid Bill allows more detailed inquiry and investigation than would be possible under the normal procedure. The Government were pushing forward a plan to create a fast train link between the capital and Birmingham and the objectors to the proposed link claimed that there was a serious impact on the environment. The adoption of a Hybrid Bill was subject to Government whipping procedures in the House of Commons, meaning that there would be inadequate time to debate the detailed and complex nature of environmental issues; and that the alternatives to the proposal would not be considered until the relevant elect committee after second reading. The Supreme Court had rejected the view that the issues raised by the applicants should be referred to the European Court of Justice. The result of the Supreme Court decision is to allow the Hybrid Bill procedure to continue and the Bill is currently at the stage of debate in the House of Lords. Lord Reed made clear that where EU law is in direct conflict with UK domestic constitutional law, it was a matter to be resolved by the UK Supreme Court. The Supreme Court accepted that there is no *acte Claire* and that the *Factortame* principle of a disapplication of a statute was not pertinent to a constitutional principle such as settled in the Bill of Rights.

The emergence of constitutional fundamentals that are unalterable by EU law and defined by the national court creates potential limitations on the general expansionist direction of the European Court of Justice. It is in line with other cases recently decided by the Supreme Court[44] and rests on the re- assertion of domestic supremacy to be found in section 18 of the European Union Act 2011. It remains unclear what the reaction of the European Court of Justice might be. The European Court of Justice may, as it has done in the past, subscribe to the view that it has the competence to settle any competing competence between EU law and domestic law of the Member States and that the national courts are obliged to follow its opinions. The European Court of Justice is increasingly of the view that in matters of EU law, national courts are behaving as European courts integral to the requirements of the Treaty obligations. Conceptually this view fits very well within the analysis that EU law is not determined within the boundaries of national states but within the conceptual framework of the jurisprudence of the EU.

5. The UK courts and devolution

The UK's unitary and non-federal state has suffered from over-centralisation for some time. Devolved arrangements, including directly elected legislative bodies, to Scotland, Wales and N. Ireland in 1998 were introduced to give different nations powers over their own regions. Devolution has resulted in important cases defining the powers of devolved legislatures. Soon after the Scotland Act 1998 came into effect questions arose in litigation as to the nature and powers of the new Parliament. In *Whaley v. Lord Watson of Invergowrie*[45] it was held by the Inner House of the Court of Session that the Scottish Parliament, being a creature of statute, does not enjoy the privilege of the UK Parliament to regulate its own proceedings (though by section 28(5) of the Act the validity of an Act of the Scottish Parliament is not affected by any invalidity in proceedings leading to the enactment).

Issues to do with devolution have been raised in the UK Supreme Court. A number of recent cases highlight the cultural distinctiveness of the Scottish legal system and the political sensitivities surrounding it. As we shall see, courts have generally upheld the powers of devolved bodies against challenge, except in relation to the primacy of EU law and interpretations of human rights, when the Supreme Court has on occasions overridden interpretations made by Scottish courts.

In *Axa General Insurance and others v The Lord Advocate*,[46] the lawfulness of an Act of the Scottish Parliament, the Damages (Asbestos-related Conditions) (Scotland) Act 2009, was challenged as to its compatibility with Article 1 of Protocol 1 of the European Convention on Human Rights and its reasonableness in terms of the general judicial review jurisdiction of the Supreme Court, in particular on grounds of irrationality and arbitrariness. The claimants were insurance companies and their claim arose from their undertaking to indemnify employers against liability for negligence. The point of the Scottish Parliament's legislation was to include under Scots law liability for personal injury claims arising from various asbestos-related pleural plaques and related conditions. The UK Supreme Court held that the claimants were entitled to make such a claim and that the courts had an overarching power to ensure that the 2009 Act was legitimate in its aims and proportionate in its response. The Court took into account the political context of the legislation, including social policy and the public interest. It found that the legislation had a legitimate purpose and that the means to achieve its aims were reasonable and proportionate. The Court rejected the claimants' case and held that the legislation was compatible with the European Convention and did not offend any of the other grounds for judicial review on which the claimants relied.

The significance of the *Axa* decision is that the UK Supreme Court indicated that it has a residual jurisdiction to consider the legality of Acts of the Scottish Parliament. Lord Hope held that the approach to the question of the Supreme Court's review powers also applied to the other devolved institutions in Wales and Northern Ireland, but that it was significant that the Scottish Parliament is 'a self-standing' democratically elected legislature. This sets an important benchmark for judicial review. Lord Hope cautioned that the courts 'should intervene, if at all, only in the most exceptional circumstances'.[47] His analysis is drawn not only from a comparative analysis of the sovereignty of the UK and Scottish Parliaments, but on the basis of the power of review itself: it constitutes an important oversight of the constitutional processes and checks and balances on the legislative programme of the Scottish Parliament and other devolved administration exercising legislative powers.

The Human Rights Act 1998 has also been relied on in cases raising devolution issues. In *Cadder (Peter) v HM Advocate*[48] the Criminal Procedure (Scotland) Act 1995, passed by the UK Parliament before the Scotland Act 1998, was the subject of judicial review on a claim by a suspect who had made admissions under caution to the police but in the absence of legal representation. The admissibility of the admissions was contested after the accused was convicted, and formed the basis of his appeal. It was argued that the absence of legal representation at the time of the police interview was a violation of Article 6 of the European Convention on Human Rights. The High Court of Justiciary refused leave to appeal on the basis of an earlier leading Scottish authority, *HM Advocate v McLean*[49] in which the argument that legal representation was a legal right had been rejected. Mr Cadder appealed to the Supreme Court of the UK. The Supreme Court followed the Grand Chamber of the European Court of Human Rights in *Salduz v Turkey* (2008)[50] in holding that a person detained by the police had the right of access to a lawyer prior to being interviewed unless there were compelling reasons to restrict that right. The Scottish court's decision in *McLean* was overruled and it was held that nothing in the Scotland Act 1998 protected the Criminal Procedure

(Scotland) Act 1995 from review. The 1995 Act could not be read compatibly with Article 6 of the European Convention on Human Rights on access to justice. The day after the Supreme Court delivered its decision, the Criminal Procedure (Legal Assistance, Detention and Appeals) (Scotland) Act 2010 was passed by the Scottish Parliament allowing a person under suspicion a right of access to legal assistance.

The Supreme Court has also held that its jurisdiction over devolution issues under the Scotland Act 1998[51] includes the power to deal with Human Rights Act claims arising in criminal – and other – cases and to determine whether the Scottish courts have correctly interpreted Article 6 rights. In *Fraser (Nat Gordon) v HM Advocate*[52] the High Court of Justiciary had refused an appeal against conviction in which the defendant sought to adduce new evidence in support of a claim that the original trial was a miscarriage of justice. The defendant claimed that the Crown's failure to disclose information to him before the trial infringed his Article 6 rights and that this raised a devolution issue as to whether the conviction was outside the powers of the Scottish courts under the 1998 Act as being contrary to the Human Rights Act 1998. The Supreme Court held that this was indeed a devolution issue over which it had jurisdiction, and that the test applied by the Scottish court was not consistent with the interpretation adopted by the Supreme Court in the leading case of *McInnes v HM Advocate*.[53] It therefore remitted the case to a differently constituted Appeal Court for consideration.

The Scotland Act 2012 addresses a number of important constitutional issues. Section 14 of the 2012 Act sets a time limit for actions against the Scottish Ministers under the 1998 Act where it is claimed that they acted incompatibly with Convention rights.[54] The jurisdiction of the UK Supreme Court over Convention rights and EU law has been clarified under section 34 of the Scotland Act 2012. This gives the Advocate General for Scotland the express power to refer a compatibility issue to the High Court of Justiciary. Under section 35 of the 2012 Act additional powers are granted to the Lord Advocate and the Advocate General for Scotland to require a lower court to refer a compatibility issue to the High Court of Justiciary or if necessary to the UK Supreme Court. Sections 36 and 37 provide the UK Supreme Court with power to hear criminal appeals from Scotland that may raise Convention rights or EU law issues.

6. Administrative and financial pressures on the UK courts

Undoubtedly the funding of judicial challenges in the courts has become highly politicised, especially as many cases are taken against the Government or public bodies. Funding arrangements for cases through legal aid are vulnerable to change. In December 2012, the Coalition Government launched a consultation process on reform of judicial review that continued until 24 January 2013, *Judicial Review: Proposals for Reform*. This was followed by an additional consultation from September 2013 until November 2013 *Judicial Review: Proposals for Further Reform*.

There are mixed motives behind the consultations and the Coalition Government's desire for reform. At one level it is to save money and prevent useless cases from being taken that are filtered out from the procedures for review. The aim is to reduce time, money and simplify procedures including shorter time limits to take cases, restrictions on the right to an oral renewal of an application where a judge has refused permission in a prior judicial process or where the claim is judged to be unmeritorious. There are proposals to limit the right to appeal to the Court of Appeal and changes in the rules relating to costs and also standing rules to prevent the taxpayer having to pay for unmeritorious cases.

One motive might be to save the Government uncertainty over judicial review through a reduction in the number of applications. This is a highly debateable point as the statistical evidence indicates that the courts are already effective in setting parameters for cases to be carefully considered.

The number of judicial review applications varies in any one year but the average[55] is around 12,000 applications lodged with the Administrative Court.[56] The bulk of applications are related to immigration and asylum cases. Only a small number of applications are granted permission to proceed to a full hearing and this is roughly about 1500 cases. Many cases are not proceeded with and nearly 50 per cent of cases were refused permission meaning that the judge was not convinced that there was an arguable case. Settlements are common and may represent a potential for changing the way in which judicial review is undertaken. There are also suggestions that some form of alternative dispute resolution might be the best way forward. This is a largely unchartered area but alternative dispute resolution would offer a way to resolve disputes in a highly cost effective way. The Pre-action Protocol for judicial review applications includes the instruction that the parties should consider alternative dispute resolution as it may offer a more suitable procedure than proceeding to litigation.

Judicial review claims that are proceeded with do not inevitably lead to the Government losing their case. Only a small number are cases where the courts find against the Government. This may not ease concern that judicial review is a 'threat' to the smooth working of Government or may be used by opponents of the Government to cause embarrassment and delays in implementing policies. Pressure groups may justify the use of judicial review as a means to test the legality of Government decisions and raise public awareness. An important part of judicial review is to check on the legality of the Government of the day as a means of upholding the rule of law.

Steps taken to reduce the workload of the administrative courts are on-going. The bulk of cases involving immigration judicial review have been moved to the Upper Tribunal (Immigration and Asylum) Chamber under section 23 of the Crime and Courts Act 2013. This is partly in response to delays in having cases heard but also the increase in the work load that made the Administrative Court less efficient than it should have been.

In planning cases the Government reduced the time limit from three months to six weeks and 30 days and in procurement cases to 30 days. In cases without any merit the right to an oral hearing was removed and the fees were increased to

£215 for oral renewals. These changes attracted criticism that they would reduce the accessibility of judicial review. The Government has gone further and decided to create within the High Court a specialist Planning Court to deal with judicial review and statutory appeals relating to nationally Significant Infrastructure Projects and other planning matters. The Criminal Justice and Courts Act 2015 creates a new Planning Court and sets various safeguards restricting judicial review in planning cases including changes to the costs arrangements for planning cases.

Judicial review is particularly vulnerable because of high costs and expenses. The complexity of legal analysis and argument makes it difficult to take cases as litigants in person. In most cases judicial review is dependent on legal aid and this has in the past been generously provided. The Coalition Government in 2013 announced restrictions on the availability of judicial review especially in certain prison cases or for applicants 'lacking a clear connection with the UK'. Legal costs are normally borne by the losing party which also enters a note of caution when taking cases. There is no absolute right to any remedy even if the application proves to be meritorious and successful. Remedies are only discretionary and may be refused and this creates a further hurdle to any application. Attempts to remove guaranteed legal aid for judicial review set out in the Civil Legal Aid (Remuneration) (Amendment) (no 3) Regulations 2014 that came into force in April 2014 was challenged as to its legality. The High Court held that this was illegal as there was no rational link between the regulations and the aim claimed by the Government to only bring cases that were likely to succeed.[57]

7. Conclusions

The UK's constitutional arrangements do not provide the courts with the power to review primary legislation nor the power to hold Acts of Parliament unconstitutional and illegal. This is unusual when compared with countries with written constitutions. Defining the democratic credentials of a representative democracy, the UK's doctrine of parliamentary sovereignty has an overriding influence over the main institutions of government and defines the pre-eminence of Parliament. The one exception is European Union law that concedes the power of illegality to be vested in the European Court of Justice. The motivation behind Brexit was largely to bring UK sovereignty to the fore and a rejection of the European Court of Justice. The other exception is the area of human rights and the rapidly developing jurisprudence of rights with its enormous potential for transforming the UK's system of public law. The UK's constitutional arrangements also should not overlook the various checks and balances to be found in the elaborate system of parliamentary oversight that defines important accountability mechanisms within the UK's constitutional arrangements. Parliament provides technical and procedural opportunities to hold government to account while acknowledging the ultimate political nature of policy making that rests in the government of the day. The recent *Miller* decision[58] affirms Parliament's role in leaving the EU.

The UK courts are under increasing pressures from mainly political perspectives about the nature of political power and its system of accountability. On human rights, the UK is certainly at risk of passing laws that are incompatible with Convention rights and are likely to be considered inconsistent with international norms. Leaving the EU brings with it the political demand for removal from the Strasbourg Courts and the enactment of a British Bill of Rights.

The rationale and justification offered for UK sovereignty is defined in terms of democratic mandates achieved through elected government. Such an explanation is convincing to a point – but as elections are single points in time, however many or how regularly held, there is little day to day monitoring of how governments behave. Trusting in Government is partly cultural, often a manifestation of social and political values and not always a reliable way to prevent abuse or misuse of power. The UK courts act as an important check on arbitrary power. The sensitivity of their role has intensified since the UK decided to leave the EU with questions about the role of the Government and the UK Parliament intensely debated.[59]

There are also financial pressures. We have also seen how the UK courts are coming under increasing financial pressures during a period of austerity finance since the financial crisis in 2008 that challenges the availability of the courts in the area of judicial review.

There are pressures on the role of the courts in terms of accountability and oversight. Expanding the role of the UK's Supreme Court is favoured by some academics[60] as a way of ensuring that judicial oversight is facilitated and improved. Constructing a constitutional court on the lines of Germany might be seen as a possible way forward. However much this possibility may be doubted it is likely to become increasingly possible as traditional constitutional orthodoxy in the UK falls under the influence of giving way to international standards that are the product of EU influences and the jurisprudence of the European Court of Justice. This is an ongoing process of evolution rather than revolutionary change. The options open to the UK include the possibility of a written constitution. There is limited support for a written constitution that would grant the UK Supreme Court the power of judicial review of legislation. There has been a noticeable use of codified manuals and explanatory documents setting out the powers of the Cabinet and Civil Service as well as the means of financial scrutiny. The devolution settlements in Scotland, Wales and Northern Ireland are being revisited with additional devolved law making powers including taxation. This is likely to transform the United Kingdom through mini-written constitutions that will ultimately require clarification of the position of England and its relationship to the devolved nations. The UK Supreme Court has shown a willingness to become pro-active on devolution issues when interpreting the limits and extent of devolved powers.[61] This is an important dimension in identifying the legality of devolved powers and ensuring that devolved governments operate within the boundaries of constitutional propriety. This falls short of ensuring a formal constitutional court that applies to UK legislation.

Strengthening the existing system of parliamentary scrutiny is ongoing but often with only limited results as the government of the day has opportunities to take overall control if not influence over parliamentary process. Overall, there are many doubts and uncertainties for the future direction of the system of public law in the UK. Unhappily the courts are at the focus of much political attention, raising some major constitutional questions about how conflicts between judges and politicians might be best resolved.[62]

Notes

1 See Hirschl (2014) 1–10.
2 See Griffith (1979) 1.
3 Waldron, (2007) 91.
4 *R (Miller) v Secretary of State for Exiting the EU etc* [2017] UKSC 5.
5 Waldron (2002) 137.
6 See Bingham (2011) 1.
7 Case C-213/89 [1990] E.C.R. 2433; [1990] 3 C.M.L.R. 1; [1990] 2 AC 85, [1991] 1 AC 603. *R. v Secretary of State for Transport ex parte Factortame Ltd., (No.2).* [1991] 1 AC 603.
8 Oliver (2013) 310.
9 Five year fixed term Parliaments in the UK are required since the Fixed-term Parliaments Act 2011 passed in 2011 under the Coalition Government but remains in force.
10 *Jackson v Attorney General* [2005] UKHL 56 [2006] 1 AC 262.
11 *R. v Secretary of State for Transport ex parte Factortame Ltd., (No.2).* [1991] 1 AC 603. H.W.R. Wade, 'Sovereignty and the European Communities' (1972) p.4. Sir William Wade (1991). Also see: House of Commons Library (2015).
12 Allison (2007) 120–123; Bradley (2007) 25–58; Allan (1997) 443; Allan (2013); Collini (2006); Gaus (1950); Hailsham (1978).
13 *Francovich v Italian Republic* C-6/90 and 9/90 [1991] E.C.R. I-5357.
14 Wade (1989) 17.
15 *Factortame* [1990] E.C.R. I-2433, [1991] 1 AC 603, 658–9.
16 Bingham (2010). 164.
17 Ibid., 164.
18 See Lord Simon in *Maunsell v Olins* [1975] AC 373.
19 Craig (2000) 211.
20 Allan (1997) 443.
21 Craig, op cit. 120–121.
22 Craig (2013) 165–8.
23 Ibid. 185.
24 Oliver (2013) 313.
25 Ibid. 335–336.
26 de Smith (1971) 614.
27 Jacob (2006) 5.
28 Ibid., page 6.
29 The Great Repeal Bill is likely to be published during the period of negotiation over the two years after Article 50 is triggered.
30 The Human Rights Act 1998.
31 *YL v Birmingham City Council* [2007] UKHL 27.
32 [2015] UKSC 19.
33 There is a rich literature on the role of the courts. John Gardner (2009); Mark Tushnet (2010); Robert Behn (1998); Antoine Bozio et al. (2015).
34 [2005] 42 ECtHR 849.
35 [2012] ECtHR 868.
36 House of Commons Library Standard Note (2015).
37 *Frith and Others v UK* [2014] 47784/09, *McHugh and others* [2015] ECHR 155.
38 See House of Commons Library Briefing Paper CBP 7461 Prisoners' Voting rights: developments since May 2015 12th January 2016).
39 Case C-650/13.

40 Interim Resolution CM/Res DH(2015) 251 adopted by the Committee of Ministers 9th December 2015.
41 Oliver (2013) 310.
42 *Thoburn v Sunderland City Council* [2003] QB 151.
43 *R (HS2 Action Alliance Ltd.) and others v Secretary of State for Transport* [2014] UKSC 3 Also see: Gaston (2014).
44 See *Osborn v The Parole Board* [2013] UKSC 61 and *Kennedy v Charity Commission* [2014] UKSC 20.
45 [2000] SC 340.
46 [2011] UKSC 46 and [2011] CSIH 31.
47 Ibid. para. 49.
48 *Cadder (Peter) v HM Advocate* [2010] UKSC 43 (SC).
49 *HM Advocate v McLean* [2009] HCJAC 97, 2010 SLT 73. See the discussion in (2011) Public Law 166.
50 *Salduz v Turkey* (2008) 49 ECHR 421.
51 See section 98 and Schedule 6, Parts I and II as amended to substitute the Supreme Court for the Judicial Committee of the Privy Council.
52 *Fraser (Nat Gordon) v HM Advocate* [2011] UKSC 24. See the discussion in (2011) Public Law 805.
53 *McInnes v HM Advocate* [2010] UKSC 7.
54 *Somerville v Scottish Ministers* [2007] UKHL 44 and the Convention Rights Proceedings (Amendment) (Scotland) Act 2009 now replaced by section 14 of the Scotland Act 2012.
55 See House of Commons Library (2013) pp. 15.
56 The Administrative Court was created out of the Divisional Court of the High Court (Queen's Bench Division) where judicial review applications are lodged.
57 Unreported case (2015) *New Law Journal* 5 (6th March 2015).
58 *R (on the application of Miller and another)* [2017] UKSC 5.
59 Ibid.
60 Allan (2004) 671; Allan (2006); Murkens (2009); McEldowney (2015).
61 See *Axa General Insurance and others v Lord Advocate* [2011] UKSC 46.
62 D'Alterio (2011) p 394–424.

Bibliography

Allan, T. R. S., 'Parliamentary Sovereignty: Law, Politics and Revolution' (1997). 113 *LQR* 443–452.

Allan, T. R. S., 'Common Law Reason and the Limits of Judicial Deference', in David Dyzenhaus (ed.), *The Unity of Public Law* (Hart 2004) 7.

Allan, T. R. S., 'Human Rights and Judicial Review: A Critique of "Due Deference"' (2006). 65 *C.L.J.* 671–695.

Allan, T. R. S., *The Sovereignty of Law: Freedom, Constitution and Common Law* (Oxford: Oxford University Press 2013).

Allison, J.W.F., *The English Historical Constitution* (Cambridge: Cambridge University Press 2007) 120–123.

Behn, Robert, 'The New Public Management Paradigm and the Search for Democratic Accountability' (1998). 1 *International Public Management Journal* 2, 131–164.

Bingham, Tom, *The Rule of Law* (London: Allen Lane 2010) 164.

Bingham, Tom, *The Rule of Law* (London: Penguin 2011).

Bozio, Antoine et al., 'European Public Finances and the Great Recession: France, Germany, Ireland, Italy, Spain and the United Kingdom Compared' (2015) 36 *Institute for Fiscal Studies* 4, 405–430.

Bradley, Anthony, 'The Sovereignty of Parliament – Form or Substance?', in Jeffrey Jowell and Dawn Oliver (eds), *The Changing Constitution* (Oxford: Oxford University Press 2007) 25–58.

Collini, Stefan, *Public Moralists* (Clarendon Press 2006) 250.

Craig, Paul, 'Public Law, Political Theory and Legal Theory' (2000). *Public Law* 211.

Craig, Paul, 'The United Kingdom, the European Union and Sovereignty', in Richard Rawlings, Peter Leyland and Alison Young (eds), *Sovereignty and the Law* (Oxford: Oxford University Press 2013) 165–185.

D'Alterio, Elisa, 'From Judicial Comity to Legal Comity: A Judicial Solution to Global Disorder?' (2011). 9 *International Journal of Constitutional Law* 2, 394–424.

De Smith, S. A., 'The Constitution and the Common Market: An Appraisal' (1971). 34 *Modern Law Review* 597 at 614.

Gardner, John, 'Can There be a Written Constitution?' (2009). Legal Research Papers Series Paper no 17/2009 (May 2009), University of Oxford.

Gaston, Ben, 'Laying the Tracks' (2014). 14–15 *New Law Journal* (4 July 2014).

Gaus, John M., 'A Theory of Public Administration Means in Our Time a Theory of Politics' (1950). *Public Administration.*

Griffith, J. A. G., 'The Political Constitution' (1979). 42 *Modern Law Review* 1–21.

Hailsham, Lord, *The Dilemma of Democracy: Diagnosis and Prescription* (London: Collins 1978).

Hirschl, Ran, *Comparative Matters* (Oxford: Oxford University Press 2014).

House of Commons Library, Judicial Review: Government Reforms SN/HA/6616 (14 February 2013).

House of Commons Library, The 1974–1975 UK Renegotiation of EEC Membership and Referendum Briefing Paper 7253 (13 July 2015).

House of CommonsLibrary, Briefing Paper CBP 7461, Prisoners' Voting rights: Developments Since May 2015 (12 January 2016).

Jacob, Francis G., *The Sovereignty of Parliament: The European Way: The Hamlyn Lectures* (Cambridge University Press 2006) 5.

McEldowney, John F., 'Public Expenditure and the Control of Public Finance', in Jeffrey Jowell, Dawn Oliver and Colm O'Cinneide (eds), *The Changing Constitution* (Oxford University Press 2015) 350–378.

Murkens, Eric Jo, 'The Quest for Constitutionalism in UK Public Law Discourse' (2009). 29 *Oxford Journal of Legal Studies* 427–455.

Oliver, Dawn, 'Parliament and the Courts: A Pragmatic (or Principled) Defence of the Sovereignty of Parliament', in Alexander Horne, Gavin Drewry and Dawn Oliver (eds), *Parliament and the Law* (Hart Publishing 2013) 309–338.

Tushnet, Mark, 'How Different are Waldron's and Fallon's Core Cases For and Against Judicial Review?' (2010). 30 *Oxford Journal of Legal Studies* 49–70.

Wade, H.W.R., 'Sovereignty and the European Communities' (1972). 88 *Law Quarterly Review* 1–5.

Wade, SirWilliam, *Constitutional Fundamentals* (Oxford: Oxford University Press 1989) 17.

Wade, SirWilliam, 'What Has Happened to the Sovereignty of Parliament?' (1991). 107 *Law Quarterly Review* 1–4.

Waldron, Jeremy, 'Legislation and the Rule of Law' (2007). 1 *Legisprudence* 91–123.

Waldron, Jeremy, 'Is the Rule of Law an Essentially Contested Concept (in Florida)?' (2002). 21 *Law and Philosophy* 137–164.

Part III

Responding to challenges on European level

14 New challenges for constitutional adjudication in Europe:

What role could the 'dialogue of courts' play?[1]

Tania Groppi

Introduction

The twenty-first century brought new challenges for the 'constitutional State',[2] that are more or less direct consequences of globalisation.

In this chapter I wish to reflect on these challenges and on the appropriate nature (or lack thereof) of the constitutional State, as we have known it, in particular in Europe since the Second World War, to provide suitable responses. In doing so, I will focus especially on constitutional judges (including supreme courts that carry out constitutional revision of laws), which represent the most distinctive institution of this form of State.

I will divide my text into two parts. In the first part I will very briefly look into some challenges and their impact on the constitutional State (of which I will give a synthetic description), underlining the repercussions on constitutional justice and on its relationship with electoral democracy. This will touch upon the controversial theme of the constitutional judge's legitimacy.

In the second part I will examine what is often called the 'dialogue of courts'; that is, the implicit or explicit circulation of case-law. This matter, as we will see, includes both 'horizontal' circulation between constitutional courts and 'vertical' circulation between constitutional courts and international or supranational courts. In the European area, we need to take into consideration the Court of Justice of the European Union and the European Court of Human Rights.

The objective of this second part will be to clarify whether such a dialogue plays or can play, in the future, a role in the search for suitable answers to new challenges and if it can contribute to strengthen the legitimacy of constitutional justice.

1. The constitutional State facing new challenges

When we mention new challenges facing the constitutional State in Europe, we usually think of the economic and financial crisis that has been affecting European economies, in particular the 'Eurozone', since 2008.

However, we need to go beyond this perspective and frame this crisis within a global scenario unfolding around the 'third revolution' (after the agricultural revolution of the Neolithic and the industrial revolution of the eighteenth century): the digital and computing revolution, that is at the basis of the more recent globalisation.[3]

From a factual standpoint, new technologies combined with the increasing mobility of persons and things determine the birth of a 'global village' to which the legal instruments of the post-Westphalian nation State and of international law – where nation States are the protagonists – have difficulty adapting in order to give appropriate legal responses. The 'territory' is not the only element affected – the 'temporal' dimension has also been impacted, for humanity has the possibility today to take decisions that might turn the future of generations upside down in a previously unknown way.

We can identify at least four fields in which there have been memorable changes: a) the globalisation of economy and finance, often the source of the globalisation of economic crises, such as the current one; b) the circulation of persons, the very obvious manifestation of which is migration; c) international terrorism, which takes advantage of the new technologies and of cyberspace; d) the environmental crisis – that is, the ever-growing impact of human activities on the environment and on human nature itself, reflected by biotechnology and the search for the genome.

What interests us in the present chapter has to do with the impact of this historical transformation on the constitutional State in its entirety: in fact, constitutional courts are only one of the many actors on the scene of the constitutional State. They are not alone. In order to understand their approach, we need to understand the institutional, political and also the economic and social context in which they act.

What do we mean by 'constitutional State' then?

Here I am referring to the State form established after the Second World War in Europe, which later, by different 'waves' of democratisation, spread throughout the world, albeit with variations. However, these variations do not prevent us from finding remarkable similarities too and, by consequence, talking about a 'model' (as 'ideal type').

In a nutshell, the constitutional State is characterised by: 1) a democratic constituent process, through which the different components of a pluralistic society agree on the foundations of their life together; 2) the presence of a constitution, as a product of that compact, which is the basis of the legal system and that is protected due to its rigidity (i.e. it has to be respected by all State powers, including the legislative power); 3) the constitutional guarantee of rights and freedoms, including economic and social rights, in the name of the principle of substantive equality; 4) the constitutional guarantee of the separation of powers, meaning the separation of the watchdog system (that includes constitutional justice) from the political decision-making process, against which the independence of the former has to be protected; 5) the electoral democracy, in terms of free elections to choose those holding the power of political decision-making; 6) openness towards international law and human rights, through constitutional provisions that allocate a special legal force to international agreements; and 7) the decentralisation of power.[4]

The great question is whether this State form on the level of institutions and values is capable of providing responses to new challenges often including the following: the need for world-wide – instead of nation-based – reactions to global phenomena; the growing importance of technology and science and, more generally, of non-legal 'sciences'; the need to take into consideration the life requirements of future generations at risk; the inevitable coexistence of very diverse groups of people, who do not share common values. All this increases the ever-present tension between 'electoral democracy' and 'constitutional democracy', that is, first of all the tension between political decision makers and constitutional courts.

In fact, political decision makers have serious difficulties, as they need to give answers that could lead to a short-term electoral consensus on a national level.[5] As a consequence, they are unfit to give coordinated answers that would take into proper consideration the international instruments, as in the field of immigration, and in the best hypothesis they act as passive executors of supranational decisions; they struggle to take into consideration the technical or scientific know-how and, even more, to adopt decisions adapted to an intergenerational time horizon. They are accountable to the present-day electorate and when external authorities do not force them – as is the case within the context of the European Union, especially in the Eurozone – they rather follow the emotions of public opinion.

In this context, a tendency to transfer the most difficult decisions to the judges can be detected, which has led to a 'judicialisation' of constitutional democracy. The term 'juristocracy' has been used to describe the growing 'power of courts' in decision-making, that goes beyond their traditional conflict-solving power.[6]

This pattern is not completely new; it started before the latest developments and some consider it to be an inherent part of the structure of the constitutional State.[7] However, it has lately intensified in the context of globalisation. As a consequence, a new burden has been put on the shoulders of the courts both nationally and internationally. In light of this new framework, we need to reflect on the instruments the courts have at their disposal to face the new challenges so that we can verify whether those instruments can be adapted or if new ones need to be introduced to avoid the collapse of the courts under this heavy burden.

2. The 'dialogue of courts': Answer to the new challenges?

2.1 A few words on the 'dialogue of courts'

Does the presumed 'dialogue of courts' have a role to play among the instruments available to support constitutional courts in the face of new challenges? The second part of this chapter is dedicated to this question. Without going into details about the 'dialogue of courts', to which many studies have been dedicated in recent years, we can say that resorting to decisions of other jurisdictions can be either optional or obligatory. The use of decisions of other national – 'foreign' – constitutional courts is always optional: it is often referred to as 'horizontal dialogue'. Whereas, the 'vertical dialogue', whereby decisions are referred by supranational or international courts, is very often obligatory, as those judgments are binding for the national jurisdictions of the Member States.[8] The vertical dialogue is generally explicit: in other words, it takes place with explicit reference to supranational court decisions. In contrast, the horizontal dialogue can be explicit if the judges feel that quoting foreign case-law may strengthen their legitimacy, or, on the contrary, it can be implicit if they feel that it would not serve that goal.

Empirical research has shown that, in this regard, there are two categories of courts: those in which foreign precedents are explicitly used and those in which, on the contrary, such situations are almost nil or at least very rare and we find only implicit references.[9] Despite the level of importance that the debate over this topic has reached, we cannot but acknowledge that there are not so many countries in which foreign precedents are often received explicitly: this practice only concerns common law systems (for example Israel, Canada, Australia, South Africa, Namibia, Hong Kong, India, New Zealand, Ireland). In contrast, the civil law systems, including most of the European countries can be allocated in the category of 'doing it but not admitting',[10] that is to say, in the category of tacit and often hidden references, except in rare and sporadic cases that do not constitute a homogenous group susceptible of being analysed, and which could be qualified as 'bricolage'.[11]

2.2 The lack of intensified 'horizontal dialogue' in 'crisis case-law'

Taking into account these considerations, if we return to 'crisis case-law' in the European legal area, we need to admit that explicit horizontal dialogue is not anymore used by constitutional courts more frequently than in ordinary circumstances.

We might figure that the considerations in the global scenario concerning the existence of an 'alliance' between courts over 'difficult issues' – expressed in mutual quotations and used to offset an evermore de-territorialised political power[12] – could be used with regard to new challenges as well. For example, regarding case-law on counterterrorism measures, there was mention of a 'judicial coalition of the willing' as 'a coordinated response on the part of a group of national courts to the coordinated counterterrorism policies of their national governments'.[13]

This is not the case. My impression, supported by non-extensive but satisfactory empirical research,[14] is that little has changed in the reasoning of constitutional courts as for the explicit use of foreign precedents. Despite the fact that the issues at hand are the same worldwide and that the courts display good knowledge of foreign case-law, they do not refer to it explicitly often than usual anymore.

This approach is obvious also in the case-law on anti-crisis measures adopted by most European countries as a consequence of the European austerity policy, which, in certain countries, even brought about constitutional revisions to insert the principle of balanced budget into the Constitution. The Lithuanian, Italian, Spanish, Portuguese and Romanian constitutional courts, as well as the Greek and Irish judges, had to review the constitutionality of these measures with regard in particular to their consequences on economic and social rights: they gave different responses but in general they sought to balance budgetary requirements and the essential content of the guarantee of constitutional rights.[15] It is, therefore, remarkable that despite the similar constitutional context between the two sides of the problem (constitutional protection of social rights on the one hand and budgetary restrictions of European origin on the other hand), they never quote each other, either to join forces or to show their differences.

The only exception is the Romanian Constitutional Court – a Court that, in its case-law, has referred in only 14 decisions out of more or less 13,000 to foreign precedents (according to a 2012 research). Of these, 4 of the 14 decisions are about anti-crisis legislation and the Court refers in them to decisions of Central and Eastern European countries' constitutional court judgments from the 1990s. Only one decision (judgment number 1533/2011) refers to the German decision of 7 September 2011 on supporting measures for Greece. Consequently, even though this reference shows an openness towards the comparative argument, which is quite uncommon in Romanian case-law, it cannot be considered as a strategy fine-tuned to a response coordinated according to the logic of horizontal dialogue.[16]

We might say that the need to face the new challenges has not altered the practice of constitutional courts regarding the techniques of reasoning as far as foreign case-law is concerned. The continental tradition seems to be much stronger than the new requirements of legitimacy.

2.3 'Vertical dialogue': What is the role of European courts?

The issue becomes more complicated when it comes to the presumed 'vertical dialogue'. Here, the word 'dialogue' is even less appropriate – effectively, it often describes mandatory interactions between constitutional courts and supranational courts. Furthermore, the communication is unidirectional because the national courts are obliged to take into consideration and often to execute the European courts' case-law without the opposite being true: thus, it lacks the parity necessary for a dialogue. Yet, even though the preliminary ruling provides an instrument for the national judges to submit their standpoint of national constitutional law to the Court of Justice of the European Union (hereinafter CJEU), there is no such instrument in the system of the European Convention pending the entrance into force of Protocol XVI. The individual appeal to the European Court of Human Rights (hereinafter ECtHR) is more configured as a way of seeking a guarantee that the national level (including the constitutional jurisdictions) cannot provide, than as a possible tool of such dialogue.

Here, we have the impression – that should also be supported by more comprehensive empirical research – that European courts are slightly more daring compared with national courts regarding measures restricting 'negative' rights and freedoms that crisis situations entail. To the extent that, in certain extreme circumstances, namely facing asylum seekers, they succeed in playing a substitute role.

There are several reasons for this attitude. In some national situations, constitutional justice struggles with structural difficulties as a result of limited possibilities of avenues to trigger the constitutional court (this is the case in Italy) or of an imperfect system of national constitutional justice (this is the case in Greece and, for different reasons, in Hungary today). However, the more obvious reason is that international courts are better placed to take decisions that often go against the will of either the government or the majority of national public opinion. In contrast, this evaluation needs to be refined when it comes to the guarantee of 'positive' rights; that is, social rights: In this field, the attitude of supranational courts does not seem more audacious than the one of national courts and they show equal respect for the role of the legislator in general.

3. Charting the relevant jurisprudence of European courts

National policies on immigration, right to asylum, the fight against terrorism – affecting the rights of disadvantaged minorities, such as illegal immigrants, asylum seekers or residents of Islamic religion – represent the privileged field of substitute role for supranational courts in the face of the default of national systems of guarantee.

In these fields, the ECtHR has developed rich case-law, which has succeeded to significantly restrict the margin of appreciation of the States, even when they invoke derogations based on Article 15 of the Convention.[17] More recently, the Court of Justice has also been seized in such questions, all the more so as the Lisbon Treaty eliminated all the obstacles hindering its intervention in that matter and the Court has been attentive to the guarantee of foreign nationals' rights.

3.1 Terrorism, immigration and the right to asylum

3.1.1 ECtHR

3.1.1.1 TERRORISM

The case-law on counterterrorism measures is very rich. The Court has succeeded to control the proportionality of derogatory measures contained by Art. 15. In *A. and others v. United Kingdom*,[18] the Court holds that the executive power and the British Parliament, using a law pertaining to foreign nationals' rights to deal with a problem that is very much a security issue, did not rationally address the threat of terrorist attacks (post 9/11), and exposed a specific group of alleged terrorists to the disproportionate and discriminatory risk of indeterminate custody. In fact, the threat came from British nationals as well as from foreign nationals and the potentially negative effects of detention without charge could affect fairly similarly British citizens and foreign nationals. The Court concludes to the violation of Article 5(1) because the derogatory measures were disproportionate in so far as they gave rise to unjustified discrimination between foreign nationals and British citizens.

A long line of cases are about Articles 2 and 3 of the Convention, which, according to the ECtHR, absolutely prohibit the deportation of a person who, in the destination State, would be in real danger of ill treatment prohibited by either of those provisions.[19]

This case-law is confirmed in terrorism cases. For example, in *Saadi v. Italy*,[20] where the appellant, prosecuted in Italy for participation in international terrorism, had been the subject of a deportation order to Tunisia, the ECtHR reaffirmed the absolute nature of the prohibition of torture pursuant to Art. 3. The Court concluded that the individual would have been at real risk of being subjected to treatments contrary to Art. 3 if he had been deported to Tunisia. The Court reiterated that the appellant's conduct and the seriousness of the charges against him were irrelevant for a review under Art. 3.

In *Aswat v. United Kingdom*,[21] the Court held that the extradition to the United States of the appellant, an individual suspected of involvement in terrorism and suffering from serious mental disorders, would give rise to the violation of Art. 3, given the uncertainty of detention conditions he would incur in the destination country. The ECtHR stated that the mental disorders the appellant was suffering from were sufficiently serious to make it necessary to transfer him from an ordinary prison to a high-security psychiatric hospital and that the medical documents clearly showed that his internment was justified by 'his own health and safety'. Therefore, the ECtHR concluded that, in the light of current medical evidence, there was a real risk that the appellant's extradition to a different country and to a different, potentially more hostile, prison environment would result in a significant deterioration in his mental and physical health and that such a deterioration would be capable of reaching the Art. 3 threshold.

In contrast, we might quote *Babar Ahmed and others v. United Kingdom*,[22] a case that involved individuals suspected of terrorist acts and threatened with extradition to the United States of America. The ECtHR held that the detention conditions in a maximum-security institution the individuals would be subjected to were compatible with Art. 3, and so was the length of the sentence they incurred.

Furthermore, the Court had to adjudicate on secret 'extraordinary rendition' operations declared to be in violation with Art. 3 and other provisions of the Convention.[23] We need to highlight that in *Nasr and Ghali v. Italy*,[24] the case in which the Egyptian imam Abou Omar was abducted by CIA agents with the cooperation of Italian nationals, and then transferred to Egypt, followed by his secret detention for months, the ECtHR decided that the principle of 'state secret' had obviously been applied by the Italian executive authority (and justified by the Italian Constitutional Court) in order to prevent those responsible in the case from being brought to account: the investigation and the case could not lead to the punishment of those responsible, so in the end there was impunity.

The ECtHR also examined the consequences that the counterterrorism measures had on other rights, as when it judged that the imposed travel ban was contrary to the European Convention on Human Rights because the person's name was on the list of suspected terrorists managed by the UN, or on a list created to prevent violations of domestic or foreign legislation on immigration. In *Nada v. Switzerland*,[25] the Swiss authorities, applying the United Nations Security Council's counterterrorism measures, put an Italo-Egyptian national residing in Campione d'Italia (Italian enclave inside Swiss territory) on the list annexed to the 'Swiss Federal Regulation on the Taliban'. Since the person's name was on this list, the applicant could not leave Campione d'Italia, and all his attempts to have his name removed from the list were rejected. The ECtHR noted that the Swiss authorities had some degrees of flexibility in the application of the UN counterterrorism regulations. It found that Switzerland had violated the applicant's rights guaranteed under Art. 8 of the European Convention on Human Rights, on the one hand, by failing to rapidly notify Italy or the United Nations Sanctions Committee that there was no reasonable suspicion against the applicant and, on the other hand, by failing to adapt the effects of the sanctions regime to the individual's specific situation. The Court also concluded to the violation of Art. 13 of the European Convention on Human Rights combined with Art. 8, since the applicant did not have effective means to achieve the removal of his name from the list.

Additionally, in *Szabó and Vissy v. Hungary*,[26] the Court held that the covert surveillance provided for under Hungarian counterterrorism legislation (which provides for the possibility to have people's homes searched and placed under covert surveillance, to open mail and parcels, to intercept electronic communications and computer data transmissions and to record all the data obtained through these methods, in order to prevent, investigate and repress terrorist acts in Hungary) represented an interference by a public authority with the exercise of the applicant's right to private life, home and correspondence. These measures, according to the legislation, may be authorised not only against identified persons but also against sets of people, which is a too broad notion that could facilitate unrestricted surveillance of large numbers of citizens.

3.1.1.2 IMMIGRATION

As regards unauthorised immigration, in the system of the ECHR, the States have the right, in accordance with a well-established principle of international law, and subject to their convention-based obligations (including those arising from the European Convention on Human Rights), to control the entry, residence and expulsion of foreigners. The case-law of the ECtHR imposes only certain limits on the right of countries to refuse entry at the border, for example, if this refusal of entry is the equivalent of rejection. In certain cases the case-law even imposes obligation upon States to authorise the person's entering in their territory if this entry is a necessary condition of the exercise of certain rights protected by the Convention, in particular the right to family life.

The strictest convictions include *Hirsi Jamaa and Others v. Italy*.[27] The applicants were part of a group of approximately 200 migrants, including asylum seekers, that was intercepted by the Italian coast guard on the high seas while it was within Malta's search and rescue region. The migrants were summarily deported to Libya in accordance with an agreement between Italy and Libya, without having had the possibility to apply for asylum. Their names and nationalities were not recorded. The ECtHR noted that the prevailing situation in Libya was well known and that it was not difficult to verify it from different sources of information. The Court thus concluded that Italian authorities were aware or would have had to be aware that, firstly, the applicants sent back to Libya as illegal migrants would have been exposed to treatment contrary to the European Convention on Human Rights and would have not enjoyed any protection there, secondly, that there was no sufficient guarantee to protect them against the risk of being arbitrarily sent back to their respective countries of origin, including Somalia and Eritrea. The Court added that Italian authorities would have had to take into account the absence of asylum procedure in the countries of return in particular and the impossibility to oblige the authorities of those countries to recognise the refugee status.

In the well-known *M.S.S. v. Belgium and Greece*[28] judgment, the ECtHR concluded to the violation of Art. 3 of the European Convention on Human Rights concerning not only the appellant's detention conditions but also the conditions of life (in the receiving country) in general in Greece. The applicant was an Afghan asylum seeker. Greek authorities were aware of the potential asylum seeker's identity and of his situation since his arrival in Athens. He was immediately taken into custody without any information about the reasons. The Court found in different reports of international bodies and non-government organisations that the systematic use of detention of asylum seekers was a widespread practice among Greek authorities. The appellant's allegations relating to the brutalities and insults he said to have suffered from the police were confirmed by numerous testimonies gathered by international organisations. The ECtHR found that the findings of these organisations also confirmed the applicant's allegations that sanitary conditions were appalling and the detention facility near Athens international airport was overcrowded. According to the Court, even if the appellant had been taken into custody for a relatively short period of time, the conditions of detention in the facility were unacceptable. The Court felt that the appellant must have had feelings of arbitrariness, inferiority and fear, thus a profound attack on his dignity, irrefutably provoked by conditions of custody equalling degrading treatments. Moreover, according to the Court, the applicant's distress had been emphasized by the inherent vulnerability of his being an asylum seeker. Thus, the Court concluded to the violation of Art. 3 of the European Convention on Human Rights.

The *Khlaifia and Others v. Italy* judgment of the Chamber[29] is along the same lines. This case concerned the detention of illegal migrants who arrived on the Italian coast in 2011 in the context of events linked to the 'Arab Spring'.They were detained in a reception centre in Lampedusa and then on vessels moored in the port of Palermo, before being deported to Tunisia. The Court held that the detention of the appellants was illegal. Lacking any legal basis, the reasons remained unknown to them and they could not challenge them. As regards their conditions of detention in the reception centre, the Court took into account the exceptional humanitarian crisis that Italy had to face on the island of Lampedusa in 2011, following the Arab Spring (55,298 migrants arrived to the island at the time the appellants were there). However, the Court concluded that the appellants' conditions of detention violated their dignity. The Court also considered that the applicants were subject to measures of collective expulsion, since their expulsion orders did not refer to their personal situation – the Court stated namely that carrying out an identification procedure was not sufficient to preclude the existence of collective expulsion. Moreover, the Court held that in that period, many Tunisian nationals were expulsed through similar simplified procedures. Finally, the Court took the view that the appellants did not have effective remedy enabling complaints because for a remedy to be judged effective when it comes to collective expulsion, Art. 13 requires that it be with automatic suspensive effect – here specifically that it suspends the expulsion measure to Tunisia, which was not the case.[30]

3.1.1.3 RIGHT TO ASYLUM

The European Convention on Human Rights does not guarantee the right to asylum as it is provided for in the Geneva Convention of 1951 and in the system of the European Union, including in Art. 18 of the Charter of Fundamental Rights. Also, the ECtHR is not entitled to examine the question whether denying or withdrawing the refugee status under the Geneva Convention of 1951 or the non-recognition of the right to asylum under the 'qualification' directive[31] are contrary to the European Convention on Human Rights. Nevertheless, the Court can consider whether the expulsion of a foreign national would put them at real risk of treatment contrary to Art. 3, which is the subject of numerous judgments.

For example, in *M.S.S. v. Belgium and Greece*, already quoted, the ECtHR concluded to the violation of Art. 13 of the European Convention on Human Rights by Greece and Belgium, combined with Art. 3 because of the violation of the appellant's right to an effective remedy. The Court held that, given that Greece did not apply the legislation in matters of asylum and that access to the asylum procedure and to remedy were hindered in the country by major structural defects, there was no effective guarantee protecting the appellant against an arbitrary expulsion from that country to Afghanistan, where he would have risk an ill-treatment. As regards Belgium, the Court held that the remedy procedure against the 'Dublin' transfer to Greece carried out in that country did not meet the requirements of its case-law in so far as it did not examine carefully and rigorously the appellant's grievances, while the expulsion of the individual to another country bore the risk of exposing him to treatment prohibited under Art. 3.

In *Hirsi Jamaa and Others v. Italy*, as we have already said, an Italian vessel intercepted potential asylum seekers in high seas. The Italian authorities led the migrants to believe that they were being taken to Italy and did not inform them of the procedures to follow in order not to be deported to Libya. The appellants thus could not address their objections under Art. 3 of the European Convention on Human Rights and Article 4 of Protocol No 4 to a competent authority, and they could neither obtain a careful and rigorous examination of their demands before the expulsion measure was executed. The Court concluded to the violation of Art.13 of the European Convention on Human Rights combined with Articles 3 and 4 of Protocol No 4. The Court recalled that the fact that the appellants did not apply for asylum and did not describe the risks they incurred because of the lack of an asylum system in Libya did not exempt Italy from respecting the obligations under Art. 3 of the European Convention on Human Rights, and that Italian authorities should have verified whether Libyan authorities respected their international obligations with regard to the protection of refugees. The Court concluded that the appellants' transfer to Libya violated Art. 3 of the European Convention on Human Rights in so far as it exposed the appellants to the risk of deportation.

3.1.2 CJEU

The CJEU has also demonstrated a very attentive attitude to the guarantee of rights in the cases referred to it, which are far fewer than those referred to the ECtHR, namely because of the lack of direct individual recourse. Moreover, in many of its decisions, the CJEU referred to the judgments of the Strasbourg Court, so we can speak of constructing a real 'multilevel' protection system.

3.1.2.1 TERRORISM

The most notorious case about terrorism remains *Kadi*.[32] Pursuant to different resolutions of the United Nations Security Council, all UN Member States were called upon to freeze the funds and other financial resources directly or indirectly controlled by individuals or entities identified by the Sanctions Committee of the Security Council as being associates of Osama Bin Laden, Al-Qaeda or the Taliban. In pursuance of these resolutions, the Council adopted a common position in the framework of the Common Foreign and Security Policy (CFSP) regarding restrictive measures against the persons affected and, on the basis of Articles 60, 301 and 308 EC, the regulation 881/2002 imposing, *inter alia*, the freezing of funds and other financial resources of these persons or entities that are also contained by the list annexed to the regulation and regularly updated based on successive UN resolutions.

Mr Kadi, resident of Saudi Arabia, and the Al Barakaat International Foundation, established in Sweden – the names of who were on the list annexed to the regulation – lodged an appeal that was rejected by the Court at first instance. The CJEU, however, considered the appeals admissible because the complete validity check by the Community courts of any legislation referred to their jurisdiction in light of the fundamental rights is the expression of a constitutional guarantee stemming from the EC Treaty. Examining the ground pertaining to the respect of the appellants' rights of defence, the Court points out that the effectiveness of judicial review implies that the Community authority is required to communicate to the person involved the reasons upon which the measure adversely affecting him is based, so that they may eventually exercise their right to seek redress. The Court admits that, the measures to freeze funds need to take advantage of a surprise effect and that thay have to be applied with immediate effect in order to be efficient. Therefore, even if the Community authorities were not bound to communicate the reasons or to hear the appellants before their names were included in the list, the authorities should have, nevertheless, done so within a reasonable period after those measures were enacted. As this was not the case, the appellants' rights of defence, in particular the right to be heard, were not respected. This violation leads also to the violation of the right to legal remedy, in so far as the appellants were also unable to defend their rights in satisfactory conditions before the Community judicature. Since the ground concerned the restriction of the exercise of the right to property, the Court nonetheless admits, on the one hand, that such restrictions could, in principle, be justified by the fight against threats to international peace and security posed by acts of terrorism. On the other hand, the Court holds that the contested regulation was adopted without furnishing any guarantee enabling Mr Kadi to put his case to the competent authorities, whereas, having regard to the general application and actual continuation of the freezing measures affecting him, such a guarantee is necessary to ensure the respect of the exercise of his right to property. Having regard to these violations, the Court was led to annul the regulation 881/2002.

3.1.2.2 IMMIGRATION

The CJEU has been seized in several cases concerning the imprisonment of third-country nationals in the framework of return procedures on grounds of irregular entry or residence.[33]

For example, in *El Dridi*,[34] the CJEU was called upon to verify whether Articles 15 and 16 of the 'return' directive were compatible with the criminal detention of a third-country national during the return procedure for the sole reason that the person resided on that territory in violation of an administrative authority order to leave the territory of that State within a given timeframe. The CJEU had to assess whether the detention could have been considered as a necessary measure for the execution of the return decision under paragraph 1 of Art. 8 of the directive, or if, on the contrary, the measure compromised the execution of that decision. Taking into account the facts of the case, the CJEU held that the detention was not compatible with the directive's scope – that is, the implementation of an effective return policy that respects fundamental rights – and it did not contribute to the removal of the third-country national from the involved EU Member State. The Court declared that if the obligation to return had not been respected within the timeframe provided for voluntary departure, EU Member States had to ensure the enforcement of the return decision in a moderate and proportionate manner, using the least coercive measures possible and respecting fundamental rights.

Furthermore, we might mention the CJEU case-law according to which EU Member States can not impose excessive and disproportionate fees for granting residence permits to long-term resident third-country nationals, nor to their family members. Such fees undermined the achievement of the objective pursued by the directive by making it ineffective. For example, in *Commission v. the Netherlands*, the CJEU held that the Netherlands (and more recently Italy)[35] had failed to fulfil their obligation arising from the directive on long-term residents, in so far as the country imposed excessive and disproportionate fees on third-country nationals. More specifically, the Court stated that the Member States did not have an unlimited margin of appreciation to impose fees on third-country nationals when issuing residence permits, and that they were not authorised to set tariffs likely to hinder the exercise of rights enshrined in the directive on long-term residents.

3.1.2.3 RIGHT TO ASYLUM

The CJEU has intervened also concerning the European system of right to asylum by establishing that the States have to ensure that the persons are not sent back to EU Member States in which the reception and asylum systems suffer from systemic problems. In certain cases where there are grave violations of the Charter of Fundamental Rights of the EU, the States can thus examine the requests even if those are not primarily their responsibility under the Dublin Regulation.

In joined cases *N.S. and M.E.*,[36] the CJEU examined the question whether the transfer of the appellants to Greece pursuant to the Dublin Regulation would have given rise to the violation of Art. 4 of the Charter of Fundamental Rights of the European Union, which corresponds to Art. 3 of the European Convention on Human Rights. When the CJEU examined these cases, the ECtHR had already concluded that the reception conditions and other living conditions of asylum seekers in Greece were contrary to Art. 3 of the European Convention on Human Rights. The CJEU held that the Member States could not ignore the systemic problems of the Greek asylum procedure and the reception conditions, which presented a real risk for the asylum seekers of beinge subjected to inhuman and degrading treatments. Emphasizing that the Dublin Regulation had to be implemented in accordance with the rights recognised under the Charter, the Court concluded that in the absence of other responsible Member States, the United Kingdom and Ireland were supposed to examine the asylum applications in question, even though the appellants had submitted them in Greece. More specifically, the CJEU issued a preliminary ruling on the question whether, in certain circumstances, a State can be required to consider an application pursuant to the sovereignty clause of Art. 3, para 2 of the Dublin Regulation II, even if, according to the Dublin criteria, the responsibility lies with another Member State of the Union. The Court specified that EU Member States had to act in accordance with the fundamental rights and principles recognised by the Charter of Fundamental Rights of the EU when exercising their discretionary power pursuant to Art. 3, para 2 and that, consequently, they shall not transfer asylum applications to Member States responsible under the Regulation when evidence indicates systemic problems in the reception conditions and the asylum procedure that the Member State cannot ignore and that could give rise to the violation of Art. 4 of the Charter (prohibition of torture). This also obliges the Member State to examine other criteria of the Regulation to determine whether another Member State is responsible for examining the asylum application. Should it be impossible to find another Member State or should the duration of the procedure enabling that be unreasonable, the Member State itself has to examine the application, in accordance with Art. 3, para 2.

3.2. Economic Crisis and the Guarantee of Social Rights

These considerations ought to be nuanced as regards the responses to the economic and financial crisis and the guarantee of social rights. Here, in fact, the European courts face several restrictions: on the one hand, as regards the ECtHR, the European Convention does not give guarantees for economic and social rights; on the other hand, as regards the Court of Justice, there is an issue with access because there is no direct individual recourse.

Nevertheless, we might mention, as we will see in the next paragraphs, several cases where the European courts ensured a level of guarantee higher than the national one: the doctrine in this regard is divided and there are authors who, on the contrary, insisted on the inability of the courts to guarantee social rights by applying the different European charters against the backdrop of the crisis, and mentioned the "solitude of the constitutional courts".[37]

In contrast, it seems to me that there are many indications that the European courts (including the Court of Justice, surprising as it may be) are less sensible to the State's budgetary requirements than the national courts. We have also noted that they had the opportunity to decide several cases pertaining economic and social rights that the national constitutional courts have never dealt with: the national constitutional jurisprudence on the economic crisis is rather jurisprudence on salary and pension cuts, but not really on the consequences of the reduction of public spending on social rights.[38]

3.2.1 ECtHR

In more recent years, the ECtHR has used several provisions of the Convention to protect economic and social rights[39] as a result of the well-established case-law, according to which,[40] notwithstanding economic and social rights depending very much on the State's situation and more specifically on their finances, the Convention "had to be read in the light of present-day conditions" and several civil and political rights protected by this instrument have extensions of economic or social nature.[41]

It is well known that the Court gave a very broad interpretation of Protocol No 1 on the right to property, to the point that included several benefits of social nature.[42] In this case-law, the Court demonstrated a tendency to give the Member States quite a wide margin of judgment in relation to the right balance between public revenue and expenditure,[43] but this margin seems to be ever more reduced in more recent years.

In *Zolotas v. Greece* (no. 2),[44] a case about a bank account, the Court specified:

> the State has a positive obligation to protect citizens and to require that banks, in view of the potentially adverse consequences of limitation periods, should inform the holders of dormant accounts when the limitation period is due to expire and thus afford them the possibility of stopping the limitation period running, for instance by performing a transaction on the account. Not requiring any information of this kind to be provided is liable to upset the fair balance that must be struck between the demands of the general interest of the community and the requirements of the protection of the individual's fundamental rights.

In two judgments concerning Hungary (*N.K.M. v. Hungary* and *R.Sz. v. Hungary*),[45] the appellants complained that the 98 per cent taxation of a part of their severance pay – pursuant to a law that entered into force 10 weeks before their dismissal – was analysed as unlawful deprivation of belongings. Despite the significant margin of appreciation that Hungarian authorities enjoyed in terms of taxation, the Court held that the means used were disproportionate to the legitimate aim pursued, namely to protect the Public Treasury against excessive severance pays.

The Court also derives certain positive obligations from other articles of the Convention, such as Articles 2, 3 and 8, when human dignity is under discussion, for example because the vital minimum is not provided.[46] In this line of jurisprudence, we might also consider the case based on Art. 3, concerning the rights of detainees towards whom the State has positive obligations that cannot be avoided by bringing arguments based on the economic crisis.[47] Other rights might be threatened by the economic crisis, such as the access to courts, trial times, execution of the judgment: here also the Court has emphasised several times the irrelevance of budgetary considerations relating to the guarantee of the rights under Art. 6.[48]

Additionally, we might consider in this regard the rigorous case-law on the non-retroactivity of laws that were at the origin of the differences with the Italian Constitutional Court controlling retroactivity in a much more flexible way and considering admissible retroactive laws justified by financial needs.[49]

We might also mention *Nagla v. Latvia*[50] in relation to the crisis – in this judgment, the Court condemns the State for violating Art. 10, as a result of the search of a journalist's home who informed the public about wages in the public sector in the context of the economic crisis.

Notwithstanding this case-law, when the Court was directly seized to adjudicate on austerity measures adopted as a result of the European Memoranda, namely by Greece and Portugal, it showed a certain reluctance to decide, as we can see in cases *Koufaki and Adedy v. Greece, Conceição Mateus and Santos Januário v. Portugal* and *da Silva Carvalho Rico v. Portugal*, relating to Article 1 of Protocol No 1 (protection of property).

In the first decision (*Koufaki and Adedy v. Greece*),[51] the Court states, relating to austerity measures adopted in 2010 in Greece, where there were 22 per cent salary cuts, that

> the restrictions introduced by the impugned legislation should not be considered as a "deprivation of possessions" as provided for by the law. The adoption of these measures was justified by the existence of an exceptional crisis without precedent in recent Greek history that required an immediate reduction in public spending. The objective of the measures were the general interest that also coincided with those of the euro area Member States, in view of the requirement to ensure budgetary discipline and preserve the stability of the zone they depend on. The margin of appreciation available to the legislature in implementing social and economic policies is a wide one.

In the second case (*Conceição Mateus and Santos Januário v. Portugal*),[52] the 2012 Portuguese public sector retirement pension cuts were on the table. The Court decided that this reduction had constituted a proportionate violation of the appellants' right to propriety. Taking into account the exceptional financial problems that Portugal was facing at the time, and the limited and temporary nature of these measures, the Portuguese government had struck a fair balance between the general interest and the protection of the appellants' individual rights to their retirement pension.

In the third case (*da Silva Carvalho Rico c. Portugal*),[53] the Court declared inadmissible as manifestly ill-founded an appeal concerning the reduction of the value of retirement pensions pursuant to austerity measures adopted in Portugal; namely the 'extraordinary solidarity contribution' introduced at the end of negotiations seeking to obtain financial support from the European Union, the Member States of the Euro Zone and the International Monetary Fund. The Court takes note in particular of the general interest at stake in Portugal in the context of the financial crisis, as well as of the limited and temporary nature of the applied measures. The Court holds, furthermore, that the reduction of the appellant's pension constituted a proportionate restriction – as the Portuguese Constitutional Court had already assessed – of his right to the protection of his propriety, aiming at the medium term economic recovery of the country.

3.2.2 CJEU

As regards the case-law of the Court of Justice, first we need to say that the Court has not been seized by national jurisdictions that had to apply austerity measures imposed by European documents, namely the Memoranda in Greece and Portugal. They could have asked for an interpretation of these documents or for the verification of their compatibility with the Treaties, first of all with the European Charter, but this dialogue, which would have been possible, did not take place.[54]

The Court rejected as inadmissible the questions for preliminary ruling that were addressed to it by the Romanian and Portuguese courts concerning the national legislation's compatibility with the Charter,[55] since the judges did not indicate any element according to which the national law was addressed to apply the law of the Union.[56]

Asking to annul legislation by way of appeal is also impossible, since the admissibility conditions laid down by the Court are too strict and the Court refused to ease them as a result of the severe impact austerity measures had on social rights, in a case referred by the Greek public sector trade union (*ADEDY and Others*).[57]

The CJEU declared that it had no jurisdiction in the case *Torralbo Marcos*[58] concerning the law that imposed on the salaried employee the obligation to pay a tax in order to be able to lodge an appeal in the framework of enforcement proceedings to obtain a judicial declaration of insolvency from the employer.

However, the Court of Justice decided important cases regarding Spain and Ireland. In *Juan Carlos Sánchez Morcillo and María del Carmen Abril García*,[59] Sanchez Morcillo and Abril García were unable to meet their obligations to make monthly repayments of the loan they took out from Banco Bilbao (secured by a mortgage on their immovable properties). The 15 April 2011, Banco Bilbao demanded payment of the entire loan together with ordinary interest and default interest and the enforced sale of the property mortgaged in its favour. The Court held that

> Article 7(1) of Directive 93/13, read in combination with Article 47 of the Charter, must be interpreted as precluding a system of enforcement, such as that at issue in the main proceedings, which provides that mortgage enforcement proceedings may not be stayed by the first instance court, which, in its final decision, may at most award compensation in respect of the damage suffered by the consumer, in so far as the latter, the debtor against whom mortgage enforcement proceedings are brought, may not appeal against a decision dismissing his objection to that enforcement, whereas the seller or supplier, the creditor seeking enforcement, may bring an appeal against a decision terminating the proceedings or declaring an unfair term inapplicable.

In *Thomas Hogan and Others*,[60] the Court decided a preliminary ruling referred by the Irish High Court concerning the loss of pension benefits of the employees because of the company's bankruptcy. The Court maintains that the domestic law recognizing 50 per cent of the employees' pensions is not in accordance with European law and that the economic situation in Ireland does not constitute an exceptional circumstance likely to justify a reduced level of protection of the employees' interests as regards their rights conferring on them immediate entitlement to old-age benefits under a supplementary occupational pension scheme.

In addition, we might mention the more and more cautious, or even restrictive case-law on access to social benefits of economically inactive EU citizens in a Member State other than their own – a problem increasingly common as a result of the economic crisis. In *Dano*,[61] the Court decided that it was in accordance with the law of the Union to exclude economically inactive citizens arriving to the territory of another Member State without seeking employment from social aid. In *Alimanovic*,[62] the Court considered a national regulation excluding nationals of another Member State seeking employment from some benefits to be compatible with Directive 2004/38 and the Treaty, whereas the same benefits were guaranteed to the Member State's own nationals who were in the same situation.

Finally, all the judgments demonstrate that, facing the economic crisis, the European courts did not alter their case-law, neither with regards the admissibility of the recourse (as demonstrates the CJEU), nor in substantial aspects (as shows the ECtHR): by doing so, they only succeed in ensuring guarantees in cases of severe violations. This is the maximum we might demand from them, 'business as usual'.

4. Conclusion

In the light of such case-law of the European courts, the question arising is that of interaction with national constitutional courts.

Several attitudes with which national courts turn to European law have been identified, ranging from the actuation and promotion through participation to reluctance, resistance and challenge.[63] In some fields the national courts tend to dedicate a level of protection to rights and freedoms higher than the one ensured by the European courts, or to show some kind of resistance (by referring to the *controlimiti*, for example) in the name of the national constitution, invoked as the expression of the 'national constitutional identity'.

In the crisis case-law, in contrast, the European courts call upon national courts to reduce the importance they dedicate to the public interest in the balancing exercise, in the name of a higher level of protection for rights. The national courts' reaction does not seem to be oriented towards resistance – except for a very limited number of cases, among which we might consider also the Italian Constitutional Court's case-law on the retroactivity of laws[64] – they rather seem open and accepting towards European case-law that often becomes the argumentative basis for the national courts' judgments.

In my opinion, the key element to understand the national courts' attitude in a crisis context, where rights are put in danger by political decisions focusing on the public interest, is exactly their relationship with the European courts. The most active and attentive national constitutional courts find in them important allies when it comes to protect rights and together they can develop a real strategy to guarantee rights. The most timid courts, on the contrary, being under the influence of political power, might have difficulties in accepting European decisions, for the same reasons as governments do.[65]

In the face of new challenges for the constitutional State, constitutional courts are called upon to assist in a growing activism. They are not always strong enough, independent enough, and legitimate enough to play this role. In this difficult task, they can be supported by an alliance strategy either with other constitutional courts or with the European courts.

The continental judicial tradition is not in favour of argumentative strategies that rely on foreign precedents. Surely, the courts might meet, organise conferences, translate and circulate their decisions, create departments of comparative law studies in their organic structure. However, all this normally produces only an implicit circulation without finding its place among the explicit arguments of the rationale.

What proves to be decisive in the European legal area is not the horizontal dialogue but the vertical one. As a consequence of the new challenges, the interaction between national courts and European courts becomes even more important: only an alliance, a coordinated response of different subjects composing a multilevel system may lead – even in hard times – to a more complete and coherent guarantee of rights and freedoms.

Coming back to the question we asked in the beginning about the constitutional State – whether it adapts or not to new challenges – we might conclude that it cannot provide effective responses, except if it is reconfigured as an 'open constitutional State':[66] constitutional courts alone are not able to take on new challenges. They can only ensure the guarantee of rights and freedoms in the framework of a response coordinated with the European courts.

Notes

1 I thank Fruzsina Orosz and Zoltán Szente for their remarks; Marco Antonio Simonelli, for his contribution to bibliographic and case-law research; Ester Stefanelli, for her support in the French version of this chapter and Floriana Plataroti, for her contribution to the final revision of the text.

2 I refer here to the concept of 'constitutional State' as it was developed by Italian and German doctrine: see in particular Häberle (2005), Häberle (2000a). In English, see Häberle (2000b) 77–94. See also Zagrebelsky (2006), Cheli (2006). In relation to this form of State, some scholars talk about 'postwar constitutional paradigm': Weinrib (2006) 89.

3 Rifkin (2011).

4 Groppi (2016a) 7.

5 For a critical approach to this kind of short-term politics, see Pope Franciscus, 'Laudato Sì' (2015) n. 178.

6 Hirschl (2004).

7 Zagreblesky (1992).

8 For these dialogue definitions, see de Vergottini (2010). See also Groppi (2015).

9 Groppi and Ponthoreau (2013).

10 Markesinis and Fedtke (2005) 11; Markesinis and Fedtke (2009).

11 Ferreres Comella (2011) 526, referring to the word 'modesty' as employed by Jackson (2009) 189. The word 'bricolage', according to the latter, was introduced by Tushnet (1999) 1225.

12 Benvenisti (2008a) 241, referring to the fight against terrorism, to the environment and to the right to asylum. These considerations were reiterated by Jackson (2009) 130.

13 Benvenisti (2008b) 255; Dyzenhaus and Thwaites (2007) 10.

14 Groppi (2010) 325.

15 Contiades and Fotiadou (2012) 660; Roman (2014) 63.

16 Tanasescu and Deaconu (2013) 321.

17 Most of the quotations of the ECtHR judgments have been taken from the thematic factsheets on the Court's case-law compiled by the Press Service of the Court.

18 *A. and others v United Kingdom* App no 3455/05 (ECHR, 19 February 2009).

19 See *Chahal v United Kingdom* App no 22414/93 (ECHR, 15 November 1996). According to the case-law of the ECtHR, Art. 3 of the European Convention of Human Rights enshrines a fundamental value of democratic society and absolutely prohibits torture and inhuman or degrading treatment or punishment, irrespective of the victim's conduct, however dangerous or undesirable it may be. Thus, in light of this article, the state also has some responsibility when proceeding to deportation despite there being substantial grounds to believe that the deported person will be in real danger of torture or inhuman or degrading treatment or punishment in the destination country. See *Salah Sheekh v the Netherlands* App no 1948/04 (ECHR, 11 January 2007); *Soering v United Kingdom* App no 14038/88 (ECHR, 7 July 1989); *Vilvarajah and others v United Kingdom* App nos 13163/87,13164/87, 13165/87, 13447/87 and 13448/87 (ECHR, 30 October 1991).

20 *Saadi v Italy* App no 37201/06 (ECHR, 28 February 2008).

21 *Aswat v United Kingdom* App no 17299/12 (ECHR, 16 April 2013).

22 *Babar Ahmed and others v United Kingdom* App nos 24027/07, 11949/08 and 36742/08 (ECHR, 10 April 2012).

23 See *El-Masri v The Former Yugoslav Republic of Macedonia* App no 39630/09 (ECHR, 13 December 2012), about a German national of Lebanese origin, allegedly the victim of a secret 'extraordinary rendition' operation in which he was allegedly arrested, held in solitary confinement, questioned, suffered ill-treatment in a hotel in Skopje for 23 days, then was handed to American CIA (Central Intelligence Agency) agents who allegedly took him to a secret prison in Afghanistan where he allegedly suffered further

ill-treatment for more than four months. See also *Al Nashiri v Poland* App no 28761/11 and *Husayn (Abu Zubaydah) v Poland* App no 7511/13 (ECHR, 24 July 2014), where two appellants imprisoned at the American naval base of Guantanamo Bay in Cuba claimed to have been held at a 'black site' of the CIA in Poland.

24 *Nasr and Gali v Italy* App no 44883/09 (ECHR, 23 February 2016). See also the Italian Constitutional Court's judgment no. 24/2014.

25 *Nada v Switzerland* App no 10593/05 (ECHR, 12 September 2012).

26 *Szabó and Vissy v Hungary* App no 37138/14 (ECHR, 12 January 2016).

27 *Hirsi Jamaa and Others v Italy* App no 27765/09 (ECHR, 23 February 2012).

28 *M.S.S. v Belgium and Greece* App no 30696/09 (ECHR, 21 January 2011).

29 *Khlaifia and Others v Italy* App no 16483/12 (ECHR, 1 September 2015).

30 *Khlaifia and Others v Italy* App no 16483/12 (ECHR, 1 September 2015) paragraph 128: 'Those factors [the humanitarian crisis situation] cannot, however, exempt the respondent State from its obligation to guarantee conditions that are compatible with respect for human dignity to all individuals who, like the appellants, find themselves deprived of their liberty. In that connection, the Court points out that Article 3 must be regarded as one of the most fundamental provisions of the Convention and as enshrining core values of the democratic societies making up the Council of Europe (see *Soering v the United Kingdom* App no 14038/88 ECHR, 7 July 1989 para 88, Series A no. 161). In contrast to the other provisions in the Convention, it is cast in absolute terms, without exception or proviso, or the possibility of derogation under Article 15 of the Convention (see *M.S. v Belgium* App no 50012/08 ECHR, 31 January 2012 para 122)'. Some of the conclusions of that judgement have been reversed by *Khlaifia and Others v Italy* App no 16483/12 (ECHR, Grand Chambre,15 December 2016), in which the Court stressed that "it would certainly be artificial to examine the facts of the case without considering the general context in which those facts arose. In its assessment, the Court will thus bear in mind, together with other factors, that the undeniable difficulties and inconveniences endured by the applicants stemmed to a significant extent from the situation of extreme difficulty confronting the Italian authorities at the relevant time".

31 Council Directive (EC) 83/2004 of 29 April 2004, successively amended.

32 Cases C–402/05P and C–415/05P *Yassin Abdullah Kadi and Al Barakaat International Foundation v Council of the European Union and Commission of the European Communities* [2008] ECR I–6351. Doubts were voiced about the Court's capability to protect the rule of law in the case of counterterrorism measures: Murphy (2012) 48.

33 Case C–430/11 *Sagor* [2012] ECR EU:C: 2012: 777, order of the Court of 21 March 2013; Case C–522/11 *Procura della Repubblica c. Abdoul Khadre Mbaye* [2011] ECR 2013–0000 (concerning a fine); Case C–297/12 *Criminal proceedings against Gjoko Filev and Adnan Osmani* [2013] EU:C:2013:569 (concerning detention based on the violation of a pre-existing entry ban).

34 Case C–61/11 *Hassen El Dridi alias Soufi Karim* [2011] ECR I-03015.

35 Case C–508/10 *European Commission v Kingdom of the Netherlands* [2012] EU: C:2012: 243 in the same line, Case C–309/14 *CGIL and INCA v Italian Government* [2015] EU:C:2015:523.

36 Case C–411/10 and Case C–493/10 *N.S. v Secretary of State for the Home Department and M.E. and Others v. Refugee Applications Commissioner & Minister for Justice, Equality and Law Reform* ECR 2011–00000.

37 Fontana (2014) Saitto (2016) 421.

38 Kilpatrick (2015).

39 Tulkens (2013) Gerards (2015).

40 *Airey v Ireland* App no 6289/73 (ECHR, 9 October 1979).

41 Guazzarotti (2013) 9.

42 See *Stec and Others v United Kingdom* App nos 65731/01 and 65900/01 (ECHR, 6 July 2005) decision on admissibility, spec. par. 51: 'In the modern, democratic State,

many individuals are, for all or part of their lives, completely dependent for survival on social security and welfare benefits. Many domestic legal systems recognise that such individuals require a degree of certainty and security, and provide for benefits to be paid – subject to the fulfilment of the conditions of eligibility – as of right. Where an individual has an assertable right under domestic law to a welfare benefit, the importance of that interest should also be reflected by holding Article 1 of Protocol No. 1 to be applicable'.

43 *Mihăieş and Senteş v Romania* App nos 44232/11 and 44605/11 (ECHR, 6 December 2011) para 21: the appellants complained referring to Article 1 of Protocol No 1 to the Convention that the remuneration they received as employees of the public sector had been reduced by 25% pursuant to an austerity programme implemented by the government. The Court held that, even if the persons involved had been holders of 'goods', the authorities did not overstep their margin of appreciation.

44 *Zolotas v Greece* App no 66610/09 (ECHR, 29 January 2013).

45 *N.K.M. v Hungary* App no 66529/11 (ECHR, 14 May 2013) and *R. Sz. v Hungary* App no 41838/11 (ECHR, 2 July 2013).

46 *Nencheva v Bulgaria* App no 48609/06 (ECHR, 18 June 2013), based on Article 2, the right to life; in this case, the defence of the government argued that the mentally and physically severely disabled children who lived in a home in the mountains died of hunger because of force majeure, as a consequence of the economic crisis in the Bulgaria of the 1990s, which had prevented the State from intervening; the Court, however, dismissed this argument.

47 See *Larioshina v Russia* App no 56869/00 (ECHR, 23 April 2002); *Khocklich v Moldova* App no 41707/98 (ECHR, 29 April 2003); *Zarzycki v Poland* App no 15351/03 (ECHR, 12 March 2013).

48 *Hornsby v Greece* App no 18357/91 (ECHR, 19 March 1997); *Scordino v Italy* (No. 1) App no 36813/97 (ECHR, 29 March 2006); *Ciovica v Romania* App no 3076/92 (ECHR, 31 March 2009); *Vassiliou Athanasiou v Greece* App no 50973/08 (ECHR, 21 December 2010); *Michelioudakis v Greece* App no 54447/10 (ECHR, 3 April 2012); *Glykantzi v Greece* App no 40150/09 (ECHR, 30 October 2012).

49 *Agrati and Others v Italy* App no 43549/08 (ECHR, 7 June 2011); *Maggio and Others v Italy* App nos 46286/09, 52851/08, 54486/08 and 56001/08 (ECHR, 31 May 2011). See also Tega (2015) 50.

50 *Nagla v Latvia* App no 73469/10 (ECHR, 16 July 2014).

51 *Koufaki and Adedy v Greece* App nos 57665/12 and 57657/12 (ECHR, 7 May 2013).

52 *Conceição Mateus and Santos Januário v Portugal* App nos 62235/12 and 57725/12 (ECHR, 8 October 2013).

53 *Da Silva Carvalho Rico v Portugal* App no 13341/14 (ECHR, 1 September 2015).

54 Kilpatrick (2014) 393; Kilpatrick (2015) 325.

55 Case C-434/11 *Corpul Naţional al Poliţiştilor v. Ministerul Administraţiei şi Internelor (MAI) and others* [2011] ECR 2011-00000, Case C-134/12 *Ministerul Administraţiei şi Internelor (MAI), Inspectoratul General al Poliţiei Române (IGPR) and Inspectoratul de Poliţie al Judeţului Tulcea (IPJ) v Corpul Naţional al Poliţiştilor – Biroul Executiv Central* [2012] ECR 2012-00000, Case C-462/11 *Victor Cozman v Teatrul Municipal Târgovişte. Portuga* [2012] ECR 2011-00000, Case C-128/12 *Sindicato dos Bancários do Norte and Others v BPN – Banco Português de Negócios SA* [2013] EU:C 2013:149; Case C-264/12 *Sindicato Nacional dos Profissionais de Seguros e Afins v Fidelidade Mundial – Companhia de Seguros SA* [2014] ECR EU: C:2014:203; Case C-665/13 *Sindicato Nacional dos Profissionais de Seguro e Afins v Via Directa – Companhia de Seguros SA* [2014] EU:C:2014:2327.

56 Kilpatrick (2014) 418.

57 Cases T-541/10 and T-215/11 *ADEDY Spyridon Papaspyros and Ilias Iliopoulos v Council of the European Union* [2012] EU:T:2012:626.

58 Case C-265/13 *Torralbo Marcos v Korota SA and Fondo de Garantía Salarial* [2014] EU:C:2014:187.

59 Case C–169/14 *Juan Carlos Sánchez Morcillo and María del Carmen Abril García v Banco Bilbao Vizcaya Argentaria, SA* [2014]. EU:C 2014:1388.

60 Case C–398/11 *Thomas Hogan and Others v Minister for Social and Family Affairs, Ireland and Attorney General* [2013] EU:C:2013:272.

61 Case C–333/13 *Elisabeta Dano and Florin Dano v Jobcenter Leipzig* [2014]. EU: C:2014:2358.

62 Case C–67/14 *Jobcenter Berlin Neukölln v Nazifa Alimanovic and Others* [2015] EU: C:2015:210.

63 Cartabia (2014).

64 On this case-law, see Groppi (2016b) 2.

65 I include in this definition the courts of countries – such as Russia, Turkey, Poland, Hungary – in which the rule of law is under attack. Nevertheless, those countries – and the democratic crisis they are facing – would require a dedicated study, also as for their attitude towards supranational courts.

66 Here I refer to the German definition of Völkerrechtsfreundlichkeit, as 'Open constitutional State': see Di Martino (2014) 109. More in general, Cassese (2015) 21.

Bibliography

Benvenisti, Eyal, 'Reclaiming Democracy: The Strategic Use of Foreign and International Law by National Courts' (2008a). 102 *The American Journal of International Law* 241–274.

Benvenisti, Eyal, 'United We Stand: National Courts Reviewing Counterterrorism Measures', in Andrea Bianchi and Alexis Keller (eds), *Counterterrorism: Democracy's Challenge* (Hart Publishing 2008b) 255.

Cassese, Sabino, 'Fine della solitudine delle corti costituzionali, ovvero il dilemma del porcospino' (2015). 1 *Ars interpretandi* 21–32.

Cartabia, Marta, 'La tutela multilivello dei diritti fondamentali. Il cammino della giurisprudenza costituzionale italiana dopo l'entrata in vigore del Trattato di Lisbona' (2014). http://www.cortecostituzionale.it/documenti/convegni_seminari/RI_Cartabia_santiago2014.pdf accessed 25 May 2017.

Cheli, Enzo, *Lo Stato costituzionale. Radici e prospettive* (Editoriale Scientifica 2006).

Ferreres Comella, Victor, 'Comparative Modesty' (2011). 7 *European Constitutional Law Review* 517–528.

Contiades, Xenophon and Fotiadou, Alkmene, 'Social Rights in the Age of Proportionality. Global Economic Crisis and Constitutional Litigation' (2012). 10 *International Journal of Constitutional Law* 660–686.

Dyzenhaus, David and Thwaites, Rayner, 'Legality and Emergency. The Judiciary in a Time of Terror', in Andrew Lynch, Edwina MacDonald and George Williams (eds), *Law and Liberty in the War on Terror* (Federation Press 2007) 10.

De Vergottini, Giuseppe, *Oltre il dialogo tra le corti. Giudici, diritto straniero, comparazione* (Il Mulino 2010).

Di Martino, Alessandra, 'The Open Constitutional State: Germany's Response to International and European Legal Pluralism', in Luca Mezzetti (ed.), *International Constitutional Law* (Giappichelli 2014).

Fontana, Giorgio, 'I giudici europei di fronte alla crisi economica' (2014). http://csdle.lex.unict.it/Archive/WP/WP%20CSDLE%20M%20DANTONA/WP%20CSDLE%20M%20DANTONA-INT/20141218-092548_fontana_n114-2014intpdf.pdf, accessed 25 May 2017.

Gerards, Janneke, 'The ECtHR's Response to Fundamental Rights Issues Related to Financial and Economic Difficulties – The Problem of Compartmentalisation' (2015). 33 *Netherlands Quarterly of Human Rights* 274–292.

Groppi, Tania, '"Business as Usual". Le dialogue judiciaire sur les affaires antiterroristes après le 11 septembre 2001', in Julia Iliopoulos-Strangas, Olivier Diggelman and Hartmut Bauer (eds), *Etat de droit, sécurité et liberté en Europe* (Editions Ant. N. Sakkoulas, Bruylant, NOMOS Verlagsgesellschaft, 2010) 325.

Groppi, Tania, 'Le « dialogue » des juges constitutionnels: entre déclin des exceptionnalismes et légitimation de la justice constitutionnelle', in Marthe Fatin-Rouge Stefanini and Guy Scoffoni (eds), *Libertés et exceptionnalismes nationaux* (Bruylant 2015).

Groppi, Tania, 'La Constitution tunisienne de 2014 dans le cadre du 'constitutionalisme globale' (2016a). 1 *Constitutions* 7–25.

Groppi, Tania, 'La jurisprudence de Strasbourg dans les décisions de la Cour constitutionnelle italienne. Une recherche empirique' (2016b). 21 *Federalismi* 2.

Groppi, Tania and Ponthoreau, Marie-Claire, *The Use of Foreign Precedents by Constitutional Judges* (Hart Publishing 2013).

Guazzarotti, Andrea, 'I diritti sociali nella giurisprudenza della Corte europea dei diritti dell'uomo' (2013). 1 *Rivista trimestrale di diritto pubblico* 9–46.

Häberle, Peter, *Lo Stato costituzionale* (Treccani 2005).

Häberle, Peter, *Stato costituzionale, I) Principi generali* vol IX, Enciclopedia giuridica (2000a).

Häberle, Peter, 'The Constitutional State and its Reform Requirements' (2000b). 13 *Ratio Juris* 77–94.

Hirschl, Ran, *Towards Juristocracy. The Origins and Consequences of the New Constitutionalism* (Harvard University Press 2004).

Jackson, Vicki C., *Constitutional Engagement in a Transnational Era* (Oxford University Press 2009) 189.

Kilpatrick, Claire, 'Are Bailouts Immune to EU Social Challenge Because They Are Not EU Law?' (2014). 10 *European Constitutional Law Review* 393–421.

Kilpatrick, Claire, 'On the Rule of Law and Economic Emergency: The Degradation of Basic Legal Values in Europe's Bailouts' (2015). 35 *Oxford Journal of Legal Studies* 325–353.

Kilpatrick, Claire, 'Constitutions, Social Rights and Sovereign Debt States in Europe: A Challenging New Area of Constitutional Inquiry' (2015). EUI Working Papers, Law 2015/34; http://cadmus.eui.eu/bitstream/handle/1814/36097/LAW_2015_34.pdf?sequence=1&isAllowed=y, accessed 25 May 2017.

Markesinis, Basil and Fedtke, Jork, 'The Judge as Comparatist' (2005). 80 *Tulane Law Review* 11–167.

Markesinis, Basil and Fedtke, Jork, *Giudici e diritto straniero* (Il Mulino 2009).

Murphy, Cian C., *EU Counter-Terrorism Law: Pre-emption and the Rule of Law* (Hart Publishing 2012).

Pope Franciscus, *Encyclical Letter Laudato Si' of The Holy Father Francis on Care for Our Common Home* (2015).

Rifkin, Jeremy, *The Third Industrial Revolution. How Lateral Power Is Transforming Energy, the Economy, and the World* (St. Martin's Press 2011).

Roman, Diane, 'La jurisprudence sociale des Cours constitutionnelles en Europe: vers une jurisprudence de crise' (2014). 45 *Nouveaux Cahiers du Conseil Constitutionnel* 63–75.

Saitto, Francesco, 'La « solitudine » delle Corti costituzionali? Sindacato sulle misure di austerity e protezione dei diritti sociali tra giudici nazionali e Corte EDU' (2016). 1 *Diritto pubblico*, 421–450.

Tanasescu, Elena and Deaconu, Stefan, 'Romania: Analogical Reasoning as a Dialectical Instrument', in Tania Groppi and Marie Claire Ponthoreau (eds), *The Use of Foreign Precedents by Constitutional Judges* (Hart Publishing 2013) 321–346.

Tega, Diletta, 'Welfare Rights in Italy', in Bruno de Witte and Claire Kilpatrick (eds), *Social Rights in Times of Crisis in the Eurozone: The Role of Fundamental Rights Challenge* (EUI Law 2015) 50.

Tulkens, Francois, 'La mise en œuvre de la Convention européenne des droits de l'homme en période de crise économique' (2013). http://www.echr.coe.int/Documents/Speech_20130125_Tulkens_FRA.pdf, accessed 25 May 2017.

Tushnet, Mark, 'The Possibilities of Comparative Constitutional Law' (1999). 108 *Yale Law Journal* 1225–1309.

Weinrib, Lorraine, 'The Postwar Paradigm and American Exceptionalism', in Sujit Choudhry (ed.), *The Migration of Constitutional Ideas* (Cambridge University Press 2006) 89.

Zagrebelsky, Gustavo, *Fragilità e forza dello Stato costituzionale* (Editoriale Scientifica 2006).

Zagrebelsky, Gustavo, *Il diritto mite* (Einaudi 1992).

15 The negotiating function of the European Court of Human Rights

Reconciling diverging interests born from new European challenges

Beatrice Delzangles

Introduction

To judge is to decide a dispute by saying what the law is.[1] How could the European Court of Human Rights (hereinafter ECtHR or Court), vested by the Convention with the function of judging, play the role of negotiator, especially when it decides a dispute affecting the new social challenges?

To negotiate is to seek an agreement between two or more interlocutors, centred on their opposing interests. If, in the common sense, to negotiate

> has always more or less evoked the very simple notion of bargaining, of agreements with reciprocal concessions,[2]

today this action refers more to

> a confrontation between closely or highly interdependent parties that are bound by a certain power balance and show at least a minimum amount of willingness to reach an agreement in order to narrow a gap or a difference, so as to build an acceptable solution with regard to their objective and the room for manoeuvre they had set for themselves.[3]

Hence the concept of negotiation has become more complex with the approach developed by game theory[4] that considers negotiation in a more restrictive way, as the search for a mutually acceptable solution in a conflict of interest situation. Behind this approach there lies the idea of the rationality of the actors and the will to seek strategies.

It is in this context that the Court exercises a negotiating function: by rendering its decision, it seeks agreement – a tacit understanding – with the Defendant State and more generally with the community of the States Parties, trying to make the various interests involved compatible. Its negotiating activity considers principally how the addressees feel about its judgements and more generally the feelings of its audience. As a result, the analysis of the Court's negotiating function is less interested in the solution found, instead it looks at the rhetoric adopted by the jurisdiction in order to reach that solution and that agreement – the tacit one – that it finds with the States. Hence the difficulty to reconstitute the message hidden behind the reasoning of the Court issuing the judgement, and its desired impact on the State receiving the decision.

The negotiating role of the Court in reconciling diverging interests is essential when questions considered 'sensitive' are at stake. In fact, some of them take the dimension of real 'challenges' of society exacerbating the divergence of interests betweeen the States and the European jurisdiction and making their conciliation even more complex. Social challenges could be defined here as the internal or external obstacles that a civilisation has to overcome in its evolution.[5] If we apply this to the European system for the protection of human rights, the challenges that the Court faces in certain disputes could point to these new economic, political, social and cultural difficulties that are of such scale that no European State could claim to find an answer to them on its own and that, in order to be overcome, deserve a focussed effort of the European States and often violate fundamental rights.

In this type of case, the Court's negotiating function is essential. Bearing in mind the importance of the issues at stake for European society – the States and their population – the way the Court chooses to apprehend them can make its authority and efficiency grow or shrink. The analysis of its negotiating function leads us first to an assessment of these political, economic, social and cultural obstacles of such significance that today they constitute a real challenge for Europe. Then we need to identify the negotiation points between the Court and the States' Parties (first part) that make it necessary for the European jurisdiction to develop different forms of negotiation (second part).

1. The challenges to jurisprudence

1.1 The challenges defined by the court

There are cases in which the ECtHR itself identifies the new challenges to be met by the States' Parties and, more generally, by European society. The Court's stance on the political, economic or social context in which a case occurs is an integral part of its reasoning. Thus, by linking the individual cases to the great challenges currently pervading European society, the Court makes considerable efforts to justify its reasoning by showing how some of these great challenges impose upon it, or, *a minima*, are taken into consideration when it proceeds to weigh the interests at stake.

The fight against terrorism led by the States' Parties is among these contextual elements interfering with its decision-making process. Besides, the European jurisdiction has adapted its discourse with the aim of better taking into account what has become a real challenge for the States since the early 2000s. It is true that since its creation, the Court has always claimed to be aware of the difficulties encountered by the States aiming to protect their population against terrorist violence. In the *Lawless* case concerning the conflict in Northern Ireland, the Court had thus concluded that there was 'a public emergency in the Republic of

Ireland threatening the life of the nation', which justified, at that time, the adoption of extraordinary counter-terrorism measures provided for in Art. 15 of the Convention.[6] But the terrorism that the United Kingdom and Ireland were faced with in the late 1950s was not perceived as a challenge to be met by all the European States. It is really only since the 11 September 2001 attacks were perpetrated on American territory that the Court has adopted a more systematic approach towards terrorism, talking about 'terrorist violence' that it has qualified ever since as 'an extremely serious situation amounting to a public emergency threatening the life of the nation'.[7] Being more sympathetic towards the arguments of the States in this matter,[8] the Court now raises the 'tremendously dangerous threat that terrorism represents for the community itself'[9] and declares itself 'fully aware',[10] even 'acutely aware'[11] of the considerable problems the States are facing in their efforts to protect their population against terrorist violence. Without labelling it a 'challenge' for the States and their population, the Court emphasised the particular context threatening European society today.

Another difficulty European States have to face is also treated as a challenge for the European *Lawless* Court: the economic crisis. Although, as its position of principle, the Court continues to assert that a State's lack of resources provides no justification to their failure to comply with the obligation to guarantee convention-based rights,[12] it did have to adapt to the economic reality of the moment and recognise the existence of a major economic downturn in Europe. In relation to the management of migratory flows and its ramifications concerning the human dignity of migrants, the Court has thus specifically taken into account the 'context of economic crisis'[13] which, coupled with the 'recent social and political changes that have particularly affected some regions of Africa and the Middle East',[14] transforms the growing flow of migrants and asylum seekers into a real challenge for European States, especially for those located on the borders of the European Union. For the Court, it is this 'general context of economic crisis' – we highlight the term 'general' that demonstrates the scale of the phenomenon – that makes it difficult not only to welcome migrants but also to access the labour market of the States most affected by said crisis. The same general approach of the crisis perceived as a phenomenon that generates economic difficulties for all European States, prevails in other cases involving Article 1 of Protocol 1, setting forth the right of ownership. Thus, as regards the decrease in officials' pensions implemented by the Greek or Portuguese government in order to restore public finances, the Court holds that these measures were 'justified by the existence of an exceptional crisis without precedent in recent Greek history',[15] by 'the economic crisis which was asphyxiating the Portuguese economy'[16] and by the 'background of an actual and unexpected budgetary crisis in Portugal'.[17] While the Court limited the crisis to Portugal in its judgements regarding the country, it finally admitted the *Koufaki v. Greece* judgement that 'a number of States' were 'in the same overall context of economic crisis' and had to make similar pension cuts.[18]

Thus, the ECtHR is aware of the challenge that the economic and financial crisis affecting Europe for the past five years constitutes for the protection of human rights. In 2013, it dedicated its opening seminar to the implementation of the European Convention on Human Rights in the time of economic crisis.[19] A year earlier at the opening of the judicial year of the ECtHR, Sir Nicolas Bratza, then President of the Court, declared that 'the economic crisis with its potential for generating political instability seems to spiral further and further out of control. All our societies are experiencing difficulties that few of us can have foreseen only a short time ago'.[20] More broadly, the Council of Europe mobilises to tackle this economic crisis, once again demonstrating the scale of the challenge.[21] It is therefore in this difficult economic context, for the moment not sufficiently brought forward by the Defendant States[22] but generally recognised by different bodies of the Council of Europe,[23] that the Court has to rule.

1.2 The academic environment of crises jurisprudence

Over the past years, the political class in France and in other States' Parties to the Convention has expressed its views several times on the judgments rendered by the ECtHR. Putting forward the issues raised by some of the questions determined by Strasbourg, these political positions often defend the idea according to which, in ruling on the new social challenges, the Court would substitute itself to the States and/or create new convention-based obligations against the States' will. Unlike the political discourse, the doctrinal discourse on European jurisprudence claims to offer a rather less polarised and better-founded analysis of the Court's decisions addressing the present difficulties of European society.

The doctrinal discourse is especially interesting for identifying the challenges set forth before the Court since it is generally intended to be more objective in presenting the diverging interests in question than politics. Consequently, the majority of authors tackling the Court's case law on terrorism, the States' migration policy and the European economic crisis or ethical questions are faced more often than the political class with the challenges these questions pose to the protection of human rights the Court is responsible for.

Thus, faced with the 'terrorism crisis',[24] the authors claim to be aware of the 'pressure from certain States' when the Court has to rule, for example, on the return of foreigners accused of terrorist activities. Some applaud, *inter alia*, the European jurisdiction's 'consistency' and 'courage' that continues, despite the current security environment, to surround the national measures for removing foreigners by the same guarantees, whatever acts they had committed.[25] Others highlight the European jurisdiction's difficulty to reconcile the efficiency of the fight against terrorism and the respect of procedural guarantees, regarding the latter as 'the main challenge ahead for European democracies and the European judge of human rights'.[26] Regarding the migration crisis, the doctrine recalls that the Court's decisions on this question are often questionably put in the 'currently very fashionable' perspective of 'Europe besieged by migrant hordes'.[27] It is easy to imagine the Court's great difficulties in managing and adjudicating practically irreconcilable interests when ruling on the more and more common state practice of outsourcing of asylum and immigration, on the conditions of detention for migrants or on their expulsion towards States where they might face risks of ill-treatment.[28]

The doctrine also perceives the European dispute born from the economic crisis as the demonstration of a new European challenge.[29] On this occasion, the Court's judgments concerning measures of economic recovery and budget consolidation adopted by certain States Parties, such as cutting the pensions for Greek civil servants or decreasing the retirement pensions in Portugal, could be qualified as 'emblematic'.[30] Faced with the government policies on fiscal restraint implemented in the assisted countries, the doctrine considered that the Court had remained 'in the background', since the Convention 'was of no help'.[31] Yet, without doubt, these policies have 'indisputably had an impact on the economic and social rights of these States' nationals'[32] and pose a real challenge to the Europe of human rights. The sensitive moment Europe is undergoing does indeed risk leading to a 'further rift within the Europe of fundamental rights'.[33] Considering the scale of the interests at stake, the doctrine focuses mostly on the Court's difficulties to achieve the 'right balance needed between the general imperatives of the community and the protection of the applicants' fundamental rights'.[34] The role it is called to play in the context of this economic crisis leads some authors to reflect more broadly on the nature of the link between the protection of human rights and economy in general. Is it effectively 'Europe's high level of protection of fundamental rights [that] may after all have something to do with the fact that Europe is still quite wealthy and prosperous' or, to the contrary, '[has] Europe [...] become wealthy because it cherished human freedom and rights'?[35] In the second hypothesis, the Court's responsibility is measured and according to whether it increases or decreases the level of protection of fundamental rights in Europe, it could affect Europe's economic decline by contributing to limit it or, on the contrary, to further accentuate it.

Finally, the doctrinal positions on the Court's case law on gestational surrogacy highlight the challenge posed by this practice to European society today but even more in the future. Because of its transnational character, gestational surrogacy (hereinafter GS) has become a European and even global issue, since third countries to the European system of human rights protection are indirectly involved.[36]

Brought before the Court, the issue of GS inevitably leads European jurisdiction to rule on a practice of considerable ethical and social implications, a practice towards which every State intends to impose its own regulations. Thus, according to part of the doctrine, not only should this practice receive a political response instead of a judicial one but, in addition, it should be handled at the European level, which Europe 'has been absolutely unable to find a common solution'[37] until now. In this context we understand that *Mennesson* and *Labassée* of 26 June 2014 condemning France for having refused to recognise the parentage legally established in the United States between the children born of GS and the couple who had resorted to this method, could give rise to very contrasting doctrinal comments.[38] The Court's argumentative stance in this case is surprising. While acknowledging that the absence of a European consensus on the way to regulate GS 'reflects the fact that recourse to a surrogacy arrangement raises sensitive ethical questions',[39] the European jurisdiction in *Mennesson* manages to keep GS on the level of a simple individual problem, reducing the diverging interests to a simple opposition between the applicants and their children and the Defendant State. Carefully avoiding to present GS as a matter of general interest facing entire modern society and transcending the applicants' and their children's person and interests, the Court does not tackle GS as a challenge for the European States and society. Should we conclude that there is no challenge in that matter or should we see it as the European jurisdiction's technique to reconcile again diverging interests?

2. Recent decisions of the Court in response to the new challenges

2.1 Conflicting decisions

The ECtHR addresses some of the social challenges with a competitive approach, seeing the State as an adversary. The Court therefore uses interpretative techniques enabling any domestic margin of appreciation, at other times, in contrast, to bow down to the State by fostering its right to its own interpretative authority. In both cases, the diverging interests are taken into account in an alternative way, so that only the Court will manage to impose its position concerning the way to perceive a current problem. The Court's arguments in support of its judgments on the matter of terrorism have long been based on this sole logic. Although today the Court has a more nuanced approach,[40] it had long positioned itself in a face-off with the States wishing to have individuals accused of terrorism extradited to States likely to engage in activities contrary to Art. 3 of the Convention. The Court states very firmly that this article 'prohibits in absolute terms torture and inhuman or degrading treatment or punishment'[41] and does not seem ready to make any concessions, not even when faced with the threat of terrorism: 'it is not possible to weigh the risk of ill-treatment against the reasons put forward for the expulsion'.[42]

By indicating with such clarity the competing objectives – protection of human rights on the one hand, fight against terrorism on the other hand – the European jurisdiction puts forth the rivalry between itself and the States over this question, as well as its distrust of the States. Thus, the Defendant State can try to give assurances of the absence of any treatment prohibited by the Convention in the host State but this is not 'a sufficient guarantee that the applicant would be protected against the risk of treatment prohibited by the Convention'.[43] Conscious of the diplomatic dimension of this type of assurance, the Court maintains that it has to verify what they generate in their practical implementation and thereby invites the States to do likewise, since 'the weight to be given to assurances from the receiving State depends, in each case, on the circumstances prevailing at the material time'.[44] Finally, the State Party itself should also be more distrustful and, so to speak, take a more conflicting approach when negotiating the reception conditions of the expulsed/extradited person with the State of destination. As for the fight against terrorism, 'mutual trust should not be applicable, in fact, when it comes to fundamental rights; only a logic based on monitoring their respect should prevail'.[45]

It is also an adversarial approach that the Court has taken towards the disagreement on acknowledging the parentage of children born of GS. In fact, only such logic could have enabled it to condemn France over this question that raises important social challenges while the Court has recognised the States must in principle be afforded a wide margin of appreciation in this respect.[46] From that perspective, *Mennesson* is akin to a real argumentative feat of the Court winning a battle that had seemed *a priori* to be lost in advance. Thanks to the concept of the 'best interests of the child', the Court manages to impose its interpretative authority in an area where the freedom of interpretation of the States' Parties was expected to prevail.[47] The Court's reasoning being based mainly on the stand-off between competing interests – the protection of health and the protection of the rights and freedoms of others perceived as 'legitimate aims' pursued by the French government on the one hand[48] and the best interests of the child in question that the Court sought to protect, on the other hand – the Court adopts a now well established process that consists of multiplying the trade-offs between conflicting interests.[49] Such trade-offs, 'inherent in the whole of the Convention',[50] have, in fact, the advantage of enabling the Court to reconcile the interests as it sees fit, sometimes outweighing the States, sometimes bowing to their margin of appreciation, depending on the issues at stake. This is how the best interests of the child could have sometimes served to justify the freedom of States to choose the most appropriate means to protect this vulnerable group,[51] and sometimes, on the contrary, to limit this freedom as in *Mennesson*. In this case, the Court could resolve its standoff with the State by transforming the interest to reconcile into a real conciliatory interest. Today it is enough that the Court puts forth the best interests of the child to orient the outcome of the dispute.[52]

The adversarial approach of diverging interests does not, however, always foster the protection of fundamental rights. For example, despite the many reminders of the Court concerning the absolute character of Article 3, the threshold of seriousness determining whether there is a breach often varies greatly and is subject to the principle of proportionality.[53] Thus, the acts of terrorism committed by an applicant and the applicant's dangerousness invoked by the Defendant State are sometimes taken into account by the Court to declare Art. 3 inapplicable.[54] In relation to the extradition of five suspected terrorists facing heavy sentences in the US, the Court found that Art. 3 was not applicable because this punishment was not 'grossly disproportionate', taking into account the terrorist deeds they were accused of.[55] Admitting from then on that in the context of extradition, a 'grossly disproportionate' sentence would violate Art. 3,[56] the Court has inevitably brought the proportionality test in the scope of this provision. In doing so, the Court can reply favourably to the States' requests in favour of relativising this provision in the assumptions of extradition and expulsion.[57] That said, paradoxically, this relativisation of Art. 3 is meaningful for the authority of the Court, concerned by the realities the States are confronted with and cannot be regarded as idealist.

Once the proportionality test has been brought under the scope of Art. 3, would the next step be the defining of the threshold of seriousness of the ill treatment inflicted on an individual depending on the economic context of the Destination State? We measure the strategic dimension of such relativisation of the guarantees contained in Art. 3 faced with the challenge currently posed by the reception of migrants by the States going through a significant economic crisis. The Court could then come to subjecting the removal or repatriation of a foreigner to different reception conditions depending on whether the Destination State is prosperous or, to the contrary, if economically it is not in a position to assume the arrival of foreigners on its territory.[58] Of course, making the respect of fundamental rights dependent on the level of public expenditures a State can assume would be unjustifiable from the perspective of fundamental rights but in the end, it could be strategic for the Court whose decisions adopted in this context of migration, paired with an economic crisis, are recently often disavowed.

Besides, is not a similar development already in motion in an entirely different area – that of property rights? The *Da Silva Carvalho Rico* decision of the Court of September 2015 on the austerity measures imposed on retired Portuguese officials establishes a particularly explicit link between the protection of social rights and the economic level of the State. Expected to make a decision on the compliance with Article 1 of the Protocol No. 1 of the pensioners' obligatory payment of a public duty, an 'extraordinary solidarity contribution', intended to contribute to the improvement of the country's public finances in the context of a budgetary crisis, the Court relied on 'the principle of the «proviso of the possible' used by the Portuguese Constitutional Court as grounds for its judgment of the provision's constitutionality.[59] Sharing this reasoning, the Court seems to be sharing the idea according to which 'a State cannot be forced to comply with its obligations in the framework of social rights if it does not possess the economic means to do so' and admitting that 'in this context', the budgetary constraints on the implementation of social rights can be accepted as long as they are proportionate to the public aim pursued and do not reduce social right's claims to purely symbolic sums. Finally, applying this principle to a specific case, the European jurisdiction holds that, on the one hand, 'the international recognition of the country's economic situation indicates that the present budgetary constraints constitute an imperative' and, on the other hand, that it 'did not reduce possessions originating in a statutory social right's claims to a level that deprives the right of its substance'.[60] Could the economic crisis have been right about the indivisibility of fundamental rights, so often defended by the Court? It is important that we remember that in principle, there is no 'watertight division' between the sphere of economic and social rights from the field covered by the Convention and that it 'sets forth what are essentially civil and political rights, many of them have implications of a social or economic nature'.[61] The principle of 'the proviso of the possible' that has appeared in the case law of the German Federal Constitutional Court,[62] however, means for the Court to make the realisation of social rights – only those are concerned in this case – conditional on 'what the individual can reasonably expect from society',[63] the assessment of the possible and the reasonable, primary obligation of the legislator. The conflict between the protection of social rights and the financial and economic constraints that the States face as a result seems to have turned in the favour of the States. Thus, should the Court's use of the 'proviso of the possible' get confirmed and, in the future, count among its many interpretation techniques, the conventionality of social rights would henceforth have a price.[64]

How can we explain the Court's need to bring this case back to the principle of the 'proviso of the possible'? In the preceding decisions on the Greek and Portuguese austerity measures, the wide margin of appreciation recognised for the States to determine their social policy had, in fact, been enough to declare the applications inadmissible, this margin of appreciation being even wider 'when the issues involve an assessment of the priorities as to the allocation of limited State resources'.[65] The Court embarked on a limited proportionality test in *Koufaki* and *Da Conceicao Mateus*, since this type of test is more often used when it comes to regulating the use of goods by the State.[66] However, it seems that in its September 2015 decision, its low intensity proportionality test in matters related to austerity measures resulting from the new adjustment programs negotiated, or even imposed, by the European Union, the European Central Bank and the International Monetary Fund to some Member States of the EU, was not sufficient anymore. In this context of economic crisis, the Court strengthens its arguments by referring also to the 'proviso of the possible' that provides a higher degree of freedom to the States in the realisation of social rights. Concomitantly, this technique enables the Court to demonstrate that it can equally show realism in the application of the Convention … . It follows that in this context of social vulnerability of certain States, "the re-emerging infernal dilemma of self-restraint or judicial activism" and certain techniques undoubtedly enable the Court to 'exercise a highly strategic self-restraint in order not to earn the wrath of the States'.[67]

Resolving conflicts of interest according to an adversarial approach does not permit the Court to increase its authority and its legitimacy in the face of the addressees of its case law. In a context of uncertainty linked to the terrorist threat, the economic crisis and migratory challenges, the States consider that the Court is lacking in realism when it continues to impose the same level of protection of fundamental rights. In contrast, when giving the States' economic and security demands a favourable reception, the Court is accused of 'selling out' the guarantee of human rights in the very context that should make it more vigilant. Whatever interests the Court chooses to prioritise, this conflicting approach brings the European jurisdiction to lose on the one hand what it had won on the other hand.

2.2 Cooperative decisions

A cooperative negotiation approach brings the Court, in conciliating the protection of fundamental rights with the States' interests, to handle the States as partners and not as adversaries. The Court then emphasises the common project that drives them and seeks a solution that is acceptable for everyone, given that the Court's results were not necessarily obtained at the expense of the States' interest, and the other way around.

The Court's arguments supporting its judgments on terrorism now fit more into this approach. The recent case law on the matter is intended to be explicit and is keen to put forth 'the difficulties faced by States in protecting their populations from terrorist violence'[68] that, according to its own wording, the Court 'considers it legitimate' for Contracting States 'to take a firm stand against those who contribute to terrorist acts, which it cannot condone in any circumstances'. Faced with the proliferation of terrorism and the States' difficulty to fight it, the Court adjusts its arguments. It takes a stand – up to now implicitly – in favour of the States, becoming their ally in this fight. The European judge pursues this objective on the same basis, as the protection of fundamental rights, eradicating terrorism thus becomes a challenge to face together, by the Court and the States Parties. Terrorist violence is seen not only as one of many 'difficulties'[69] to take into account to be able to rule, but 'constitutes, in itself, a grave threat to human rights'.[70] It is difficult not to make the connection between the development of the European jurisprudence and the rise in terrorism of recent years in Europe and in the world, as well as the increasing criticism of the States Parties to its jurisprudence – notably of the United Kingdom – regarding the prohibition to extradite/expulse persons accused of terrorist acts, which would want to have greater discretional powers to defend their homeland security in the face of this complex threat.

Faced with this new challenge, the Court now seeks to put forth the interests and values it shares with the States. Thus, in the older case law, it was the response to terrorism and not terrorism itself that constituted a real threat to democracy.[71] But the increasing and more and more generalised attacks have forced the Court to change paradigm and finally admit that these are acts of violence that constitute a threat for democracy.[72] Thus, on this issue, the Court tackles the requirement of democracy not as the necessary condition for the protection of the convention-based rights and freedoms but as a goal to reach and that legitimises a certain pattern of behaviour of the States.

In a different area, that is, the economic crisis, the Court also seeks to join the efforts – notably financial ones – of the States challenged to resolve the violations of the Convention, especially when the violations are structural and systemic and pose the risk of generating many applications. Repetitive cases do raise significant difficulties for both the Court that was already overloaded and the States because of the budgetary consequences arising from the execution of the Court's judgments. Hence, the pilot judgment procedure has been in place for over a decade, enabling the Court to help the States identify the structural or systemic problems, and to adjourn the related cases for a period of time, on the condition that the Government acts promptly to adopt measures to tackle those problems.[73] We should not forget that this technique was used in the case of *Broniowski* on the subject of properties which concerned some 80,000 people,[74] the *Hutten-Czapska* case related to the housing of 100,000 people[75] or the *Kuric* case where 26000 people's social rights were at stake.[76] While the pilot judgments against Greece may relate to only a few thousand applications, in reality they involve close to a million cases in which a reasonable time has been exceeded.[77] Consequently, as far as repetitive cases are concerned, 'the Court's work, (...) no longer consists solely in dealing with individual applications but means finding solutions to major societal problems affecting large categories of persons'.[78] Thus, in 2009, the first year of the economic crisis in Greece, the assessment of violations of the Convention by this State showed clearly that budgetary shortages were the main cause of over 90 per cent of the violations found by the Court.[79] That year, the Greek State budget, totalling around 125 billion euros, recorded a deficit of 37 billion euros, or roughly one third, to be able to comply with the European Convention.[80] Without explicitly recognising the financial effort this State in the midst of an economic and financial crisis has to make in order to increase the number of magistrates, build new courthouses, computerise the domestic courts' registry services – while making no secret of the benefit the pilot judgment procedure could have for the Court by avoiding the influx of applications[81] – delivering such judgments means for the Court to implicitly admit the serious financial consequences of its case law on the State's public finances.

A final example illustrates how the Court seeks collaborative solutions to resolve the disagreement with the States: On the subject of the expulsion/extradition of persons accused of terrorist activities, the Court now proposes streamlined criteria to accept the diplomatic arrangements invoked by the Defendant State that gives assurances that the affected person's reception conditions in the Destination State are in compliance with the Convention. Aware that 'there is widespread concern within the international community as to the practice of seeking assurances to allow for the deportation of those considered to be a threat to national security', but, at the same time, wishing to avoid at all costs to rule upon 'the propriety of seeking assurances' or 'to assess the long term consequences of doing so',[82] in the end the Court decided to systematise the requirements towards the assurances obtained in Art. 3 expulsion cases hitherto scattered in its different judgments and decisions. Thus, such systematisation enables it to respond to the criticisms of those for whom these assurances are rarely sufficient to altogether remove any real risk of ill treatment but also to fulfil the wishes of the States, which have no other means to obtain the commitment of the Destination State.[83] This streamlining of the Court's jurisprudence related to diplomatic assurances obtained in expulsion cases benefits both the States Parties and the individuals, while guaranteeing judicial security.

3. Conclusion

The jurisprudence of the Court enables it to identify the important social challenges that resonate with the courtroom. Other discourses that are exterior to the European system of human rights protection, either political or doctrinal, can also constitute indicators that permit isolation of the questions creating a real challenge for the States Parties and the European society among all of the political, economic, social or cultural questions brought before the European jurisdiction.

Adopting the perspective of the ECtHR's relationship with the States, the chapter has identified and explained the negotiating points around the current social challenges. Its focus was on the way the Court's jurisdiction puts an end – in specific cases – to the difference of interests and defines what the law is in the individual cases.

The chapter analysed that Court's judgments range from conflicting decisions showing confrontation between the Court and the Defendant State, and cooperative decisions seeking an understanding between the two stakeholders. The ECtHR's arguments thus reveal a swaying between these two poles, which sometimes occurs successively in a single case.

New decisions reflecting to the challenges show that there is change in the jurisprudence of the Court, just take the 'proviso of possibility' as an example or the emergence of the 'proportionality' doctrine in cases where identically it was not present before. I argued that this change must be better understood if we accept that the negotiating function of the Court in the European environment in these highly sensitive questions will highly determine the approach of the Court to the individual cases. Respect for the jurisprudence of the Court depends not only on the doctrinal quality of the decisions but also on how cautious the Court is of different interests while defining what the law is in these highly conflictual and politically heated situations.

Notes

1 See for example Cornu (2014) 714.
2 Bellenger (2015) 27.
3 Idem 19.
4 With Game theory, 1944, outcome of mathematician J. von Neumann's and economist O. Morgenstern's reflection, the art of speculation has become a science.
5 *Le Petit Robert* (2012) 648.
6 *Lawless v. Ireland no 3* App. no 332/57 (ECHR, 1 July 1961).
7 *A. and Others v. United Kingdom* App. no 3455/05 (ECHR, 19 February 2009).
8 See for instance *Saadi v. Italy* App. no 37201/06 (28 February 2008) §114 where the Italian government asked from the Court that account 'be taken of the scale of the terrorist threat in the world of today and of the objective difficulties of combating it effectively'.
9 *Daoudi v. France* App. no 19576/08 (ECHR, 03 December 2009) §65.
10 *A. and Others* §246.
11 *Daoudi.*
12 On this subject, see also Tulkens (2013) 8.
13 *M.S.S. v. Belgium and Greece* App. no 30696/9 (ECHR, 21 January 2011) §223; *Hirsi Jamaa and Others v. Italy* App no 27765/09 (ECHR, 23 February 2012) §122; *Sharifi and Others v. Italy and Greece* App. no. 16643/9 (ECHR, 3 November 2014) §176.
14 *Hirsi Jamaa and Others* §176.
15 *Koufaki and Adedi v. Greece* App. no 57665/12 and 57657/12 (ECHR, 7 May 2013) §37.
16 *Da Conceicao Mateus and Santos Januario v. Portugal* App. no 62235/12 and 57725/12 (ECHR, 31, October 2013) §25.
17 *Da Silva Carvalho Rico v. Portugal* App. no 13341/14 (ECHR, 24 September 2015) §44.
18 *Koufaki* §44. Interestingly enough, it does not generalise the economic crisis in the *Da Silva Carvalho* decision.
19 Implementing the European Convention on Human Rights in time of economic crisis (2013).
20 Opening of the judicial year of the ECHR (2012); www.echr.coe.int/Documents/Annual_report_2012_FRA.pdf

21 In its report entitled 'State of democracy, human rights and the rule of law in Europe' of 2014, the Secretary General of the Council of Europe, Mr. Thorbjørn Jagland, stressed that 'European societies have suffered the effects of the recent economic crisis, which has deeply affected social cohesion in many member States, and which may eventually threaten both the rule of law and democracy. See State of democracy, human rights and the rule of law in Europe (2014). Further evidence of the challenge that today the economic crisis constitutes for Europe: the Committee of Ministers of the Council of Europe instructed the Steering Committee for Human Rights to study "the feasibility of new activities, as well as the revision of existing instruments, on the impact of the economic crisis on human rights in Europe (...)" see Reference Document (2013). This request led to a study released in June 2014 on "The impact of the economic crisis and austerity measures on human rights in Europe', updated in 2016.

22 Nevertheless, the argument pertaining to the economic difficulties encountered by a State is often invoked. For example, see *Mahamad v. France* App. no 48352/12 (ECHR, 15 April 2015) §18 or *Preda and Others v. Romania* Application nos. 9584/02, 33514/02, 38052/02, 25821/03, 29652/03, 3736/03, 17750/03 and 28688/04 (ECHR, 29 April 2014) §92. By contrast, the present economic crisis in Europe is not (yet?) among the Defendant States' arguments.

23 The impact of the crisis on the protection of human rights is thus one of the European Union's main concerns as well: see for example the Annual Conference of the European Union Agency for Fundamental Rights on the 'Challenges and opportunities for access to justice in austerity' (2012) or the 2012 annual report of the Agency for Fundamental Rights published in 2013.

24 Marguénaud and Mouly (2013) 346.

25 Hurpy and Afroukh, (2015) 11.

26 Milano (2015) 7.

27 Tinière (2012) 8.

28 V. Labayle (2014) 501.

29 Tulkens (2013) 8.

30 Aktypis (2014) 1027.

31 Fines (2014) 20.

32 Idem.

33 Idem.

34 Aktypis (2014) 1027.

35 Mälksoo (2013) 20–21.

36 Duguet, Prudil and Hrevtsova (2014) 46–51.

37 Hauser (2014) 617.

38 *Mennesson v. France* App. no 65941/11 (EHCR 26 June2014.).

39 Idem §79.

40 Cf infra.

41 *Saadi* §127.

42 Idem §138.

43 Idem §148.

44 Idem.

45 Weyembergh (2002) 179.

46 *Mennesson* §79.

47 Idem §84.

48 Idem §62.

49 Delzangles (2009) 292.

50 *Sporrong and Lönnroth v. Sweden* App. no 7151/75 and 7152/75. (ECHR, 23 September 1982) §69.

51 See *Margareta and Roger Andersson v. Sweden* App. no 12963/87 (ECHR, 25 February 1992) §95 A226-A and *Johansen v. Norway* App. no 17383/90 (ECHR, 7 August 1996) §§77, 78.

52 E. g. *X. and Y. v. Holland* App. no. 8978/80 (ECHR, 26 March 1985) §27 A91 and *Siliadin v. France* App. no 73316/01 (ECHR, 26 October 2005).
53 *Caloc v. France* App. no 33951/196 (ECHR, 20 July 2000) §98 or *Galotskin v. Greece* App. no 2945/07 (ECHR, 14 January 2010) §38.
54 E.g. *Ramirez Sanchez v. France* App. no 59450/00 (ECHR 27 January 2005) §149.
55 *Babar Ahmad and Others v. The United Kingdom* App. no 24027/07 (ECHR 10 April 2012) §244.
56 Idem §235.
57 The third intervention of the United Kingdom in *Saadi* is particularly explicit (117,123).
58 See Sarmas (2013) 16.
59 *Da Silva Carvalho Rico* §44.
60 Idem.
61 *Airey v. Ireland* App. no 6289/73 (ECHR, 9 October 1979) §26 A41.
62 BVerfGE 33, 303, 333; 43, 291, 314.
63 Idem.
64 Paraphrasing Didier Ribes expression in '*la Constitution, combien ça coûte?*' (2008).
65 *Koufaki* §31 or *Da Conceicao Mateus and Santos Januario* App. no 62235/12 (ECHR, 8 October 2013) §22.
66 Sudre (2015) no 363.
67 Burgorgue-Larsen (2012) 144.
68 *Othman (Abu Qatada) v. United Kingdom* App. no 8139/09 (ECHR, 9 May 2012) §183.
69 *Öcalan v. Turkey* App. no 46221/99 (ECHR, 12 May 2005) §179.
70 Idem. See also *Trabelsi v. Belgium* ECHR in 2014, reproduced in *Ouabour v. Belgium* App. no 26417/10 (ECHR, 2 June2015) §63.
71 E.g. Soulier (1989) 30.
72 On this question, compare *Klass and others v. Germany* App. no 5029/71 (ECHR, 6 September 1978) §49 A28 and *Zana v. Turkey* App. no 181954/91(ECHR, 13 February 2008) §55.
73 This is how the pilot judgments are presented on the Court's website.
74 *Broniowski v. Poland* App. no 31443/96 (ECHR, 22 June 2004) §162.
75 *Hutten-Czapska v. Poland* App. no 35014/97 (ECHR 19 June 2006) §239.
76 *Kuric and Others v. Slovenia* App. no 26828/06 (ECHR, 26 June 2012).
77 *Michelioudakis v. Greece* App. no 30226/09 (ECHR, 9 October 2014).
78 Sarmas (2013) 16.
79 Sarmas (2010) 44.
80 Sarmas (2012) 36.
81 E. g. *Broniowski v Poland* App. no 31443/96 (ECHR, 22 June 2004) §190.
82 *Othman* §186.
83 Idem §188.

Bibliography

Aktypis, Spyridon, 'Chronique de jurisprudence de la Cour européenne des droits de l'homme' (2014). *Journal de droit international*, 1027.

Bellenger, Lionel, *La négociation* (Presses universitaire de France 2015).

Burgorgue-Larsen, Laurence, 'Actualité de la Convention européenne des droits de l'homme (juillet-décembre 2011)' (2012). *L'Actualité Juridique Droit Administratif*, 144.

Cornu, Gérard et al., *Vocabulaire juridique* (10th edn, Presses Universitaires de France, 2014).

Delzangles, Béatrice, *Activisme et autolimitation de la Cour européenne des droits de l'homme* (LGDJ, 2009).

Duguet, Anne-Marie, Prudil, Lucas and Hrevtsova, Radmyla, 'Gestation pour autrui pratiquée à l'étranger: conséquences pour les couples français et évolution du cadre légal dans certains pays' (2014). 125 *Médecine et Droit* 46–51.

Fines, Francette, 'L'atteinte aux droits fondamentaux était-elle le prix du sauvetage de la zone euro ?' (2014). 20 *Revue des Droits et Libertés Fondamentaux*; http://www.revuedlf.com/droit-ue/latteinte-aux-droits-fondamentaux-etait-elle-le-prix-du-sauvetage-de-la-zone-euro/, last accessed on 18 January 2016.

Hauser, Jean, 'Etat civil: après l'enfant conventionnel, un autre nouveau-né, l'enfant fait accompli !' (2014). *Revue trimestrielle de droit civil*, 617.

Hurpy, Hélène and Afroukh, Mustapha, 'Eloignement des étrangers terroristes et article 3 de la Convention européenne des droits de l'homme' (2015). 11 *Revue des Droits et Libertés Fondamentaux*; http://www.revuedlf.com/cedh/eloignement-des-etrangers-terroristes-et-article-3-de-la-convention-europeenne-des-droits-de-lhomme/, accessed 18 January 2016.

Labayle, Henri, 'Droit d'asile et confiance mutuelle : regard critique sur la jurisprudence européenne' (2014). 50 *Cahiers de droit européen*, 501–534.

Le Petit Robert (2012). Dictionary Le Robert, Paris.

Marguénaud, Jean-Pierre and Mouly, Jean, 'Le Comité européen des droits sociaux face au principe de non-régression en temps de crise économique' (2013). *Droit social*, 346.

Milano, Laure, 'Garanties du procès équitable et lutte contre le terrorisme' (2015). *Revue des Droits et Libertés Fondamentaux, No.* 7; http://www.revuedlf.com/cedh/garanties-du-proces-equitable-et-lutte-contre-le-terrorisme/, accessed 18 January 2016.

Ribes, Didier, 'La Constitution, combien ça coûte?' (2008). *Nouveaux cahiers du Conseil Constitutionnel*, No. 24.

Sarmas, Ioannis, 'Les 60 ans de la Convention européenne des droits de l'homme – spécificités nationales: le cas grec' (2010). 254 *Les Petites Affiches* 44.

Sarmas, Ioannis, *The Greek Crisis and the Role of Audit* (Ant. N. Sakkoulas Publishers 2012).

Sarmas, Ioannis, 'Implementing the European Convention on Human Rights in time of economic crisis', background paper (2013).

Soulier, Gerard, 'Lutte contre le terrorisme', in Mireille Delmas-Marty (ed.), *Raisonner la Raison d'Etat* (PUF 1989).

Sudre, Frédéric, *Droit international et européen des droits de l'homme* (12th edn, PUF, 2015).

Tinière, Romain, 'L'externalisation des contrôles migratoires et les juridictions européennes – 1ère partie' (2012). *Revue des Droits et Libertés Fondamentaux*, No. 8; http://www.revuedlf.com/droit-ue/lexternalisation-des-controles-migratoires-et-les-juridictions-europeennes-1ere-partie-lexternalisation-en-europe/, accessed 18 January 2016.

Tulkens, Françoise, 'La Convention européenne des droits de l'homme et la crise économique. La question de la pauvreté' (2013). *Journal européen des droits de l'homme, 1*, 8.

Weyembergh, Anne, 'L'impact du 11 septembre sur l'équilibre sécurité/liberté dans l'espace pénal européen', in Emmanuelle Bribosia and Anne Weyembergh (eds), *Lutte contre le terrorisme et droits fondamentaux* (Bruylant, 2002) 119.

16 The crisis, judicial power and EU law

Could it have been managed differently by the EU Court of Justice?

Márton Varju

This chapter examines the contribution of the EU Court of Justice – affecting both the European and the national level – in addressing the challenges and the consequences of the global financial and economic crisis. It assesses the treatment in the jurisdiction exercised by the Court of legal claims posed against the EU mechanisms adopted to manage the crisis and of claims advanced in the context of local pressures arising from the crisis. Its main contention is that the Court of Justice – an influential institutional actor in the EU political arena – could have engaged with the crisis and its consequences in a different manner. The contrasting judicial approaches followed in different cases reveal that the socio-economic impact of the crisis on individuals and the rights and interests of individuals could have been given a different treatment in the judgments, which – by providing a close reading of the applicable legal provisions – ultimately confirmed the political consensus developed at the European level concerning the management of the crisis.

The present chapter is structured as follows. It first examines the nature of EU judicial power and the related question of whether the EU Court of Justice can be expected to engage with the pressures and the dilemmas that may arise from the socio-economic context of its operation. This provides the basis of the ensuing analysis of the Court's recent crisis-related jurisprudence which emerged in two distinct domains. Firstly, the judgments delivered in the judicial review of EU (European) measures adopted in order to manage certain causes or consequences of the crisis are examined. Secondly, a scrutiny of the jurisprudence dealing with developments at the level of the Member States is provided, which sheds new light on the controversies of the Court's contribution to the management of the effects of the crisis, especially those arising at the level of the individual.

1. The crisis as a context and the Court of Justice

The current financial and economic crisis put significant pressure on and confronted with heavy dilemmas the European economic system and the European and national regimes of socio-economic governance. The management of the crisis involved – among others – the introduction of support measures addressed to states in financial difficulties, the active use of monetary policy instruments to secure financial and economic stability, the adoption of bailout measures and state aid in support of failing industries or individual economic operators, and a strong political commitment to a policy of fiscal constraint (sound budgetary policies).[1] For European societies and individuals, the crisis brought with itself an economic meltdown, collapsing public finances, skyrocketing public debt, shrinking employment opportunities, social deregulation, reduced access to welfare and to public services, social deprivation and cost of living and private debt crises, and intensifying internal and external economic migration.[2] While responses were expected predominantly from the political process and from governance, the legal issues of the crisis and its management, and with them its pressures and dilemmas, eventually found their way to national and European judicial forums, including the European Court of Justice, and provoked their involvement.[3]

Addressing matters of economic and monetary policy and public finances, and engagement with the consequences of economic and social changes, are not evident tasks of the judiciary.[4] The same holds true for judicial power addressing politically and socially highly charged cross-border developments, such as the stability of the common European currency, the implementation of sound fiscal policy by each Member State government, or the management of the local consequences of intra-EU economic migration.[5] In these domains, courts are expected to respect the decisions made in the political process (defer to legislative intent) and to discharge their functions, especially their review and control functions, on the basis of a close reading of the applicable legal provisions. However, within the bounds of their competences and in the judicial function bestowed upon them, it is not excluded that the judiciary engages more intensively with the socio-economic context of the applicable legal rules. The declared policy and other objectives of those rules and broadly formulated general principles of law, especially those which provide protection to individuals and their rights, can enable more expansive judicial approaches.[6]

In the case of the EU Court of Justice, the expectation that in the exercise of its powers the context of legal rules and the rights of individuals may play a defining role looks back on decades of such previous practices.[7] The discourse on the Court as a relevant institutional actor in the EU political arena committed to advance the agenda of European integration positioned specifically the Court as an institution which is prepared to understand its judicial function broadly.[8] In a similar vein, the literature on the activism of the Court and the related practices of judicial interpretation presented the EU Court of Justice as an actor that is aware of the purpose of the broader context provided by European integration and the particular objectives pursued.[9] The EU Court of Justice has, however, also been associated with a strong tradition of legal formalism which as opposed to judicial engagement with the context and an expansive judicial involvement in the protection of individuals stood for a more restricted judicial approach whereby the Court's contribution to European integration was restricted to emphasizing the legal nature of the obligations undertaken by the Member States and arguing for an effective implementation and enforcement of those obligations.[10]

With this background, the scope for the Court's engagement with the challenges and the consequences of the crisis seems fairly limited. The policy domains affected – monetary policy, economic policy and fiscal policy – allow only a limited room for judicial interference which can be reduced even further by the detailed legal regulation of policy objectives, the of synergies between those objectives, and of powers and instruments made available for the implementation of the policies in question. Challenges at the political level, such as cross-border tensions between different Member States, local political pressures and demands, or the impact of political decisions at the level of individuals are also shielded from judicial intervention. A more constructive judicial involvement is, however, not excluded. The objectives of the applicable legal measure may enable the Court to enhance the protection available to individuals in the context of the management of the crisis. The same may follow from broadly formulated principles of law, which may be codified as in case of the fundamental rights protected in the EU Charter of Fundamental Rights (hereinafter, the EU Charter). Judicial powers thus exercised can be readily contrasted to a judicial approach which closely follows political intent and that interprets policy objectives and the relevant legal rules close to the wording of the legal text.

The dilemma of whether to engage in the jurisprudence with significantly deteriorating social and economic conditions is not new to the EU Court of Justice. In the wake of the global economic crisis of the late 1970s, it was confronted by the measures adopted by the EEC and the Member States in response to the crisis, and the exercise of its review powers was criticised by commentators on the basis of expectations that it would enable the Court to 'play its part in the search for remedies to the evils which beset their contemporaries'.[11] Among others, they wanted the Court to revisit areas of its case law which reduce Member State policy-making opportunities, place more emphasis on areas of law which enhance the protection of individuals, such as social or consumer protection, and, in general, to use its review powers constructively taking into account industry needs in times of an economic meltdown. The Court, however, never lived up to these expectations. It continued with the strict enforcement of Member State obligations and its review powers were used within their normal legal bounds.

2. EU (European) crisis measures and the Court of Justice

For individuals, the powers available to national courts and the EU Court of Justice presented practically the only effective means for influencing post-crisis European political processes and socio-economic governance. The legal claims advanced contesting the lawfulness of EU (European) crisis management measures aimed at ensuring that the Union and the Member States stay within the boundaries of the competences available for common monetary and economic governance. At the level of the individual, not only the low democratic credentials of decision-making emerged as problematic, but also the issue that the instruments adopted focused solely on the common objectives and their synergies determined in the Treaties.[12] The Court's treatment of these claims confirmed in effect that other avenues for crisis-management following alternative policy directions are not available in Europe.

In *Pringle*,[13] which concerned the legality under EU law of the ESM (European Stability Mechanism) Treaty, the Court made it clear that the Member States were not prevented from taking governance responses to the crisis outside of the EU political and legal framework. The bottom-line exposed by the judgment was that the bailout of euro-zone Member States by the other Member States, which is subject to the condition that the economic policy changes required by the EU are implemented, cannot be criticised under EU law because it observes the synergies established in the Treaties between the policies affected and because it separates in law adequately and effectively the parallel policy areas.[14] In this connection, as recognised by the Court, the circumstance that the bailout mechanism is organised outside of the EU in the international arena had no relevance.[15] In delivering its legal conclusions, the judgment placed significant emphasis on EU law recognising the general objective of sound national budgetary polices,[16] which enabled not only a light-touch judicial review of the political decision to tie the bailout of Member States to implementing economic policy changes at the national level but also that judicial reasoning did not have to consider the actual impact of the ESM on individual Member States – neither at a societal level, nor at the level of the individual.

The judgment, which read closely the objectives pursued by the measures in question under the relevant competences regulated in the Treaties,[17] was evidently unprepared to pursue the more broadly framed legal claims. The claim under Article 4(3) the Treaty on European Union (TEU) was rejected on the grounds that the ESM does not violate the relevant provisions of EU law and that there are sufficient legal guarantees that the operation of the ESM will comply with EU law,[18] which can be criticised for providing a rather restrained judicial reading of the loyalty principle. The alleged violation of the right to effective judicial protection, also provided in Article 47 of the EU Charter, was rebutted having regard to the horizontal provisions of the Charter which determine its scope of application.[19] With this judicial solution, the Court avoided a thorough assessment of situations in which judicial protection under EU law within the scope of the ESM may have to be provided to individuals.

The Court held with rigour[20] that the ESM mechanism cannot violate the relevant Treaty provisions as it does not relieve the Member State concerned of its responsibilities towards its creditors or provide a guarantee for the debts of the recipient Member State.[21] It was satisfied that the limited availability of assistance and the requirement of strict conditionality requiring the implementation of an economic policy programme by the Member State concerned ensure that assistance under the ESM does not undermine the sound national budgetary policy and the related financial stability objectives under the EMU framework.[22] Following a close reading of the relevant legal provisions, it rejected that the ESM Treaty would unlawfully affect the relevant EU rules or amend their scope.[23] It, thus, concluded that neither the objective of providing Union financial assistance to a Member State facing difficulties as expressed in Article 122(2) Treaty on the Functioning of the European Union (TFEU), nor the ability of the EU to exercise its competences 'in the common interests' are jeopardised with the adoption of the ESM Treaty.[24]

In the judgment in *Gauweiler*,[25] which concerned the challenge before the German Constitutional Court against decisions adopted under the OMT (Outright Monetary Transactions) programme of the European Central Bank (ECB), the reasoning of the Court indicated that there was no issue of arguing for a crisis-management response which would have balanced the relevant interests differently or have taken into account other interests. As in *Pringle*, the case turned on the Court confirming on the basis of the Treaties that there were obvious policy synergies – those between the monetary policy objectives and the objective of sound budgetary policies – which were duly exploited by the relevant policy instruments that involved the implementation of economic policy reforms at the national level. The ultimate conclusion was that as a matter of legal interpretation following closely the objectives of the relevant legal provisions the OMT decisions cannot be regarded as instruments of monetary financing, nor of economic policy.

The Court addressed the central legal issue of whether the 'no monetary financing clause' under Art. 123 TFEU precluded the financial assistance offered under the OMT programme by providing a close reading of that provision. It held that while providing financial assistance by the ECB to a Member State is prohibited, the purchasing in the open market from creditors of Member State bonds previously issued by that state is not excluded under EU law.[26] In supporting this argument, the Court referred to the nature of open market purchasing operations and the objective pursued by them.[27] This latter was determined by the Court on the basis of the objectives laid down in EU law for Art.123 TFEU which is to encourage the Member States to follow a sound budgetary policy and to avoid using the ECB to finance public deficits or to provide privileged financing for the Member States.[28]

The safeguards regulated in law for the OMT mechanism to prevent the violation of the monetary financing clause were central to the Court's scrutiny.[29] The judgment produced a lengthy list of direct and indirect safeguards and other legal guarantees[30] and dismissed claims that the OMT programme would lessen the impetus for the Member States to follow a sound budgetary policy.[31] As in *Pringle*, it argued in this regard that the financial assistance available is bound in legal regulation to purposes specific to EU monetary policy, such as safeguarding the monetary policy transmission mechanism and protecting the singleness of monetary policy.

The question of whether the operation of the OMT programme concerns monetary policy and falls within EU competences was settled following a similar judicial reading of the relevant legal provisions. In the absence of a Treaty-based definition, the Court relied on the objectives and instruments provided in the Treaties to define the scope of EU monetary policy[32] and referred, specifically in connection with the OMT programme, to the content of the relevant press release which associated the OMT mechanism with explicit monetary policy objectives.[33] Based on the interpretation provided (and the interpretative approach followed) in *Pringle*, the Court also ruled that the conditionality regulated for the implementation of the OMT programme requiring the adoption of economic policy correction measures under the relevant EU frameworks cannot alone render the

OMT decisions in question falling outside the scope of EU monetary policy.[34] It pointed to the inevitable policy synergies as expressed by EU law; namely, that the conditionality requirement is available to ensure that the implementation of monetary policy does not undermine the effective implementation of economic policies in the Member States and that conditionality is necessary to give effect to the parallel legally recognized objective that the Member States follow a sound budgetary policy.[35]

As opposed to the judgment in *Pringle*, the Court engaged in a detailed scrutiny of claims based on broadly framed principles of EU law; here, the principle of proportionality regulated under Art. 5(4) TEU. This, however, did not entail a different approach to judicial interpretation in the case as the appropriateness of the OMT programme to achieve the objectives of EU monetary policy was assessed on the basis of the provisions laid down in the relevant documents, such as the earlier mentioned press release.[36] The Court also deferred to the expert assessment carried out by the ECB when it accepted that the economic analysis produced prior to the adoption of the OMT decisions under scrutiny was prepared 'with all care and accuracy' and without a manifest error.[37] As regards the suitability of the instruments, it was ready to accept that they reduced the risks which were capable of jeopardising the stability of the Euro area.[38] The explanations provided in the press release also proved to be crucial in the Court declining that the OMT decisions were excessive[39] and that the state bonds affected by the intervention would have been selected in an arbitrary manner.[40]

3. The crisis at the national level and the Court of Justice

The engagement of the Court of Justice with crisis-related developments in the Member States in some respects resembles that experienced in connection with European crisis management measures. However, some of the rulings, where the immediate legal environment enabled the Court to take recognition of the rights and interests of the individuals affected, indicate that an alternative judicial approach may be available in addressing the consequences of the crisis. Although the judgments analysed below were adopted in different legal and factual settings, the strong contrast between the different interpretative routes followed, especially when compared with the judgments in *Pringle* and *Gauweiler* above, suggest that the Court of Justice may indeed be equipped to assess in law the socio-economic impact of the crisis, primarily those affecting individuals. The difference was essentially that in one group of cases the broadly formulated legal principle in question – EU citizenship – was interpreted narrowly following the relevant legislative provisions closely and in the other the broadly framed principles – the protection of consumers and the protection of fundamental rights – gave way to a reading of the law which in effect internalised the impact of the crisis on individuals.

The ruling in *Dano*,[41] which concerned the social entitlements of EU citizens in the host Member State, produced a controversial, nonetheless, legally formally justifiable engagement by the Court of Justice with what is essentially poverty-driven intra-EU migration.[42] The judgment, which read the applicable legislative provisions closely and generally correctly,[43] refused to consider – on the basis of the politico-legal concept of EU citizenship – whether under EU law the Member States – individually and collectively – have responsibility towards the citizens of other Member States beyond that legislated for the economically active and for those with sufficient means.[44] By dutifully following the relevant distinctions laid down in the applicable EU rules and in the implementing national measures, the Court confirmed the prerogative of the Member States to differentiate as a matter of rights and social entitlements between EU migrants on the basis of the particular set of factors laid down in law, which may not include those which made the individual concerned to emigrate from his/her home Member State.[45]

In the Court's reading, EU citizenship was reduced to the right to non-discrimination on grounds of nationality,[46] which was then interpreted and applied exclusively in the light of the provisions of the applicable EU legislation.[47] It emphasised that while the non-discrimination principle applies to social assistance provided by the Member States, the entitlements following therefrom are subject to derogations.[48] The judgment pointed out that the right to non-discrimination in regards social assistance applies only to persons who are covered by the personal scope of the applicable EU legislation, which meant in practice that the particular entitlement which follows from EU citizenship was reserved for a narrower cohort of persons, mainly for the economically active.[49] The claim based on the EU Charter was rejected just as in *Pringle* on the basis of the horizontal provisions (Article 51), the Court arguing that the case concerned Member State action outside the scope of EU law.[50] This seems like a particularly narrow interpretation of what constitutes the implementation of EU law by the Member States[51] which, however, is consistent with the narrow interpretative approach followed in the judgment that led to a reduced legal construction of EU citizenship.[52]

In *Alimanovic*,[53] another controversial case concerning the social entitlements of EU migrants in the host Member State, the Court reaffirmed the interpretative approach followed in *Dano*.[54] Firstly, it established on the basis of the applicable EU legislation that the benefits in question constituted 'social assistance' in the meaning of EU law intended to cover the subsistence costs for persons who cannot meet those costs themselves.[55] This meant that the entitlement of citizens of other Member States for such benefits depended on their qualifying as EU citizens as a matter of the rights provided under EU law. In this regard, the judgment confirmed the principle clarified in *Dano* that the equal treatment of Union nationals – in the social domain – depends foremost on whether their residence in the host Member State is lawful as a matter of EU law.[56] It held that the rights enjoyed by EU citizens must be defined with reference to the applicable EU legislation (the EU Citizenship Directive)[57,58] which position clearly reflects the political understanding shared among Member State governments and expressed in EU legislation that the citizens of other Member States cannot become an unreasonable social burden for the host Member State.[59] The judgment, thus, deprived the equal treatment principle and EU citizenship of their legal relevance as general principles of law capable of guaranteeing rights and imposing obligations independent from the rights and obligations laid down in the detailed provisions of EU legislation.[60]

The judicial approach followed in these judgments must be contrasted with that emerging in a series of cases concerning – in the context of local real-estate market and banking crises in Southern and Eastern Europe – the unfairness of mortgage agreements and the lawfulness of their enforcement under EU law. While the immediate legal environment of these cases under EU law, which involved the interpretation and application of broadly framed legal principles rather than detailed EU legislation, is different from that of the earlier EU citizenship cases, the judgments demonstrate the potential inherent in the bolder judicial assessment of general principles of EU law, especially when the rights and interests of individuals are at stake. The Court, relying on the principles laid down in the relevant EU directives, argued for the expansive reading of the protection available for individuals under those measures, and it was also prepared to engage with broadly framed provisions of EU law, such as the rights protected in the EU Charter, so as to give expression to the social context of the legal disputes dealing with the repossession and the loss of family homes.

The early judgment in *Aziz*[61] concerning the lawfulness of the Spanish procedural environment[62] in which the unfairness of the mortgage contract being enforced was claimed set the tone for the jurisprudence. Having established the protection of consumers as the central objective of the applicable EU legislation (Directive 93/13/EC),[63] the Court – on the basis of the general principles of EU law concerning national procedures and remedies – condemned the national procedural environment and the capacities of the institutional actors operating therein as failing to provide adequate opportunities for individuals to raise the unfairness of contractual terms.[64] The judgment found reinforcement for its conclusion in the circumstance that the mortgaged property in question was the 'family home of the consumer' and the damage inflicted upon the consumer by national procedural law would have caused the 'definitive and irreversible loss of that dwelling'.[65]

A similar procedural shortcoming in Spanish law was the subject-matter of the judgment in *Morcillo*,[66] where the different availability for consumers and for sellers or suppliers of legal remedies in mortgage enforcement procedures was claimed to violate EU law. Starting from the same interpretative premise as in *Aziz* concerning the objective of consumer protection,[67] the judgment held that taking into account especially the principles which 'lie at the basis of the national legal system', such as the rights of the defence, legal certainty and the proper conduct of judicial procedures, and having regard to the right to effective judicial protection secured under Article 47 of the EU Charter,[68] national law provided insufficient protection to the consumer as a matter of the rights derived from Directive 93/13/EC.[69]

In the judgment in *Kásler*,[70] the Court ruled on the substantive question relating to the unfairness of the contractual terms in question[71] as well as the issues concerning the general procedural environment of the domestic case. This was achieved with the ruling ultimately favouring a very large consumer cohort, which had taken out loans from domestic banks in a foreign currency, affected by a significant depreciation of the domestic currency during the crisis. The judgment made it clear that the requirement under Article 4(2) of Directive 93/13/EC that a contractual term must be drafted in plain intelligible language entails that the relevant economic specifications (the 'economic consequences' which follow from the contractual term for the consumer) must be described in a transparent manner.[72] In particular, consumers must be informed in sufficient detail of the functioning of the mechanism of conversion for the foreign currency in which the loan is provided to the local currency and of the relationship between that mechanism and that provided for by other contractual terms relating to the advance of the loan.

The same judicial approach focusing on the objective of providing a high level of consumer protection and the right to effective judicial protection[73] as provided by the EU Charter led to confirming the lawfulness of the contested national rule in *Kušionová*.[74] The Court found that adequately regulated national procedures operating with reasonable procedural time-limits and offering effective protection to the rights of the affected parties, for example by providing sufficient powers to the court proceeding in the case to safeguard the rights of consumers, are compatible with EU law.[75] Providing protection against the loss of a dwelling (a 'family home'), which was interpreted as capable of not only seriously undermining consumer rights, but also placing the family of the consumer concerned in a particularly vulnerable position,[76] again played a crucial role in judicial interpretation determining the level of protection which must be provided by national law. The judgment relied extensively on the applicable fundamental rights principles as provided in ECHR and EU law,[77] and it concluded ultimately that the protection of the principal family home required in particular that interim protection must be available with a view to ensuring the effectiveness of the protection provided to consumers under EU law.[78]

4. Conclusions

This chapter analysed the engagement of the EU Court of Justice, within the jurisdiction available to it and in the context of the cases brought before it, with European and national measures adopted to manage the crisis and also with the socio-economic consequences of the crisis, especially those emerging at the level of the individual. In the judgments examined, the prevalent judicial approach followed was to read the relevant legal provisions as closely as possible and, thus, to give effect to the intent of the legislator and respect the intergovernmental political compromise expressed in law. The broadly framed principles of EU law, such as fundamental rights or EU citizenship, which would have enabled the Court to offer a more engaging assessment of the impact of the crisis, played only a residual role. There were, however, evident instances of the EU Court of Justice taking notice of the particular socio-economic context of the crisis and ensuring that its consequences for individuals are duly appreciated within the available legal frameworks. This latter development suggests that the EU judiciary had choices in developing its responses to the crisis.

Notes

1 IMF (2009); OECD (2009).
2 Habermas (2012); Schweiger (2014).
3 On the Hungarian Constitutional Court's engagement of the crisis, see Varju and Chronowski (2015) and Chronowski and Varju (2016).
4 See, inter alia, Sólyom (1994); Sajó (1996); Tushnet (1999); Goldmann (2014).
5 See Kelemen (2001); Schmidt and Kelemen (2013).
6 See, inter alia, Bickel (1962); Ackerman (1991); Allan (1994); Tremblay (2003). In the context of the euro-crisis, Fabbrini (2014); Fahey and Bardutzky (2013).
7 For a comprehensive analysis, see Weiler (1991).
8 Burley and Mattli (1993); Mattli and Slaughter (1995); Garrett (1995); Garrett, Kelemen and Schulz (1998); Stone-Sweet (2004).
9 See Tridimas (1996); Conway (2012); Beck (2012); Dawson, de Witte and Muir (2013).
10 Weiler (2012). See also Barents (2004); Williams (2010); Dickson (2012).
11 Mertens de Wilmars and Steenbergen (1984).
12 For a critical account of these legal developments and the judgments below, see de Witte and Beukers (2013); Craig (2013); Schwarz (2014); Hinajeros (2015).
13 Case C-370/12 *Pringle* EU:C:2012:756.
14 See *Pringle* (n 13) paras 110–113, 125–126.
15 Contrast with a more hostile treatment under EU law in *Kadi* (Joined Cases C-402/05 P and C-415/05 P *Kadi* EU:C:2008:461) of developments in the international arena when they interfere with, and not enhance as in case of the ESM Treaty, the effectiveness of EU action.
16 The objective was not tested substantively or explained what it may entail, but was used as a generic legal label so as to confirm that the bailout of the Member States can legitimately come with demands for concrete policy changes at the national level. Nonetheless, the Court was correct to reach the concluding argument that the mechanisms in place do not affect the responsibility of the Member State concerned for its debts.
17 The claim based on the violation of the 'no monetary bail out clause' under Article 125 The Treaty on the Functioning of the European Union was rejected on the ground that having regard to the objectives of maintaining budgetary discipline in the Member States and of maintaining the financial stability of the monetary union financial assistance granted by the EU or by the Member States, which prompts the implementation of sound monetary policy in the Member State concerned and does not affect its commitment to remain responsible towards its creditors, is acceptable under EU law, *Pringle* (n 13) paras 130–137.
18 Ibid para 151.
19 Ibid paras 179–180.
20 It made it clear at the outset on the basis of the relevant legal provisions that the ESM does not concern EU monetary policy and, in fact, monetary policy objectives, ibid paras 95–96, and rejected an expansive reading of the relevant Treaty provisions and rejected that any instrument which has an effect on price stability would be covered by them, ibid para. 97.
21 Ibid paras 138–141. See also ibid paras 144–146 concerning the rules of capital calls addressed to the Member States under the ESM.
22 Ibid paras 142–143.
23 Ibid paras 100–105.
24 Ibid para 106.
25 Case C-62/14 *Peter Gauweiler and Others v Deutscher Bundestag* EU:C:2015:400.
26 Ibid para 95.
27 Ibid paras 96–98, it cannot have an "effect equivalent to that of a direct purchase of government bonds".

28 Ibid paras 99–101.
29 Ibid paras 102–111.
30 Ibid paras 116–120.
31 Ibid paras 112–115.
32 Ibid paras 42–46 and 53–55.
33 Ibid paras 47–49. Basically, according to the Court there was an obvious connection between the specific objectives of the OMT programme and the general objectives of EU monetary policy, see para 50.
34 Ibid paras 57–59, 62–65.
35 Ibid paras 60–61.
36 Ibid paras 71–73.
37 Ibid paras 74–75
38 Ibid paras 76–78.
39 Ibid paras 81–82. The Court again made a list of safeguards which put limits to the implementation of the OMT programme, see paras 83–88.
40 Ibid para 90.
41 Case C-333/13 *Dano* EU:C:2014:2358.
42 For criticism, see Thym (2015); Verschueren (2015); Nic Shubine (2015); O'Brien (2016).
43 *Dano* (n 41) paras 46–54.
44 Ibid para 81 made it clear that only these categories of EU citizens are provided a right of residence in another Member State under EU law and, thus, a right to non-discrimination.
45 The central conclusion was that economically inactive EU citizens cannot use the welfare system of the host Member State 'to fund their means of subsistence', ibid para 76.
46 Ibid paras 57–61.
47 Ibid para 62.
48 Ibid paras 63–64.
49 Ibid paras 65–72, 73–75. The only concession allowed was that the assessment whether the person concerned has sufficient resources to qualify for a right of residence in the host Member State must be carried out on a case-by-case basis, ibid para. 80.
50 Ibid paras 86–89 (the laying down in their own competences the conditions for vindicating the right to social assistance).
51 Contrast with the interpretation provided in Case C-617/10 *Fransson* EU:C:2013:280.
52 An alternative interpretation of EU citizenship which would have taken into account factors other than those specified in EU legislation as relevant (e.g., the personal causes of migration) would have meant that national legislation affecting these factors may fall under the scope of the Charter.
53 Case C-67/14 *Jobcenter Berlin Neukölln v Nazifa Alimanovic and Others* EU:C:2015:597.
54 For a critical analysis, see Iliopoulou-Penot (2016); O'Brien (2016).
55 *Alimanovic* (n 53) paras 43–44. It covers the minimum subsistence costs necessary to lead a life 'in keeping with human dignity', paras. 45–46.
56 Ibid para 49.
57 Directive 2004/38/EC OJ L158/77.
58 See, in particular, in ibid paras 52–54 concerning the rights of job seekers and in paras 59–62 concerning the assessment of whether the person concerned places an unreasonable burden on the local social assistance system.
59 Ibid para 50.
60 See ibid para 51.
61 Case C-415/11 *Mohamed Aziz v Caixa d'Estalvis de Catalunya, Tarragona i Manresa (Catalunyacaixa)* EU:C:2013:164. See also Order in Joined Cases C-537/12 and C-116/13 *Banco Popular Español SA v Maria Teodolinda Rivas Quichimbo and Wilmar Edgar Cun Pérez and Banco de Valencia SA v Joaquín Valldeperas Tortosa and María Ángeles Miret Jaume* EU:C:2013:759.

62 Contrast with the outcome in Case C-280/13 *Barclays Bank SA v Sara Sánchez García and Alejandro Chacón Barrera* EU:C:2014:279, paras 38–45.
63 Directive 93/13/EC on unfair terms in consumer contracts, OJ L95/29.
64 *Aziz* (n 61) paras. 44–60.
65 Ibid para 61.
66 Case C-169/14 *Juan Carlos Sánchez Morcillo and María del Carmen Abril García v Banco Bilbao Vizcaya Argentaria SA* EU:C:2014:2099. See further Case C-8/14 *BBVA SA v Pedro Peñalva López and Others* EU:C:2015:731; Order in Case C-342/13 *Katalin Sebestyén v Zsolt Csaba Kővári and Others* EU:C:2014:1857; Joined Cases C-381/14 and C-385/14 *Jorge Sales Sinués and Youssouf Drame Ba v Caixabank SA and Catalunya Caixa SA (Catalunya Banc S.A.)* EU:C:2016:252; *BPE* (n 61); C-618/10 *Banco Español de Crédito SA v Joaquín Calderón Camino* EU:C:2012:349; Case C-49/14 *Finanmadrid EFC SA v Jesús Vicente Albán Zambrano and Others* EU:C:2016:98; Joined Cases C-482/13, C-484/13, C-485/13 and C-487/13 *Unicaja Banco, SA v José Hidalgo Rueda and Others and Caixabank SA v Manuel María Rueda Ledesma and Others* EU:C:2015:21; Case C-76/10 *Pohotovos⊠ s.r.o. v Iveta Korčkovská* EU:C:2010:685.
67 *Morcillo* (n 66) paras 22–24.
68 The Charter's applicability was not contested under the horizontal provisions as the case concerned the application of Directive 93/13/EC.
69 *Morcillo* (n 66) paras 31–47. The fundamental rights aspect of the decision was further reinforced with a reference to the principle of equality of arms, and, thus, to the right to a fair hearing, which led to the Court establishing that the incomplete and inadequate national provisions had failed to provide equal protection to the rights of the consumer, on the one hand, and the rights of the seller or supplier, on the other, paras 47–50.
70 Case C-26/13 *Árpád Kásler and Hajnalka Káslerné Rábai v OTP Jelzálogbank Zrt* EU:C:2014:282.
71 See further *Aziz* (n 61) paras 73–75; *Rueda* (n 66) para. 43; *Pohotovos⊠* (n 66) para 63; Case C-34/13 *Monika Kušionová v SMART Capital, a.s.* EU:C:2014:2189, paras 70–80.
72 *Kásler* (n 70) paras 61–75. See also *Pohotovos⊠* (n 66) paras 44–53, 65–76.
73 As in the cases above, the law on national procedures and remedies provided the framework of assessment, see *Kušionová* (n 71) para 50.
74 *Kušionová* (n 71) para 68, the national measure must make the protection of the rights of consumers excessively difficult or impossible in practice.
75 Ibid paras 55–61.
76 Ibid paras 62–63.
77 Ibid paras 64–65. The judgment referred explicitly to the relevant Strasbourg jurisprudence concerning the right to respect for the home and the loss of a home, para. 64.
78 Ibid para 66, with reference to *Aziz* (n 61).

Bibliography

Ackerman, Bruce, *We the People: Volume 1. Foundations* (Harvard University Press 1991).

Allan, T.R.S., *Law, Liberty, and Justice* (Clarendon 1994).

Barents, Rene, *The Autonomy of Community Law* (Kluwer 2004).

Beck, Gunnar, *The Legal Reasoning of the Court of Justice of the EU* (Hart Publishing 2012).

Bickel, Alexander M., *The Least Dangerous Branch* (Yale University Press 1962).

Burley, Anne-Marie and Mattli, Walter, 'Europe before the Court: A Political Theory of Legal Integration' (1993). 47 *International Organization* 41–46.

Chronowski, Nóra and Varju, Márton, 'Two Eras of Constitutionalism in Hungary' (2016). 8 *The Hague Journal on the Rule of Law* 271–289.

Conway, Gerard, *The Limits of Legal Reasoning and the European Court of Justice* (CUP 2012).

Craig, Paul, 'Guest Editorial: Pringle: Legal Reasoning, Text, Purpose and Teleology' (2013). 20 *Maastricht Journal of European and Comparative Law* 3–11.

Dawson, Mark, de Witte, Bruno and Muir, Elise (eds), *Judicial Activism at the European Court of Justice* (Elgar 2013).

Dickson, Julie, 'Towards a Theory of European Union Legal Systems', in Julie Dickson and Pavlov Eleftheriadis (eds), *The Philosophical Foundations of EU Law* (OUP 2012).

Fabbrini, Frederico, 'The Euro-Crisis and the Courts: Judicial Review and the Political Process in Comparative Perspective' (2014). 32 *Berkeley Journal of International Law* 64–123.

Fahey, Elaineand Bardutzky, Samo, 'Judicial Review of Eurozone Law: The Adjudication of Postnational Norms in the EU Courts, Plural – A Case Study of the European Stability Mechanism' (2013). *Michigan Journal of International Law* (MJIL Emerging Scholarship Project) 101.

Garrett, Geoffrey, 'The Politics of Legal Integration in the European Union' (1995). 49 *International Organisation* 171–181.

Garrett, Geoffry, Kelemen, Daniel and Schulz, Heiner, 'The European Court of Justice, National Governments and Legal Integration in the European Union' (1998). 52 *International Organization* 149–176.

Goldmann, Matthias, 'Adjudicating Economics? Central Bank Independence and the Appropriate Standard of Judicial Review' (2014). 15 *German Law Journal* 265–280.

Habermas, Jürgen, *The Crisis of the European Union* (Polity 2012).

Hinajeros, Alicia, *The Euro Area Crisis in Constitutional Perspective* (OUP 2015).

Iliopoulou-Penot, Anastasia, 'Deconstructing the Former Edifice of Union Citizenship? The Alimanovic Judgment' (2016). 53 *Common Market Law Review* 1007–1036.

IMF, *Global Financial Stability Report: Responding to the Financial Crisis and Measuring Systemic Risks* (International Monetary Fund, 2009).

Kelemen, Daniel, 'The Limits of Judicial Power: Trade-Environment Disputes in the GATT/WTO and the EU' (2001). 34 *Comparative Political Studies* 622–650.

Mattli, Walter and Slaughter, Anne-Marie, 'Law and Politics in the European Union: A Reply to Garrett' (1995). 49 *International Organization* 183–190.

Mertens de Wilmars, J. and Steenbergen, J., 'The Court of Justice of the European Communities and Governance in an Economic Crisis' (1984). 82 *Michigan Law Review* 1377–1398.

Nic Shuibne, Niamh, 'Limits Rising, Duties Ascending: The Changing Legal Shape of Union Citizenship' (2015). 52 *Common Market Law Review* 889–938.

O'Brien, Charlotte R., 'Civis Capitalist Sum: Class as the New Guiding Principle of EU Free Movement Rights' (2016). 53 *Common Market Law Review* 937–978.

OECD, *Responding to the Economic Crisis* (OECD, 2009).

Sajó, András, 'How the Rule of Law Killed Hungarian Welfare Reform' (1996). 5 *East European Constitutional Review* 31–41.

Schmidt, Susanne K. and Kelemen, Daniel (eds), *The Power of the European Court of Justice* (Routledge 2013).

Schwarz, Michael, 'A Memorandum of Misunderstanding – The Doomed Road of the European Stability Mechanism and a Possible Way Out: Enhanced Cooperation' (2014). 51 *Common Market Law Review* 389–424.

Schweiger, Christian, *The EU and the Global Financial Crisis* (Elgar 2014).
Sólyom, László, 'The Hungarian Constitutional Court and Social Change' (1994). 19 *Yale Journal of International Law* 223–237.
Stone-Sweet, Alec, *The Judicial Construction of Europe* (OUP 2004).
Thym, Daniel, 'The Elusive Limits of Solidarity: Residence Rights of and Social Benefits for Economically Inactive Union Citizens' (2015). 52 *Common Market Law Review* 17–50.
Tremblay, Luc B., 'General Legitimacy of Judicial Review and the Fundamental Basis of Constitutional Law' (2003). 23 *Oxford Journal of Legal Studies* 525–562.
Tridimas, Takis, 'The Court of Justice and Judicial Activism' (1996). 21 *European Law Review* 199.
Tushnet, Mark, *Taking the Constitution away from the Courts* (Princeton University Press 1999).
Varju, Marton and Chronowski, Nóra, 'Constitutional Backsliding in Hungary' (2015). 6 *Tijdschrift Voor Constitutioneel Recht* 296–310.
Verschueren, Herwig, 'Preventing "Benefit Tourism" in the EU: A Narrow or Broad Interpretation of the Possibilities Offered by the ECJ in Dano?' (2015). 52 *Common Market Law Review* 363–390.
Weiler, John H.H., 'The Transformation of Europe'. (1991) 100 *Yale Law Journal* 2403–2483.
Weiler John, H.H., 'Deciphering the Political and Legal DNA of European Integration: An Exploratory Essay', in J. Dickson and P. Eleftheriadis (eds), *The Philosophical Foundations of EU Law* (OUP 2012).
Williams, Andrew, *The Ethos of Europe* (CUP 2010).
de Witte, Bruno and Beukers, Thomas, 'The Court of Justice Approves the Creation of the European Stability Mechanism Outside the EU Legal Order: Pringle' (2013). 50 *Common Market Law Review* 805–848.

Part IV

Constitutional courts under pressure – A European comparison

17 Constitutional courts under pressure – An assessment

Zoltán Szente and Fruzsina Gárdos-Orosz

Introduction

If we look at the legal systems of the countries discussed in this book, many doubts can be raised as to whether any comparison may be made between them. They operate in different constitutional contexts, they belong to different legal cultures, and they must face various challenges, or the same challenges in different ways. Even the same constitutional courts rarely deal with the same questions, which makes any comparison difficult. Furthermore, the study of the practice of the European courts introduces new elements to the comparison, since they do not operate within a nation-state framework, and their primary function is not the judicial review of legal acts. Hence, because of this, it is important to clarify what the basis for the present comparison actually is. As we showed in the introductory chapter, our work deals with the major trends in constitutional adjudication, seeking answers to questions whether the contemporary challenges, that frequently put unusual or even unprecedented pressure on the courts, trigger changes in constitutional jurisprudence or not. That is, whether or not these social developments have led to the replacement or thorough modification of previously established judicial constructions and interpretive practices. In other words, the judicial strategies are the focus of our attention. We think that these strategies can rationally be examined and the constitutional imprints of the crisis situations in the various legal systems (including the European legal regimes) can be compared with each other.

However, due to the lack of objective criteria for the measurement of changes in judicial responses to different challenges, it is impossible to create a ranking between the examined countries based on a scale or extent of changes. Still, the occurrence and directions of changes can plausibly be exhibited and evaluated by qualitative analysis and comparison of the old and new judicial practices.

In analysing the national situations as they have been described in this book, we found that a simple three-variable scheme assumed on a strictly logical basis can provide a more or less suitable analytical framework for identifying and instantiating the contemporary major trends of European constitutional adjudication, even though not all cases can be classified in these categories. The latter will be discussed separately below as 'special cases'.

The first group includes those countries where constitutional jurisprudence has changed significantly in the areas affected by the challenges described above. The opposite stance is the stability/continuity of the judicial practice as far as constitutional review is concerned. And there is an intermediate position that can be characterised by moderate changes and the co-existence of the old and new concepts and designs. In this regard, we repeat that constitutional practice, including the jurisprudence of the competent courts, is developing in every legal system. Even a rich and well-established jurisprudence cannot give solutions to every case, as the continuously changing conditions of social life demand new and adequate answers from the courts. Thus, 'stability' in the context of this work means the relative 'unchangingness' of the mainstream constitutional jurisprudence that preserves the previously developed legal constructions, judicial attitudes and conventional paths of adjudging constitutional controversies. Conversely, in our understanding, 'changing' jurisprudence does not mean that all elements of constitutional adjudication have changed. Even the most fluid or versatile practice cannot dispense with certain structural and procedural continuity (without the serious risk of losing trust or legitimacy). Consequently, there are no rigid frontiers between these categories, as the positioning of the particular countries or legal systems is also relative and selective. While a constitutional system may preserve its fundaments inasmuch as the protected sphere of privacy is at stake (in domestic security issues, for instance), it can vary when reacting to the legal problems of migration, etc.

1. Constitutional responses to challenges – Major judicial strategies

1.1 Changing constitutional jurisprudence

As to the first category, among the countries we have examined, France and Spain have changed the constitutional jurisprudence to the greatest extent. In France, as Hourquebie claims, the Constitutional Council (*Conseil Constitutionnel*) has taken into account the 'reality' both in inland security and social welfare cases, which has led it to adopt a 'pragmatic' approach in its jurisprudence.[1]

It is to be noted, however, that in both countries the constitutional court had to face and resolve unaccustomed problems. In France, shocking terrorist attacks put huge pressure not only on the legislature and the government but also on the Constitutional Council in adjudicating the constitutionality of the anti-terrorism legislation, and, indirectly, to upkeep the 'fundamental laws of the Republic'. These fundamental laws were at stake when the deprivation of nationality as a sanction against terrorism was suggested, which concerned directly such substantial liberties as the equality or the right to citizenship. In some controversial issues – for example, the ban on the wearing of headscarves or the concealment of the face in public space – unprecedented legislative measures were adopted in the protection of public order, and the *Conseil Constitutionnel* had to establish a new balance between the freedom of religion and the public security interests.

The Spanish Constitutional Court (*Tribunal Constitucional*) has also developed a special 'crisis jurisprudence' in those areas affected by major challenges. Although the Constitutional Court expressed quite early that "[t]he objective of guaranteeing the security of the constitutional State at any cost, via preventive controls, puts the constitutional State itself seriously at risk",[2] the social climate that has surrounded the fight against terrorism has influenced the relating practice of the Court. It is particularly interesting, as this country has had experience in this regard. As far as foreigners' rights are concerned, the previous constitutional doctrine imposed the obligation upon the legislature to respect the substance of fundamental rights. On this basis, the core area of the basic rights should have been extended to foreign citizens in an equal way as they are applied to Spanish citizens. However, as Balaguer Callejón reports,[3] the Constitutional Court has accepted the government's policy to make a difference between the immigrants on the basis of their authorisation to stay or reside in Spain. So, this interpretation breaks the coherence of the Court's earlier way of argumentation to place certain rights on the basis of human dignity and the 'essential content' doctrine. In this way, the Court has enabled the Government to grant different rights and entitlements to the various groups of immigrants.

In the constitutional review of the laws related to the economic crisis, the Spanish Constitutional Court practically confirmed all policy measures of the other branches of government. According to Balaguer Callejón, discovering the 'economic interpretation of the Constitution', the Court has shown strong deference to policy choices and has not afforded due consideration to the constitutional impacts of austerity measures, in so far as social rights have been interpreted from the perspective of the requirements of balanced budgets and economic austerity, and certain principles and rights have been subject to financial considerations.

In Spain, the secessionist efforts in Catalonia mean a special challenge to the constitutional system of high account. In this area, the jurisprudence of the Constitutional Court has not been very mutable compared with the previous practice, as its very recent decision on the Catalan independence referendum shows.

1.2. 'Swinging jurisprudence' – between continuity and change

As mentioned above, in a lot of countries the outcomes and major directions of constitutional adjudication show signs of both continuity and change. It means that although in some areas the Constitutional Court has developed new doctrines in response to crises, in other respects it can be characterised by continuous practice preserving the validity of the earlier constructions and interpretive patterns.

Greece is a great example of this, because this country was hit by an extremely extensive economic crisis affecting almost all areas of social, political and economic life. As Vlachogiannis reported, nothing has remained unchanged, and this has generated new and rich constitutional case-law. Here the stability of the old constitutional principles and values, as well as the fortitude of constitutional judges, has been tested on a number of occasions. The Supreme Court, which has the power of constitutional review of legislative acts, started from the theoretical basis of a 'holistic interpretation' that has provided a sufficiently flexible tool for the body to keep a room for manoeuvre in each controversial issue. The principle of proportionality, as a frequently used judicial instrument, has also offered a desirable flexibility: although it is well-established interpretive method, it has not been applied in the same way as before. This theoretical and methodological background made it possible that 'the Court has oscillated between, on the one hand, reaffirming well established doctrines, on the other hand, introducing in its legal reasoning the concept of "emergency situation"'.[4]

However, this variation of adaptation and maintenance of previous practice was not a persistent judicial behaviour. In the initial stage of the economic and financial crisis, the Court showed a deference to the Government austerity policy, discovering new and less stringent constitutional standards, like the concepts of 'decent living standard' (allowing restrictions on personal incomes and allowances), 'core of the state' (legitimising new Government functions and empowerments), or reshaping its earlier approaches, like the extended use of the concept of 'general interest' (of which the category of 'budgetary interest' was deduced). While many objected this frequent recourse to emergency laws, the Court often 'failed to protect adequately certain rights', like property rights or equality.[5] At the peak of the judicial self-restraint, the 'public' or 'general interest' emerged with so great a weight in the justification of Government measures that it seemed to trump every individual right. It is an extreme position in relation to the stability/change dichotomy; if there is a danger of the collapse of the national economy so that is the survival of the state is at stake, any device is allowed to be used that is necessary to avoid this cataclysm. Just because of this approach, Greece should be included in the group of those countries where constitutional jurisdiction rapidly changed when the crisis management laws were on the agenda of the judiciary. However, as time has passed, and the efficiency of crisis management became more and more questionable, the attitude of the Supreme Court also altered towards the crisis-led legislative initiatives. As Vlachogiannis claims, the Court 'has inaugurated an era of strong form of judicial review of socio-economic legislative measures, extending the scope and increasing the intensity of the control exercised'.[6] This shift comprised, among others, the creative interpretation of some constitutional provisions in order to defend certain constitutional values, or the adherence to stricter justifications of restrictive social policy measures instead of complacency with a plain reasonableness.

On the imaginary 'continuity/change' scale the next country is Italy, where the Constitutional Court (*Corte costituzionale*) has showed different levels of rigidity in its legal acts on the various issues of crisis management. As we saw from Ciolli's study, although the Court succeeded to maintain its earlier level of rights-protection, even for immigrants, it upheld some unusual legislative pieces in the area of the fight against terrorism. The effective control over public expenditure proved to be the upmost argument in the course of constitutional review of the regulatory power of the legislature and the Government. Although the Court could lean on the solid foundation of the principle of 'balanced budget' that had been just introduced into the Italian Constitution, sometimes even the retroactive nature of statutory regulation was not enough to declare a law unconstitutional.[7]

Besides all this, Italy belongs to the group of countries where the Constitutional Court has had to face quite special challenges. One of these was the sensitive relationship between the Parliament and the Government, and the point was how the Court would adjudge the shift of balance toward the executive power. It seems that the Court did not impede the development of the 'presidentialisation' of the Government, though the constitutional context had not changed in this respect. The *Corte costituzionale* supported also the central Government's efforts to strengthen its own power *vis-à-vis* the regions, albeit the restructuring of the vertical division of power has taken place without constitutional change. Ciolli's study shed light on a special challenge to the decentralised government structure of Italy which has been tested by the economic depression, as the successful crisis management demanded the centralisation of resources and competences at the expense of the regional governments.

Portugal was also severely hit by the negative effects of the world financial crisis. Some constitutional issues emerged from both the national economic stability and growth policy and from the international bailout programme. These challenges to the Portuguese constitutional system were special in two respects. First, the economic and social rights are considered full-fledged fundamental rights in the Constitution, rather than mere state aims providing general guidelines or policy purposes for the government. Second, Portugal was in need of international financial aid, the conditions of which were determined by external actors, namely, the so-called *Troika* (consisting of the European Commission, the European Central Bank and the International Monetary Fund). In addition, these economic and financial requirements were set more or less in a loose, political form. Incidentally, the proposed and applied tools aiming at economic and financial recovery were typical and well-known restrictive measures – from pay-cuts of public sector workers to curbing social and welfare services.

While, as Canotilho argues, the Constitutional Court was frequently criticised for its 'unprecedented judicial activism' as well as for, in some cases, its unpredictable and illegitimate practice, the Court invoked certain constitutional values such as equality or legitimate expectations, which proved to be sufficiently strong in defending individual rights. Probably, the major ambition of the Constitutional Court was to find compromise solutions when budgetary interests collided with individual claims for social rights. This attitude was manifested, for example, when the Court repealed the law imposing an additional pay-cut on public employers, but only with *ex nunc* effect, which meant that the contested recovery measure could prevail for some time. This special 'yes–but' approach is also reflected in it upholding some controversial legislative acts, but only under special conditions; such as the temporary effect and exceptional nature of these measures causing only proportional rights limitations. Economic crisis management inspired the development of new judicial constructions and case-law concerning for instance, the proportionality review, the content of legitimate expectations or the 'essential core of minimum guarantees [for social rights]'. Basically, the Court has recognised a wide discretionary power of the government to determine the way and instruments of crisis management without renouncing the protection of the rights of those people who, in part as a consequence of the economic crisis, are in the worst financial situation. Besides these developments, Canotilho also emphasises that 'the Court mainly followed its previous paths and methods, as well as some of its most important jurisprudential lines'.[8]

1.3. Preferring stability and continuity in crisis-related jurisprudence

Obviously it can be safely claimed that the real question is not whether the constitutional jurisprudence has changed as a result of the global challenges in the various European countries, but how much change has happened, or what kind of adaptation has been achieved. Within this framework, the results of our research show that some national courts succeeded in preserving their previously developed standards and doctrines and found that the new challenges can be effectively managed by the established practice and case-law. Certainly, it does not mean that the continuity of jurisprudence would have prevailed in all cases or areas.

In Gardasevic's report on Croatia it is argued that the Constitutional Court has not significantly departed from its own previous case-law. As Gardasevic concluded, the 'constitutional protection of fundamental rights and freedoms in Croatia in the past 15 years has constantly been evolving in a way as to give those rights a position of judicially enforceable constitutional rules', which suggests an unbroken practice. It is reinforced by the finding of this study that in contrast with the real war situations in the early 1990s, when 'the Court showed extreme deference to emergency measures', in the cases relating to domestic security in recent years, it took a different position.[9] The Court insisted, for example, to upkeep the traditional proportionality review even in cases of 'state measures for prevention and suppression of terrorism' [striking down a law limiting the freedom of assembly for such reasons]. However, we must be careful in assessing the relevant achievement of this Court, as some of the new-generation security measures have not been brought before the body. Therefore, the situation in this field, as Gardasevic says, is 'far from clear and any general conclusion on how the Court could really act in future cases of imminent and serious threat to the constitutional order might be quite premature'.[10] The Court, then, seems to apply a 'process-based' approach concentrating mainly on procedural matters, rather than proceeding with substantive reviews.

As to the economic crisis, the Croatian Constitutional Court has made it clear that the 'social state', 'social justice' or 'social rights', even they appear in the constitutional text, are only policy guidances for the legislator and do not enjoy special protection.

All in all, though the Constitutional Court did not have to make significant changes in its crisis-related practice, the main reason for this relative continuity was that the constitutional foundations offered enough room for it to respond to the new challenges after the war experiences of the country, and the original low constitutional rank of social rights.

All signs show that the jurisprudence of the German Federal Constitutional Court (*Bundesverfassungsgericht*) has changed the least with regard to the crisis-led legislation in the countries we have investigated in this book. As it is well-known, this Court has developed an extremely rich case-law and has some experience concerning certain challenges from the past, like terrorism and migration, which are such acute problems today. The recent jurisprudence of this Court is also interesting because it has had to face a similar problem brought about by economic crisis as its Portuguese and Greek counterparts, though from a different point of view. The Federal Constitutional Court had to adjudge the constitutionality of 'rescue packages' that provided financial assistance (mainly credits and loans) to some EU member states that found themselves in a difficult budgetary position. However, Germany stood on the creditors' side, and from this one could conclude that the German Constitutional Court had to resolve basically different constitutional problems than the courts of the countries that as debtors had been beneficiaries of these recovery programmes. Despite this, in Germany too, the core issue was the protection of national sovereignty as well as the major properties of the democratic decision-making process. More specifically, the constitutional issue concerned the scope of the *Bundestag*'s budgetary rights in relation to financial transactions whose content was defined by international institutions. The Court held that any transfer of the budgetary powers of the lower house of Parliament is constitutional only if the *Bundestag* has the opportunity to control the process that imposes financial obligations on Germany. In doing so, the Constitutional Court rejected the idea that the necessity demands extraordinary solutions or rules. As Mehde stresses in his chapter, it was 'almost unthinkable that the Court could explicitly distance itself from previous judgements'.[11] He sees in the present case-law the uninterrupted continuation of the practice followed since the Maastricht decision of the Court in 1993. Although the Constitutional Court has not dealt with every conceivable problem, the well-established necessity–proportionality test was used also for the case on the constitutionality of an anti-terrorism-data-gathering system. Maybe the only real innovation was that the Constitutional Court in a case – the first time in its history – asked for a preliminary ruling of the European Court of Justice, but this in itself can hardly be regarded as a disruptive change in jurisprudence.

1.4 Special cases

1.4.1 National pathways under special reasons

There are some countries that cannot be clearly classified into any of the three groups. It is a great temptation to suppose that the relevant constitutional jurisprudence of the United Kingdom should be included in the second class where the judicial practice fluctuates between change and continuity depending on the nature of the case before them. However, the jurisprudence of the British courts germane to the crisis-related legal acts cannot be characterized as being 'intermediate' or 'halfway' on the scale from continuity to transformation. Birkinshaw's study argues that in the areas of foreign, defence and security policy the British courts can be characterised by deference to executive expertise in choosing the best policy solutions, and they are reluctant to intervene in decision-making process when 'general interest' is invoked. One can easily get the impression that the courts are steadily retreating in reviewing the antiterrorist legislative acts, which means that they give green light to more and more extension of government influence over privacy, and give up some traditional positions in the area of police and secret service investigations.

If in the UK the judicial practice is constantly changing in domestic security issues, McEldowney's study reveals that the British courts persist in their distrust of the supremacy of the European human rights law. As he claims, the jurisprudence of the European Court of Human Rights and the European Union law have challenged 'the UK's constitutional orthodoxy',[12] creating a dilemma between the traditional principle of parliamentary sovereignty and the claim for primacy of the European law. This leaves its stamp on the judicial review as well. McEldowney argues that one of the motivations behind Brexit could be to regain UK sovereignty, which prefers judicial deference to policy making having basically political nature. Eventually, whereas the judicial practice on antiterrorism legislation has gradually changed in recent years, the traditional deference of the courts to the inherent autonomy of political branches in policy making will probably win in the long run.

The Hungarian and the Polish examples belong to the special cases for conspicuously different reasons. While the jurisprudence of both of the Hungarian Constitutional Court (*Alkotmánybíróság*) and the Polish Constitutional Tribunal (*Trybunał Konstytucyjny*) in crisis-led cases show many similarities to the decisions and solutions of other constitutional courts, the most important issues have not had precedents to be compared with. Although both courts have had rich experiences in dealing with temporary and unprecedented situations (think of the constitutional challenges of transitional justice after the fall of Communist regimes in these countries), their jurisprudence was not as wide-ranging, diversified and elaborated as in those countries where the constitutional review has much longer traditions.

The comparison of the jurisprudence of the Hungarian Constitutional Court with the practices of other courts is difficult, because the competence of the Constitutional Court has been reduced nowhere else in the way as it was reduced in this country. The special reason is the harsh reduction of the power of the Hungarian Constitutional Court, namely the abolition of the Constitutional Court's power to review the constitutionality of public finance laws. Although the Hungarian Constitutional Court had elaborated in detail the constitutional requirements of public finances in the 1990s, due to this power reduction the Court has not been able to enforce them against the political will of the parliamentary majority in recent years.

Still, there are some legal areas and constitutional issues where we can compare previous and new practices. In doing so, we can observe judicial deference to the executive power in handling crisis situations. For example, the balanced budget has proven to be a major public interest in both countries and which was considered sufficient justification for extensive state intervention in the sphere of economy and property rights. This is especially true in Hungary, where there was a significant reduction in the level of protection of fundamental rights and the rule of law compared with the previous jurisprudence. As a result of the curtailment of the Court's jurisdiction and the court-packing replacing the old judges with new members who are loyal to the Government, the Constitutional Court became a quasi-Government agency usually providing formal legitimacy for the Government's will.

Besides the difficulties of comparison, the other reason why Hungary and Poland cannot be classified as countries where constitutional jurisprudence of crisis-related legislative acts has significantly changed in the past few years is that the changes of case-law were not really motivated by the responses to the challenges examined by us, but by the shift towards authoritarian governance that shocked the position of the constitutional courts and made them a subordinate to the governmental will (in Hungary), or is in the process of so (in Poland).

1.4.2 The European scene

The practice of the European courts can hardly fit in the groupings we propose. First, they do not perform classical judicial review of normative legal acts and, second, they are in a special position from another point of view as well – though the Court of Justice of the European Union (CJEU) has been reached only by cases related to the economic crisis, the European Court of Human Rights (ECtHR) deals only with legal disputes of individual rights under the European Convention of Human Rights (ECHR). However, the persistence or changeability of their practice can be explored and compared with the development of the national-level constitutional jurisprudence.

As Groppi points out, in as far as the use of foreign law as an instrument in the hands of constitutional courts is concerned, the need to face new challenges has not changed the interpretative practice of national courts, which means that they have not had to resort to the jurisprudence of the European courts or foreign judicial rulings or more intensively than before the crises.[13] Nevertheless, there are significant differences between the national courts as to how courageously they use or refer to the Court's case-law. At the same time, the European courts have fought their own battles in relation to the effects of global challenges, since all of the problems discussed in our book have also European dimensions, and it is a widespread view that these challenges can only be managed successfully on a European level.

Analysing a number of recent judgments of the Strasbourg court, Groppi shows that in most fields the European Court of Human Rights reaffirmed its earlier jurisprudence insisting, for example, on the absolute nature of the prohibition of torture, or on the appellants' right to effective remedy even in such sensitive cases like the treatment of suspected terrorists or asylum seekers. In some cases, it was disposed even to confront the more permissive national judicial practice, when certain basic rights were at stake. Thus, while the Hungarian Constitutional Court did not see anything wrong with the legal mandate of national security authorities to use covert surveillance of the private life of 'sets of people' in order to prevent, investigate or repress terrorist acts, the ECtHR found it a too broad empowerment without sufficiently specified reasons.

For the ECtHR, it was more difficult to give protection for those who had been affected by the negative effects of the world financial crisis. The ECHR does not recognise the economic and social rights as basic rights providing effective protection for these interests. However, in some areas, the Court applied a wide reading of several civil and political rights protected by the ECHR, using them as tools for recognizing some protection for those who are the losers of economic crisis. Thus, the broad interpretation of the right to property might restrict the central government interventions in the economic sphere, providing an effective tool against illegitimate restrictive financial measures. The scope of judicial protection of individual rights became wider when the financial crisis affected other rights highlighted by the Convention such as the access to courts or the right to a fair trial. However, when such rights were not affected, the Court was reluctant to narrow the margin of appreciation of the national legislatures to take social and economic policy measures. According to Groppi, this deference was constantly justified by referring to the existence of an exceptional crisis without precedents. This kind of caution was noticeable in certain areas in the case-law of the Court of Justice of the European Union as well, for example when the access to social benefits of EU citizens of other Member States or other foreigners was concerned. In reality, only a few relevant cases reached the CJEU, and even in these procedures the Court often referred to the judgments of the ECtHR.

In sum, Groppi concludes that the recent jurisprudence of the European courts demonstrates that under the circumstances of the economic crisis, these courts 'did not alter their case-law, either as regards the admissibility of the recourse (…), or in substantial aspects'. It is another question that this continuity of practice was sufficient to ensure guarantees only in extreme cases and severe violations of individual rights.

Beatrice Delzangles claims that the ECtHR has elaborated a more systematic practice on terrorism cases since 9/11, acknowledging that the 'terrorist violence', as 'an extremely serious situation amounting to a public emergency threatening the life of the nation' is a legally relevant concept. While the Court firmly refused some sorts of justification for rights limitations (e.g. the lack of sufficient resources of state) and insisted on some absolute limits for state intervention (like the absolute prohibition of torture), it was willing to accept the relevance of the 'exceptional' and 'unexpected [economic] crisis' as recognisable circumstances of restrictive government actions. The general references to the principle of proportionality or to the requirement of legitimate aims for any state actions were only conventional parts of reasoning without any meaningful impact. Delzangles stresses, for instance, that the 'low intensity proportionality test in matters related to austerity measures (…) was not sufficient anymore', and that the ECtHR basically pursued a self-restraining stance. In her approach, the relevant case-law of the Court can plausibly be understood in the framework of a 'cooperative negotiation approach' in which the ECtHR is continuously trying to work together with the national courts to find the proper functions of all judicial bodies as stakeholders.[14]

In view of the Court of Justice of the European Union, Varju argues that the Court's practice can be characterised by deference to legislative intent respecting the policy decisions. According to the CJEU position with regard to the underlying political process of decision-making in the affected policy domains, there is only a limited room for judicial intervention that is even more restricted when detailed legal regulation exists – as is quite usual in the affected policy areas (like monetary or fiscal policy). The Court, using a close reading of the relevant legal provisions, has never given up its strategic aim at enforcing the Member States' obligations and promoting the general objectives of the European Union.[15]

2. Major judicial strategies in responding to legal challenges

2.1 General trends in Europe

If we look at the interpretative tools and argumentative techniques that the constitutional courts used for justifying the changes in their case-law, we can find a lot of instruments and ways, though their application certainly varied from court to court and from case to case. The categorization of the national courts according to the change/stability dimension could be a useful theoretical tool for a sketchy comparison of the various jurisdictions and for a description of the possible judicial strategies in responding to the modern challenges. Apart from this, we can identify certain general behavioural patterns that the constitutional courts used to follow when they faced the constitutional problems of global challenges.

First, we have to notice that all global challenges discussed here are complex social phenomena with a lot of different effects most of which have never been brought to a court. Second, we have to notice that the various challenges have not equally been addressed by the constitutional court in different countries. However, the more serious social problems came from a challenge, the greater the chance to have its legal aspects reaching the courts.

One of the most frequently discussed challenges was the financial crisis, which raised several constitutional issues, such as the scope of budgetary and taxation powers of certain public bodies or the legitimate limitations of social and property rights. Indirectly, other basic rights could also be affected, like equality (e.g. when economic or financial burdens were distributed in an unequal way) or the freedom of enterprise and business activity (e.g. when the government monopolised certain economic branches or activities).

As a result, the economic and financial matters have been judicialised to a degree never seen before. But, before we conclude that through the legal responses to the financial crisis the constitutional courts have largely increased their power *vis-à-vis* the political branches and institutions in this field, we must also add that the courts mostly occupied a deferential position in these questions, leaving wide discretionary power for central governments to choose the policy measures for handling economic crisis. The qualitative analysis of the courts' decisions in European crisis management tools also shows that judicial institutions were generally supportive of new mechanisms and measures of financial stabilization and economic recovery.[16]

Some examples demonstrate (e.g. in Greece) that over the years, as the negative effects of the economic crisis were gradually overcome, the courts became less and less lenient towards restrictive government measures. This shows that there might be a link between the strictness of the courts and the severity of the consequences of crises. The longer the economic austerity policy lasts, the courts show less and less deference to the rights limitations. In other words, in case of long-term constraints, it is difficult to convince the constitutional courts of the necessity of restrictive governmental interventions. In a number of countries, although the constitutional courts were willing to accept the constitutionality of extraordinary measures (for example, cuts in the payments to public employees), they were less disposed to approve policy measures that had long-term effects or that unequally divided the burdens of crisis management. Consequently, the courts most frequently show deference to governmental measures of economic and financial crisis management, but this permissiveness had limits. In this way, the constitutional courts usually followed a half-way strategy trying to find a long-term balance between the reasonable extraordinary powers of the government and the protection of individual rights. This balance evidently depends on the political and constitutional contexts of the individual countries.

Basically, we can draw similar conclusions if we examine the constitutional adjudications in relation to domestic security and antiterrorism laws. Most constitutional courts have proved to be appreciative actors towards these legal acts, even in countries that were not directly affected by terrorist attacks. Although neither the legislators nor the courts have not yet transgressed certain borders (e.g. torture or mass expulsions have not been proposed), it is worrying that the government interventions and restrictive policy actions have no firm limits or borders and that counter-terrorism measures seem to fit into an open-ended process, and that the courts constantly fall back, giving up certain guarantees (see the examples of Hungary or the UK).

The judicial practice is the least elaborated on the issue of mass migration. The influx of migrants in 2015 and the later flows of migrant people took place too fast to allow constitutional courts to give the right legal answers to the relevant constitutional questions, or to establish sound jurisprudence in this issue. While the ordinary courts have had to cope with a lot of individual cases, trying to distinguish refugees from economic immigrants, the relevant constitutional problems were only rarely addressed to the constitutional courts (raising the problem of social rights of migrant people, for example). Furthermore, since the handling of this challenge requires a common European (or, more exactly, an EU-level) solution, the national courts have been mostly reluctant to deal with these issues. Still, the EU-level treatment of mass migration has produced sovereignty problems in some countries, where (as in Hungary) the constitutional courts addressed this topic as an issue of the (national) constitutional identity.

In other special challenges we have found fluctuating judicial practices. While the relevant courts have resolutely tried to defend certain pillars of the traditional bastions of national legal system in the UK (protecting parliamentary supremacy from the influence of European law) and in Spain (confirming the unity and territorial integrity of the country), they have contributed to considerable changes of the form of government in Italy (in strengthening the executive *vis-à-vis* the other power branches and the regions) and in Hungary (in dismantling the system of the rule of law).

2.2 *The tools of creativity*

The continuation of the previous or traditional case-law self-evidently did not require any particular justification and it was sufficient to invoke the well-established precedents or constructions. On the basis of a well-elaborated jurisprudence, it can be easier to justify why no special authorisation is required, or why there is no need to give up or abandon the well-admitted constitutional standards.

However, changing the old case-law apparently required more thorough justifications. The results of qualitative research of the various national judicial practices show that the courts deployed several different reasons and argumentative tools for this purpose.

In the first instance, we found that the constitutional adjudication has nowhere been placed on completely new theoretical bases; that is, the constitutional courts have not replaced the traditional methods of constitutional interpretation with a new judicial philosophy or interpretative theory. As a matter of fact, none of the courts has offered any coherent theory of the 'emergency constitutionalism' either, precisely determining the frontiers of the special empowerment of the other power branches or defining the constitutionally permissible tools and instrument in such situations. Under these circumstances, the simplest reasoning for the alteration to the previous case-law was, in theory, the pure reference to the state of necessity or exigency, which needs new and unusual responses, as it was so meaningfully and explicitly expressed by an earlier president of the Hungarian Constitutional Court.[17]

One technique in the courts' toolbox was the reinvention of 'sleeping' provisions of the constitution. This means that an old rule is used in a new way; this happens, for example, when the court declares the unconstitutionality of a statute based on a provision that it has never been used in this way in the past. Another means is to use a special (and unaccustomed) method of constitutional interpretation in individual cases (or in a special group of cases)– such as a 'holistic' or 'economic' interpretation' (of which we can see examples in Greece or Spain, respectively). It is a closely related methodology to create or deduct new constitutional concepts and doctrines that can provide new justifications for rights limitations or other purposes. Sometimes, these newly discovered constitutional ideas and requirements emerged as magic words serving for the justification of the changing practice. Above all, the 'public' or 'general' interest, usually specifying it as the maintenance of the functioning of state or protection of public order, and the 'balanced budget' (provided that it was not explicitly recognised by the constitution) played such a role in constitutional reasoning.

Some constitutional courts were ready for reshaping existing constitutional doctrines and constructions in order to use them for resolving the new conflicts.

The great advantage of this method was that it could conceal the minor changes in the court's perception or case-law. In particular, the necessity–proportionality or 'balancing' test was an appropriate tool for such purpose; first, because it was a generally accepted interpretative method in almost all countries, and, second, it always gave a certain flexibility to the constitutional courts to draw almost any conclusion they want to declare. Another way of changing judicial practice was to invent new tasks and functions for governmental institutions. This can be seen in the coordination of public finances in Italy, which has backed up the government's centralisation efforts, or in the government's obligation to ensure the functioning of state in a number of other countries discussed in this book. For this purpose, the crisis situations provide good reference points for the courts to argue that unprecedented difficulties necessitate the authorisation of the political branches to exercise special powers to overcome them. In doing so, perhaps the consideration by constitutional judges could play a role in that it is better to give a short-term, exceptional and strongly controlled authorization for the governments than to introduce a state of emergency or siege (as the 'terrorism state of emergency' was put into the constitutional text in Hungary, where even the 'considerable and direct danger of a terrorist act' may base the promulgation of the special legal order).

In certain cases, paradoxically, the reference to a more abstract danger of basic rights was used as an argument for approving rights limitations. Pursuant to this kind of reasoning, the intensified state intervention is justified by the public interest for the maintenance of the functionality of the state, where, for instance, the state's solvency or the balance of state budget is indispensable to guarantee the basic rights and liberties of the citizens. It must be added to this that constitutional courts often refrained from thorough investigation as to whether such references were well founded, since it was considered that the definition and ranking of the public interests at this general level is the task of policy makers. It is a recurrent argument for judicial deference that courts are not structurally well-prepared to solve complicated problems, as they do not possess the proper expertise to overrule complex budgetary or anti-terrorist legislation. Furthermore, the self-restraining courts frequently postulate that judges may not replace the government's policy measures with their own choices because it is not their function. Another set of arguments readily reflect the underlying logic of emergency powers accepting the presumption that extraordinary circumstances need extraordinary tools to be overcome.

Whereas the reference to the necessity as a fact triggered by a crisis situation became a part of the *ratio decidendi* in a lot of constitutional court rulings without further investigation, the constitutional jurisprudence was changeable [or mutable] in assessing the proportionality of the legal means employed in such cases.

3. Reasons and explanations of jurisprudential change and stability – Justifications for jurisprudential changes

Jurisprudential changes and their reasons can be followed up and identified from the published decisions, and, possibly, from the available concurring and dissenting opinions of the constitutional and other high courts. It is more difficult, however, to reveal the reasons for these changes, and the motifs that have encouraged a court to make changes in its case-law or to overrule an earlier precedent or doctrine.

In the first place, it is important to state that jurisprudential changes can have external or – from the point of view of constitutional courts – 'objective' reasons. In recent years, special crisis-driven constitutional amendments have been adopted in some European countries.[18] First and foremost, these were so-called 'debt-brake' rules; that is, constitutional guarantees against the government indebtedness, or for the obligatory reduction of the existing state debts. Another constitutional innovation was to entrench or interpolate fairly general requirements into the basic laws, primarily the principle of 'balanced' or 'transparent budget'. Such new-generation rules emerged, for example, in the French, Italian, Hungarian, and Spanish Constitution. Certainly, the modifications of the constitutional text may seemingly lead to changes in the jurisprudence of the constitutional courts too. However, it does not mean that the courts are not obliged to justify their decisions made on the basis of the new provisions, even if the simple reference to the textual changes can be an attractive and comfortable solution and was not unprecedented in the practice of the examined courts.

An additional external factor was a new phenomenon of the European 'constitutional mutation' extending the scope of EU institutions to economic governance that induced a 'mirror effect' at national level introducing new constitutional doctrines in the member states judiciaries, like the acceptance of the diminution of the national budget autonomy.[19]

The involvement of the European institutions, including the supranational courts, may affect the national-level constitutional jurisprudence in other areas as well. The constitutional courts can be reluctant to overtake or overrule the emergent EU-level policy in mass migration; or, otherwise, they can get into an awkward situation, as with the Hungarian Constitutional Court, when their judgements were condemned or neglected by their international counterparts.

However, as we have seen, one can often find significant changes in the constitutional adjudications without any alterations in the constitutional text. We can say that in most cases, the constitutional courts did not need textual changes or changing intention of the constitution-making power for accomplishing significant changes in their jurisprudence. Nevertheless, the experience shows that even the courts that changed their case-law to the greatest extent, have not deliberately converted to a new philosophy of constitutional interpretation. Rather, they applied odd and several different techniques that were case-dependent or problem-oriented solutions, while the dominant or usual methods of constitutional interpretation as such were not changed or replaced.

As we have seen, there are no general national replies to the constitutional challenges or behavioural patterns that would be followed in all arising matters. The countries (and their legal systems) under examination in this book are very diverse, and the most significant global challenges affect them in such different ways. In light of this, it seems unlikely that a comprehensive theory can be developed that can give a general explanation of the different constitutional courts' strategies and judicial behavioural patterns in relation to the pressures put on them, and which could reliably predict how the jurisprudence of the various constitutional courts will change in the future. Such a general theory could be based on the correlation between certain common features of the constitutional systems under review or their challenges (as independent variables), and the nature of the constitutional replies given to such challenges by the constitutional courts (as dependent variables). Such independent variables may be the traditions and embeddedness of democratic values in the various countries (making a difference between the 'old' democracies and the 'new' ones in post-Communist states), the place of the particular countries according to political geography (in centre-periphery dimension), legal culture (distinguishing common law and civil law systems), or the institutional settings of constitutional adjudication (whether there are specialised/centralised constitutional courts, or not). Moreover, the clusters of challenges (like the threat of terrorism, migration flow or economic crisis) might trigger different legal responses in the dimension of the stability/change dichotomy. Obviously, the level or degree of jurisprudential changes or continuity as outcome are the dependent variables.

However, according to our assessment, such kinds of connections cannot be detected in any of these aspects. As a matter of fact, significant reforms or alterations can be demonstrated in both the 'old' and 'new' democracies (e.g. in France and Hungary), while the relative stability of the constitutional jurisprudence can also be exemplified in traditional and post-Communist political systems (as the examples of Germany and Croatia show). Hence, the intensity and direction of changes have taken place regardless of whether the respective countries belong to the centre or the periphery in European political landscape.

Consequently, our major finding is that there is no any specific independent variable determining the stability or variability of constitutional jurisprudence in a particular country, but the special context of the national legal systems can explain how the judicial branch reacts to the major challenges. Even within the same country, it is very unlikely that there would be a dominant cause for the development of case-law in this respect. Of course, there are several factors that in many countries have a significant influence on how the courts respond to constitutional challenges. Thus, the institutional interests of the supreme judicial bodies, such as to build or preserve the legitimacy of the judiciary or to maintain the room for manoeuvre, could be significant considerations in the interplay between the constitutional courts and other public bodies. The courts must justify continuously that they apply consistently the constitutional principles and rules to constitutional litigation and to other cases, and that they do not use their power arbitrarily. The individual attitudes of constitutional judges may also play an influential role in choosing judicial strategies. Judges may be reluctant to assume responsibility by approving unpopular measures and, *vice versa*, they may be tempted to prevent such measures being implemented.

As to the country-specific reasons, perhaps it is too early to draw general conclusions, and only a few authors of this book have undertaken to give an explanation for the very recent development of the constitutional case-law. Vlachogiannis, for example, argues that the Supreme Court in its crisis-induced practice followed the changes of public opinion. Though at the beginning, the Court feared the possible consequences of striking down the laws adopted in the course of economic crisis management, as the popular opinion started to become distrustful of the efficiency and fairness of the restrictive policies, the Court's position also began to harden.[20] In spite of this attitude, the German *Bundesverfassungsgericht* has scrupulously maintained that crisis management does not require extraordinary means that overturn the constitutional balance between state bodies or lead to significant legal restrictions of basic rights. As Mehde argues, this position derived from the self-identity of the Constitutional Court as being itself an institutional guarantor of stability.[21]

The change of the jurisprudence of the French Constitutional Council has been probably promoted by the heightened social atmosphere begotten by the brutal and bloody terrorist attacks in Paris and Nice. In this country, where some actions were committed by second- or third-generation immigrants who had been born and grew up in France, the fight against terrorism is also an integration problem. If it is at all possible, this sort of 'neighbour terrorism' is even more frightening than those attacks that are committed by aliens or 'professional terrorists', and in a certain sense, these types of attacks can have deeper consequences, as extremely violent forms of behaviour draw the attention to the failures of social integration or multiculturalism. Moreover, 'Islam fundamentalism' as a phenomenon produces a major challenge to the balance between the religious freedom and the public interest of domestic security, and to the traditional secularism.

Some scholars have tried to import the theory of 'new constitutionalism' and the idea of 'weak judicial review'[22] from the Anglo-Saxon political philosophy and to apply them to the Hungarian circumstances.[23] This approach presumes that all developments including the deep transformation of the institutional settings as well as the functioning of the Constitutional Court have been nothing else than a shift from the 'legal' to the 'political constitutionalism'. Although the detailed analysis of these arguments goes far beyond the scope of our book, it can be noted that this approach seems to be a misconception in Hungary's political and constitutional context, as the theory of political constitutionalism presumes and supports the ultimate power of the representative bodies against the judiciary within the framework of constitutional democracies; accordingly, this tenet is hardly suitable to justify the dismantling of the democratic procedures and institutions.

In Hungary, an empirical research shows that political orientation is the most decisive factor in explaining judicial behaviour; the individual judges follow their personal choices on the politically controversial issues and there is an extremely strong correlation between the voting behaviour of the judges and the political standpoints of the parties that had nominated them.[24] But this is only a consequence of a long process of authoritarian tendencies that has taken place there since 2010. Therefore, the significant and in-depth change in the jurisprudence of the Constitutional Court has not been the consequence of the legal and political responses to the challenges, but it has rather been an outcome of the decline of the rule of law.

The risk of over-politicisation of constitutional courts was posed also by Balaguer Callejón, Canotilho and Granat for Spain, Portugal and Poland, respectively.

Remarkably, constitutional judges are often divided along professional or ideological cleavages. However, if these courts are polarised by political camps or extra-legal attitudes, their whole legitimacy may be imperiled, because it is questionable what use is a constitutional court which operates on a political basis besides the democratically elected institutions.

In addition, the strength and intensity of the various challenges may also influence what legal answers are given by constitutional courts in the particular countries. When the question is addressed whether survival or collapse of the state, whether casualties or protection of human lives, the courts may show greater deference as in Greece for economic austerity programmes or in the UK or France when the whole society was shaken by brutal terrorist attacks.

Certainly, we cannot exclude that the old judicial practice was not appropriate to be applied successfully to new challenges, and its comprehensive review was really necessary and justified. For example, as we referred to it in the Introduction, some European countries have had to face unprecedented forms of terrorism, and others have been hit by serious economic depression endangering the normal functioning of the state. It can hardly be denied that constitutional culture and national legal traditions also influence whether a constitutional or other high court consistently upheld its relevant case-law, or opened the way for new constitutional standards and conventions. Maybe the most typical example for this definite role of legal culture is the longstanding fight of the British courts with the supranational European law, and their enduring strife to preserve the old and traditional ways of law application.

As the Hungarian and the Polish cases show, the state and conditions of constitutional democracy can be a new potential variable to explain what responses are given by the constitutional justice to the new crises. Earlier we rejected the idea that the strength and embeddedness of constitutional democracy is a major criterion of change or stability of constitutional jurisprudence, as this presumption cannot be justified by the qualitative analyses of our research. The examples of some old democracies, like Britain or France, where the judicial practice has exhibited a lot of change, and, conversely, the relative immutability of the Croatian constitutional case-law demonstrate that there is no direct link between the variability of constitutional practice and the strength of the institutional system. This is not surprising, as neither change nor continuity itself is a negative thing. However, it does not mean that the state of development of the rule of law or the constitutional democracy do not have any influence on the reaction of the judiciary to crisis situations. It is obviously not by accident that the authoritarian tendencies in two post-Communist countries have materialised, and the constitutional courts have not been able to resist the political pressure of political branches. Still, judicial deference is discernible also in strong democracies too, as the crisis-related case-law of the French Constitutional Council or the UK courts show.

4. Epilogue: What next?

Because how the constitutional courts cope with challenges is not a closed process, our findings offer only an early insight into the very recent developments and trends. And, although these are basically path-dependent processes, unforeseeable, radical turns may also occur, as demonstrated by the decline of Hungarian or Polish constitutional adjudication. In spite of such theoretical possibilities, we think that there is much to be learned from the crisis-oriented jurisprudence of the constitutional courts.

As we highlighted above, neither the change nor the stability of constitutional jurisprudence is valuable in itself, but to judge whether the evolution of case-law or the performance of a constitutional court is appropriate or not, depends on a number of factors. However, the unfounded changes of case-law, the escape from the responsibility for serious decisions, the hasty rulings and unelaborated new doctrines or interpretive solutions, and, in general, the unreasonable deference may act as a warning of the weaknesses of constitutional adjudication. These phenomena give cause for concern for the future, as other global challenges – from environmental crisis to special problems caused by the technological development – can produce repeatedly new tasks for constitutional courts to be solved. Conversely, if a judicial body, often bearing the responsibility for the ultimate decision on matters that may essentially influence the life of the whole society, is able to guard over the constitutionality and to enforce the constitutional principles and requirements, this is an important guarantee of successful management of global challenges. To do so, there may be a need to revise and reshape existing constitutional doctrines and overrule long-standing precedents, to invent new rights and concepts adapting the living law to the new circumstances, or, *vice versa*, only the preservation of the well-established judicial constructions and interpretative tools may contribute to the successful crisis management.

In studying the judicial responses to the global challenges and the very recent development of the constitutional adjudication in some European countries, perhaps the most important lesson is that courts are not static institutions and their functioning and achievement depend more on the social environment and the political context than has been believed so far.

The constitutional courts' performance will surely influence their image and in the longer term may contribute to the increase or decrease of their legitimacy. Some authors of this book have already indicated that this issue has arisen in their country, not only for some of their fiercely debated decisions, but also questioning their traditional role and functions. If we look at the very recent trends of constitutional adjudication in Hungary and Poland, the frequent claim about the 'triumph' of constitutional review,[25] at least for the Central European countries, now seems to be a hasty conclusion.

Of course, the controversy about the most effective way of protecting constitutional values and individual rights is a legitimate debate in which all the 'dialogue between national and European courts',[26] the strengthening of the role of supranational institutions,[27] the 'political constitutionalism' or the 'weak judicial review'[28] can be viable and rational options. But it is worth pointing out that even if in some cases the constitutional courts were weak to resist the external pressures put on them, or that they gave wrong or ineffective responses to the challenges, this is not enough reason to impair or abandon judicial review as a basic instrument of controlling public power. This is especially the case when the alternative of judicial review is to build up an uncontrolled governmental power arguing that extraordinary challenges and tasks require extraordinary means and powers. In fact, the strengthening of constitutional review is a much more plausible solution to its occasional weaknesses.

Notes

1 Hourquebie in this book.
2 STC 62/2011 of 5 May 2011.
3 Balaguer Callejón in this book.
4 See Vlachogiannis in this book.
5 Ibid.
6 Ibid.
7 See Ciolli in this book.
8 Canotilho in this book.
9 See the chapter of Gardasevic in this book.
10 Ibid.
11 Mehde in this book.
12 McEldowney in this book.
13 Groppi in this book.
14 See Delzangles' chapter in this book.
15 See Varju's chapter in this book.
16 Fabbrini (2016) 100–101.
17 See Szente and Gárdos-Orosz in this book.
18 For a detailed analysis on this see Contiades and Alkmene (2013).
19 Tuori and Tuori (2014) 204.
20 Vlachogiannis in this book.
21 See Mehde in his chapter in this book.
22 Tomkins (2012), Bellamy (2007).
23 Pócza (2012) 48–70 and Antal (2013).
24 Szente (2016).
25 See e.g. Paris, Marie-Luce, Setting the scene: elements of constitutional theory and methodology of the research, in Bell, John and Paris, Marie-Luce (eds.), *Rights-Based Constitutional Review. Constitutional Courts in a Changing Landscape*, Edward Elgar (2016). 2.
26 Groppi and Ponthoreau (2013) and Halmai (2014).
27 Jakab and Kochenov (2017).
28 Gyorfi (2016).

Bibliography

Antal, Attila, 'Politikai és jogi alkotmányosság Magyarországon' (2013). 22 *Politikatudományi Szemle* 3, 48–70.

Balaguer Callejón, Francisco, 'Constitutional Courts under Pressure – New Challenges to Constitutional Adjudication. The Case of Spain', in Zoltán Szente and Fruzsina Gárdos-Orosz (eds), *New Challenges to Constitutional Adjudication in Europe – A Comparative Analysis* (Routledge 2018).

Bellamy, Richard, *Political Constitutionalism. A Republican Defence of the Constitutionality of Democracy* (Cambridge University Press 2007).

Birkinshaw, Patrick, 'National Security and the Limits of Judicial Protection', in Zoltán Szente and Fruzsina Gárdos-Orosz (eds), *New Challenges to Constitutional Adjudication in Europe – A Comparative Analysis* (Routledge 2018).

Canotilho, Mariana, 'Constitutional Law and Crisis: the Portuguese Constitutional Court Under Pressure?', in Zoltán Szente and Fruzsina Gárdos-Orosz (eds), *New Challenges to Constitutional Adjudication in Europe – A Comparative Analysis* (Routledge 2018).

Ciolli, Ines, 'Global Markets, Terrorism and Immigration: Italy Between a Troubled Economy and a Constitutional Crisis,' in Zoltán Szente and Fruzsina Gárdos-Orosz (eds), *New Challenges to Constitutional Adjudication in Europe – A Comparative Analysis* (Routledge 2018).

Contiades, Xenophon and Fotiaou, Alkmene, 'How Constitutions Reacted to the Financial Crisis' in Contiades, Xenophon (ed.), *Constitutions in the Global Financial Crisis. A Comparative Analysis* (Ashgate 2013).

Delzangles, Beatrice, 'The Negotiating Function of the European Court of Human Rights: Reconciling Diverging Interests Born from New European Challenges', in Zoltán Szente and Fruzsina Gárdos-Orosz (eds), *New Challenges to Constitutional Adjudication in Europe – A Comparative Analysis* (Routledge 2018).

Gardasevic, Djordje, 'Croatian Constitutional Adjudication in Times of Stress', in Zoltán Szente and Fruzsina Gárdos-Orosz (eds), *New Challenges to Constitutional Adjudication in Europe – A Comparative Analysis* (Routledge 2018).

Fabbrini, Federico, *Economic Governance in Europe: Comparative Paradoxes and Constitutional Challenges* (Oxford University Press 2016).

Granat, Mirosław, 'Constitutional Judiciary in Crisis. The Case of Poland', in Zoltán Szente and Fruzsina Gárdos-Orosz (eds), *New Challenges to Constitutional Adjudication in Europe – A Comparative Analysis* (Routledge 2018).

Groppi, Tania and Ponthoreau, Marie Claire (eds), *The Use of Foreign Precedents by Constitutional Judges* (Hart 2013).

Groppi, Tania, 'New Challenges for Constitutional Adjudication in Europe: What Role Could the 'Dialogue of Courts' Play?', in Zoltán Szente and Fruzsina Gárdos-Orosz (eds), *New Challenges to Constitutional Adjudication in Europe – A Comparative Analysis* (Routledge 2018).

Győrfi, Tamás, *Against New Constitutionalism* (Elgar 2016).

Halmai, Gábor, *Perspectives on Global Constitutionalism: The Use of Foreign and International Law* (Eleven Publishing 2014).

Hourquebie, Fabrice, 'Remarks on the Case-law of the French Constitutional Council in Relation to New Challenges', in Zoltán Szente and Fruzsina Gárdos-Orosz (eds), *New Challenges to Constitutional Adjudication in Europe – A Comparative Analysis* (Routledge 2018).

Jakab, András and Kochenov, Dimitry (eds), *The Enforcement of EU Law and Values* (OUP 2017).

McEldowney, John, 'The UK Supreme Court and Parliament: Judicial and Political Dialogue', in Zoltán Szente and Fruzsina Gárdos-Orosz (eds), *New Challenges to Constitutional Adjudication in Europe – A Comparative Analysis* (Routledge 2018).

Mehde, Veith, 'Beware of Disruptions – The *Bundesverfassungsgericht* as Supporter of Change and Anchor of Stability', in Zoltán Szente and Fruzsina Gárdos-Orosz (eds), *New Challenges to Constitutional Adjudication in Europe – A Comparative Analysis* (Routledge 2018).

Paris, Marie-Luce, 'Setting the Scene: Elements of Constitutional Theory and Methodology of the Research', in John Bell and Marie-Luce Paris (eds), *Rights-Based Constitutional Review. Constitutional Courts in a Changing Landscape* (Edward Elgar 2016).

Pócza, Kálmán, 'Alkotmányozás Magyarországon és az Egyesült Királyságban' (2012). 5 *Kommentár* 35–51.

Szente, Zoltán, 'The Political Orientation of the Members of the Hungarian Constitutional Court between 2010 and 2014' (2016). 1 *Constitutional Studies* 1.

Szente, Zoltán and Gárdos-Orosz, Fruzsina, 'Contemporary Challenges to Constitutional Adjudication in Europe', in Zoltán Szente and Fruzsina Gárdos-Orosz (eds), *New Challenges to Constitutional Adjudication in Europe – A Comparative Analysis* (Routledge 2018).

Tomkins, Adam, 'In Defence of the Political Constitution' (2012). 22 *Oxford Journal of Legal Studies* 1, 157–175.

Tuori, Kaarlo and Tuori, Klaus, *The Eurozone Crisis. A Constitutional Analysis* (Cambridge University Press 2014).

Varju, Márton, 'The Crisis, Judicial Power and EU Law: Could it have been Managed Differently by the EU Court of Justice?', in Zoltán Szente and Fruzsina Gárdos-Orosz (eds), *New Challenges to Constitutional Adjudication in Europe – A Comparative Analysis* (Routledge 2018).

Vlachogiannis, Apostolos, 'From Submission to Reaction: The Greek Courts' Stance on the Financial Crisis,' in Zoltán Szente and Fruzsina Gárdos-Orosz (eds), *New Challenges to Constitutional Adjudication in Europe – A Comparative Analysis* (Routledge 2018).

Index

For Product Safety Concerns and Information please contact our
EU representative GPSR@taylorandfrancis.com Taylor & Francis
Verlag GmbH, Kaufingerstraße 24, 80331 München, Germany